The Urban Pattern

The Beginnings of Civilization   (photo by Richard K. Eisner)

The Urban Pattern

City Planning and Design

Fourth Edition

Arthur B. Gallion, FAIA
Simon Eisner, APA, AICP

 D. VAN NOSTRAND COMPANY

New York • Cincinnati • Toronto • London • Melbourne

To Arthur B. Gallion

Arthur Gallion loved and respected the people of this world. He traveled to many lands and observed the basic goodness of all he met. As an educator, he devoted much of his life to the betterment of young seekers of knowledge. He expressed concern for honesty on the part of those who determine the character of the environment. His enthusiasm and critical dialogues inspired and motivated all who knew him.

Development of this Fourth Edition of *The Urban Pattern* without the creative contributions of Arthur Gallion has been a lonely task.

Simon Eisner

If you can look into the seeds of time,
And say which grains will grow and which will not,
Speak then to me. . . .

—*Shakespeare*

Cover photograph of contrasting subdivision development, Rancho Mirage, California, courtesy of Webb Engineering, Palm Springs, California.

D. Van Nostrand Company Regional Offices:
New York   Cincinnati

D. Van Nostrand Company International Offices:
London   Toronto   Melbourne

Copyright © 1980 by Litton Educational Publishing, Inc.

Library of Congress Catalog Card Number: 79-65550

ISBN: 0-442-26261-2

Published by D. Van Nostrand Company
135 West 50th Street, New York, N.Y.   10020

10   9   8   7   6   5   4   3   2   1

PREFACE

No one can fail to observe that, despite the marvels of man's inventive genius and the material comforts enjoyed by many, the spiritual and cultural lives of many people in the modern world are still improverished. All the expenditure of thought and money that has been devoted to planning has not substantially improved our environment. The authors of this book do not presume that planning will solve all the ills of the urban community or that planning by itself will be adequate to preserve or conserve our natural resources. Without creative planning, however, we will not begin to achieve an environment conducive to the good life we aspire to.

The Fourth Edition of *The Urban Pattern* has been designed for students and for those who are active in professional offices. We hope that the book will encourage readers to fulfill their professional potentials and expand their ability to serve the public they represent. The reorganization of the book's parts is in response to the manner in which many professionals conduct their practice and, therefore, should be useful to both the novice and the professional.

The current comprehensiveness of the planning profession has broadened the horizons for persons in or entering the field. No longer concerned only with the regulation of land use, professionals must now be increasingly involved in related fields. The "Comprehensive Planner" must bring together many related factors affecting the complicated and often conflicting interests of urban life.

The Fourth Edition of *The Urban Pattern* responds to many of the new opportunities and concerns. It focuses on areas where innovation and experimentation affect the public and private sectors. These include growth management regulations, which communities need as they begin to feel the stress of growth without the substantial economic base required to support the needs and demands of new residents. The environment within and around urban areas is also discussed, with respect to the increasing concern for health and security in those urban areas subject to careless treatment of resources. Environmental impact studies are cited as efforts to mitigate potential problems. Detailed attention is paid to the role of geography in determining the location and nature of urbanism so to enable students to understand the importance of this factor in the growth and development of communities.

The problems confronting the increasing number of aging persons are of

v

paramount importance to planners both in the United States and abroad. New materials on planning of housing for the elderly deal with this subject as it is treated in many nations.

Policy planning, the current emphasis of many university programs in urban planning, is reviewed in reference to the recent pronouncement by the President and the adopted Policy Statement of the American Institute of Planners (now the American Planning Association).

New material deals with implementation of plans through the utilization of zoning, land subdivision, and capital improvement. The required consistency between the Comprehensive Plan and zoning is cited as an example of the new laws affecting the planning process.

The various roles of persons and organizations involved in planning by the public and private sectors are described to demonstrate the forces and potential conflicts in the struggle between the regulators and the regulated. The function of the planning advocate is described: the role of representative of the interests of the poor and minority groups before the decision-making agencies.

The scope of the book has been broadened to include new materials dealing with New Towns In-Town, urban design, historical preservation, shopping centers, industry, regional planning, and many other related subjects.

The authors are grateful to the many contributors to the earlier editions of *The Urban Pattern*. Their work continues to add constructively to the educational process. In addition, we wish to thank others who have made it possible to extend the scope of the fourth edition. These include: Editors of Time Life Books, Inc.; David Bonavia, author of *Peking*; Professor John Friedmann, UCLA, and William Alonzo; Lawrence E. Pavlinski, Chief, Pedestrian and Cyclist Branch, National Highway Traffic Safety Administration; Hong Kong Government Information Services; Nien-Ting Chang, graduate student at UCLA; Robert S. Holmes, President, Eno Foundation for Transportation, Inc.; David I. Davis, Highway Engineer, Federal Highway Administration; Denise P. Frank, Caseworker, Foster Homes Program, Bucks County, Pennsylvania; Michael J. Frank, Chief, County Planning Division, Bucks County, Pennsylvania; Anglo-Chinese Educational Institute, London, England; Lewis Mumford; Sylvia Stern, graduate student, UCLA; Joan Robinson, Professor Emeritus of Economics, University of Cambridge, England; Harvey S. Perloff, Dean, School of Architecture and Urban Planning, UCLA; American Institute of Planning; American Society of Planning Officials; American Planners Association.

We also extend our appreciation to many persons who contributed to the text by their suggestions and editing of the material. Special thanks to the staff of D. Van Nostrand Company, whose courtesy and consideration added to the pleasure of the preparation of the manuscript.

Simon Eisner, APA, AICP

CONTENTS

PART 1 THE CITY IS BORN

mentalism · The Baroque City · Behind the Façades ·
Colonial Expansion—America · From Radials to Gridiron

PART 2 THE CITY IN TRANSITION

PART 3 THE PLANNING PROCESS

PART 4 PLANNING FOR THE FUTURE

PART 5 IMPLEMENTATION

PART 1

The People, Yes,
Out of what is their change
from chaos to order and chaos again?
—*Carl Sandburg*

The City
Is Born

1

The Dawn of Urbanization

The simplest definition of urbanism might be

> The confederation or union of neighboring clans resorting to a center used as a common meeting place for worship, protection, etc., hence the political or soverign body formed by such a community.

Another definition is that an urban area is a composite of cells, neighborhoods, or communities where people work together for the common good. The types of urban areas, therefore, can vary greatly as persons participate in production, the trading of goods, transportation, delivery of a variety of services, or a combination of all of these activities.

A third definition says that urban areas are locations where there is opportunity for a diverse type of living environment and life styles. People live, work, and enjoy themselves, in social and cultural relationships provided by the proximities of an urban area.

Urban areas can be simple or complex. They can have a rural flavor or that of an industrial workshop. They can be peaceful places or filled with all types of conflicts. They can be small and easy to maintain or gargantuan, filled with strife and economic problems.

FROM THE CAVE TO THE VILLAGE

Contrary to popular belief, urbanism did not begin when people left their caves. It probably started in the caves themselves where people gathered for protec-

3

tions against the elements or for defense against nomadic tribes who might kidnap them or rob them of their shelter and food.

Lewis Mumford states in his article "The Natural History Of Urbanization":

> Though permanent villages date only from the Neolithic times, the habit of resorting to caves for the collective performance of magical ceremonies seems to date back to an earlier period; and whole communities, living in caves and the hollowed out walls of rock, have survived in widely scattered areas down to the present. The outline of the city as both an outward form and inward pattern of life might be found in such ancient assemblages.[1]

These places of communal living gave way to the village. The village was a by-product of the development of agriculture on fertile soils where there was an adequate water supply. On many occasions these areas were adjacent to the Mediterranean Sea and the Nile, Tigres, and Euphrates Rivers. Mumford holds that the newly created urban areas and the rural hinterland, the city and country, were part of an interlaced whole that was essential to the sustenance of human and animal life, which in turn promoted agricultural production.

Early villages were located on sites that offered natural protection. Some natural defenses were elevated terrain, islands, and peninsulas. Otherwise, villages were surrounded by barricades or moats. One of the earliest known villages was built upon piles in a Swiss lake.

People have always been gregarious beings. They have sought companionship and devised group entertainment and sports. The village was also an appropriate sanctuary for the altar of their deity, a meeting place for assembly, and a center for trade. As the environment became increasingly populated, urbanization resulted.

As cities have taken on added functions and have grown, the care of fertile land has become to some extent ignored. Lands, still used for agriculture, have been infused with so many artificial fertilizers that the soil has become a vehicle for these chemicals. These fertilizers are the main nutrients for fruit and vegetable crops. Concern for protection of fertile soils has been slow to develop, but increasing attention is now being focused on conservation. Some Indian communities, for example, opposed urban developments on their reservations, favoring instead the protection of their land and culture, despite the greater cash return resulting from urbanization.

The city, as opposed to the village, came about as the result of crop growing and stock breeding on a somewhat permanent basis. The production of hard grains that could be stored from year to year offered stability as it provided insurance against starvation. The ability to preserve food made it possible for a people to diversify its activities. Urban areas became known for the type of food they could conserve, wheat and rye in the European areas, rice in the orient.

---

[1] *Man's Role in Changing the Face of the Earth,* ed. William L. Thomas, Jr., U. of Chicago Press, 1956.

With the development of a diversified economy not totally dependent upon the production of food, it was possible to attract people into a labor pool, thus providing employment in a variety of forms. When this occurred, villages or hamlets enlarged into towns and cities. They operated on a different political and economic basis than was possible in the simpler forms.

Newly created cities bore many of the physical and social characteristics of their earlier form of urbanism. There are agricultural centers today with their food supply still located in the fields that surround them. These particular urban centers have had little reason to grow beyond the limited size that their basic functions have dictated.

While many changes have taken place in some rural areas, great parts of the developing countries of the world still live in a Neolithic age insofar as economy and standards of living are concerned. The natives wrest what food they can from poor land, constantly remaining on the verge of starvation.

The People's Republic of China made its greatest step forward when it freed itself from the danger of famine. In that nation a large-scale commitment to agriculture is the primary planning goal. A tremendous amount of manpower has been allocated to that end due to a lack of mechanical equipment.

THE NATURE OF CITIES

The word "city" implies a concentration of people in a geographic area who can support themselves from the city's economic activities on a fairly permanent basis. The city can be a center of industry, exchange, education, government, or involve all these activities. These diverse areas of opportunity attract people from rural areas to cities.

Thus we find that cities tend to become big if their economic base is wide. The smaller cities are usually satellites that depend on larger cities to sustain their economic life. Thus central cities have multiple functions, whereas the bedroom communities surrounding the cities have mainly the purpose of housing the more affluent members of the work force.

Cities also have circulation systems that unite the different areas of the city and provide routes for bringing commodities from the farms to the city's distribution centers. Multiple forms of transportation and transit are often available in large cities.

Cities have many obvious faults insofar as their services to people are concerned. They can be overcrowded, contain large amounts of substandard housing, be centers of unemployment, and have corrupt government officials. Taxation tends to be high and services less than adequate. However, with all of these faults, cities are here to stay. The charge to planners, at all levels, public and private, is to find ways of making these essential elements in our social system work better, more efficiently and thus make our cities better places to live in.

GEOGRAPHY OF URBAN AREAS

In studying the urban areas in the world one can observe certain phenomena regarding their location. The larger cities, with some exceptions, are found where the climate is relatively moderate. Few of any great size are located north of the 60th or south of the 45th parallels. This does not mean that there are no great temperature extremes within these boundaries. For instance, the great Sahara Desert and the frigid winter climate in parts of Canada, the United States, and the Soviet Union lie in this moderate temperature zone. However, for parts of the year, the climate is inhabitable so that life exists or even flourishes.

Geographic studies also indicate that urban areas seldom form in areas where the topography is steep. There are some cities at high altitudes, but the slope of the land in these urban areas is relatively level. Cities such as Denver, Colorado, and Mexico City are more than 5000 feet above sea level, but the terrain at these sites is relatively flat. It is only owing to the "bull dozer," a recent invention, that steep areas have been leveled to permit urban development.

Accessibility to other places usually determines the location of larger cities. Thus most of the largest cities of the world are located on or near major waterways. New York, Seattle, Boston, Rio de Janeiro, and Chicago demonstrate this principle. Some of these cities are terminals for external transportation, while others, like Chicago and Kansas City, are the crossing points for networks of internal transportation. Geographic studies of cities also take into account the relationship among people, types of housing, densities and concentrations of population, the rates of growth, and the impact of growth upon the land and all other resources.

IMPACT OF URBANISM ON THE ENVIRONMENT

Urban growth can effect many changes. Urbanization alters a climate as the result of buildings occupying land, pavements covering streets, and smoke from factories pouring into the air.

Even the seemingly most trivial of human activities can bring about vast environmental changes. The construction of a simple irrigation canal from the Colorado River to the fertile Imperial Valley of California caused the Salton Sea to form in 1905 after a heavy rainfall in the upper reaches of the river. Thus a body of water about 40 miles long and 10 miles wide exists today where in 1904 there was only desert land.

In recent years this huge body of water has been contaminated by the rivers flowing into it. They bear effluents from the sewerage in Mexico and pesticides and fertilizers from the agricultural areas that the rivers flow through. The saline content of the water has been increasing, thereby increasing the chances that the fish in the sea will be harmed.

Recent ventures in the Alaskan wilderness may bring about long term adverse effects on the life cycles of human and animal life there. Where a perfect balance in nature existed, today the advance of "southern civilization" has replaced the dog sled with the gasoline motored automobile. The once limited pathways that did not disturb the permafrost have been replaced by the trenches cut by the many heavy vehicles. The pattern of migration of the caribou and other large animals may be disrupted by the hundreds of miles of the oil pipeline. Each of these incidents may not be critical to the survival of the Alaskan Eskimos, but the sum of these changes may be as great as those that created the Sahara Desert.

The future presents all humanity—not just urbanites—with the problem of coping with technological change. Among the problems that we will have to confront are the disposal of nuclear wastes, the filling of the skies with aerosols, and the development of artifical rain through the use of iodides. The latter development not only changes the microclimate, but may ultimately affect the inhabitability of our planet.

TYPES OF URBAN COMMUNITIES

From earliest times, each urban community has filled a special mission in the social and economic structure. They all have had particular functions to perform, some singular and others multiple. Thus we find:

The Cross Road.   This has been the simplest form of community that expands or contracts as traders travel from one area to another. It is place for rest, food, relaxation, and exchange of merchandise and ideas. The location can be at a transporation terminal or at the port on a body of water.

The Primary Agricultural Community.   This is the service area for rural activities. It is here that essentials for agricultural activities are acquired and that the harvest is brought for shipment to processers and ultimately consumers.

The Commercial City.   It is here that the business ventures, the exchanges, the dealing in commodities takes place. There is a wide range of retail merchandise for the consumer to select from.

The Industrial City.   Raw or partly processed materials are turned into finished goods for shipment to the market places of the world.

The Transportation City.   This is at the center of the transportation web, where goods are brought from far off places to be distributed to other far off places.

The Recreational City.   Cities that attract large numbers of people because of their climate or special offerings. These include health resorts, gambling centers, recreational, or scenic areas.

Educational Cities.   Cities where a major educational institution or group of institutions constitute the primary functions of the urban area. Examples of such places are Claremont, California, Davis, California, and Princeton, New Jersey.

Mining Communities.   Here the extraction of minerals forms the economic base. Mining communities in South Africa are of this type.

Retirement Communities.   These include cities where the principal export capital comes from income and pensions. The communities in the sun belt are examples.

Governmental Centers.   These are centers of governmental activity where the principal employer is the government.

Combination (Regional) Cities.   A few cities perform all or many of the above functions. They are, therefore, larger and more complex than any of the above types of communities.

POLITICAL FOUNDATION

The village brought something new to the lives of primitive people. It introduced the necessity for mutual responsibility and co-operation. Social and political organizations resulted from this need.

People, however, did not adjust themselves easily to the self-discipline that community life requires. Personal rivalry flared within the village, and the most powerful individual assumed the role of tribal leader. When there was rivalry between villages, armed conflict often ensued. Several villages might come under the domination of the victorious tribe with the tribe's leader rising to the position of ruler. In time, empires were created and rulers took the titles of king and emperor.

SOCIAL STRUCTURE AND AESTHETICS

Society has been forged in the crucible of natural forces. Because they are part of nature, people have suffered from many of the evils they have inflicted on the environment. They have faced the necessity to improve economic security, correct social maladjustments, discard mass superstitions, or resist seizure of power by autocrats bent upon personal glory and self-aggrandizement. The conflicts have created varying degrees of pressure upon humankind under a variety of circumstances.

What distinguishes the early city from the primitive village is its higher degree of political and social organization. The more sophisticated social structure allows people to live together in relative peace. Social, economic and political organization are essential to the growth and development of a city.

As a result of the advanced social structure, bold aesthetic changes took place. Temples and other structures of the ruling group became permanent. Tremendous amounts of energy were expended to produce great edifices, such as palaces and cathedrals, which became a source of pride to the public and the seat of power for its rulers. In the meantime, the homes of the people were mud huts. They were without any amenities and situated on unpaved streets. This situation still exists in a large part of the world where great numbers of people live in slums, favellas, and barrios, many of which are in urban areas.

EVOLUTION OF PHYSICAL FORM

Evolving from these conflicts the development of cities has marked the culture of a people. Sensitive to the surge between oppression and justice, the physical form of cities has been shaped by the economic, social and political forces of society. The degree to which freedom or slavery has dominated human life, the manner in which war has been waged, the instruments of destruction and defense, the tools for peaceful pursuits and the way they have been used, the consideration, neglect, or disdain people have shown their fellows, all account for the kind of cities people have built for themselves, and their effect on urban development may guide us in charting our future enterprise in city building.

Historians have attempted to isolate and codify the variations in the patterns of cities. However, their development almost precludes such classification. Adjectives like organic and inorganic, irregular and geometrical, magical and mystical, formal and informal, medieval and classic, are often so obtuse they obscure rather than clarify the distinctions, or they describe a form without the substance. The primary distinction in the pattern of cities is marked by the transitions from a slave to a mercantile economy and from slingshot to gunpowder warfare.

Two basic urban forms are discernible: the walled town and the open city. Within these basic forms a wide variety of patterns has been woven, each color and design shaped by the character of society at the time.

Few cities in which great cultures thrived began with a plan. They developed by a process of accretion—the growth was irregular in form, sensitive to changes in the habits of people, and dynamic in character. They began as free cities which were settled voluntarily. Geometrical form was introduced according to the structure of the land or the manner in which the land was apportioned among the inhabitants. Colonial cities founded by great states were given a formal pattern predetermined by a ruling authority. Privileged landowners plotted their land for allocation to settlers, the plots being generally regular in form, almost static in character.

Within these various patterns we may find similar social, economic, and political habits and customs. Neither the presence nor the absence of geometrical form has affixed itself upon a people or a period as a conclusive expression of society. It is rather the manner in which the forms have been manipulated and the purpose for which they have been devised that give significance to the physical patterns of cities.

With the ebb and flow of civilization the irregular and geometrical patterns have been grafted one upon the other. Villages which grew into cities because of geographic, economic, or social advantages may show evidence of geometrical forms superimposed upon an irregular pattern, or an informal system may have been grafted upon a city having an original pattern of gridiron streets. Cities have been subjected to the process of continuous remodeling through the ages, and the variety of forms is the result of forces which dominated during the successive periods of their history. We find the motives of city builders, from emperors to subdividers, reflected in the designs they have stamped upon the city.

We have been accustomed to measuring a civilization by the monuments it produced. Certain cultural characteristics are revealed by these structures, but it is not enough to observe the monuments alone. The city is not the palace, the temple, or a collection of art objects. If we are to discern the characteristics of a civilization, we cannot confine our attention to the rulers; we must observe the affairs of the people. The city means the whole people who inhabit it, the entire collection of the houses the people live in, the shops in which they work, the streets they traverse, and the places in which they trade. To separate the palace from the dwellings of the populace is like removing a phrase from its context. When the palace is related to the lives of the people, it may provide quite a different interpretation than when it is observed as an isolated monument.

More than the great structures that impress us, it is the dwellings of the people that mark the culture of cities. Civilization is not measured by inventions alone; it is measured rather by the extent to which the people share the benefits these inventions make possible. Progress is not guaged by comparison of an aboriginal village with a modern city; it is more accurately appraised by the degree to which the people have participated in the advantages of each. Standards and quality are relative, and it is the contrast between the environment of the privileged and that of the poor which provides the yardstick of the freedom and happiness enjoyed by the people in any period.

History reveals a lag between moments of great social ideals and the structures that reflect them. Institutions of social and political justice or oppression gather a momentum which carries beyond their zenith. The substance of these institutions, the freedom they have nurtured or denied, may have altered or vanished by the time the physical structure of the urban environment they engendered is finally completed. Frequently, the powerful human forces which produced a city have begun to change or disappear but the physical form of the city has never been modified. An environment which emerged from a society of high ideals may then become the dramatic scene of decline.

Stability, in the sense of a sameness of human conduct, a *status quo* of human institutions, has not long endured. Humanity must continuously have new cultural food upon which to nourish, or it decays. Civilization has not remained static for any protracted period. During periods in history when the social and political institutions were molded to the welfare of the people they provided the very climate of freedom in which the baser instincts of humanity could forge and wield the tools of oppression, inequality, and injustice. Unless this tide was stemmed, civilization turned in the direction of decline. We observe these trends in early villages, in ancient cities, in medieval cities, in the Baroque Period, and there is evidence of their presence in our cities today.

CITIES OF ANCIENT LANDS

Early civilization spread along the fertile valleys where food, water, and transportation were at hand. A series of great and small empires rose, waged wars, and fell. Supremacy shifted from one kingdom to another, each adding its contribution to the evolution of the civilized world, but one characteristic was shared in common by all these civilizations. All possessions of the kingdom, the land, and its benefits were subject to the will of the ruling monarchs and their appointed emissaries.

In Egypt the lives of the people were dedicated to the Pharaoh. The towns they built in the third millennium B.C. were erected upon his order. They housed the slaves and artisans engaged in building the great pyramids—the royal tombs of kings and nobles. Like huge barracks the cells and compartments of sun-dried bricks were crowded about common courtyards. Narrow lanes served as open drainage sewers as well as passageways to the dwellings. Walls surrounded the towns. Because the kingdom was broad and mighty, they were probably built primarily for protection from seasonal floods rather than the armies of invading enemies.

Concurrent with the Pyramid Period of Egypt, permanent towns of burned brick were built along the Indus Valley. In Mohenjo-Daro and Harrapa the streets were arranged in a regular pattern and, as in Egypt, the dwellings were compactly built about interior courts. The heights of buildings were established in proportion to the width of streets, one and two stories predominating. Sanitation was of a relatively high order; a system of underground sewers extended about the towns, and there is evidence that disposal lines were connected to the dwellings. But all trace of the civilization that produced these cities has apparently vanished, and it remains a matter of conjecture whether the peoples who occupied them influenced the city-building of the Near East in subsequent centuries.

In the second millennium B.C. Egyptian pharaohs built temple cities on the banks of the Nile. Monumental avenues, colossal temple plazas, and rock-cut tombs remain as mute testimony to the luxurious life of the nobility in Memphis, Thebes, and Tel-el-Amarna, but few snatches of recorded history describe the city of the people. Time and the elements have washed away the clay huts and tenements in which the people dwelled. The dramatic Avenue of the

Sphinxes in Thebes and the broad temple enclosure, one-third mile wide and one-half mile long, in Tel-el-Amarna tell a vivid story of powerful autocrats, while historians piece together fragmentary remains of the homes of people and conclude that slums spread about the towns.

A series of empires rose in Mesopotamia, and humble villages along the valley of the Tigris and Euphrates Rivers became monumental cities of the kings. Each was heavily fortified to resist the seige of many enemies. The stately palace-temple dominated the city, and the people lived their urban existence in the shadows of slavery and superstitious religion. Economic hardship added to the burden of the masses. According to Bemis and Burchard a skilled artisan in ancient Sumeria could obtain housing for 5 or 6 per cent of his income, but the poorest dwellings cost unskilled workers as much as 30 and 40 per cent of their subsistence allowance.[2]

Seeking to improve the lot of the common people, the great King Hammurabi, in 2100 B.C., codified his laws of justice. In Old Babylon we observe the dawn of building regulations. The codes of Hammurabi meted harsh punishment to irresponsible builders. According to the king's decree, if the wall of a building should fall and kill the son of the occupant, the life of the builder's son would be sacrificed—the doctrine of "an eye for an eye, a tooth for a tooth."

Out of the slums of thriving imperial cities were carved triumphal avenues connecting magnificent city gates. King Sennacherib built his temples and palaces in seventh-century Nineveh. The processional avenues, great walls, monumental gates, and hanging gardens of Nebuchadnezzar's palace were the vivid spectacle of Babylon in the sixth and fifth centuries described by Herodotus. This Greek historian also told of the narrow streets lined with the three- and four-story dwellings of the populace. Behind the avenues, laid in regular pattern at right angles to each other, were the crowded houses of the people. Of more concern to the vanity of rulers was the monumental spectacle of the great edifices with which they adorned their cities.

Perhaps the physical environment of the home did not weigh heavily upon the people in ancient times. Undoubtedly a beneficent desert climate cleansed the insanitary surroundings in these southern lands. But, human nature being what it is, we can reasonably suspect that the violent contrasts in social caste, the servitude in which the multitude languished, and the restriction from participation in public affairs were as responsible for the continuous wars, revolts, and conquests, as the insatiable appetite of kings for power.

A more enlightened society appears to have been cultivated in the islands of the Aegean Sea. Kings reigned over city-states, but these rulers were apparently not accorded the distinction of deification as in eastern lands. In contrast to the austere detachment of royal palaces in Mesopotamia, the palace served as a center of community life in Aegean culture. On the island of Crete the town sites

[2]Albert Bemis and John Burchard, *The Evolving House,* volume 1 of *A History of the Home,* MIT Press, Cambridge, Mass., 1933-36.

offered natural protection. Ancient cities, like Knossos, were not surrounded by walls. The people enjoyed free access to the sea and entered into trade with other lands. On the mainland of Greece, however, cities needed the protection of ramparts; the cities of Tiryns and Mycenae were heavily fortified.

These early cities of the Aegean were irregular in form. Meandering streets followed the rugged topography of the sites. The streets were narrow lanes but they were paved with stone. Excavations have revealed highly developed systems of water supply, sanitation, and drainage for the palace and many of the houses. Most dwellings were one-story in height and, although densely built, the towns did not reach the great size and congestion which were apparent in cities of the Near East.

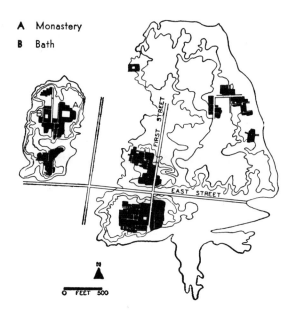

A Monastery

B Bath

MOHENJO-DARO

Excavations at Mohenjo-Daro in the Indus Valley have revealed the remains of a large city built about 3000 B.C. It is apparent that a relatively advanced civilization flourished in this city. Houses ranged in size from two rooms to mansions with numerous rooms. The map shows the archeologist's assumption that a major street ran in the north-south (First Street) and east-west (East Street) directions. Areas shown in black have been excavated and indicate the intricate plan of narrow roads. Buildings were of masonry, streets were paved, and considerable evidence of sewer drainage from dwellings has been uncovered. The principal buildings excavated are a public bath and a monastery.

KING SOLOMON'S TEMPLE AND CITADEL, Jerusalem, c. 900 B.C.

The splendor of the temples and palaces of the kings in contrast to the congested dwellings of the populance. (Restoration by Dr. John Wesley Kelchner).

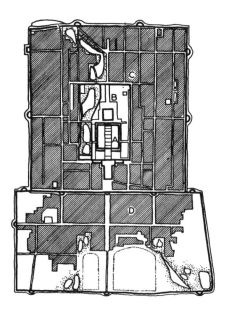

PEKING

A Forbidden City
B Imperial City
C Tartar City
D Chinese City

Within each of the cells surrounded by streets in the sketch is a maze of narrow minor roads, also laid out in rectilinear form.

Peking.   The City of Peking was started during the eighth century B.C. on approximately the same site that the city occupies today.

The present plan of Peking, however, stems from the eleventh century A.D. The original city of the Tartars was extended with the addition of the Chinese city. The Forbidden City of the Emperor lies in the center of the city. The dwellings are cramped along an intricate system of regular alleys, but the royal gardens and lakes occupy a large area of the city.

The city of the Ming Dynasty covered an area approximately 3¼ miles long and 4 miles wide, about 8,300 acres. This is known as the inner city within which the Imperial Palace was located.

In spite of its rapid growth in recent years, the city accounts for only a small portion of the 6,600 square miles that now bear the name of Peking. Within the broader definition of the city there are the satellite towns and agricultural communities.

The changes that have taken place in the city since 1949 have been greater than anything that occurred during the previous 500 years.

Author David Bonavia writes:

> Geographically Peking occupies roughly the same position in China as does New York in North America—both verging on the 40th parallel, both having comfortable temperatures in the autumn and spring. But there the similarity ends. Located on the edge of the North China Plain, Peking is essentially a huddled city, sheltered behind hills and mountains to the north and west, and gazing proudly but a shade wistfully toward the warm and fertile plains of Southern China. It stands neither on a significant river nor beside the sea.[3]

The city is in the form of a grid, oriented according to cardinal points, the form finalized during the 15th century. Straight streets and avenues were laid out around the central palace known as the "Forbidden City." The Forbidden City (Imperial Palace) reflects the power and energy of the ancient authorities. A great museum of historical structures and artifacts, it stands at the head of Tien An Men Square surrounded by public buildings.

LuKang, Taiwan.   LuKang, the old port town in ChangHua County, was the place where Chinese culture first landed on Taiwan.[4] The name LuKang means "deer-port". Today it is a town of 70,000 people with a total area of about 15,000 acres. With the silting up of its harbor, the shipping of rice, hemp, and deerskin from the port ceased. Today, LuKang is a backwater town but it has something no other place in Taiwan can boast of: a human and intimate scale.

Crooked streets mark the town. It is, however, an easily walkable community with tangible signs of old China, such as the ancient temples and shops

---

[3] *Peking,* Time-Life Books, 1978.

[4] Nien-Ting Chang, "LuKang, an Old Port Town in Taiwan," unpublished paper, UCLA.

in which artisans worked and musicians performed. Large farmhouses and small factories are located outside of the town. The linear commercial area is located along the main street as are the two major temples. Beyond the residential section is the agricultural area and the fish ponds.

The south-north and east-west streets that divided the ancient town into blocks performed the function of social control. Each block was surrounded by walls that formed a self-contained area. In conventional Chinese architecture, people and space should be in harmony. This concept is crucial to understanding the Chinese city.

LUKANG, TAIWAN

Taipei

Lukang

Taiwan

Hong Kong

SOUTH CHINA SEA

2

The Classic City

GOVERNMENT BY LAW

On the mainland of Greece the virile shepherds from the north mingled with the Aegean peoples, merged with their city-states, and gradually absorbed them within their culture. A wealthy landowning noble class rose in power, and during the eighth century B.C. leaders from this group appropriated much of the influence previously exercised by the kings. The palace citadel disappeared, and temples dedicated to the gods of their religion replaced them upon the acropolis. The nobles assumed the power of kings, dominated the cities, and brought oppression to the peasant class. Seeking relief in other lands, the peasant group opened new avenues of colonization and trade. A merchant middle class emerged. Feuds between this new economic group and the city-dwelling nobles forced the selection of a common leader, and in the seventh century the Tyrants of Athens came into power.

Although they were themselves of the noble class, the Tyrants maintained their leadership by their support of the common people. Estates of the nobles were redistributed among the people, and a strong land-holding peasant class developed. Under the successive leadership of Solon, Pisistratus and Clisthenes, the principle of law evolved as a basis of social conduct. A new form was given to political organization of the community: a government of laws determined by the people.

During the fifth century B.C. with the inspired leadership of Pericles, democracy and a high order of morality took root in Athenian citizenship. Political education was extended by way of free speech and assembly. Magistrates were elected to execute the laws, and public service was vested with dignity. Sovereignty of the people was assured and protected by a body of laws to which all agreed and were subject. The deep sense of individual responsibility was expressed in the vow of Athenian citizenship:

I will not dishonor these sacred arms; I will not abandon my comrade in battle; I will fight for my gods and my hearth single-handed or with my companions. I will not leave my country smaller, but I will leave it greater and stronger than I received it. I will obey the commands which the magistrates in their wisdom shall give me.

17

I will submit to the existing laws and to those that the people shall unanimously make; if anyone shall attempt to overthrow these laws or disobey them, I will not suffer it, but will fight for them, whether single-handed or with my fellows. I will respect the worship of my fathers.

THE DEMOCRACY OF ATHENS

Inspired by the political genius of Pericles the democracy of Athens in the fifth century acquired a soul. It required wise citizenship to retain this quality, and philosophers like Socrates strove to cultivate the wisdom and intelligence. Although Socrates sometimes disapproved of the laws and thought some of them bad, he insisted upon the obligation of the citizenry to abide by them until they were revised. Esteem for the law was expressed in the words of the great orator Demosthenes:

> The whole life of men, whether they inhabit a great city or a small, is ordered by nature and the laws. Whilst nature is lawless and varies with individuals, the laws are a common possession, controlled, identical for all. . . . They desire the just, the beautiful, the useful. It is that which they seek; once discovered it is that which is created into a principle equal for all and unvarying; it is that which is called law.

Athenian democracy of the fifth century was described by Glotz

> as the exercise of sovereignty by free and equal citizens under the aegis of law. The law, which protects the citizens one against the other, defends also the rights of the individual against the power of the State and the interests of the State against the excesses of individualism. Before the last years of the fifth century there is no sign that liberty has degenerated into anarchy or license, nor is the principle of equality carried so far as to entail the denial of the existence of mental inequalities.[1]

Democracy in the Age of Pericles produced that inherent dignity of the individual born of free speech, a sense of unity with one's fellowman, and a full opportunity for participation in affairs of the community. The Athenian citizen experienced the exhilaration of freedom and accepted the challenge of responsibility it thrust upon him with honor and with pride. The discovery of freedom gave impetus to the search for truth as honest men desire it. Philosophy was nurtured, and there were no depths which the wise and intelligent were afraid to plumb. Reason was encouraged, logic invited, and science investigated. There was no truth which might be discovered and remain undisclosed. Inspired by this atmosphere it was no wonder great philosophy was born; only in freedom can such greatness be cultivated, not freedom from care but freedom of the spirit. This was the environment of culture which produced Socrates, Plato, and Aristotle.

---

[1] Gustave Glotz, *The Greek City and Its Institutions,* Kegan Paul, Trench, Trubner & Company, 1929.

The affinity between freedom and spiritual values was symbolized in the temples built upon the acropolis. In them was reflected the exalted stature of democratic man. Some four centuries later another philosopher, this one from Bethlehem, was to recreate the spiritual values demonstrated by the Greeks at the height of their democracy.

THE HUMBLE CITY

During the early years when democracy was flowering, the Greek city was a maze of wandering unpaved lanes lacking in drainage and sanitation. Water was carried from local wells. Waste was disposed of in the streets. There were no palaces and, with the execption of the temples, public buildings were few and simple. The common assembly place was the *pnyx*, an open-air podium where the citizens met to consider affairs of state. The agora, or market place and center of urban activity, was irregular in form. There was little distinction between the dwellings of the well-to-do citizen and his less privileged fellowmen. The few rooms that comprised the house were grouped about an interior court behind windowless facades facing the random streets. Most towns were surrounded by protective walls.

For the Greek citizen the temple was the symbol of his democratic way of life, the equality of men. Upon the temples he lavished all his creative energies, and in them we find a refinement of line and beauty of form that expressed the dignity and humility of the Athenian. In later and less happy days Demosthenes reflected upon this period of the fifth century. "These edifices," he said, "which their administrations have given us, their decorations of our temples and the offerings deposited in them, are so numerous that all efforts of posterity cannot exceed them. Then in private life, so exemplary was their moderation, their adherence to the ancient manners so scrupulously exact, that, if any of you discovered the house of Aristides or Miltiades, or any of the illustrious men of those times, he must know that it was not distinguished by the least extraordinary splendor."[2]

HIPPODAMUS

It was natural that an atmosphere of philosophy should impel a search for order in the city. It was a topic that engaged the attention of teacher-philosophers and politicians alike. In the latter part of the fifth century an architect from Miletus, by the name of Hippodamus, advanced positive theories about the art and science of city planning. He has been credited with the origination of the "gridiron" street system, although this is not entirely accurate. A semblance of geometrical form had been present in early towns of Egypt, Mesopotamia, and

[2] Glotz, p. 302.

THE ACROPOLIS, Athens

The temple rather than the palace of rulers dominated the ancient Hellenic city and a meeting place for political assembly of the people—the pnyx—was added to the urban pattern. As the power of kings diminished and democracy expanded, the houses of the people and the community facilities established for their use assumed greater importance in the city plan. (Trans World Airways photo)

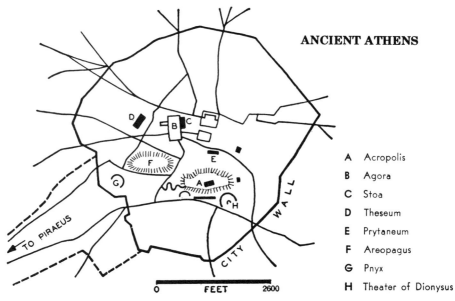

ANCIENT ATHENS

A Acropolis
B Agora
C Stoa
D Theseum
E Prytaneum
F Areopagus
G Pnyx
H Theater of Dionysus

the Indus Valley, and a formal rectangular pattern was used, in part, for rebuilding some Greek cities after their destruction by the Persians in the sixth century. The gridiron pattern was vigorously applied by Hippodamus to obtain a rational arrangement of buildings and circulation.

The city plan was conceived as a design to serve all the people. The individual dwelling was the common denominator. Blocks were shaped to provide appropriate orientation for the dwellings within them. The functional uses of buildings and public spaces were recognized in the arrangement of streets. They provided for the circulation of people and vehicles without interference with the orientation of dwellings or the assembly of people in the market place.

Superimposing the rigid geometrical form of the Hippodamian street system upon the rugged topography of the sites occupied by most Greek cities created numerous streets so steep they could be negotiated only with steps. Since the movement of people was almost entirely on foot, this did not present the problem we might assume today although there were probably some puffing Grecians who reached the top of a long climb to attend a political meeting in the assembly hall. The principal traffic streets, however, were placed to allow the circulation of the few horse-drawn vehicles which entered the town.

PUBLIC SPACE

The expanding affairs of government required appropriate facilities. The agora, or market place, was the center of business and political life, and about it were lined the shops and market booths. Accessible from the agora square, but not facing upon it, were the assembly hall (*ecclesiasteron*), council hall (*bouleuterion*), and council chamber (*prytaneum*).

The agora was usually located in the approximate center of the town plan, with the major east-west and north-south streets leading to it. It was designed to accommodate all the citizens who would have business in the market place or attend public functions in the adjacent public buildings. The open space enclosed by the agora occupied about 5 per cent of the city area, the dimensions being approximately one fifth of the width and breadth of the town itself.

The plan of the agora was geometrical in form. Square or rectangular open spaces were surrounded by colonnaded porticoes sheltering the buildings about the square. The plan was arranged to avoid interference between the movement of people across the open space and those who assembled for trade and business in the market. Streets generally terminated at the agora rather than crossing it, the open space being reserved primarily for pedestrian traffic and circulation.

Common open space in Greek cities was largely confined to enclosure for public buildings. Because the city was small in area, the city dweller was not far removed from the open countryside about the town. Olive groves flourished outside the walls and here the philosophers founded the academy and the lyceum. In these quiet groves they met their pupils and set the pattern for later institutions of higher learning. From these academies came the first university, the Museum of Alexandria.

PRIENE

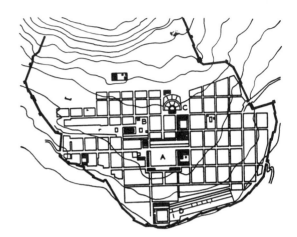

A Agora

B Temple of Athene Polias

C Theater

D Stadium

These cities demonstrate the Hippodamian plan as it developed toward the end of the Hellenic Period. The agora occupies the approximate geographical center of the town. About it are the temple shrines, public buildings, and shops. The dwelling blocks are planned to provide the appropriate orientation of houses in a manner similar to that shown at Olynthus. Recreation and entertainment facilities are provided in the gymnasium, stadium, and theater. The contours of the site indicate that some of the streets were very steep, steps being frequently required, but the main streets connecting the gates and the agora were generally placed so that beasts of burden and carts could traverse them readily.

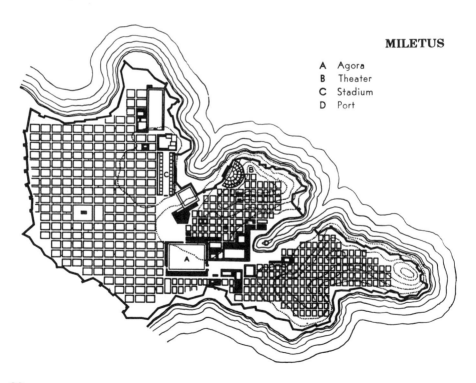

MILETUS

A Agora

B Theater

C Stadium

D Port

Evidence of attention to building regulations is recorded in the chronicles of various Athenian writers. There is reference to laws restricting buildings from encroachment upon the streets and prohibitions against the projection of upper floors beyond the first floor walls. These are forerunners of the present-day "rights-of-way." Windows were not permitted to open directly upon the street, and water drains were not allowed to empty into the street. Though primitive when judged by the standards acceptable today, the Greek towns demonstrated a conscious effort to improve the environment for the whole people, the final test of genuine civic responsibility.

It was in the colonial cities founded by the city-states on the shores of the Mediterranean that the planning theories of Hippodamus found their fullest expression. It is recorded that Hippodamus himself planned Piraeus, the port city of Athens, as well as Thurii and Rhodes. The old established cities were remodeled in parts, the agora assuming a more orderly form as new buildings were erected for public affairs, but the colonial cities had the benefit of planning prior to their settlement. Although they were founded by a mother city-state, they enjoyed a degree of political autonomy, becoming a part of the confederation of Greek cities which comprised the Athenian "Empire."

THE SIZE OF ANCIENT CITIES

Athens, in the fifth and fourth centuries, had a citizen population of some 40,000 and a total population of between 100,000 and 150,000 including slaves and foreigners. Most Greek cities, however, were relatively small. Only about three towns exceeded 10,000 persons during the thriving Hellenic Period. It was a theory of Hippodamus that this was an appropriate size, and Plato later concluded it should range between 5,000 and 10,000. In the settlement of colonial towns it was customary to dispatch about 10,000 colonists from the mother city-state. The glorious metropolis with its teeming millions is undoubtedly an exaggerated description of the actual number of people who dwelt in urban communities in ancient times. The metropolis, as we know it, is of comparatively recent origin.

A number of factors bore upon the size of a city and the population it could support. The food and water supply was a primary consideration. The tools for cultivating the soil, the means for transporting the products, and the source and methods for distributing the water supply established limits on the urban population which could be accommodated in a single group. As long as people were dependent upon the primitive hand plough, the horse-cart, and gravity flow of water, it was not feasible to gather in great numbers and maintain adequate standards of urban hygiene. Hellenic towns relied primarily on local water-courses, wells, and springs, but supplemental supply was sometimes available through conduits from more remote sources in higher surrounding hills.

THE DWELLINGS

In their houses the Greeks sought quiet privacy. Most of the social contacts and all business affairs were carried on outside the home. Small merchants frequently had shops adjacent to their houses, but business and politics were generally conducted in and adjacrnt to the agora. Sports and recreation were concentrated in the gymnasium; drama and festivals in the theater. Feasts and other celebrations seldom occurred in the private dwelling. There was usually a small altar in the home, but religious exercises and worship took place in the temple precincts. Consequently, the house was unpretentious in its appointments and, as has been previously mentioned, there was little distinction between the dwellings in the town. A display of affluence was not consistent with the tenets of democracy in the fifth century.

Early houses were enclosed about a central hearth. A hole in the roof allowed the smoke to escape and it also permitted the collection of rain water in the cistern. In late Hellenic towns sanitation was improved by the pavement of streets and installation of underground drains from dwellings. The town maintained reservoirs, but there was no distribution system. With the improvement of drainage, however, there was an increasing number of homes with private baths. Disposal of sewage was apparently not provided for, and the portable latrine and private cesspool continued in use. Terracotta braziers supplemented the hearth as a source of heat in the larger houses.

Care in planning the dwelling was not less because of its simplicity. On the contrary, as the center of family life, the proper arrangement of rooms in relation to the site received attention from builders and philosophers alike.

The climate urged emphasis upon orientation of the dwelling. The maximum amount of sunshine that could be invited into the dwelling was desirable in the winter months, and if the rooms were shielded from the cold north winds, heat could be conserved. Conversely, the heat in summer was relieved when the direct rays of the sun were excluded. These criteria were satisfied in the plan of the Greek house.

The principal rooms were faced to the south, opening upon the private courtyard. A colonnade projected from the rooms to shelter them from the high summer sun. The north wall of the house was punctured with only a few small windows. This plan form was used in practically all dwellings in the town, whether the street entrance occurred on the north, south, east, or west.

Chroniclers of the period referred to the importance of proper orientation. Aristotle wrote, "For the well-being and health ... the homesteads should be airy in summer and sunny in winter. A homestead possessing these qualities would be longer than it is deep; and the main front would face south." According to Xenophon in his *Memorabilia*, Socrates applied the following reasoning to the dwelling arrangement. "When one builds a house must he not see to it that it be as pleasant and convenient as possible? And pleasant is to be cool in summer, but warm in winter. In those houses, then, that look toward the south, the winter sun shines down into the *paestades* [court portico] while in summer, passing high above our heads and over our roofs, it throws them in shadow."

The effect of these criteria was a planning system that sprung from the elements of the individual unit—the home—applied uniformly throughout the town plan. This consistent treatment is unique in urban planning; we do not find it recurring for 2,400 years when a similar relation between the dwelling and the site was recognized in the vast housing program in Europe following the First World War.

DECLINE OF THE CITY

It cannot be assumed that political affairs always ran smoothly in the Age of Pericles. Teachings of the Sophists were disturbing to some of the well-established customs. A little man by the name of Socrates subjected many of the prevailing habits to severe questioning. He insisted upon inquiry and application of reason to the activities of men. He desired that the individual should cultivate an insight into truth, that he should become neither stronger than the state nor subservient to it. Socrates raised some questions about the existence of the gods.

There were some good democrats who believed he was wrong in raising these questions; they had suffered from uprisings of the oligarchic party and feared lest the faith in democracy be weakened. They brought charges against Socrates for impiety and subverting the youth of Athens. There were those who loved this wise man whose only ambition was the quest for truth. They appealed to him to flee his accusers as was the custom, but Socrates would not. He had suggested changes in the habits of men which would improve their lot, and if these were unlawful he would remain to face the people. Found guilty, he was sentenced to die, and in 399 B.C. he drank the hemlock.

The lesson of Socrates has been repeated in history. The institutions of men must change or decay, grow or wither. Socrates showed a way for men to continue command of their destiny by seeking truth. He strove to improve the institutions that they might better serve the people, and for this his fellowmen found him guilty of treason. More confidence in the strength of democracy would not have caused him to be so accused; more confidence might have saved democracy itself.

During the fourth century there was evidence of growing indifference toward the responsibility of government. Accustomed to liberty the people were taking it for granted, and they inclined to allow affairs to run themselves. Freedom guaranteed by democracy was coming to mean that "the people has the right to do what it pleases." Some people were, in the words of Demosthenes, "even building private houses whose magnificence surpasses that of certain public buildings."

Well-to-do citizens spent more of their time in their country villas, whereas the common people found the difficulty of earning a living more absorbing than participation in public affairs. The middle class was disappearing, and a wide gap was growing between those with money and those without it. Plato and Aristotle saw a degeneration of the democracy of Pericles. They perceived a growing abuse of individual liberty and became increasingly critical of democracy itself. Others

were gripped with cynicism while maintaining the fight for democracy.
Demosthenes said:

> The objection may be raised that it was a mistake to allow the universal right of
> speech and a seat in the council. These should have been reserved for the cleverest,
> the flower of the community. But here again it will be found that they are acting
> with wise deliberation in granting even the baser sort the right of speech, for
> supposing only the better people might speak, or sit in council, blessings would fall
> to the lot of those like themselves, but to the commonalty the reverse of blessings.
> Whereas now, anyone who likes, any base fellow, may get up and discover
> something to the advantage of himself and his equals. It may be retorted, "And
> what sort of advantage either for himself or for the people can such a fellow be
> expected to hit upon?" The answer to which is, that in their judgement the
> ignorance and baseness of this fellow, together with his good will, are worth a great
> deal more to them than your superior person's virtue and wisdom, coupled with
> animosity. What it comes to, therefore, is that a state founded upon such insti-
> tutions will not be the same state; but given democracy, these are the right means
> to secure its preservation. The people, it must be borne in mind, does not demand
> that the city should be well governed and itself a slave. It desires to be free and to
> be master. As to bad legislation it does not concern itself about that.

Glotz gives the following description of the alarming developments of this
period in the fourth century:[3]

> But in Greece as a whole there existed almost everywhere a glaring contrast
> between the equality promised by the constitution and the inequality created by
> social and economic conditions.
>   The power of money was spreading and corrupting morality.... Agriculture
> was commercialized to such an extent that by progressive eviction of small
> peasants and the concentration of estates in the same hands the system of large
> estates was recreated. Rhetoricians, advocates and artists, who had formerly
> reckoned it a dishonor to commercialize their talent, now felt no scruples in selling
> their goods as dearly as possible. Everything could be bought, everything had its
> price, and wealth was the measure of social values. By gain and by extravagance
> fortunes were made and unmade with equal rapidity. Those who had money rushed
> into pleasure-seeking and sought every occasion for gross displays of luxury. The
> newly rich were cocks of the walk. Men speculated and rushed after money in order
> to build and furnish magnificent houses, to display fine weapons, to offer to the
> women of their family and to courtesans jewels, priceless robes and rare per-
> fumes, to place before eminent guests and fashionable parasites fine wines and
> dishes prepared by a famous chef, or to commission some popular sculptor to carve
> their bust.
>   What happened to public affairs when "love of money left no one the smallest
> space in which to deal with other things, to such an extent that the mind of each
> citizen, passionately absorbed in this one purpose, could attend to no other
> business than the gain of each day" (Plato). Politics also was a business concern;
> the most honest worked for a class, the others sought for themselves alone the

[3] Glotz, pp. 311, 312.

profits of power and barely concealed their venality. We are dealing with a time when "riches and rich men being held in honor virtue and honest men are at a discount," when "no one can become rich quickly if he remains honest" (Plato). Were these merely the capricious outbursts of a philosopher in love with the ideal or of a character in a comedy? Listen to the terrible words uttered before a tribunal: "Those who, citizens by right of birth, hold the opinion that their country extends wherever their interests are, these obviously are people who will desert the public good in order to run after their personal gain, since for them it is not the city which is their country, but their fortune."

The struggle between democracy and oligarchy was renewed, and Isocrates sums up the growing conflict between the widely separated classes:

Instead of securing general conditions of well-being by means of mutual understanding the antisocial spirit has reached such a pitch that the wealthy would rather throw their money into the sea than relieve the lot of the indigent, while the very poorest of the poor would get less from appropriating to their own use the property of the rich than from depriving them of it.

THE HELLENISTIC CITY

The Peloponnesian Wars weakened Athens financially, and corrupt politicians began to gnaw at the moral fiber of the people. Athens became easy prey for a conqueror and succumbed to the Macedonian armies of Alexander the Great. But the essential qualities of wisdom, logic, and reason, the sensitive, esthetic character of democratic days, had sunk its roots deep into the soil of Athens. The Greeks were conquered by mighty armies, but their culture dominated the conqueror. Greek influence spread throughout the Mediterranean shores, and the Hellenistic period brought new city building—the planning and architecture patterned after the great works of the Greeks.

Old cities flourished and new cities were founded. Pergamon, Alexandria, Syracuse, and Candahar grew large and populous; the humble quality of the Hellenic city vanished. The city became the scene of luxury, ruddy with the display of empire. Magnificent public buildings—the odeion, the treasury, the library, the prison—were added to the agora. The assembly retained its traditional place among these monumental structures, but it remained, as Percy Gardner[4] expressed it, for the citizens "to exercise such functions (a mere show of autonomy) as the real rulers of the country ... left to them." Baths, palaestrae, and stadia were built for entertainment and festival. Gardens and parks were introduced from the Orient. An entourage of royalty built fine villas in the urban environs, and distinctions in caste grew more apparent.

Small kings, wealthy families, and ambitious foreigners desirous of acclaim within this frame of monumental splendor bestowed generous gifts upon the

[4] Percy Gardner, *The Planning of Hellenistic Cities.*

city. Empty honors were accorded for their beneficence. The great stoa at Priene was the gift of a king of Orophernes of Cappadocia. Here, one by the name of Zosimus staged a festive dinner for the whole citizen population of the city in return for receipt of the "dignity of Stephanephorus." According to Pausanias the *bouleuterion* at Megalopolis was named after Thersilius who dedicated it, and the donor of the *bouleuterion* at Elis was one by the name of Lalichmium.[5] Inscriptions bear a quantity of evidence of the surge for popularity through these magnanimous gestures of philanthropy. The genuine character of the Hellenistic city was, in the third and second centuries B.C., degenerating into a hollow form of a decaying social structure.

ROMAN PROWESS

In their early migrations to the Italian peninsula, the Greeks had founded cities. Like other peoples on the shores of the Mediterranean, the Romans drew upon the Greek culture planted there. They grafted Hellenic forms upon the irregular patterns of their villages and used these forms for the new towns they founded in the near and far reaches of their broad empire.

The Romans were calculating organizers. They excelled in technical achievement and were skilled engineers and aggressive city builders. But they had not the philosophy of the Greeks. Preoccupied with conquest, administration was their prime business and they devised political organization which has continued to this day. Intense builders with a flair for gargantuan scale, their works were not graced with the refinement of line and form or the creative spirit of the Athenians. Greek forms were reduced to mechanical formulae which could be readily applied like parts arranged upon graph paper.

With inventive genius the Romans solved technical problems created by the congregation of great numbers of people in cities. They developed water supply and distribution, drainage systems, and methods of heating upon which the health of the masses depended. The great aqueducts for transport of water over tremendous distances and the underground sewers like Cloaca Maxima were feats of engineering skill and prowess. The great highways paved with stone represented the tireless efforts of intense builders.

MONUMENTS AND DIVERSION

The Forum Romanum of the Republic had a human scale. Its proportions and form undoubtedly caused the citizen to feel he was a part of the activity that took place there. Here the individual and his identity were merged with "Rome". The buildings were not so overwhelming in size that they humbled the individual.

[5] William A. McDonald, *The Political Meeting Places of the Greeks,* Johns Hopkins U. Press, Baltimore, 1943.

The common people had their share of hardships, but one can imagine the Gracchi pleading their case in the Senate for an equitable distribution of the land and its benefits. The citizen understood the religion of his temples, and he was proud of the triumphs of the Roman legions abroad. He could participate in the business affairs of the basilica and perhaps engage in the money-lending enterprise carried on there. He felt himself to be one of the actors in this drama as a Greek had been in his assembly and agora.

This citizen of early Rome saw gracious living like that in Pompeii and Herculaneum or the busy life and fashions of Ostia. He observed distinctions in class among the dwellings but took these for granted in a day when a slave economy was all he had thus far witnessed in history. If the citizen was not blessed with wealth, he could nevertheless indulge himself in the various common forms of entertainment the community offered—the gay combat in the colosseum, the drama in the theater, or a festival in the forum.

But the scene changed for the Roman citizen. World conquest was the ambition of Rome, and the citizen saw great riches flow into his capital. He saw intrigue absorb the military and political leaders and he saw the public lands and wealth won in campaigns appropriated by them. He saw monuments erected in dedication of great victories, and the triumphant entry of generals from abroad.

The Roman citizen saw emperors crowned and he saw them build new fora which dwarfed his Forum Romanum. He saw each new forum exceed in size the one that preceded it. The Forum of Augustus was greater than the Forum of Julius Caesar; the Forum of Vespasian matched that of Augustus; and the Forum of Trajan was the most magnificent of all. He saw the Palace of Augustus crown the Palatine and the Golden House of Nero span acres.

The Roman citizen saw institutions of pleasure, rather than culture, built to divert his attention from social and economic inequities. He saw the huge Colosseum where carnal displays and bloody gladiatorial combats were staged for the excitement of a populace which might otherwise have grown restless. He saw the Circus Maximus, where he could join 150,000 of his fellow citizens to witness the drama of daring chariot races.

The scale of all these structures, the spaces they enclosed, and the architectural fitments with which they were adorned appalled the Roman citizen. It was not the plan of a city which he saw emerging, but a series of ever greater monuments to the glory and deification of his rulers. Even the colonial cities followed the form of the military camp.

SLUMS AND DECAY

Diversion was afforded the citizen, but he saw his city grow congested. He saw men, like Crassus, profess to be civic leaders but speculate in the land and build huge tenements. He saw the city crowded with slums to become fuel for disastrous fires. The height of buildings reached six, seven, and eight floors and Emperor Augustus found it necessary to decree a limit of 70 feet for all tenements. According to the Constantin Regionary Catalog there were 46,602 blocks of apartments and only 1,797 private houses in Rome in the fourth century after Christ.

This Roman citizen saw nobles, the returning heroes, and the rulers move to great estates and comfortable villas in the country. The Empire had grown so broad and so fat no enemy could reach them. Luxury and display were imported from the Orient, and the leaders grew soft. The city-dweller lived in slums while the affluent enjoyed leisure in the country. No strong and healthy men with convictions remained to defend the Empire, and Rome gradually merged with the camp of barbarians from the north. Civilization descended into the Dark Ages.

The lesson of Rome and the cities it built is well stated by Henry Smith Williams:

> During the entire ages of Trajan and the Antonines, a succession of virtuous and philosophic emperors followed each other; the world was in peace; the laws were wise and well administered; riches seemed to increase; each succeeding generation raised palaces more splendid, monuments and public edifices more sumptuous, than the preceding; the senatorial families found their revenues increase; the treasury levied greater imposts. But it is not the mass of wealth, it is on its distribution, that the prosperity of states depends; increasing opulence continued to meet the eye, but men became more miserable; the rural population, formerly active, robust, and energetic, were succeeded by a foreign race, while the inhabitants of towns sank in vice and idleness, or perished in want, amidst the riches they had themselves created.[6]

[6] Henry Smith Williams, *The Historian's History of the World,*The Outlook Company, 1904.

3

The Medieval Town

OUT OF THE DARK AGES

By the fifth century after Christ the Roman Empire had crumbled under the weight of luxury, pomp, and ceremony. Western civilization declined, trade disintegrated, and the urban population returned to rural life. Cities shrank in size and importance, and social and economic confusion followed.

Barbaric rulers established city-states and formed the nucleus of future nations. The economy was rooted in agriculture, and the rulers parceled their domains among vassal lords who pledged military support for the kingdom. The people were dependent upon the land for their subsistence and entered a state of serfdom under their lords. The feudal system was the new order.

Wars among the rival feudal lords were frequent. Strategic sites were sought for their castles, and within these fortified strongholds the serfs of the surrounding countryside found protection. Through centuries of the Dark Ages monasteries served as havens of refuge for the oppressed, and the church strengthened its position during these trying times. This influence combined with the power of the feudal lords renewed the advantages of communal existence within the protective walls. Invention of the battering ram and catapult increased the danger from enemies, forced the construction of heavier walls, and gave increased impetus for a return to urban life. The countryside was not safe, and fortifications were extended to include the dwellings that clustered about the castle and monastery.

CASTLE, CHURCH, AND GUILD

Movement to the towns brought a marked revival of trade about the eleventh century. Advantages accrued to the feudal lords—in return for protection they collected higher rent for their land. Many new towns were founded, and sites of old Roman towns were restored. Urban life was encouraged by the lords; they granted charters which secured certain rights and privileges of citizenship to the urban dwellers. This new form of freedom was attractive to those who had lived their lives in serfdom.

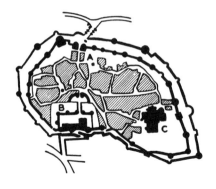

CARCASSONNE

A   **Market Square**
B   **Castle**
C   **Church of Sr. Nazaire**

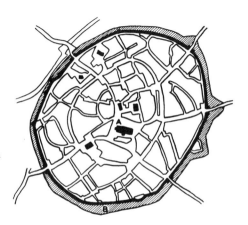

NOERDLINGEN

A   **Cathedral Plaza**
B   **Moat**

Medieval cities of the twelfth and thirteenth centuries usually had irregular street patterns and heavy walls. Carcassonne was restored by Viollet-le-Duc in the nineteenth century. In it we see the castle (B) with its own moat and walls, the market place (A), and the Church of St. Nazaire (C). The plan of Noerdlingen shows the radial and lateral pattern of irregular roadways with the church plaza as the principal focal point of the town. The city of the Middle Ages grew within the confines of the walls. While the population was small, there was space in the town, but when it increased the buildings were packed more closely and the open spaces filled. Sanitation and water supply remained the same. The result was intolerable congestion, lack of hygiene, and pestilence.

Then the merchants and craftsmen formed guilds to strengthen their social and economic position. Weavers, butchers, tailors, masons, millers, metal-workers, carpenters, leatherworkers, glassmakers, all established regulations to control their production, maintain their prices, and protect their trade. A new social order was in the making—a wealthy mercantile class was rising to challenge the power of the feudal lords.

The early medieval town was dominated by the church or monastery and the castle of the lord. The church plaza became the market place and, with

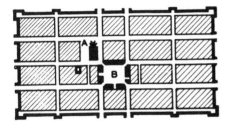

MONTPAZIER

A   Cathedral Square
B   Market Square

During the thirteenth and fourteenth centuries colonial cities were founded by young empires to protect their trade and provide military security. They were plotted for allocation of sites to settlers and the regular plan is a distinct contrast to the informal development of the normal medieval town.

citizenship bestowed upon the people and merchant guilds established, the town hall and guild hall were built on or adjacent to the market plaza. The castle was surrounded by its own walls as a final protection in the event an enemy penetrated the main fortifications and entered the city.

Distinction between town and country was sharp, but this demarcation and the small size of the city provided ready access to the open countryside in times of peace. Aiding the protection of cities, the town sites were usually on irregular terrain, occupying hilltops or islands. The town was designed to fit the topographic features. The circulation and building spaces were molded to these irregular features and naturally assumed an informal character.

The roads radiated generally from the church plaza and market square to the gates, with secondary lateral roadways connecting them. The irregular pattern was probably consciously devised as a means to confuse an enemy in the event he gained entrance to the town. Although the battering ram and the catapult were instruments for assault upon the heavy fortifications and hot oil poured from the battlements was a means for mass defense, hand-to-hand combat was the principal form of military action. In the maze of wandering streets the advantage rested with the inhabitants against an enemy unfamiliar with the town arrangement.

THE PICTURESQUE TOWN

The abbés and artisans were sensitive to the form and materials of the buildings they erected. Under their guidance, care was exercised in the placement of, and relation between, the structures of the town. Buildings assumed a functional character in both form and location. They were not built to be "picturesque"; that quality emerged from the consideration given to town building by its builders. Accidents of vista and contrasts of form and color resulted from the contours of the land and the ingenious selection of the sites for each structure. The commanding position of the cathedral or church gave a singular unity to the town, a unity strengthened by the horizontal envelope of the encircling walls.

The entire town was treated with a structural logic that characterized the architectural treatment of the Romanesque and early Gothic buildings. Open spaces—the streets and plazas—developed as integral parts of the sites upon which the buildings were erected. With the exception of a few main roads between the gates and the market place, streets were used as pedestrian circulation about the town rather than traffic arteries as we know them today. Wheel traffic was generally absent on all but the main roadways.

MEDIEVAL DWELLINGS

Conservation of heat in the cold climates and the restrictive area of the town caused the houses to be built in connected rows along the narrow streets. Behind these rows of dwellings open space was reserved and in them the domestic animals were kept and gardens cultivated. The workshop and kitchen occupied the ground floor of the dwelling. Here the merchants and craftsmen operated their enterprises and manufactured their goods. There was little distinction between classes among the population of the early medieval town. The workers lived in the homes of their employers as apprentices in the trade or business. The living and sleeping space was on the second floor of the dwelling. The simple plan provided little privacy within the house. Some of the burghers enjoyed separate sleeping rooms, but the accommodations were universally simple and modest in their appointments. The chimney and fireplace replaced the open hearth of the ancient house. Windows were small and covered with crude glass or oiled parchment. Facilities for waste disposal within the dwelling were not usually provided, although some of the houses were equipped with privies. Construction was of masonry or wood frame filled with wattle. Thatch covered the roofs, and the fire hazard caused some towns either to prohibit this type of roofing or to encourage fire resistant materials by offering special privileges for the use of fireproof materials. Streets were usually paved and maintained by the owners of property facing upon them. This may account, in part, for their narrow width.

MEDIEVAL INSTITUTIONS

Meditation and study characterized the monastery. It was extended to research by scholars intent upon the cultivation of professional skills. Monasteries and the guilds combined to form the university, and here were welcomed those who desired to study in withdrawal from the market place. Here also were conducted research and training in law, medicine, and the arts. Universities were assisted by the growing wealth of the merchant class. The universities at Bologna and Paris were founded in the twelfth century and those at Cambridge and Salamanca in the thirteenth century. The churches also established hospitals in which the sick could receive care and treatment not theretofore available to the people.

Life in medieval cities had color, a color visible to all the people. The church provided pageantry and gave drama to the life of every man. It was an institution in which all men could participate, giving inspiration and adding a measure of beauty to the existence of the people. It lifted people above baseness and encouraged better deeds. It offered music and meditation. The sense of participation produced a picturesqueness in life reflected in the picturesqueness of the towns. The people—merchants, artisans, and peasants—mingled in the market place, the guild hall, and the church; a human scale pervaded the informal environment of the city of the people.

There were innumerable hardships suffered and endured by the people of the Middle Ages, but in the early towns they did not lose the sense of intermingling. Each man had the feeling of being an active citizen in his community. This attribute of the urban environment—a social well-being—was, however, soon to be dissipated.

4

The Neoclassic City

MERCANTILISM AND CONCENTRATION

The number of towns increased rapidly during the Middle Ages, but they remained relatively small in population. Many had only a few hundred people, and the larger cities seldom exceeded 50,000 inhabitants. The physical size was restricted by the girth of the fortifications, water supply, and sanitation, the distance across the town seldom exceeding a mile. Water was available at the town fountain. There was no sewage disposal, and all drainage was by way of the streets.

As long as the population remained small, these apparent deficiencies presented no serious problem. Communication between towns was slow, facilities for transport were cumbersome, and necessity for mutual assistance in times of conflict urgent. The towns were built within ready reach of each other. Most were within a day's journey apart and frequently a round trip to a neighboring town could be made on foot in a single day.

World travel and trade, however, brought a concentration of people to centers situated on main crossroads. During the fourteenth century Florence grew from 45,000 people to 90,000 people, Paris from 100,000 to 240,000, and Venice reached 200,000. Successful merchants consolidated their interests in several towns, and moneylending helped their enterprise. Commerce increased between towns and countries. The danger of military aggression gradually diminished, and safety for travel increased.

The mercantile economy expanded, and the power of the feudal lords declined. Ownership of the land gradually shifted to a new caste of noblemen, the wealthy merchants. The church accumulated a vast domain and there emerged two privileged classes, the nobles and the clergy. The guilds declined and medieval serfdom disappeared, but the facilities for processing materials and goods—the mills, ovens, presses—came into the possession of the noble class. The peasants were required to pay tolls of various sorts for the use of these facilities. The feudal economy had been rooted in the land, and the new economy was dominated by the possession and control of money.

CONGESTION AND SLUMS

The growing population forced a congestion within the cities not present in earlier days. The traditional height of two stories for dwellings changed to three and four stories. The upper floors were projected beyond the first floor, and the roofs often spanned the street width. Open space within the interior blocks of dwellings was built up. Population density increased without change in the systems of water supply or sanitation.

Wheel traffic increased. The narrow streets became congested, dark, and filthridden from refuse thrown from dwelling windows, and provision for elimination of waste remained inadequate. The call of *gare de l'eau* was familiar in France and, contracted to the anglicized "gardy loo," it became equally familiar in Edinburgh. Excreta were disposed of in cesspools beneath dwelling floors; there or in the streets it was left to ripen for fertilizer. Odors from filth in the streets were overcome by keeping the windows or shutters closed. Ventilation was by way of the chimney only. Disease spread rapidly in times of epidemic; in the fourteenth century the Black Death, a pestilence of typhus, took the lives of nearly half the urban population.

During this period the cities reverted to a condition inferior to the days of Rome a thousand years before. The manor house of the nobleman grew spacious while the typical dwelling of the poor remained cramped and was moved higher into the attic. The first sewer was installed in London after the Black Death. Water closets were not introduced until the sixteenth century in Spain, France, and England, and it was early in the seventeenth century when water supply was connected to dwellings in London. Fire hazards were prevalent everywhere. As a precautionary measure an ordinance in London, in the thirteenth century, required that slate or tile roofs replace the usual reed and straw. It is interesting to note a similar order that appeared in the American Colonies at a somewhat later date. It read:

New Amsterdam, 15 *December* 1657:
The Director General and Council of New Netherland to All, who shall see these presents or hear them read, Greeting! Know ye, that to prevent the misfortunes of conflagrations, the roofs of reeds, the wooden and plastered chimneys have long ago been condemned but nevertheless these orders are obstinately and carelessly neglected by many of the inhabitants. . . . The said Director General and Council have decided it to be necessary, not only to renew their former ordinances, but also to amplify the same and to increase the fines. . . [1]

[1] Straus and Wegg, *Housing Comes of Age,* Oxford University Press, New York, 1938.

Overcrowding within the small dwellings of the poorer people further increased the hazards to health and the spread of epidemics. In 1539 an Act of Parliament mentioned that "great mischiefs daily grow and increase by reason of pestering of houses with divers families, harboring of inmates, and converting great houses into tenements, and erection of new houses."

GUNPOWDER

In the fourteenth century gunpowder was invented, and new techniques of warfare were introduced. The feudal lords had relied upon citizen-soldiers to man the crenellated parapets in time of siege, but the new weapons of attack and defense required larger numbers of trained professional soldiers. Military engineering became a science. Fortifications were extended, and heavy bastions, moats, and outposts were built. Extension of the area occupied by the fortifications created a "no-man's land," and separation between town and country became more distinct. Open space outside the walls was further removed from the urban dweller. People came to the cities in large numbers to participate in the expanding commercial enterprise and fill the ranks of professional armies.

THE RENAISSANCE

In France the kings achieved a semblance of national unity in the fifteenth century. Elsewhere cities remained provincial dukedoms with wealthy merchant families wielding control over them. It became the ambition of rulers to display their affluence and power by improving their cities. They engaged in intellectual pursuits, drawing upon the classic heritage of Rome for this cultural activity. The noble families of Florence, Venice, Rome, and Lombardy desired to embellish their cities; the Medicis, Borgias, and Sforzas built themselves new palaces on which were draped the classic motifs. A formalism was grafted upon the medieval town although the buildings retained the characteristic fortress quality of the Middle Ages. The basic form of cities did not change, but the structure was decorated with façades of classic elements.

The Church participated in this movement. Residence of the Popes was re-established in Rome, and work on the Vatican Palace was begun. Pope Julius planned to replace the old basilica of St. Peter with a great church which would become the center of Christendom.

Feverish preoccupation with the arts gripped the merchant princes, church-men, and the kings. Practice of the arts became a profession. The system of apprentice training in Italy prepared men to work in a variety of artistic fields. An apprentice to a painter would also work in the shop of a goldsmith; a sculptor would study architecture. Versatility was a characteristic of the artists and their services were given encouragement. Leonardo da Vinci practiced all the arts and became a planner, military engineer, and inventor as well. Kings, merchant nobles, and popes were patrons of the arts and bid heavily for the services of the growing number of practitioners.

The strange anonymity of the master-builders of medieval towns no longer prevailed in the Renaissance. Robert de Luzarches, William of Sens (Canterbury Cathedral), Geoffrey de Noyes (Lincoln Cathedral), Jean-le-Loup, and Henrico di Gambodia (Milan Cathedral) are seldom recorded in the history of medieval town building, whereas a host of individuals received personal recognition in the Renaissance and later periods. The names of Brunelleschi, Alberti, Bramante, Peruzzi and Sangallo in Italy, and Bullant, de l'Orme, Lescot in France, are as well known as their works. Many others achieved world renown; their names were more prominent than the patrons who commissioned their works. Mansart, Bullet, Blondel, Lemercier, de Brosse, Le Notre, Percier, and Fontaine in France; Bernini, Longhena, Borromini, Palladio, Michelangelo, Raphael in Italy; Inigo Jones, Christopher Wren, the Brothers Adam in England; all these artists enjoyed the confidence and patronage of popes, kings, and merchants.

VIENNA

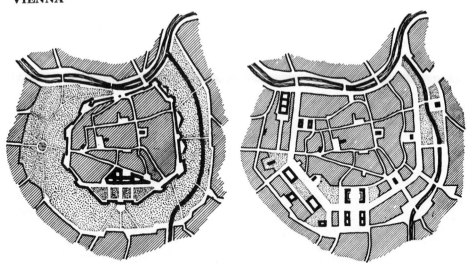

Vienna before 1857   **Vienna after 1857**

In the late 18th and early 19th centuries long-range artillery was greatly improved and the old systems of walls, moats, and ramparts were reduced in effectiveness for military defense, and the form of the city underwent drastic alterations. The walls and ramparts were levelled, the moats were filled in and boulevards were built in the open space as in the famous Ringstrasse encircling the original town of Vienna. These spaces separated the old town from the surrounding suburbs but, as in Paris, they were gradually built up in response to the ruthless speculation of the late 19th century and open space disappeared from the city.

PIAZZA OF ST. PETER, ROME

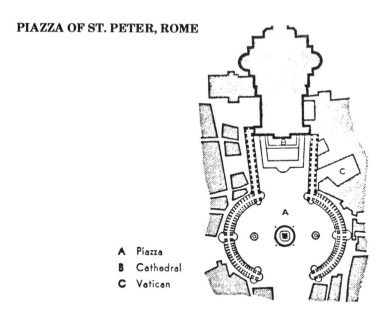

A Piazza
B Cathedral
C Vatican

Formal plazas of the Renaissance were carved out of the medieval town and given monumental scale and form reminiscent of classical antiquity. Exterior space was enclosed with formal façades, and the shapes were modeled like sculptural pieces, isolated from the rest of the city.

Tien An Men Square in Peking, China represents one of the largest plazas in the world. It originally covered 27 acres but in 1958 was enlarged to include 98 acres. It is surrounded by huge public buildings that appear small against the background of the open space.

TIEN AN MEN SQUARE, PEKING

MONARCHY AND MONUMENTALISM

The monumental character of the classic returned to the city. Every form had its centerline, and every space its axis. The structural quality of the Middle Ages was replaced by a classic sculptural form, modeled symmetrically. The "barbaric" art of medieval cities was forsaken. With haughty disdain Molière called it:

> The rank taste of Gothic monuments,
> These odious monsters of the ignorant centuries,
> Which the torrents of barbarism spewed forth.

The axis and the strong centerline symbolized the growing concentration of power. Kings of France became monarchs, wealthy merchants in Italy became autocratic dukes, large landowners in England became lord barons, and the popes became benevolent partners of all. Louis XIV of France gave voice to the spirit of the times when he shouted his famous words, *"L'État, c'est moi."*

Out of the cramped medieval town were carved formal "squares." The modeling of spatial forms absorbed the attention and skills of designers and planners, and classic elements were ingeniously assembled to form the spaces. Michelangelo created the Campodiglio on the Capitoline Hill in Rome, Bernini designed the huge Piazza of St. Peter's, the Piazza di San Marco in Venice was completed, Rainaldi built the twin churches on the Piazza del Popolo, the Place Royale (now Place des Vosges) and Place des Victoires were built in Paris.

Long-range artillery removed the advantage of the old walls for military defense. Louis XIV ordered Vauban, his military engineer, to redesign the defense system. Vauban tore down the walls and built earthwork ramparts beyond the city. Within the leveled space of the old walls boulevards and promenades were laid. The famous Ringstrasse of Vienna occupied the open space left when the city walls of that city were demolished. Cities were opening up, and the city of the Middle Ages was being released from its clutter. Transition from the Renaissance Period to the Baroque Period was in process.

Originally, a narrow winding street led to St. Peter's. The suddenness with which the vistor was thrust into this magnificent open space made the square seem even more beautiful.

With Paris in mind, the dictator Mussolini ordered that the path to St. Peter's be opened, and so the medieval buildings that had lined the approaches were removed and the axial avenue from the castel St. Angelo to St. Peter's came into being.

THE BAROQUE CITY

An air of grandeur permeated the courts of kings. Louis XIV ordered Le Notre to design the gardens of Versailles. Here was space of unparalleled proportions, scale of incomprehensible size. Here was the conception of a man who, having achieved domination over the lives of men, confidently set about to become the

PIAZZA OF ST. PETER, ROME (photo by Richard K. Eisner)

THE BAROQUE CITY

The centerline and the axis symbolized the mighty power of the monarch. Louis XIV ordered the removal of his palace from the congested city of Paris to the open hunting grounds of Versailles, and he ordered the avenues to radiate from his magnificent palace. The entire city of Karlsruhe was designed to revolve about and radiate from the Prince's palace. After the fire of 1666 Christopher Wren proposed a monumental plan for the rebuilding of London. He conceded the new power dominant in England by placing upon the major focal point the Stock Exchange. But the plan was not accepted; the necessary adjustment of property boundaries and prices could not be resolved.

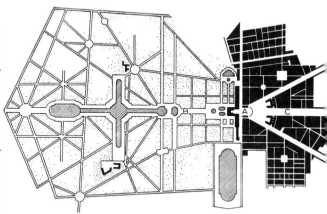

VERSAILLES

A Palace

B Gardens

C Town

42

A   Palace
B   Gardens
C   Town

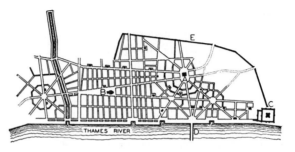

KARLSRUHE

A   Stock Exchange
B   St. Paul's Cathedral
C   Tower of London
D   London Bridge
E   Old Walls

LONDON   (Christopher Wren's Plan)

master of nature. The egotism of rulers knew no limitations, nor could it brook a hint of equality; Louis XIV threw the wealthy financier, Foucquet, into prison for his temerity to build a château almost as fine as the king's.

In the eighteenth century the Baroque City expanded, and dominance of the ruler intensified. The avenues of Versailles focused upon the royal palace, whereas the whole city of Karlsruhe as well as Mannheim revolved about the palaces and great gardens of the royalty.

Plazas of the seventeenth century had been designed as isolated, enclosed spaces. They were now opened and less confined, as though moved by a desire to recapture the space of the countryside. Design shifted from walled-in architectural forms to an extension and expansion of open space. Jules-Hardouin Mansart, architect for the palace buildings at Versailles, designed the Place Vendôme with greater dimensions than previous squares in Paris. The three squares by Héré de Corny in Nancy were connected, the continuity of open space emphasized by colonnades and enhanced by a tree-lined avenue.

Probably the most dramatic example of the new surge to penetrate the city with open space was the Place de la Concorde designed by Jacques-Ange Gabriel during the reign of Louis XV. In this square, space is almost completely released.

It flows from the gardens of the Tuileries and the Louvre on one side into the broad avenue of the Champs Elysées begun by Louis XIV to connect Paris with his palace at Versailles. The scale is further amplified by the Seine river lying along one side. Opposite the river is the only group of buildings facing this tremendous square.

Another departure in urban design was the Piazza del Popolo in Rome designed by Valadier. A three-dimensional transition of space was obtained with a series of terraces linking the lower level of the square and the gardens of the Pincio Hill above. Continuity replaced the enclosure of open space as the new direction in civic design.

In England the classic revival came later than elsewhere, the Tudor style having absorbed the Renaissance shock. Recoiling from the hazards of over-hanging upper stories, a building ordinance in 1619 decreed that the walls of buildings would henceforth be built vertically from foundation to roof. Timed with the onrushing wave of classic formalism, this law aided the introduction of the "Italian Style" ushered in by Inigo Jones, its leading exponent.

The landowning class had tempered the rise of monarchy in England and the monumentalism of the "grand plan" did not quite take root there. Christopher Wren attempted it in his plan for rebuilding London after the fire of 1666. He went so far as to place the Stock Exchange at the symbolic focal point of his plan instead of the traditional palace or cathedral. Even this acknowledgment of the domination of mercantilism in England was not enough to offset disagreement over the necessary reapportionment of property values destroyed in the fire.

Formalism permeated the English Renaissance, but it was expressed in terms of quiet repose rather than striking grandeur. This quality is observed in the simple curved building forms facing broad open spaces of the Circus and Royal Crescent in Bath designed by John Wood, the younger. The same quality was built into the undulating surfaces and free curving forms of Lansdowne Crescent, also in Bath. John Nash carried on these curving plan forms overlooking spacious open parks in his designs for the Park Crescent and Regent's Park developments in London.

Formalism was unobtrusively introduced in the enclosed squares of London during the eighteenth century. They were intended not as impressive plazas, but as places for the quiet relaxation of the surrounding residents. These simple, though formal, open spaces were created largely by builders who would be classified today as "speculators"; they were in the business of subdividing land and building homes. Many are unknown, as in the case of Lansdowne Crescent in Bath, but two prominent builders in London were James Burton and Thomas Cubitt and they lent a dignity to their profession by the work they performed.

BEHIND THE FAÇADES

The fine rows of formal dwellings and squares in England, the monumental vistas, royal gardens and the palaces of France, the well-modeled piazzas in

Italy, all had been built for the upper classes, the wealthy merchants, and the kings. The lot of the people of lesser means had not been substantially improved. It was not the purpose of the builders of the Baroque town to engage in reforms. They were concerned with such improvement of the urban environment that would maintain the prestige and glory of their exalted position in society. The broad avenues provided more than satisfaction of the ego and vanity in despots, more than delightful promenades for the elegant carriages of the aristocrats; they were strategic means with which to impress the populace with the power and discipline of marching armies.

Behind the fine façades of the plazas and wide avenues dwelt the congested urban population. The city lacked sanitation, sewers, water distribution, and drainage. Epidemics and pestilence were frequent, and poverty was appalling. A breach was widening between the aristocracy and the masses. Fratricidal wars of religion and social restlessness of the seventeenth century were followed by the stamp of the despotic heel and the courtiers. Oppression brought revolutions in the eighteenth century. The Baroque city had unfolded its grand open spaces and they were overlapping upon the people. Another change was taking place: machines were replacing handcraft methods for making goods for trade.

COLONIAL EXPANSION—AMERICA

Aided by the mariner's compass, courageous explorers in the fifteenth and sixteenth centuries extended the net of colonial empires over the face of the globe. The eyes of people everywhere looked toward the new world in North America for relief from oppression and chaos. Colonies in the Americas were settled by pioneers impelled by a burning desire for freedom. Far removed from the mother-countries and with a whole great land as an ever-widening frontier to the west, the settlements did not grow as permanent fortified towns. Strong forts were established at some early settlements—Havana, San Juan, St. Augustine, New Amsterdam—but the barricades thrown up as protection from attack by Indians offered no impediment to the development of villages in the way that fortifications had restricted the growth of medieval cities in Europe.

The initial settlement was sometimes irregular in plan; the Wall Street District in Manhattan retains the pattern of the early settlement of New Amsterdam about 1660, and Boston streets meandered about the Common. But most of the towns were plotted in advance for allocation of the land to settlers. The people who ventured across the sea to this new land sought opportunities from which they had been deprived in their homeland. Freedom meant the right to their land and possessions for their households. The principal occupation was agriculture; the towns were small and within walking distance from all parts to the countryside about them.

The quiet New England towns reflected the modest character of the puritan. The center was the meeting house and the common, and each family had its own dwelling, albeit humble. The environment was one of beauty in simplicity—communities of neighbors. In the South the towns were settled by folks also eager to improve their lot, but they reflected the stamp of the Crown. Class distinctions, while dormant for a time, were retained, and formality characterized the life and pattern of the towns.

In Williamsburg, Virginia, the quiet though formal repose of an English town was transplanted to a new land. Through the beneficence of John D. Rockefeller, Jr., it was recently restored and offers an impression of the early

NEW AMSTERDAM

The Dutch settlement of New Amsterdam was built on the tip of what is now known as Manhattan, New York City. The pattern of its streets in 1660 still exists—Broadway (called Breedeweg by the Dutch), Broad Street, and Wall Street. The almost medieval irregular street plan and the canal are reminiscent of the Dutch towns in Europe.

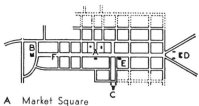

A   Market Square
B   The Capitol
C   Governor's Palace
D   College of William and Mary
E   Bruton Parish Church
F   Duke of Gloucester Street

WILLIAMSBURG

Settled in 1633, the town of Williamsburg was founded in 1699 as the capital of the Virginia Colony. It was laid out by the surveyor Theodorick Bland. The main street, Duke of Gloucester Street, was 99 feet wide and extended from the College of William and Mary to the Capitol. The land was subdivided in lots of about one-half acre in size. The town had a population of between 3,000 and 4,000 people. The quiet formality of the town was English. The spaces are not "grand"; they have a human scale.

colonial town. Williamsburg was settled in 1633, and in 1693 the College of William and Mary was granted a charter and located there. The town became the capital of the Virginia Colony in 1699.

The surveyor, Theodorick Bland, laid out the city with formal axes adapted from the aristocratic mode in Europe. The Duke of Gloucester Street was the main avenue, extending from the College to the Capitol building. A "green" was placed at right angles to this street and terminated at the palace. The town was subdivided into residence lots of one-half acre each. It was a formal plan, but it neither revolved about monumental features nor was it overpowered by them. A human scale pervaded the environment; the town appeared to exist for the people who lived there rather than the rulers who dominated it.

Early Philadelphia and Baltimore may have enjoyed this quality, but it is not apparent in their plans. The City of Brotherly Love was planned by the surveyor, Thomas Holme, for William Penn in 1682. It was a rigid gridiron street pattern extending between the Delaware and Schuylkill Rivers. Two main streets, Broad and Market, bisected the plan in each direction and intersected at the public square in the center of the town. A square block was allocated for a park in each quadrant.

The plan had little distinction. Penn expected it to be a town of single houses and shade trees. By the middle of the eighteenth century, however, it was common practice to build the houses from lot line to lot line and the open spaces were lost within the walls of brick that lined the gridiron streets. Continuous rows of buildings shut off access to the rear of the property, and alleys were cut through the center of the blocks. Then dwellings were built along the alleys, only to become the quaint and narrow business and residential streets for which the city is known today.

The aristocratic paternalism that characterized the early settlements in the southern colonies was reflected in the plan of Savannah, Georgia. Laid out in 1733 by James Oglethorpe, the plan was a rectilinear street system liberally interspersed with park squares along the avenues. The streets linked these parks and created continuity of open space when the town was built with single houses. It has since been forsaken by the intensive building coverage of the intermediate blocks.

Trade and shipping thrived in the North and settlers flocked to the colonies. Landowners opened subdivisions and platted lots for sale and lease. Rights to pasture and timber on adjacent land were sometimes granted to purchasers of lots in the new towns. Such a development was Lansingburgh on the Hudson, surveyed by Joseph Blanchard for the large landowner, Abraham Lansing. This, like many others, was a speculative venture; the plan was a gridiron with a Common reserved in the center as in the New England villages. Profiting from the precedent in Philadelphia, alleys were platted in the original subdivision.

The gridiron plan adopted for these towns was not only the simplest form to survey, but it was not an unsatisfactory form for the small village. A sense of unity was maintained by the close relation of all dwellings to the town square and to the agricultural land on the outskirts. It was when this same pattern was

PHILADELPHIA

William Penn commissioned the surveyor Thomas Holme to lay out the city in 1682. A rigid gridiron plan was adopted. Two major streets crossed in the center of the town and formed a public square. A square block park was placed in each of the four quadrants. The early dwellings were single-family houses. In the middle of the eighteenth century it became a common practice to build dwellings on the side lot lines resulting in continuous rows of buildings which cut off access to the rear yards. Alleys were then cut through the center of the blocks. These alleys have since become streets.

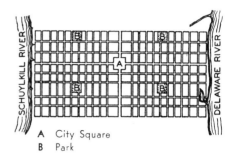

A   City Square
B   Park

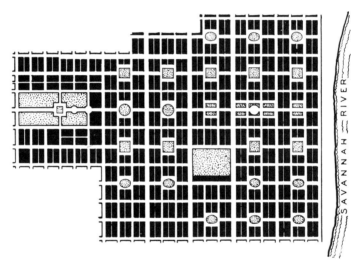

SAVANNAH

Laid out in 1733 by Oglethorpe, Savanah was a regular pattern of rectangular streets with park squares liberally spotted in alternate blocks. The plan is similar to Philadelphia with a more generous allocation of open spaces.

extended endlessly that the monotony of the checkerboard lay heavily upon the town.

A small settlement begun in 1649 on the banks of the Severn River in Maryland received the name of Annapolis in 1694. It was the first city in America to adopt diagonal avenues and circles as the basic plan form but was followed by a more dramatic display, the classic plan for Washington, D.C., by Major Pierre Charles L'Enfant.

FROM RADIALS TO GRIDIRON

After deliberation of an appropriate location for the capital of this new nation, it was decided to avoid existing urban centers such as New York and Philadelphia. Ambitious for the future of their newly founded country, the founding fathers selected a site along the banks of the Potomac River, removed from the commercial environment of established cities. L'Enfant, a young French designer, was commissioned to prepare a plan for the new capital city. With his background in the baroque atmosphere of Paris and inspired by the spirit of the American cause, it was natural that he should conceive of this new city on a grand scale woven into a pattern of geometrical order. Such a plan appealed to the aristocratic tastes of men like Washington and Jefferson, and it was such a plan that was adopted by them in 1791.

Following the example of their capital city, a number of cities wrapped themselves in the radial plan, a system of diagonal streets overlaid upon a gridiron pattern. Joseph Ellicott, brother of Andrew Ellicott who surveyed Washington, D.C., planned the city of Buffalo in 1804. He adopted a form of diagonal streets crossing a gridiron pattern at the central square near the Lake Erie waterfront. After the fire of 1805, Judge Woodward and Governor Hull in 1807 prepared a plan for Detroit. It was a grand complex elaborated with concentric hexagonal streets and containing most, if not all, the myriad forms used in Washington, D.C. To implement the plan, owners of property destroyed in the fire were ceded larger sites conforming to the new layout. New plans in 1831 and 1853 drew away from the original idea and, with the exception of a few spots like Grand Circus Square, there is little apparent form in the city today.

Among the other cities with diagonal streets were Indianapolis and Madison. Both these cities were based upon the gridiron, but diagonals ranged from the center to the four corners of the plan. The center in Indianapolis was an open circle; in Madison the focal point was the Wisconsin State Capitol building.

In the midst of this wave of radial planning a significant development occurred in New York City. In 1800 the city surveyor and architect, Joseph Mangin, proposed a plan for extension of the city to the north. His plan provided for major north-south streets with squares and plazas somewhat reminiscent of Washington, D.C. It also suggested a treatment for the waterfront about Manhattan. But Mangin's plan was not adopted.

Instead, an official commission prepared a plan in 1811. This commission was composed of three members, two of whom were lawyers and landowners and the third a surveyor. They proposed a rigid gridiron street system to be laid over the entire island irrespective of the topography and extensive waterfront. Only one angular street was retained—Broadway. The position of the commission was quite clear: "Straight-sided and right-angled houses," they reported, "are the most cheap to build and the most convenient to live in."[2]

---

[2] Turpin Bannister, *Town Planning in New York State,* American Society of Architectural Historians.

DETROIT

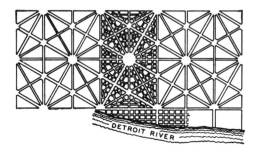

Judge's and Governor's Plan for Detroit, 1807.

BUFFALO

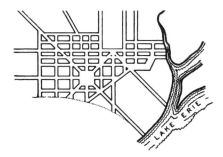

    In 1804 Joseph Ellicott, a surveyor, laid out the city of Buffalo on the shores of Lake Erie. He copied the diagonal streets of Washington, D. C., with the plazas and circles of that city.

NEW YORK CITY

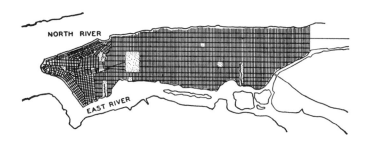

    After turning down a proposal of the city surveyor and architect, Joseph Mangin, in 1800, a commission was appointed to arrive at a plan in 1811. Their plan was a rigid gridiron street pattern laid upon the irregular topography of the city. Open space was not generously allocated. A military parade ground of 69 acres, 55 acres for a public market, and 5 small parks were the only open areas provided in the plan. Despite the "uncommonly great" price of land, explained as the reason for the economy of open

The matter of economy obviously guided the commission in its delibera-
tions and dictated its conclusions. They found that "the price of land is so
uncommonly great," and their proposal for retention of open space was indeed
frugal. A reservation of 69 acres for a military parade ground, 55 acres for a public
market, and five small parks was the limit of open area the commission deemed
feasible.

Assuming that the major traffic would continue to move back and forth
between the Hudson and East Rivers, the east-west streets, 60 feet in width, were
spaced but 260 feet apart. This extravagance was offset, however, by economy of
streets in the opposite direction; north-south streets, 100 feet wide, were spaced
at distances ranging from 600 to 900 feet.

The commission's appraisal of traffic flow was hardly accurate as the
reverse direction it has since taken readily attests. Nor did it reflect particular
optimism for the future of this great city. But it is the economy of the commission
that poses the most pertinent issue because it bears strong resemblance to that
practiced in later and less happy days of urban planning.

*space, the layout of streets can hardly be construed as economical; they occupy some 30
percent of the land area. This harsh and uncompromising plan is reflected in the city of
today in which open space has all but completely vanished. It was not until the middle
of the nineteenth century that the great Central Park was definitely established in the
plan.* (United Press International photo)

It will be recalled that Peter Minuit purchased the entire island of Manhattan from the Indians in 1626. At that time he paid the astounding sum of $24. When the commission laid out its plan in 1811, most of the land was still devoted to agriculture. The commission, however, considered that the price of land was then "uncommonly great." Guided by the economy of a surveyor's rod and chain, the island was mapped in a huge checkerboard. The ultimate cost of fitting the topography, "broken by hills and diversified by watercourses," to this pattern of land subdivision was overlooked, to be sure, and the reservation of 30 per cent of the land for streets was possibly explained by the extensive frontage it provided for the sale of lots. But can the omission of ample open space be construed as economy?

The commission surely expected the city to continue the growth it was then enjoying: they obviously did for they so mapped it for subdivision and sale. Even though the land had been developed with single-family houses on individual lots, the open space in the 1811 plan would have been inadequate. Forty-five years later (1856), 840 acres were purchased for Central Park, and it cost the taxpayers of the city $5,500,000.

This is the variety of economy that distorts the planning of our cities today. It is this experience in the practice of economy from which we are obliged to learn and profit. Is it economical to avoid the reservation of open space in the name of practical planning only to find the land value has become so dear we cannot afford the space when the need is urgent? The value of learning from yesterday is to prepare today for a better tomorrow.

There were those who protested the formlessness of the commissioner's plan. Many agreed with Henry R. Aldrich when he claimed its inspiration was "the great facility which it provides for the gambling in land values and ready purchase and sale of building blocks" which had "wrought incalculable mischief." It was an omen of the fate to befall the American city in subsequent years.

PART 2

Sir, if you wish to have a just notion of the magnitude of this city, you must not be satisfied with seeing its great streets and squares, but must survey the innumerable little lanes and courts.

—Samuel Johnson

The City in Transition

5

The Industrial
Revolution

HANDCRAFT TO MACHINES

With the nineteenth century came the dawn of the Machine Age. Until that time all goods had been processed and assembled by hand. Shops were modest and generally located in the home of the proprietor. The number of employees was small, and there was maintained a close relationship between worker and employer.

There had always been those who worked with inventions. The Renaissance had been such a period; gunpowder, the printing press, and the processing of various materials were important developments of that time. Ways were devised to improve the simple hand machine, but in 1765 Watt invented the steam engine and, with it, mechanical power became independent of hand operation. Enterprising proprietors applied this power to the work in their shops, and production of goods increased. With production increased, trade expanded, the shop moved from the home into separate quarters—the factory—and the distinction between employee and employer widened.

In 1776 Adam Smith set forth his theories of capitalism. With the advent of machines driven with mechanical power a new era was born. Mercantilism moved into the capitalism of the industrial system. The number of employees in proportion to the owners increased rapidly, and trade unions among workers, in contrast to the medieval guilds of proprietors, were formed.

Invention of the machine touched off feverish activity; belt-line production absorbed the attention of industrial management, and repetition of operations replaced the variety of handcraft. Each machine had its job, and each man his machine. With each new device production per worker jumped; mass production made it possible for more people to have more things than had ever been available to them before. The size of factories grew and the number of workers employed by each factory owner also increased. The factory was like a magnet, drawing about it an ever-increasing belt of workers' dwellings, schools, and shops.

TRANSPORTATION

The industrial system was dependent upon the transportation of raw materials to the factory and finished products to the consumers. Before the invention of the steam engine, goods were hauled in wagons and towed on river barges. Beginning in 1761 the inland waterways were linked by a system of canals in the United States, and in 1809 Fulton built his steamboat, the *Clermont.* In 1825 the first steam railroad was operated for public transportation in England, and a line was laid in the United States in 1829. Industrial production increased while domestic and foreign commerce expanded. Between 1850 and 1880, export trade from the United States increased from $17,000,000 to $100,000,000.

In the crowded city, the horse-drawn carriage trundled the people leisurely about the streets. The *voiture-omnibus* for passenger transportation was introduced to Paris in 1819 and was adopted, as the "horse-car," in New York City in 1831. In 1832 some rail lines were used by the horse-car, but the rail-less vehicle continued in use for a long time.

Traffic congestion paralleled the increase in population density, and in 1867 an elevated cable car was built in New York City. A steam train replaced the cable in 1871, but congestion was hardly diminished. Extending their rails beyond the city, the steam railroads offered some relief. Suburbs sprung up along them and invited those commuters who could afford the time and luxury of escape from the city centers.

The electric street railway replaced the horse-car about 1885, and thenceforth became the principal urban transport. By 1917 there were 80,000 cars and 45,000 miles of track in American cities. As a result, the population scattered somewhat about the periphery, but congestion persisted. In 1895 an electric elevated line was installed in Chicago and, shortly thereafter, in New York and Philadelphia.

Still failing to untie the knotty problem of traffic and transportation, the electric railway went underground. In 1897 a short line was built in Boston, and the first major subway was started in New York City in 1904. As we are sadly aware today, these developments aided and abetted congestion. The cities spread, population grew, and transportation only intensified concentration in the urban centers.

When Daimler invented the internal combustion engine in 1885, transportation was beginning another step into the tangle of urban traffic. There were four automobiles registered in the United States in 1895; in 1900 there were 8,000; in 1972, 97,000,000. The automobile split the city open at the seams, and to this day we are frantically trying to hold it together with patches on a worn-out fabric.

It is recorded that Leonardo da Vinci tinkered with a toy flying machine, but in the nineteenth century men themselves took to the air and by 1903 they were flying in heavier-than-air machines. In 1927 Lindbergh spanned the Atlantic Ocean, and in 1938 Howard Hughes flew around the world in 3 days, 19 hours, 8 minutes, and 10 seconds. Today commercial planes are traveling to every part of the earth, carrying 300 passengers at 600 miles per hour, and soaring into the stratosphere. How long can the city remain congested?

COMMUNICATIONS

Civilization has moved at the rate man has communicated his ideas. In ancient times men sent their messages by "runner." The printing press and postal service were initiated in the fifteenth century, and the thoughts of men could be recorded for all to see and read. Their transmission, however, depended upon the carrier on foot or horseback.

The industrial revolution sprung wide the door of man's inventive genius. The will to communicate with each other hung by a strand of copper wire. By 1850 messages were being ticked off on a telegraph key. Then, on March 10, 1876, Professor Alexander Graham Bell sat in his laboratory and spoke into a gadget. His assistant, listening at the other end of a wire, heard the words, "Mr. Watson, come here, I want you." Men could talk to each other on the telephone, and the effect of space and time was drastically altered.

By the end of the first quarter of the twentieth century the miracle of radio not only further changed time and space, it exploded them in the face of civilization, and adjustment is still far from complete.

PUBLIC HEALTH AND SAFETY

In ancient times the tragedy of epidemics aroused rulers to improve the physical environment. Primitive though they were, there were efforts to provide drainage and distribute water in the cities of Crete and the Indus Valley. It was not until the cholera plague of the Middle Ages had violently reduced the urban population in Europe that sanitary sewer connections and water distribution were provided as a public service.

Measures for the public health and safety were extended during the nineteenth century. The first system of water supply by gravity flow was installed in Boston in 1652. By 1820 pumping systems were in general use, and methods for the disposal and treatment of sewage were improved. The heavy coverage of buildings on the land reduced the natural drainage of the city, but extensive street paving permitted effective cleaning and storm sewers augmented the sanitary equipment. Urban hygiene in the factory town did not lag for lack of facilities. It was simply outstripped and nullified by the congestion of people and the intensity of land use.

Public thoroughfares in towns of the Middle Ages were dark and foreboding lanes. An occasional oil lamp hanging from a corner building was the only light to guide the stranger through the night. Artificial gas lighting appeared in London in 1812 and by 1840 was in common use for lighting city streets. The first central generating plant for distribution of electricity was placed in operation in 1882. Thenceforth electricity replaced gas for street lighting.

Electricity illuminated the highway and residential street. It made the "great white way" that brightens the city of today, but it also brought the gaudy display of signs and advertising that flash at night and droop hideously by day. With degenerate taste they sell the wares of commerce and industry but reduce the city aspect to that of a cheap bazaar.

Services for the health, safety, and convenience of the urban population advanced farther in a period of less than 100 years than in all past history. This tremendous progress and the actual living and working conditions of the industrial city present a bewildering contrast. Glorification of the industrial system and the fruits of its new-born activity blinded people to the ruin and havoc spreading across the urban community.

THE FACTORY TOWN

The steam locomotive extended its rails between the raw products, the factory, and the cities of consumers all over the land. The railroad with its sprawling yards penetrated the town with a network of tracks. Every amenity of urban life was sacrificed to the requirements of industrial production. The factory with its tentacles of railroads and shipping was the heart and nerve center of the city. Port cities on the ocean, lakes, and rivers prospered, drawing to them ships laden with coal and ore and sending from them shiploads of manufactured goods. Railroads and ships joined at the factories, and the waterfront became the industrial core of the city,

The impact of the industrial revolution was first felt in England. The new industrial economy brought exploitation of the poor and, with poverty, came the slums. New slums, mechanical slums, row upon row of crowded workers' houses in the shadow of the factory, all were added to the traditional slums of the seventeenth century in Europe. The degraded environment of the factory town hung like a cloud over urban life for the next century and a half. Engrossed in the technical processes of industrial production, the homes of the people were neglected. Writing in 1865, Dr. Clifford Allbutt described the slums he saw:

This is no description of a plague-stricken town in the fifteenth century; it is a faint effort to describe the squalor, the deadliness, and the decay of a mass of huts which lies in the town of Leeds, between York Street on the one side and Marsh Lane on the other; a place of "darkness and cruel habitations" which is within a stone's throw of our parish church and where the fever is bred. These dwellings seem for the most part to belong to landlords who take no interest whatever in their well-being. One block perhaps has fallen years ago by inheritance to a gentleman

   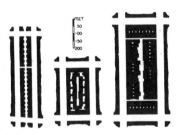

| The Seventeenth Century City | The Nineteenth Century City | The Twentieth Century City | London | Vienna | New York |

Among the deplorable slums of the nineteenth-century factory town in England, the two-story row-house predominated. Stretching in long rows with small backyards and narrow streets, the living environment was dreary and monotonous. Crowding on the continent, however, was even more severe as indicated in the sketch of a tenement block in Vienna. Built to a height of four and five floors, it was typical to place a double row of dwellings within the block, the interior row facing on a narrow interior court on both sides. While it has been customary to assume that European slums were more crowded than housing in this new world, the tenement block in New York City does not confirm such a notion. The sketch shows a combination of the "railroad" and the "dumbbell" tenements, many of which still remain despite the fact that they were outlawed in 1901.

THE INDUSTRIAL REVOLUTION AND THE NINETEENTH CENTURY CITY

STOKE-ON-TRENT, England (British Information Service)

59

in Lancashire, Devonshire, or anywhere; another to an old lady; a third, perhaps, to an obscure money-lender. Meanwhile, the rotten doors are falling from their hinges, the plaster drops from the walls, the window frames are stuffed with greasy paper or old rags, damp and dung together fester in the doorways, and a cloud of bitterness hangs over all. To one set of houses, appropriately named Golden Square, there is no admission save by alleys or tunnels, which are only fit to lead to dungeons: so that for perhaps half a century or more the winds of heaven have never blown within its courts.

In the new land across the sea there was a vast source of natural resources and an energetic people inspired by a new-won freedom. The industrial revolution swept across America unimpeded by traditions. Then one could hear the echo of events in Europe. As the economy shifted from agrarian to industrial, the people and the resources were soon to experience the throes of exploitation and the struggle for a decent living environment.

The air of American towns became polluted with smoke and grime from belching chimneys of the new age. Railroads ate into the core of cities, water-fronts were ruined, soot covered the village, and sewage flowed into the streams and lined the beaches. Buffalo, Chicago, Detroit, St. Louis, all devoted their splendid sites on lakes and river waterfronts to the industrial plants, the railroads, and the tankers of the new factory system. The land was platted and advertised as "desirable sites for industry."

Immigration from foreign lands invited the building of tenements. Into them the newcomers crowded, grateful for some place to live in this country of promise. Industrial growth in the large centers induced the people to remain in cities rather than migrate to the more healthful environment of rural communities, and the inevitable result was the creation of slums.

There was an exception to the concentration in congested cities. A large supply of labor was needed to obtain the raw products for manufacture, and "company towns" sprung up at mining and lumber camps in various parts of the country. They occupy an infamous place in the annals of American town development. Living in deplorable shacks and shanties, the workers' families were subject to the will of a single employer for their livelihood. Shelter, food, and clothing were supplied through and at terms prescribed by the mining company.

6

The City of Contrasts

LAST OF THE BAROQUE

Repeated uprisings of the people caught in the tangled industrial city were a source of annoyance to the ruling class in Europe. In the midst of the orgy of urban expansion, a development of monumental proportions was undertaken in Paris. Sensitive to the restlessness of the working classes, Napoleon III proposed to open broad avenues through the slums in which discontent festered. In devising his plan he was not unmindful of the advantage these open spaces would provide his soldiers in controlling mob violence.

Georges-Eugène Haussmann, a bureaucrat in the city administration, was selected, in 1853, to take charge of the huge program. The result was an amazing demonstration of administration and organization. The entire boulevard system of Paris was planned and executed in a period of seventeen years and under the most strenuous circumstances. Haussman was resisted, on the one hand, by a city council reluctant to appropriate the necessary funds and, on the other, by bourgeois property owners affected by his broad strokes of planning.

Haussmann was aware of the need to design for the traffic of a new industrial age. He laid out the new streets in long sweeps cutting through the maze of winding medieval lanes. With these avenues he connected old plazas and created new plazas. He laid out the radiating avenues across the open fields from the Place de L'Étoile, the Bois de Boulogne, the monumental Avenue de L'Opéra, and many other grand boulevards.

The program engineered by Haussmann was stupendous. It transformed Paris and gave it much of the color of that great city. But can it properly be called planning? A series of masterful projects were executed. Haussmann intended to improve the circulation of traffic, and the broad avenues that were opened through the congested districts were an improvement. He had the conception of scale appropriate for the new city: he saw it as a complex wanting unification. But the tradition of monuments was deeply rooted in the process of city building. It was not long since the revolution against tyranny, and an emperor was again the ruler. The tree-lined avenues and vistas meant to impress rather than serve the people.

The time was not ripe for solving the new urban problems. Mixed land uses were not changed, and the avenues became continuous shopping streets along the ground floor with dwellings on the upper floors. There was no separation between land uses as in the earlier London residential developments about Bloomsbury, which were by-passed by traffic arteries and shopping streets. The scheme of Haussmann was gargantuan in scale, but it was too late to become an effective monument to the ego of a monarch, and too early to solve the planning of the industrial city. It was the swan song of the Baroque city.

PARIS

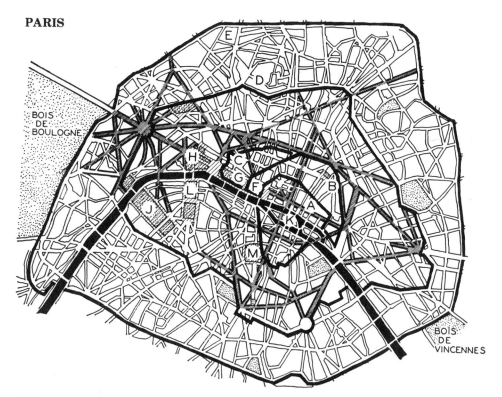

The dark-shaded streets show the Haussmann Program

Wall **A**	Built by Philip Augustus, Twelfth century	**G**	The Tuilleries
Wall **B**	Built by Charles V, Fourteenth century	**H**	The Champs Élysées
Wall **C**	Built by Louis XIII, Seventeenth century	**J**	The Champs de Mars
Wall **D**	Built by Louis XV, Eighteenth century	**K**	The Île de la Cité
Wall **E**	Built by Napoleon III, Nineteenth century	**L**	The Invalides
F	The Louvre	**M**	The Luxembourg

DEVELOPMENT OF PARIS

Beginning as a fortified town on the small island in the Seine River, Paris was known as Lutetia by the Romans. At the time of the Norman invasion in the ninth century the town had expanded beyond the original *Île de la Cité* and was fortified on both sides of the Seine. The fortifications were extended by Philip Augustus in the twelfth century. The left bank (south) was the principal location for churches and colleges, the commercial center lying on the right bank. The kings made their residence on this bank, and in the fourteenth century Charles V built a wall to contain more adequately this growing part of the city. At the east end of the town was the tower known as the Bastille; at the west end, on the banks of the Seine, was the Louvre which became the royal palace.

The Louvre was extended in the sixteenth century under Henry II, and the Tuileries Gardens were created. The power of the monarch was growing, and the Renaissance was ushered in. Henry IV built the Place Royal, and in the seventeenth century Louis XIII had the walls expanded to contain the Tuileries Gardens.

During the reign of Louis XIV, the Sun King, Paris grew rapidly and court life extended its influence. Vauban reduced the fortified walls, and the ramparts were transformed into promenades, the first of the *Grands Boulevards*. The Tuileries Gardens and the Louvre were enlarged, and the initial stage of the Champs Élysées was built into the "suburbs" to the west. The Place des Victoires and Place Vendôme were built. Monumental quais were created along the Seine. King Louis XIV, however, moved his court and residence to Versailles where he built the great palace and gardens.

The city expanded further under Louis XV who built the Place Louis XV (Place de la Concorde), Rue Royale, and Church of the Madeleine. Streets were widened and new avenues built for fine residences. The Champs de Mars was also established, and in the latter part of the eighteenth century a new wall was built to contain the growing city.

Following the Revolution the industrial development of the city increased. The outskirts of the city were built up, and a new wall was built in 1840. Under Napoleon III, the huge program by Baron Haussmann was carried out. Many new avenues were cut through the city and boulevards created on the sites of old walls.

As Paris developed, the city underwent remodeling under each of the monarchs but the greatest projects in each successive period were those along the fringe of the city. The great open spaces that distinguish the city today were developed in advance of the city expansion and the walls extended to include them as the city spread about them. Even as late as Haussmann, boulevards were carved out of the city, but the most expansive spaces were those like the Champs Élysées and the Place de l'Étoile, and boulevards radiating from them were laid across open fields. The rapid growth of Paris has spread the city in all its suburbs and absorbed the open spaces including those created when the walls of 1840 were leveled in the latter part of the nineteenth century.

MID-VICTORIAN MEDIOCRITY

There was a depressing consistency about the factory town of the nineteenth century. It bred mediocrity in every aspect of life; mediocrity was its characteristic. Vast areas of mean dwellings lay under a pall of smoke; an atmosphere of haze hung over the environment. Peaks of creative inspiration were few and far between. Monotonous order was a natural result of rigid organization of people and things. The mid-Victorian Period signifies bad taste and dull, routine life. Here and there a pseudo-gaiety pierced the haze, but it was fluffy with gray frills touched more with half-concealed vulgarity than genuine pleasure. The urban environment reflected the bawdy "can-can" rather than the graceful waltz. A film of grime and soot covered it, and the wide range from wealth to poverty meant little more, in a cultural sense, than the difference between more or little bric-a-brac in the cluttered surroundings. The cultural energy of the city was sapped by the gigantism of industrial development. The factory was like a monster that spewed forth its products and then reached out to clutch them in its expanding claws.

Glorification of the machine was complete, and man had created a master. This was significant to him. He had proved his power. Here was a creature of man that could produce anything. It had no need for a brain; it was automatic. It had no limitations; it could even destroy man himself. And man was tremendously proud of his achievement.

Proof of the mediocrity of the age were the few who recognized it. William Morris and John Ruskin cried out against it: Charles Dickens wove it into his classic stories; muckraking reporters like Lincoln Steffens exposed it; Octavia Hill and Jane Addams fought it with vigorous social work. They saw the dulling of man's creative spirit, the shift from quality to quantity as a measure of success. They perceived it in all its shabby elegance and grime—the nineteenth century industrial city.

Apparently, human beings can move in an atmosphere of mediocrity for just so long, and then an awareness of a cultural vacuum dawns. Unfortunately they may only peer, rather than search, for the absent quality, and they often fabricate a substitute, an artificial air of pomposity that serves rather well and takes much less trouble than the search for culture. To achieve culture it might be necessary to forego temporarily some material advantages in which we so firmly believe. So we ingeniously contrive to have both.

This happened in the transition twilight of the nineteenth century.

THE CITY BEAUTIFUL

World fairs had proved a great way to place the products of industry before the people and it was proposed to hold one in Chicago in 1893. The Columbian Exposition, as it was called, was to demonstrate amply the great industrial empire and to give pedigree to this new empire. What more natural way to accomplish this than by clothing it in the robes of classic form? Had this not been the "cultural" drape for the great days of the past? Was this not an appropriate cloak for a new era when men could produce more than at any time in history? With this new power men could reproduce classic structures that would surpass the emperors. This was a natural conclusion in the nineteenth century and it was true. Mediocrity had taken its toll in taste as in exploitation. A reaction was inevitable, and it was violent.

It was a natural paradox that out of the smoke, soot, and grime of the cities, this Fair would be called "White City." Cities were cramped, monotonous, and ugly; the Fair would be big, broad, and beautiful. The Fair would be everything the urban environment was not, and it was a huge success. It did all the things it purported to do and something more. It launched a movement of "classic revival" in this country which was to portray all the contrasts conceived in the nineteenth century and born in the twentieth.

Daniel Burnham, the chief architect for the Columbian Exposition, uttered the magic words that marked the new era: "Make no little plans." The fair rolled up a tidal wave of "city planning" and it swept across the land. Every large city planned to become the "City Beautiful." Burnham was commissioned to prepare a plan for San Francisco after the earthquake and fire of 1906. The Commercial Club of Chicago engaged him for the plan of that city in 1909. He did one for Manila and Baguio in the Philippines, and he was an active member of a commission of architects who renewed the plan of Washington, D.C.

Other cities followed suit. Plans were of colossal scale with monumental proportions. Axes shot off in all directions terminating with proposed buildings that put the visions of past kings to shame. Great plazas and broad avenues, generously punctuated with monuments, were almost a civic obsession. The "City Beautiful" was the Grand Plan reincarnate; the *École des Beaux Arts* in Paris was the fountainhead for the designers of this period and the plans had to be big to be beautiful.

Civic centers became a popular theme. Nearly every city had its Civic Center Plan—open space landscaped in the traditional fashion, fountains distributed about plaza and garden, public buildings limited in number only by the size and ambition of the city, topped off with a frosted dome terminating a long and broad vista.

All this activity was performed in something of a vacuum. An air of haughty detachment pervaded the planning, an isolation from the affairs of people and community activities. A monument or public building blithely placed in the middle of an important traffic artery suggests the characteristic paradox. It was as though the planners had determined that the people must adjust themselves to the mighty formal arrangement. It failed to occur to them that the entire development of a city was essentially a derivative of human needs. The Civic Center conception was one of removal from the life of the community rather than a functional entity within it. Removed from channels of enterprise, civic affairs had an air of divorcement. The grandiose buildings were imposing, not inviting. They held the spellbound citizen at arm's length. They did not fit the city, its life, its habits, or its manners; theirs was an air of disdain rather than dignity.

Then these great structures became so laden with excess "architectural" expense, it was almost too much to bear. The citizen could really not afford the sums of money they cost. There were some grand gestures made and executed, but the lavish plans were largely destined for respectable storage in the archives of a more modest city hall. Most of the work that reached the stage of execution was necessarily and haphazardly remodeled later to fit the requirements of traffic and circulation ignored in the original planning.

The seeds of city planning had nevertheless been planted. Planning organizations sprung up in various parts of the country. A Town Planning Board was established in Hartford, Connecticut, in 1907. In 1909 the first National Conference on City Planning was held. This was followed in 1911 with the founding of the National Housing Association. By 1913 there were official planning boards in 18 cities in the country, and in the same year Massachusetts led off with the first state legislation that made city planning a mandatory responsibility of local governments: all cities with a population of 10,000 or more were required to establish a Planning Board.

THE CITY OF COMMERCE

Meanwhile the real city was shoving its sprouts through these pleasant but fortuitous efforts. The technical "know-how" of industrial production had been learned. The industrial system was no longer primarily a technical problem; it was now a commercial process. Financing and distribution were the new emphasis. Selling the rapidly produced merchandise and financing the expanding facilities to produce more were transforming the system into a financial empire. Factory management turned its attention from production of goods to commercial organization, banking, national and world-wide trade associations. The nature of commodities and their production methods gave way to ticker-tape and figures in a set of books. The businessman—the tycoon of commerce—became the main cog in the new era. Statistics, business cycles, bookkeeping, financing, and the stock market were the stock-in-trade of those who strove for success. Trade in commodities rather than the commodities themselves was what counted now. The city began to bristle with buildings, sheltering acres of floor space for business. The skyscraper was the dramatic manifestation of the commercial city.

It was apparent that affairs must be operated on a practical basis. Cities must work, the ornamental must be discarded, and only the useful could be tolerated. Land cost money, buildings cost money, services cost money, and so did time. These required attention of practical men, not dreamers. It was well and good to have ideas about a "City Beautiful," but it was far more important that they pay dividends.

To answer these demands there emerged the "city engineer," the practical man who could make surveys and calculations, determine the size of sewer, water, and drainage systems, lay out rail lines, streets, walks, curbs. City planning became an engineering process engaging practical men free from dreams. These qualifications appealed to civic and business leaders and instilled confidence in their judgment and businesslike manner. It was this individual that businessmen desired for the responsibility of planning within budget limitations. They had received a huge dose of grand planning, proposals to embellish the city with architectural trappings costing more than the problems they were intended to solve.

There was merit in this position; the "City Beautiful" was not frowned upon, it was simply too expensive. Awed by the monumental dreams, impressed by the vision, it was not with disrespect that the proposals were sidetracked. These great designs had simply lost all connection with the commercial city that was growing up in the twentieth century. It was a thing apart, detached, unrelated to the affairs of men. It solved no problems, and there was a sub-conscious recoiling from the classic mold into which it would cast the physical environment.

The city was a business proposition, and it must pay dividends. Land took on a new value. There was a time when it was sold as "lots." The value was later measured in terms of street frontage, a price per front foot. It was now being measured by the *square* foot. Every square foot of land had a value and none could be wasted. Building coverage was intense; layer upon layer of floor space was piled upon the land.

Despite resistance to the monumental planning of the "City Beautiful," the classic treatment had made a deep impression. It gave an appearance of pedigree which was itself an asset to the business world. The value attached to every square foot of land for commercial use opposed the fine balance between the buildings and open space of classic planning. But the appearance could be captured, however, so remnants of the classic revival were hung upon the façades of buildings and each thus became a fit associate for its neighbor along the street. It was a sham, to be sure, but the street assumed a stylish front and the value of land behind the façades was protected.

As in architecture and the arts, city planning acquired a Queen Ann front and a Mary Ann back. The street became a canyon embellished with a galaxy of styles cutting through mountains of building bulk. The appearance of dignity was achieved without the loss of a square foot of land.

Washington, D.C. is not a typical American city, but it dramatically displays the contradictions of the twentieth century. The job of government in a great democracy attracted an expanding population to the capital city. With the people came commercial enterprise, and the forces of conflict were set; the commercial city and the classic city were diametrically opposed.

The pseudo-classic planning for activities of the Federal government was vigorously maintained. In 1901 the MacMillan Commission was appointed to restore the original character of the L'Enfant plan. Some results were obtained. The railroad which had been cut across the Mall was removed, and the present site for the Union Station was established. There was agreement on a uniform limit for the height of future buildings. To preserve these accomplishments the National Commission of Fine Arts was appointed in 1910 by President Theodore

Roosevelt. It was followed in 1926 by creation of the National Capital Park and Planning Commission.

These commissions performed yeomen services to the preservation of the classic city, but that city had changed. A new age had arrived, immature but nonetheless a moving force. Commercialism with its entourage of shops, hotels, office and loft buildings, entertainment and residential development, traffic and transportation descended upon the city. Above all, the evaluation of land and the intensity of development that had overtaken other cities could not be denied in the capital city.

Commercial enterprise paid respects to the monumental street system which had been laid down. Into this framework the features of the new city were squeezed and fitted. Classic façades were likewise draped upon the street fronts, but behind these fronts formless building space was heaped upon the land, even as in other cities.

The contradiction between the classic and the commercial city was clearly apparent. To protect its character of monumental buildings and planning, the Federal reservation was necessarily isolated from the remainder of urban development. With this separation the prescription of uniform building height and style, building sites, forms, and open space could be rigidly controlled.

The paradox of the city was substantially complete. The execution of a plan for the capital of a great democratic government could be accomplished only by freezing its form into a preconceived and inflexible mold. The reason for the paradox had apparently escaped notice.

It was falsely assumed that a planning "style" could be transferred from another age and adapted to a new set of conditions. It was overlooked that periods of culture in the past have been identified by the special stamp of character they evolve from within the framework of each. Great cultures have not been so recognized because of their similarities with previous periods, but because of the distinctive qualities they have contributed to the progress of civilization.

The false premise upon which the plan of Washington, D.C., has evolved is magnified by the design of the structures themselves, the insistence upon classic forms without regard for the essential arrangement of interior space. Exterior space is equally oblivious to the functional elements of the city. The classic courtyards, their prototypes treated with fine paving or gracious gardens, have in Washington become oil spotted parking lots filled with automobiles. The Federal reservation of classic monumentalism is hollow and unnatural; the commercial city, warped into the pattern of its streets, is equally artificial.

THE NEED FOR REGULATION

Laissez-faire took deep root in the affairs of men as the commercial city formed. The new attitude of practicality presented something of a contradiction in urban building. It became increasingly apparent that if freedom was to avoid license

NEW YORK CITY

New York illustrates the contrasts, conflicts and chaos of modern commercial centers.

WASHINGTON, D.C.

Fairchild Aerial Surveys

A city of monumental compromise between the classic and the commercial city. The Capitol is near the center of the photograph. It is encircled (left and counterclockwise) by the House Office Building, Library of Congress, Supreme Court, and Senate Office Building. To the right is Union Station. The Mall extends from the Capitol to the Washington Monument, from which the Reflecting Pool leads to the Lincoln Memorial.

some order must be established. In practical terms this meant the adoption of rules and regulations which, in turn, implied certain curbs upon *laissez-faire.*

We have observed that regulations over city building were not new in the annals of history. King Hammurabi codified his rules of justice in 2,000 B.C. The Greeks had regulations pertaining to the building of dwellings. The Romans established height limits for tenements. Towns of the Middle Ages adopted various regulations against fire hazards and projecting upper stories.

The sad condition of housing that developed with the factory system in the nineteenth century forced the enactment of many laws to curb abuses. Restrictions applying to commercial and industrial buildings were rare, and with the advent of the skyscraper the need for appropriate regulations became more and more apparent.

Regulations for light, air, and lot coverage, though lax, were accepted for residential buildings, but commercial structures were permitted to occupy as much as 100 per cent of the lot area for the entire height. Steel construction and elevators pushed buildings higher. Light and air could penetrate on the street frontage only, and this diminished as buildings rose, floor upon floor, into the air.

Regulations increased in number and scope during the early part of the twentieth century. Codes establishing standards of construction, mechanical, and electrical installations were adopted to protect the public health and safety. Fireproof construction was required where congestion was most acute. Protection was assured for public rights-of-way.

Mixed land uses, the indiscriminate placement of stores and shops in residential areas, induced premature depreciation of land values and residential neighborhoods. The necessity to exercise some measure of public control over land use was pressing.

EARLY ZONING

There was some precedent for zoning. When town walls in Germany were leveled in the nineteenth century, building regulations designated "belts" in which apartments and single houses could be built about the periphery of the ramparts. Protection from encroachment of undesirable land uses had been attempted in America. Exclusive residential sections in some middle-western cities were planned as courts entered through monumental gates and "block ordinances" were framed to restrict improvements to high-class residences. Height limits were placed on buildings in Boston in 1903—125 feet in the central district and 80 feet elsewhere. In 1909 Los Angeles adopted a regulation dividing the business area into seven "industrial" districts. The remainder of the city was declared to be residential and in this area "laundries" were excluded. After a piece of land, in which a brick industry was located, was annexed to the city another ordinance was enacted to prohibit brickyards in residential districts. Both these ordinances were upheld in the California courts.

These cases were hardly more than experimental gestures, but the chaotic growth of cities made it imperative that positive steps be taken to bring some order into the urban pattern. It is a fortunate characteristic of humankind that when leadership is needed there is usually available someone willing and capable of assuming the responsibility. Such a man was Edward M. Bassett, an attorney in New York City. To Mr. Bassett goes credit for a public service on behalf of the urban population. He undertook a thorough investigation of the power of the people to regulate their own destiny and worked diligently on the preparation of a legal instrument whereby the people could exercise effectively their powers to control the use of land in the urban community.

Mr. Bassett defined zoning as "the regulation by districts under the police power of the height, bulk, and use of buildings, the use of land, and the density of population." With this clear-cut purpose, the first comprehensive zoning ordinance in this country was enacted by New York City in 1916. There is no better testimony to the remarkable thoroughness of Mr. Bassett and his colleagues than the subsequent history of zoning in the courts. Tested in a number of cases in later years, the principle of zoning was upheld in every court.

One of these cases is particularly significant. It fairly confirmed the democratic nature of planning, and established it as an instrument with which the people could order the destiny of their cities. In his opinion on the "Euclid Case" Justice Sutherland of the U. S. Supreme Court said:

> Until recently urban life was comparatively simple; but with the increase and concentration of population, problems have developed, and constantly are developing, which require additional restrictions in respect to the use and occupation of private lands in communities. Regulations, the wisdom, necessity and validity of which, as applied to existing conditions, are so apparent that they are now uniformly sustained, a century ago, or even a half century ago, probably would have been rejected as arbitrary and oppressive.[1]

Little need be added to the words of Supreme Court Justice Sutherland.

Zoning had a profound effect upon American cities. For the first time there was created an instrument with which to control the use of land in urban areas. It is characteristic of this technique that it protects the general welfare of the people by protecting that of each individual citizen.

There was nothing in the nature of zoning that confined it to urban development alone. It was essentially a device for planning—the execution of a plan—and as such could be applied at any scale and for any land requiring public control over its use. It has been applied to counties in a manner similar to that of cities, and it has been adapted as a means for conservation of natural resources. In 1929 the State of Wisconsin empowered counties to establish districts in which agriculture was excluded from submarginal lands and forestry and recreational development encouraged within these privately owned lands.

Zoning is a vital part of the urban machinery, but it can fail through abuse, misuse, and resistance to essential changes in the urban pattern for the general welfare.

[1] *Village of Euclid, Ohio* v. *Ambler Realty Company,* 272 U. S. 363 (November 22, 1926).

EXTENSION OF PUBLIC SERVICES

The industrial revolution changed the city into a metropolis. The urban population became the multitude, and the supply of basic human wants to this multitude required highly organized services. Transportation via common carriers, roads, water supply, sewage disposal and drainage, communications, power and illumination, all vastly expanded the scope. Their impact upon the public health and safety increased accordingly. Being thus colored with the public interest, some of these services were subject to public regulation; others were embraced in public ownership.

Public works to control or harness natural resources for the community at large were not new. We will recall the dikes, reservoirs, and irrigation projects along the Nile; the aqueducts, sewers, and roads built by the Romans as public projects. This responsibility disappeared for a time during the Feudal Period but returned toward the end of the Middle Ages. Limited though they were, water supply and sewage disposal were then considered public responsiblities.

In the early history of this country many of the highways were private toll roads. They were transferred to public ownership and control, and the sewerage system and drainage remained a public responsibility. There are other public services, however, which are owned and operated as private enterprises. Because of their impact upon the common welfare, the continuity of their service is essential and they enjoy a monopoly guaranteed by franchise. Known as *public utilities,* they are subject to regulation by public authority.

The railroads, street railways, and other forms of common carriers, the telephone, telegraph, and radio are with some exceptions regulated public utilities. The same is true of electric power, illumination, and gas distribution. The supply of water is generally owned by the public, although there are exceptions.

The "social" control of utility services is an important factor in the future of urban development. It is therefore pertinent to understand the position of our courts in dealing with this phase of democratic procedures.

In 1876 Chief Justice Waite of the U. S. Supreme Court set forth the theory of public interest in private property. The case was that of a grain operator who violated a local statute controlling the rates for storage. The court held that the enterprise was "affected with the public interest" because of the dependence of the public upon it and the consequent right of the public to exercise authority over its operations. Justice Waite stated,

> When, therefore, one devotes his property to a use in which the public has an interest, he, in effect, grants to the public an interest in that use, and must submit to be controlled by the public for the common good, to the extent of the interest he has thus created.[2]

<hr />

[2] *Munn* v. *Illinois,* 94 U. S. 113.

Chief Justice Taft confirmed this position in a later case with this opinion:

In a sense, the public is concerned about all lawful business because it contributes to the prosperity and well-being of the people. The public may suffer from high prices or strikes in many trades, but the expression "clothed with the public interest" as applied to a business means more than that the public welfare is affected by the continuity or by the price at which a commodity is sold or a service rendered. The circumstances which clothe a particular kind of business with a public interest, in the sense of *Munn* v. *Illinois* and other cases, must be such as to create a peculiarly close relation between the public and those engaged in it, and raise implications of an affirmative obligation on their part to be reasonable in dealing with the public.[3]

It will be observed that enterprise engaging in public service assumes a dual obligation. The first is to supply all the needs of the public implied by the nature of the service, and the second is to provide the services at a cost reflecting reasonable but not excessive profit. This status of a public utility—a public service for which it enjoys a monopoly—imposes obligations beyond the scope of the usual private enterprise. Public utilities became an integral part of city planning, and successful development of the city is largely dependent upon the effectiveness of their operations.

[3] *Charles Wolff Packing Company* v. *Court of Industrial Relations of the State of Kansas*, 262 U.S. 522 (1923).

7

Betterment of Living Conditions

The depths to which urban communities sank in the nineteenth century, and in which many still remain, is a shameful blot on the world scene. Building tenements for rent was a profitable enterprise in the nineteenth century. Excessive building coverage on the land and crowding of dwellings within the buildings brought about population congestion with unbelievable acceleration. The population density in London was 265 persons per acre in 1870. It was 23 per cent higher than this in New York City, 326 persons per acre, which then had only one-third the total population of London.[1]

Standards of land use were lax. The first law to regulate tenement building came to New York in 1867, but only faint improvements were forced upon speculators. Planning persisted at a deplorably low level; the "railroad" plan was typical of the early tenements and it had no more evil rival in the world. The usual lot width was 25 feet, with a depth of 100 feet. Built to the side property lines of these narrow lots, the "railroad" plan covered as much as 90 per cent of the area. The small space remaining at the rear was used for privies, no sanitation being provided within the building. With four apartments on each floor, and five or six stories high, only one room in each dwelling enjoyed light and air; all other rooms had no exterior exposure.

The unbearable living conditions imposed on the poor did not go unnoticed. A competition was sponsored in 1879 by the "Plumber and Sanitary Engineer" for a "model" tenement. The results were touched with irony. The winning plan, by James E. Ware, Architect, was the prototype of the later accursed "dumbbell" plan which covered 85 per cent of the lot and resorted to a narrow

[1] *American Cyclopedia,* 1875, Vol. XII, p. 382.

interior light shaft along the property lines. Despite subsequent legislation "outlawing" these buildings, innumerable still remain to afflict the City of New York.

THE UTOPIANS

The industrial city was shrouded in gloom. Class distinctions of the eighteenth century were present, but the new economy forged links between them. The fate of the privileged classes was inextricably woven with the welfare of the masses. The upper classes recognized this, and philanthropy assumed new proportions. Efforts to relieve the burdens of the working classes pierced the haze all through the nineteenth century.

As early as 1797 the Society for Bettering the Conditions of the Poor was formed in England. While there were nostalgic recollections of the formal city, the struggle to improve the living environment of the working people moved steadily on. The depressing condition of housing for the poor impressed some industrial leaders who sensed the problems it presented to the future of the industrial economy. The first half of the century was marked by protests against the "sordidness, filth, and squalor, embroidered with patches of pompous and vulgar hideousness," and a number of Utopian communities were proposed. One such scheme was that of Robert Owen.

Owen was the proprietor of a cotton mill at New Lanark. He was familiar with the problems of industrial management, having successfully introduced reforms in the working conditions, hours, and wages for employees in his plant. However, Owen saw beyond these reforms and, in 1816, he set forth an unusual plan for a co-operative community combining industry and agriculture.

Dwellings were grouped about a large open space in which he located the communal buildings. Surrounding the dwellings were large gardens, and this entire area was encircled by a main roadway. On one side of the compound were the factories and workshops. Beyond, on all sides, was the agricultural belt ranging from 1,000 to 1,500 acres. The village was designed for about 1,200 people. Owen intended his plan for the unemployed, assuming that the community would become self-supporting and thereby reduce the heavy cost of public relief.

Another of the Utopians was J. S. Buckingham who, in 1849, wrote a treatise entitled *National Evils and Practical Remedies*. In this work he displayed his plan for a "model" town for an "Associated Temperance Community of About 10,000 inhabitants." Buckingham adhered to the current distinction of class, placing the finer houses near the center of his plan, receding in class to the humble dwellings and workshops about the periphery.

The Utopian proposals were not executed, but they focused attention upon the growing evils of the urban environment. In 1844 the Rochdale Pioneers formed the first consumers' co-operative organization. In the same year the first Royal Commission on Health and Housing was appointed in England and the first Public Health Act was passed in 1848.

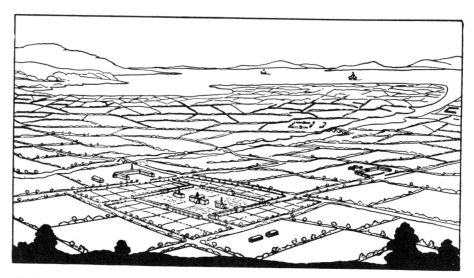

PROPOSED SELF-SUPPORTING INDUSTRIAL TOWN

In 1816 Robert Owen, an English industrialist moved by the problem of the ill-housed industrial workers and increasing unemployment, proposed a plan for a community which he believed could become self-supporting and reduce the heavy cost of public relief. Owen further proposed that similar communities could be established at appropriate intervals in the countryside. Communal buildings for each community were situated in the center of a broad Common. About the Common were rows of dwellings, and surrounding the dwellings were large gardens. The main road encircled the entire compound and the factories and workshops were located along the outside boundary of the community. Designed for about 1200 people, each community was surrounded by an agricultural area of between 1000 and 1500 acres to supplement industrial employment.

PLAN OF A MODEL TOWN FOR AN ASSOCIATED TEMPERANCE COMMUNITY OF ABOUT 10,000 INHABITANTS

Proposed in 1849 by architect J. S. Buckingham, this Utopian plan specified a multitude of features within the community and recommended that industries using "steam engines" be situated at least one-half mile from the town. It was also suggested that sites would be reserved for "suburban villas" in the agricultural land surrounding the town.

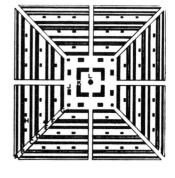

A 1000 houses 20 feet wide

B Arcade for workshops

C 560 houses 28 feet wide

D Retail shops

E 296 houses 38 feet wide

F Winter promenade arcade

G 120 houses 54 feet wide

H Schools, baths, dining halls

J Public buildings, churches

K 24 mansions 80 feet wide

L Central square

By the middle of the century severe epidemics were spreading over England and continental countries. The ruling classes could insulate themselves from many undesirable features of urban living, but they were not immune to disease. Spurred by alarm, the royalty engaged in a few paternal developments. Prince Albert in England, Louis Napoleon III in France, and the Berlin Building Society under Prince Wilhelm in Germany built some "model" dwellings.

These projects represented two extremes. In the congested areas, six-and seven-story tenements were repeated with little improvement in plan and design over previous buildings; they could only decay into more slums with the passing of time. The other extremity was the suburb of single houses built on the outskirts of the cities. The intention of these dwellings was encouragement of home-ownership. Being too expensive for the vast number of low-paid workers, they reverted to the usual middle-class suburbs. The prospect of selling these dwellings at handsome profits further removed them from the income group most in need of improved housing. Consequently, there were no solutions in these spurts of activity.

THE MODEL TOWNS

Recognizing the desirability of good housing for their workers and stimulated by the unexecuted proposals of the Utopians, some "model" communities were undertaken by industrial owners. One of the earliest of these "towns" was Bessbrook, built in 1846 for workers in the linen mills near Newry, Ireland. In 1852 Sir Titus Salt built Saltaire for some 3,000 workers in his textile mill near Bradford, England. Extensive community facilities were introduced in this development. In 1865 the Krupp family began the first of several "model" villages for workers in their munitions and iron factories in Essen, Germany.

George Cadbury, a chocolate manufacturer, moved his plant from Birmingham to a rural site and began the town of Bourneville in 1879. While this community was initiated as a "company" town it was converted to an autonomous village about 1900 and has some 2,000 dwellings today. The land has remained in the single ownership of the village. In France, another chocolate manufacturer, M. Menier, built a workers' colony at Noisel-sur-Seine near Paris in 1874. Similar communities were built in France by the Anzin Mining Company for mine workers at Valenciennes, and M. Schneider et Cie., for their Creusot Steel Mills near Fontainebleau. Others were developed at the Crespi Cotton Mills near Capriate, Italy, and Agneta Park near Delft, Holland, in 1883 for the Van Marken Yeast and Spirit Works.

In 1886, Lever Brothers, famous makers of soap, built Port Sunlight near Liverpool. The site for this project was 550 acres, and large blocks were employed with interior gardens and play areas, a forerunner of later planning. Another project that foreshadowed subsequent developments was Creswell, built by Percy Houfton in 1895 for his Bolsover Colliery. A hexagonal pattern was used, the houses facing inward on the gardens. Sir Joseph Roundtree, cocoa manu-

PORT SUNLIGHT, England. "Model" Town by Lord Leverholm, 1886.

facturer, built Earswick near York in 1905. This, like Bourneville, was made a community trust. It was planned by Barry Parker and Raymond Unwin, architects prominent in the new direction of town planning.

Some industrialists in America sought to improve the housing for their workers, probably the best known being Pullman, Illinois, built in 1881. It was built as a permanent town in conjunction with the plant for manufacture of Pullman sleeping cars.

The "model" towns of the industrialists in the nineteenth century were so few in proportion to the real problem of housing in the factory centers that they contributed little to the solution of that problem. They were flavored with a paternalism similar to the "model" dwellings built by the royalty at an earlier date. They did demonstrate some planning arrangements from which later communities were to profit, but the rarity of the projects rather emphasized the disparity between the living standards which were possible in the industrial era and the low level to which housing for most of the urban population had degenerated.

There can be no claim to city planning during this era. The fervor for industrial expansion had blotted out the original plans for cities in America, and only remnants can now be seen. Ambitious proposals like the Judges and Governors plan for Detroit remained as diagrams of what might have been. Even the distinction between major and minor arteries established in the early Detroit plan, for example, was abandoned in favor of a standard street width of 66 feet.

The gridiron plan of New York City was the beginning of a sterile urban character. The movement "Westward ho!" gripped the pioneers and with them strode the land surveyors. By the time this great trek had moved across the United States the vast land had been mapped in a gargantuan gridiron of mile-square sections. The pattern of land division was thoroughly bound in a legal straight jacket of readily recorded deeds. Natural features, rivers, mountains, and valleys were ignored. Henceforth the grid became the basic pattern of farms, villages, towns, cities, and counties. Desirability of the land was measured by its prospects for quick and profitable turnover. Subdivision practices were conveniently designed to enhance these prospects, and the pattern of future development of cities was fairly sealed in this package of the gridiron plan.

THE HORIZON OF IMPROVEMENT

As the nineteenth century wore on governments in Europe assumed more and more responsibility for the improvement of the city. The British Housing Law of 1890 empowered the state and local authorities to condemn land and build dwellings for rent to the working class. In response to the growing strength of the trade union movement in Germany a law of 1889 granted privileges to co-operative housing developments, using funds derived from social insurance which had been inaugurated by Bismarck. At an earlier date, legislation was enacted in Holland to provide for the loan of public funds to "public utility societies" engaged in housing, and a similar program was begun in Stockholm, Sweden, in 1879. The "public utility society" is somewhat similar to the "limited dividend company" in the United States, but was subject to closer state supervision in Europe because of the greater amount of financial assistance it received from the government.

These various measures set the stage for the more enlightened era to follow in the next century. There also began a program of social work on behalf of decent housing which was to extend into the twentieth century. Miss Octavia Hill launched her crusade for the underprivileged in London in the latter part of the century—a practical program based upon the idea that good and continuous management could improve living even in existing tenements.

Stirred by the gallant efforts of such crusaders as Jacob Riis, there developed a growing protest against the congested tenements in America. The hideous "railroad" and "dumbbell" tenements on 25-foot lots had spread over New York City, but there were signs of mild and spotty reforms. As early as 1871 the Boston Co-operative Company began a modest program of rental houses for city workers, and other "model" dwellings were attempted.

In 1894 the publication of some plans for tenements by the architect Ernest Flagg aroused wide interest. These plans provided broader light courts than the standard practice, reduced the length of interior corridors and improved the exposure of the rooms. A competition for better housing was held by the Improved Housing Council in 1896. It was won by Mr. Flagg with a plan requiring a lot 50 feet in width but accommodating the same number of apartments per floor as the "dumbbell" plan on the same area of land. The rooms in each apartment were larger, and their exposure and arrangement were enhanced.

With this impetus to improve low-cost housing, the Tenement House

Committee of the Charity Organization Society conducted a competition in 1899. The program specified certain basic planning standards to be followed by the competitors. Among the prescribed requirements were a maximum lot coverage of 70 percent, large light courts, and a minimum volume of air per occupant within the dwelling. The winning design was submitted by the architect, R. Thomas Short.

This competition spurred renewed efforts for reform and culminated in the passage of the Tenement House Act of 1901, commonly known as the "New Law" in New York City. The act was modeled after the standards of the competition, and fairly established the 50-foot lot in subdivision practice.

Progress became more visible when the twentieth century opened. Several organizations were formed for the purpose of building better housing for the low-income worker. One of the most notable was the City and Suburban Homes Company of New York. Starting business in 1896 and assisted by Ernest Flagg, it has since built some 3,500 apartment units. The by-laws of the company were worthy of note; its purpose was "to offer to capital a safe and permanent investment and at the same time to supply wage earners improved homes at current prices."

In 1879 the Washington Sanitary Improvement Company was established in Washington, D.C. It was followed in 1904 by the Washington Sanitary

BERN

The early medieval town had space within and about it. With the increase in trade and the rise of mercantilism the city form remained the same, but open space was built up. The methods of water supply, drainage, and waste disposal remained the same, but more and more people were crowded into the city. It has continued to grow in population as have other cities, but, while it extended its boundaries, the process of congestion has increased in intensity of land use. Current undesirable congestion has been bearable only with the vast improvement in water distribution, public utilities of gas, electricity, sewage disposal, and mechanical inventions.

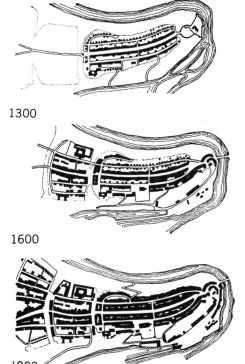

1300

1600

1800

Housing Company and these organizations have built nearly 1,000 apartments for rental to families of low income in the capital city.

MOVEMENT TO THE CITIES

The factory system brought more and more people to the urban centers. While rural areas in England were decreasing in population from 10,000,000 in 1821 to 9,500,000 in 1936, cities were gaining from 4,000,000 to 37,000,000. In Germany the rural population dropped from 23,000,000 in 1821 to 19,000,000 in 1936, and urban population increased from 2,000,00 to 48,000,000 in the same period. The industrial metropolis and congestion became synonymous. Between 1800 and 1900 urban population in Europe grew between 300 and 400 per cent. At the beginning of the nineteenth century, London had a population of 1,000,000; at the beginning of the twentieth century it was 7,000,000. During the same period Paris grew from 700,000 to 3,000,000, and Berlin from 172,000 to 4,000,000.

The population of the United States was largely agrarian at the beginning of the nineteenth century. Only about 5 per cent of the people lived in towns, and they were small communities. In 1790 there were but two cities with a population as large as 25,000. The inauguration of regular steamship service between Europe and America in 1840 helped to feed the factory system with immigrants seeking the freedom of this land. By the middle of the century 20 per cent of the people lived in cities. From that time forward the acceleration was rapid, and in 1940 there were 3,464 urban communities with 56.5 per cent of the total population of the country. Four hundred and twelve cities had more than 25,000

NEW HAVEN

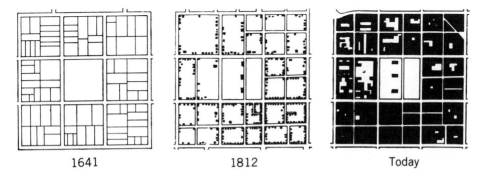

| 1641 | 1812 | Today |

Just as the medieval town became crowded with the increase in trade, the new towns gradually became congested with the development of commercialism. The plan of New Haven shows it as an open residential community until the industrial revolution. In the last hundred years, however, the street system has changed only slightly, but the land has been built up until little open space remains.

population. Of these, twenty-three ranged between 250,000 and 500,000; nine were between 500,000 and 1,000,000, whereas five exceeded 1,000,000.

LIVING ENVIRONMENT

Ever present among the complicated urban activities of the nineteenth century was the effort to improve the living environment. Urban speculation and its disintegrating effect upon the environment of man had aroused the public consciousness during the century. The critical essays of eminent men in the literary world—John Ruskin, Thomas Carlyle, Lord Shaftesbury, Charles Dickens, Engels, and Benjamin Disraeli—shed light on the issues with the force of their insight and talent.

Among those who spoke out against the evils at the turn of the century was Patrick Geddes. In 1892 Geddes founded the Outlook Tower in Edinburgh, a center in which he could study the whole complex of urban life. He insisted upon a view of all phases of human existence as the base of operations, an integration of physical planning with social and economic improvements.

This principle does not sound unfamiliar today, but it was new when Geddes expressed it. As a contemporary of his said: "There was a time when it seemed only necessary to shake up into a bottle the German town-extension plan, the Parisian Boulevard and Vista, and the English Garden Village, to produce a mechanical mixture which might be applied indiscriminately and beneficently to every town in this country. Thus it would be 'town-planned' according to the most up-to-date notions. Pleasing dream! First shattered by Geddes, emerging from his Outlook Tower in the frozen north, to produce that nightmare of complexity, the Edinburgh Room at the great Town-Planning Exhibition of 1910."

Patrick Geddes gave voice to the necessity for what was later to become Regional Planning.

THE GARDEN CITY

There was another who rose above the throng at the end of the century. He was Ebenezer Howard. Disturbed by the depressing ugliness, haphazard growth, and unhealthful conditions of cities, he had an idea which he set forth in a little book entitled *Tomorrow,* published in 1898. The idea was the Garden City.

In this book Howard described a town in which the land would remain in the single ownership of the community. The dwellings would be distributed about a large central court in which the public buildings would be located. The shopping center would be on the edge of the town and industries on the outskirts. The city would have a population of some 30,000 people in an area of 1,000 acres. Surrounding the entire city would be a permanent belt of agricultural land of 5,000 acres.

Rather than failing of execution as did the proposals of the early Utopians, Ebenezer Howard, before his death in 1928, saw his idea become reality. The Garden City Association was formed in 1899 and in 1903 the First Garden City,

Limited, a limited dividend society, obtained 4,500 acres of land 34 miles from London and began the city of Letchworth. It was designed for a maximum population of 35,000 with an agricultural belt of 3,000 acres. In thirty years this town had grown to a population of 15,000, with more than 150 shops and sixty industries, and had paid 5 per cent dividends on the invested stock. At a later date a second garden city, Welwyn, was started. The site was 2,400 acres and it was designed for a population of 40,000. In fifteen years it had a population of 10,000, with fifty industries.

These cities followed the scheme of Ebenezer Howard, the agricultural belt remaining a permanent protection and not a reservation for continued expansion of the urban area usually considered the only usefulness of vacant land on the periphery of cities. These towns have had the added advantage of retaining, for the benefit of the population itself, the increment of increased value of land created by a growing and prospering community.

There is a difference between the usual joint-stock company and Garden City, Limited, which developed Letchworth. The principal object of the latter is to create a town for the benefit of the community. In so doing, the rights of the shareholders to dividends on their stock are limited (5 per cent in Garden City, Limited) and profits earned above the dividends are applied to the benefit of the whole community. The company is in a position of public trustee rather than a private landlord. It has proven a sound, but not a speculative, investment. Land for all development purposes is leased for a period of ninety-nine years. The town government is the Urban District Council of fifteen members, elected by the residents, and of these, five members retire annually and are eligible for re-election.

Another feature distinguishes Letchworth. Development and growth of the Garden City are reversed from the practices of the usual speculative city. Aside from the merits of planning in either type of town, zoning in Letchworth determines the use of specific areas and only those uses are permitted; only factories and workshops are built in the industrial zones, and shops in the commercial zones. In the speculative town any use of a lesser economic character is permitted in its zoning provisions; dwellings are found in industrial and commercial zones, and these mixed uses are largely responsible for the sad state of the urban environment. The overdeveloped center and underdeveloped periphery of the speculative town are absent in Letchworth. Open spaces remain for development as the need arises and for the appropriate use provided in the plan.

Of the 1,500 acres of the town contained within the rural belt, 935 acres are reserved for residential use, 170 acres for industry, 60 acres for shopping, and the remainder for parks and roads. There are some 4,000 dwellings in the town of which the Urban District Council has built 1,300 cottages for workers.

THE COMMON DENOMINATOR

The house a family lives in is the common denominator of the city; it is the fiber of the city. The link between it and city building is so close the two are almost synonymous. Industrial and commercial enterprise strengthen the structure of the city, but it is the community of homes that marks the health, even the civilization, of a people.

Haussmann ripped through the slums of Paris with his boulevards, civic centers were planned for American cities, the impressive garb of classic façades was hung on the streets of the commercial city, and zoning was devised as the legal instrument to lend stability to the urban framework. But housing, the manifestation of the inner structure of civilization and the culture of people, remained as always the "left-over" in the urban plan.

Had zoning come early rather than late the urban predicament might have been much different. It is not exactly practical to plan a city after it has been built. Planning implies a program before an act, but zoning was adopted after the city had taken shape and zoning could hardly accomplish more than freeze the mixture. There was no chance to prescribe the ingredients before they had been poured together and well stirred. It was inevitable that housing should become the excrescence of urban land use.

City planning was first an urge to improve the esthetic pattern of the urban environment. Then zoning made of it a statistical exercise and a marathon of prognostication. These movements were necessary and valuable, but they did not improve the environment of the people and that is the purpose of city planning. Housing has thus become the principal instrument to attain that objective. It brings into focus the social, economic, and esthetic aims and needs of the urban population. It consequently becomes a political responsibility.

After World War I the housing shortage became a major crisis in Europe. Building inactivity through the war years had left the people of all countries with not only a shortage of dwellings, but monetary systems that, through inflation and war debt, needed transformation. It was essential that governments take a hand.

Public policy with respect to housing had made considerable progress in European countries during the nineteenth century. The groundwork for public assistance had been laid. Financial aid was available to private enterprise through public utility societies and trade union co-operatives. Local public authorities were empowered to provide housing for the lowest income families. The exercise of condemnation by public authorities was an accepted instrument to enforce housing improvement, and cities in a number of countries had acquired large areas of vacant land outlying the built-up city.

The housing program reminded men that standards of living are more than a load of mechanical equipment surrounded by walls of a building and covered by a mortgage. The family and its dwelling had been engulfed by the tidal wave of the industrial revolution. It emerged from the war as the primary unit of design in city development.

The record of the program is of historic importance. The performance in each country assumed similar characteristics, but each deserves some attention for the remarkable progress it represents in the total pattern.

8

Environmental Improvement

ENGLAND

In England the Housing Act of 1919 superseded the Act of 1890 in response to the "Homes for Heroes" campaign. It provided for subsidies by the Ministry to local authorities for clearance of slums and building low-cost housing. During the twenties and early thirties the purposes of this Act were consolidated and extended. Compensation to owners in built-in areas declared ready for clearance was restricted to the market value of the land, and no payment was made for the substandard structures on the site. Standards of occupancy were established to prevent overcrowding of families within dwellings, and local authorities were vested with police power to order improvements in physically substandard dwellings or their demolition.

The housing program had given strong impetus to enactment of the Housing and Town Planning Act of 1909 which, with subsequent amendments, became the Town and Country Planning Act of 1932. This was a comprehensive piece of legislation. Local authorities were not only empowered to prepare and enforce plans for the urban area, but typical of the British pride in their rural countryside, the Act provided for the preservation of rural areas and important buildings. It further implemented the co-operative planning for two or more separate political subdivisions—cities and counties—where they required such treatment as a region.

The Housing Act of 1936 brought the relationship between housing, slums, and city planning into clearer focus. The local authority is required to prepare a plan for redevelopment of blighted areas, in which these areas are related to the general plan for the city. Such an area may then be declared suitable for redevelopment and the authority is empowered to acquire the land, in whole or in part, and arrange for its rebuilding by private enterprise or public authority.

The terms on which this declaration may be made are that at least fifty working-class houses are contained in the area; at least one-third of the dwellings are overcrowded or physically unfit, congested, or unsatisfactory for renovation; that the area is suitably located for housing, in part, for industrial workers; and that redevelopment of the entire area is necessary to establish adequate standards of low-rent housing in the area.

The effectiveness of the British program is demonstrated by performance. According to the 20th Annual Report of the Ministry of Health, there were 3,998,366 dwellings built in England between the end of the war and 1939. Of this number, 2,455,341 were built by private enterprise, 430,481 were built by private enterprise with some degree of government assistance, and 1,112,544 were built by local authorities.

Slum clearance was an important phase of the program in England. However, apartment buildings three to five stories in height were considered necessary in order to restore ample open spaces in the residential plan, and this was contrary to the traditional dwelling of the English people. The cottage and garden was the type of dwelling close to the heart of the Englishman. The most successful housing developments were, consequently, those in which this type predominated.

THE SATELLITE GARDEN TOWN

Two great projects were undertaken in this period—Becontree, a satellite community for 25,000 families on 2,770 acres near London, and Wythenshawe, adjacent to Manchester.

Sir Ernest Simon has called Wythenshawe a satellite garden town in contrast to a garden city such as Letchworth and Welwyn. The two have similar characteristics: a residential area of low density of not more than twelve families per acre, factory and shopping areas, parks, schools, and other civic buildings, and protective buffers of permanent agricultural belts on the periphery. However, a garden city is intended to be a self-contained and self-sustaining community whereas the satellite garden town is situated close to a large city in which the residents of the garden town may have their work and places of business.

The city council of Manchester appointed a Housing Committee in 1926 to consider the possibility of a satellite garden town to relieve the congested slums in the city. An estate of about 2,500 acres in single ownership adjacent to the city on the Mersey River was recommended as the site. It was later increased to 5,500 acres, and after some opposition locally and in Parliament the entire area was incorporated in the city in 1930, most of the land being finally purchased at agricultural value. Mr. Barry Parker, Architect, was invited to prepare plans for the estate. An agricultural belt of 1,000 acres was reserved, and the original grounds of the estate were retained as a 250-acre park. A golf course of 100 acres was also provided. Two broad parkways run through the town connecting with the city. The residential areas which border these parkways are separated from the roadways by an open space 150 feet wide. Side roads give access and ingress

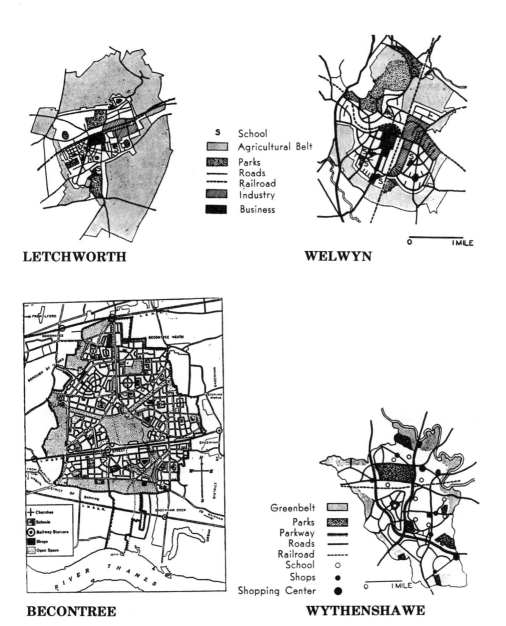

S   School
Agricultural Belt
Parks
Roads
Railroad
Industry
Business

LETCHWORTH   **WELWYN**

0   1 MILE

Greenbelt
Parks
Parkway
Roads
Railroad
School   ○
Shops   ●
Shopping Center   ●

0   1 MILE

BECONTREE   **WYTHENSHAWE**

THE GARDEN CITY AND THE SATELLITE TOWN

Reflecting the ideas of Ebenezer Howard, the Garden City of Letchworth was begun near London in 1903 and Welwyn soon followed. Limited in their initial planning to an ultimate maximum population, the garden cities were surrounded by agricultural fields similar to the original proposal by Robert Owen. The satellite towns of Wythenshawe and Becontree are similar to the garden cities with the primary exception that the latter are self-contained, each having its own industry, whereas the former are dependent upon the larger industrial cities, to which they are attached, for industrial employment.

87

to abutting property and the main road has been confined to through-traffic with limited access. The residential area is 3,000 acres with a maximim density of 12 houses per acre; 25,000 houses are planned with an ultimate population of 100,000.

The land on which Wythenshawe is built remains in the ownership of the city of Manchester. Both the city and private enterprise may build on the estate and by 1935 a total of about 4,800 dwellings had been completed. Of these the city built some 4,600. It is planned that about two-thirds of the residential area will be used for municipal housing, and one-third for private housing. About 500 acres are reserved for industrial, commercial, and civic buildings.

Some criticism was leveled at the city council of Manchester for ex-travagance in purchasing a large tract of land and reserving large areas for permanent open space. Sir Ernest Simon, a staunch leader for improved housing in England, has defended the policy of the city with a comparison of the method pursued in the usual procedure:

Let us consider first the question of the bulk purchase of land. The question is whether the City Council has been wise to purchase so large a block of land straight off, or whether it would have been more economical to continue its previous policy of purchasing relatively small plots of land as and when required. It has in fact, since the War, purchased nearly 2,000 acres at a cost which has been gradually rising, but which must average about 400 pounds an acre, giving a total of about 800,000 pounds. In Wythenshawe, on the other hand, the original purchase of 2,500 acres was at 80 pounds an acre. Since then prices have gradually increased. As development has proceeded and as it has become known that the Corporation was in the market for more land, the prices have been put up, and the average price paid for the whole 3,500 acres is perhaps in the neighborhood of about 100 pounds an acre, or a total of say 350,000 pounds.

If at Wythenshawe the Corporation had pursued its old policy, first of all developing main roads and main drainage, then gradually buying pieces of land as they were required for housing and became ripe for building, there is not the least doubt that they would have had to pay a similar average price to that paid in the rest of Manchester; that is to say about 400 pounds an acre.

The effect of the bulk purchase therefore is that the land has been purchased at an average price of 100 pounds per acre as against an average of 400 pounds. So far as the 2,000 acres are concerned which are to be used for municipal housing, nobody denies that this land was needed for housing, and that it would, at some time, have had to be bought for that purpose. The economy through buying in bulk has therefore been 300 pounds an acre, or a total of 600,000 pounds for the 2,000 acres. Against this saving must of course be set the annual loss in owning the land up to the time of development; say 4 per cent for interest charges. This amounts to 8,000 pounds per annum. From this must be deducted the rents receivable from the agricultural land (less cost of management) which would bring the net burden down to a figure of say 6,000 pounds per annum, that is to say, against a total saving of 600,000 pounds there is an annual charge, so long as the land is wholly undeveloped, of 6,000 pounds. The period of delay before full development is, of course, uncertain, but if Manchester proceeds with its programme of building 3,000 houses a year, most of them being necessarily built at Wythenshawe, the estate will be fully developed in less than ten years. Assuming, however, that twenty years were required, the burden of interest, beginning at 6,000 pounds per annum and gradually falling to nothing, would amount in the whole period to 60,000 pounds. The net saving on the housing estate owing to the early purchase would therefore be no less than 540,000 pounds.

Let us now turn to consider the 1,500 acres purchased for factories, shops, public buildings and private enterprise houses. Development is still in its early stages, and no particulars have been published as regards the terms on which this land is being leased for these different purposes. We are informed, however, that the ground rents which are being obtained are such that they represent on the average a capital value of at least 300 pounds per acre above the bare cost of the land. When these 1,500 acres are fully developed there will therefore be a profit on the capitalized value of the land of at least 300 pounds an acre, or 450,000 pounds on the whole area. Against this item also there will be a set-off representing the interest charges during the period of development, which on the assumptions previously made should certainly not exceed 50,000 pounds, leaving a net gain of 400,000 pounds.

Taking the landlord account as a whole (covering the 3,500 acres) we come, therefore, to the following conclusion: that the bulk purchase of 3,500 acres by the Corporation as against the old policy of hand-to-mouth buying of the land required for housing, and not buying any land for other purposes, will, if the estate is fully developed in twenty years or less, show a capital advantage to the Corporation of approximately 1,000,000 pounds.

Accusations of extravagance against the City Council for the bulk purchase of land are, therefore, the exact reverse of the truth. The fact is that the City Council has shown a high degree of business foresight in making the purchase, which will ultimately be of great benefit to the ratepayers.

There is only one other aspect of the Wythenshawe development which has been called extravagant: the generous reservation which has been made in the plans for the agricultural belt, parks, parkways and the preservation of spinneys. Admittedly, the area reserved is an advance on what has previously been done; but the difference between the normal practice of reserving 10 per cent of the area for parks, on the one hand, and what has been done at Wythenshawe on the other, is not great. The total expenditure on open spaces in the whole three parishes of Wythenshawe, even if the whole agricultural belt is actually purchased by the City Council, will certainly not reach 200,000 pounds; it must be admitted that the necessary open spaces could have been provided for perhaps 50,000 pounds less. But this extra expenditure will make a big difference to the amenity of the estate. Can anybody seriously call this extravagance when it is set off against the 1,000,000 pounds which will be gained on the landlord account?[1]

SWEDEN

Mature policies of land acquisition by cities in the Scandinavian countries resulted in aggressive participation in the supply of housing by private enterprise

[1] Sir E. D. Simon, *The Rebuilding of Manchester*, Longmans Green, New York, 1935.

via the public utility societies and housing co-operatives. Copenhagen in Denmark, Stockholm in Sweden, and Oslo in Norway made outstanding progress in both urban and rural housing and standards were maintained at a relatively high level. It is estimated that 10 per cent of the population in Stockholm lived in housing produced by the co-operative societies alone, and a fifth of the people in Copenhagen and Oslo are accommodated in co-operative and public utility housing.

The industrial revolution did not reach Swedish cities until electrical power had been developed as a major power source. As a consequence congestion did not afflict Swedish cities to the extent suffered by other cities on the continent. Decentralization was feasible—power was brought to the people rather than the people congregating at the source of power. While migration to cities during the nineteenth century had increased ten- to twenty fold elsewhere, the increase of population in town and country was stable in Sweden. During the nineteenth century rural population increased from 1,000,000 to 2,000,000, and urban population increased from 2,000,000 to 4,000,000.

The central district of Stockholm contained its share of slums, but they did not constitute the relatively large problem prevailing in continental cities. The principal problem in Sweden was overcrowding within dwellings, undoubtedly due to the rigorous climate and the heating problem it created. More than 50 per cent of the families occupied apartments of one and two rooms.

Since Sweden was a neutral country during World War I the economy had not only escaped suffering but had fared quite well. A shortage of housing occurred because construction had lagged, but the government was in a satisfactory financial position to render all needed assistance to correct it. From 1917 to 1920 municipalities subsidized public utility societies and co-operative groups that were building low-cost housing to the extent of one-third the cost. In 1920 this subsidy was reduced to 15 per cent of the cost because of increased wages and resulting capacity to pay higher rents. With stability generally restored by 1923 the subsidies were discontinued. Interest rates on mortgage money were high, and the State Dwelling Loan Fund was set up to make loans for second mortgages at low interest rates to offset the high first mortgage costs.

It was a tradition in Sweden for citizens to have the greatest possible freedom from government aid or interference. This tradition had not only been strengthened by, but was largely due to, the vigorous and aggressive co-operative movement. It became an effective and progressive instrument for the maintenance of democratic procedures and economic freedom. In order to remove itself from housing operations as much as possible, the government created an independent agency in 1929 to administer the Swedish Housing Loan Fund. This agency loaned government funds at low interest and long terms to continue the building of housing for low-income families. The successful operation of co-operatives soon obviated any need for these loans, and financial responsibility was shifted to the co-operative societies. By 1934, 10 per cent of the people in Stockholm lived in housing developments sponsored by the co-operative societies.

The co-operatives were of two major types. The S.K.B. (*Stockholm*

Kooperativa Forbundet, or Stockholm Co-operative Society) was engaged in the production of various consumer goods. Housing built by this society was primarily for its member employees. The H.S.B. (*Hyresgasternas Sparkassa och Byggnads-forening,* or Tenant Savings Bank and Building Society) was an organization specifically organized to build dwellings for members of the society, and membership was not restricted to any particular occupation. Careful research in planning was carried on by this society, and the projects it developed introduced advanced techniques in planning, equipment and community facilities.

Since 1904 the city of Stockholm had purchased 20,000 acres of land surrounding the city. This land was incorporated and planned for "garden suburbs." The city installed streets and utilities, and sponsored a program for working families to lease lots and build their own dwellings. Loans were available from the municipality up to 90 per cent of the value of each unit. The loans were in the form of materials purchased by the city, the balance (10 per cent) being the owner's contribution in labor. Standard plans for the dwellings, ranging from 700 square feet to 1,000 square feet in floor area, were prepared by the city, and skilled supervision was provided during construction. It was a popular and successful program, offering an opportunity for low-income families to leave the congested slums.

Rebuilding of cities was aided by the Town Planning Act of 1931 which required all urban communities, regardless of size, to prepare a rebuilding plan. All improvements thereafter were obliged to conform to the plan.

In 1935 encouragement was given to rehousing slum dwellers by means of rent rebates ranging from 30 per cent of economic rents according to family size. There were other forms of housing improvement such as joint rehabilitation of substandard buildings by owners of contiguous property for which the municipality advanced loans. Housing for the aged and for single women were also included within the scope of municipal programs.

The methods employed in Sweden to maintain good housing were varied. Public policy was always flexible enough to be adjusted as changing conditions warranted, and private enterprise, through the co-operatives and housing societies, was courageous and astute with its investments.

FRANCE

Epidemics of cholera generated some activity in the nineteenth century to correct substandard housing in France, and the threat of mob violence moved Napoleon III to build wide avenues through the slums as a means to control them. But it was not until 1894 that serious legislation was enacted. The Act passed at that time was similar to the Belgian Law of 1889 which made funds available from the government at low interest rates for houses to be sold exclusively to industrial employees. In 1912 the *Office Public d' Habitations à Bon Marché* (Public Office for Low-cost Housing), an organization of local authorities, was empowered to loan funds for, and subsidize, low-cost housing.

It was augmented several times later until the Loucheur Act of 1928, which concentrated further upon production of housing for low-income families and expanded financing through public authorities and private enterprise. Nearly half the dwellings provided by the Public Office after World War I were concentrated about Paris.

Despite ambitious plans to rebuild the congested slums—the *ilots insalubre*—a blot was dropped on the housing program in Paris. When the city walls were razed, it was expected that the open space would be reserved and the surrounding slum belt cleared and rebuilt with appropriate standards of planning. It was another idle dream. When the fortifications were leveled, the land was leased to speculative enterprise in 1930 and some 20,000 dwellings crowded into tightly planned tenements eight stories high were built in the open space. The adjacent slums remained.

There was some encouragement in the late thirties. The Department of the Seine planned a series of *cité jardins* in the outlying areas of Paris. While literally translated as "garden cities," these developments were designed as satellite garden villages somewhat similar to Wythenshawe in England. In the words of M. Henri Sellier, Administrator of Housing Office of the Department of the Seine, the *cité jardins* were planned as "essential elements of the City of Greater Paris."

Another blow befell the program. The necessity for co-operation from public utility agencies in the successful development of the city was amply demonstrated. Lack of proper arrangements for transportation meant failure for some of the *cité jardins* outside Paris and near failure for others. The interesting project at Drancy La Muette remained vacant because transportation was not provided. Chatenay Malabry, planned for 20,000 people, and Plessis Robinson were partly occupied, but transportation was not completed.

The post-war housing program in France hardly set a standard to serve as a guide for urban development. The plan for the *cité jardins* about Paris was courageous, but, as indicated above, it was not enough for success. Urban planning is complex, and the variety of public services makes the difference between success and failure.

GERMANY

Certain policies had been well established in Germany prior to World War I. Public utility societies and trade union co-operatives were recognized as effective instruments in the housing field. State financial aid was an accepted method; during the last half of the nineteenth century Bismarck had inaugurated social insurance, and this source supplied funds for housing loans for many years. Local governments had also assumed responsibility for housing government workers and financing public utility societies.

During his tenure of office in 1902, Mayor Adickes of Frankfurt obtained passage of a law (*Lex Adickes*), permitting the city government to pool private property, rearrange it to conform to the city plan, and redistribute such land for redevelopment. In this process the city was further authorized to retain 40 percent of the land without compensation to the owners, for streets, parks, and other public uses. Pursuant to this enactment in Frankfurt, a policy was adopted in numerous German cities to acquire outlying vacant land on the periphery. The purpose of this policy was protection from the inevitable speculation and resulting boom in land prices which accompanied the rapid increase in urban population.

This policy was fully rewarded after World War I when the need for housing, production of which had come to an abrupt halt, became most acute. The cities were then in a position to lease large quantities of these public lands to private and co-operative organizations for the construction of housing without the penalty of excessive land costs. In seventy German towns with more than 50,000 population, more than 6,000 acres of city-owned land were leased between 1926 and the rise of Hitler. Similar policies were adopted in other countries, Austria, Switzerland, Holland, and Denmark, and 15,000 acres outlying Prague in Czechoslovakia were made available for housing.

The first world war left Germany impoverished. Inflation upset the monetary system, an inactive building industry left a serious housing shortage, and the country was undergoing transition from imperial to republican government. High financing costs rendered it difficult for private enterprise to cope with the housing problem. Interest on mortgage money had more than doubled, moving from 4 per cent to as high as 10 per cent. Rents had quadrupled while wages had increased only 50 per cent. It became imperative for state and local governments to finance a large part of the housing program.

Property owners had become beneficiaries of the inflation which had the effect of liquidating all previous mortgages. As a consequence the *Hauszinsteuer* (House Rent Tax) was adopted in 1921. Prewar rents were used as the base for a tax levy ranging from 10 to 50 per cent of the rents, and the funds thus derived were used to finance second mortgages at a very low interest rate (generally 1 per cent) to compensate for the high cost of first mortgage money. Administered by local government, these funds were loaned to public utility societies and co-operatives for housing. The effectiveness of this policy is evident in the production of some 3,000,000 dwellings between the war and the rise of Hitler. More than three-quarters of these dwellings received financial aid from the government. The housing problem was not solved, a sufficient supply of dwellings was not provided and the slums remained, but the program represents a remarkable achievement for what it did accomplish.

German cities had suffered the same kind of chaotic growth experienced by other cities on the continent during the nineteenth century. It was obviously necessary to reconsider land utilization and planning if the tremendous housing program were to result in a permanent asset to the communities in which it was built. It is a significant contrast with our own experience in the United States. Emergencies have been the excuse to postpone urban planning in our country; the emergency in republican Germany was considered the sound reason to engage in the most serious planning. Despite the shadows cast over that country since Hitler's rise to power and the national frustration it brought, the housing program of the 1920–30 decade looms as an example of aggressive, though immature, democracy in action.

The pressing demand for new dwellings gave neither the time nor the funds for a real program to clear the slums; this was necessarily postponed until an adequate supply of dwellings could be built. Two effective means were brought into play in the early twenties: the public utility society (limited-dividend company) and the co-operative society. The public utility society, though comparable to the limited dividend company in this country, was subject to careful supervision by the state and was eligible to receive the benefits of several

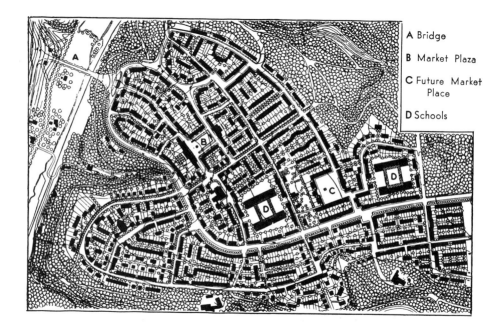

A Bridge

B Market Plaza

C Future Market
Place

D Schools

MARGARETHEN-HOHE, Essen, George Metzendorf, Architect

Emerging from the Garden City movement, this village was developed in 1912 by the Krupp family for workers in the industrial steel plants in Essen. The community was planned for 2,000-2,500 dwellings (12,000-16,000 population). It illustrates a number of planning features. Surrounded by forest, the principal connection with the city is by way of the bridge (A) on the north boundary. Rather than bisecting the plan in the usual manner, the main traffic street swings around the village and bypasses the market plaza (B). This shopping center and the future principal market place (C) are conveniently located within the dwelling area rather than upon the periphery. The schools (D) are situated within blocks of dwellings rather than upon the traffic roads. The road system is designed to fit the topography of the site but is arranged to avoid through-traffic on any but the main roadway. It will also be observed that buildings are generally set back at the road intersections to avoid obstruction of traffic vision at the corners.

It is a curious paradox that this development to improve the living environment of the working people of Essen was dedicated to the same member of the Krupp family for which the powerful military cannon "Big Bertha" was named a few years later.

forms of subsidies found necessary to implement a large supply of new housing. They were formed for the purpose of building low-cost housing and, in spite of state supervision, exercised a high degree of initiative and ingenuity in the planning of their projects. The co-operatives, or self-aid societies, were largely organized by trade unions as a means to supply housing for their members. These companies enjoyed privileges similar to public utility societies and assumed the same obligations. The effectiveness of these groups is demonstrated by the extensive operations of the three largest which built 71,000 dwellings up to 1929. These three, known as "Dewog," "Gagfah," and "Heimat," were among some 4,300 co-operatives societies in operation.

In addition to large organizations there were a number of smaller private companies engaged in the program, but they contributed to a much less degree than the above mentioned companies. The government created various agencies under jurisdiction of the several provinces and municipalities, for research in the technical phases of planning, construction, and financing. The results of this research were made available to all private and public organizations in the housing field.

With few exceptions, planning prior to 1925 had been confined to the usual city blocks. Inadequate building regulations had permitted an excessive density for population and building coverage within these confines. The first step away from high density in the postwar program was the arrangement of buildings about the perimeter of the usual city block with building coverage reduced within the center of the block. This "hollow square" form enclosed recreation and service areas, the buildings being mainly apartments of three and four stories in height. Many large-scale developments were placed upon tracts of vacant land. Here freedom from the subdivision of the gridiron system led to more informal planning and the "row house" was adopted where density was not a prerequisite. Main traffic streets were confined to the periphery of the projects, and the internal residential roads were bordered by parallel rows of dwellings. Apartments of three and four stories were also included along the marginal areas of the site.

Research in planning techniques soon led to a rational consideration of orientation. Sunlight in every room was a rule, and the orientation of all buildings to provide east and west exposure became mandatory. The preferable exposure was west light for living rooms and east light for bedrooms. The attention devoted to the proper orientation for all dwellings at this time is reminiscent of the fifth century B.C. in Greece.

The process was like modern planning hygiene. The final step in this rationalization was directed to the relation of the buildings to the streets. Buildings located in parallel lines along each side of a street did not provide equal privacy for living areas nor quiet for sleeping rooms. The new site planning produced uniform orientation for all dwellings but did not give them uniform exposure upon the open spaces surrounding the buildings. The next step in planning technique was the placement of all buildings at right angles to the streets. The space between buildings was thereby free of vehicular traffic, although the walks were designed to permit access for small trucks to facilitate movement of goods and service. This arrangement provided privacy for all living units, safety for play and recreational areas, and uniform orientation for all dwellings.

Strict adherence to this planning theme produced a rigid uniformity that increased during the late twenties, but it served to overcome some of the traditional inhibitions of the gridiron street system. These principles of planning were recognized as guides to challenge the designer, and some projects developed in 1931 and 1932 demonstrated some liberation from the previous regimentation. A more plastic and flexible treatment was emerging, but progress was interrupted by the political domination of Nazism.

Recreation space for children and adults, shops, meeting rooms for common use, and kindergartens were provided in the housing developments. Home laundry was customarily performed by the housewife. In early projects laundry facilities were placed upon the roof of two-story buildings, one-half being roofed and one-half open drying space. This practice carried over to apartment buildings until the adoption of central heating systems encouraged central laundries or "washeries" in conjunction with them. Private gardens were provided to the extent that space permitted but were usually confined to the single-family row houses. Some subsistence plots were included in a few of the large developments.

Probably the most outstanding example of integrated planning occurred in Frankfurt-am-Main. Ernst May, the architect-in-charge, and his associates undertook a comprehensive plan for the entire city in preparation for the housing program. May subscribed to the principle of satellite communities about the periphery of the city. The housing developments were surrounded by permanent open spaces but were planned as part of the city expansion rather than detached and self-contained garden cities.

The best and most enlightened professional talent was brought into play in

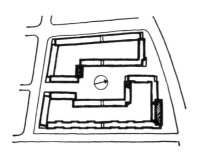

POSSMORWEG, Hamburg

Built in 1927-28 on plans by Schneider, Elingius, and Schramm. A variation of the "hollow square" planning characteristic of the early housing program in Germany. Under the direction of the city architect, Fritz Schumacher, this type of planning continued in Hamburg. The large space in interior courts was a vast improvement over high land coverage, but orientation of the dwellings was compromised.

the program. Planning techniques were subjected to a complete revaluation. While this was a natural result of critical material shortages and high building costs, it encouraged the evolution of planning methods which had a profound effect not only upon housing alone but on urban planning and architecture. Stirred by the necessity to reach basic solutions of social and economic problems, there came a renaissance of architectural and planning thought. It can be said that a new concept of the urban environment emerged. A new sense of freedom was expressed. It had not yet reached maturity when it was halted by the insidious spread of Nazism and suppression.

HOLLAND

At the turn of the century, the Act of 1901 in Holland required that every city with a population of 10,000 or more prepare a comprehensive town plan, in which new areas for housing were to be allocated. Housing standards were to be established by the local authorities who were charged with responsibility to ascertain compliance with them, exercising the power of condemnation where necessary. The local authorities were also empowered to build low-cost housing. Government funds were made available to public utility societies at low interest rates and limited dividends.

During and following World War I these powers were extended and the housing program was accelerated. In the ten years after the war some 500,000 dwellings were built in Holland. Because careful attention was directed throughout the program to meet the needs of the various income levels, it was possible to confine the "public" housing primarily to the problem of direct slum clearance.

SOVIET UNION

Since the revolution of 1917 planning and housing in the U.S.S.R. have been treated with vigor. The contrast between Imperial Russia and the Soviet Union is apparent. Vast plans for industrial development were made and many were carried out. New cities were built and portions of old cities rebuilt.

There appears to be a distinction, however, between the tremendous activity and the standards of construction utilized by the Soviets. The latter does not measure up to expectations suggested by the former. A city plan like that proposed for Stalingrad, a linear city, suggests hopeful prospects for the reorganization of the urban pattern. The executed housing developments, on the other hand, are extensive, but the technical inadequacies, the small apartments in multistoried buildings, leave much to be desired and offer little to warrant particular attention.

The form of government in the Soviet Union and the economic structure are so different from governments in the western world that comparisons are ineffective. The political processes occupy such an integral part of urban development that experience and accomplishments in planning in the Soviet Union are not subject to satisfactory appraisal.

AUSTRIA

Austria emerged from the Empire period and World War I financially bankrupt. Inflation had reduced to a minimum the capacity of private capital to produce housing. Municipal government was forced to take the major role and Vienna undertook an energetic program. Public funds were not available, and it was necessary to obtain them by a tax on rents. This was inaugurated in 1923 and launched an active program, approximately a quarter of the revenues from taxes being devoted to housing in 1928.

SWITZERLAND

Switzerland had a housing shortage following World War 1, and local governments rendered financial assistance to co-operative organizations as encouragement to produce an adequate supply. However the situation in Switzerland did not present as serious a problem as most countries because of stable policies of private finance that prevailed during most of its history. The advantages of democratic capitalism had always been more evenly distributed in Switzerland, and the excesses suffered in many countries had been absent to a marked degree. The result was that this little country had not sunk to such low depths that violent action was required to restore balance.

PEOPLE'S REPUBLIC OF CHINA

Planning in the People's Republic of China is now supposed to take place in consultation with the people. The degree to which this actually transpires is uncertain for most planning decisions seem to be decided by the central authorities. The degree to which there is freedom to vary from national policies, at the local level is the only valid criterion by which democracy in Chinese planning can be measured.

Planning Functions. Joan Robinson portrays planning in China as follows:

> There are several phrases always used in connection with the system of economic planning—'two initiatives, of the top and the bottom'; From the bottom up and from the top down; and leaving leeway, which means allowing room for adjustment as production goes on.[2]

---

[2] *Economic Management in China*, monograph, Modern China Series, No. 4, Anglo-Chinese Educational Institute, 1976.

That is, representatives of the provinces meet with the Planning Commission in Peking to review the various programs proposed by the provinces. The Planning Commission, after evaluating these programs, assigns priorities and funds for their implementation.

Robinson also delineates the various planning bureaucracies in China:

There are various departments concerned in drawing up a provincial plan. The plan for agriculture gives targets for the major crops and for fisheries and forestry. It is also concerned with promoting mechanization.

The plan for industry gives all major products in quantities and minor ones as a global sum. It makes allowance for trial production of new items.

There is a plan for communications and transport within the provincial orbit. The plan for commerce covers the volume of purchases of consumer goods to be supplied through the shops and matches the value of sales against total purchasing power.

The plan for capital construction sets out all major projects and the additional productive capacity that they will provide.

There is a plan for the labour force and the wage bill, showing the number of new jobs that will be created.

There are departments concerned with education, culture and health, dealing with enrollment in schools and colleges and with the medical service, sanitation and the arts.

The plan covers the distribution of materials and the products of agriculture and industry.

Finally, there is a department concerned with finance, dealing with revenue and expenditure and setting targets for reduction of costs of production. This bureaucracy is performing the functions, not only of the civil service in the capitalist countries, but also of a large part of private business.[3]

[3] Robinson, *Economic Management.*

9

Search for the Good City

The population of the world is exploding. Mechanization is attracting multitudes of people to the cities. The rising flood of urbanization is surging outward from the center and engulfing the surrounding countryside. Congestion festers within and eats about the edges. Communications are breaking down. Medical science is sustaining health and prolonging the life span. Famine and pestilence are no longer the levellers of excess population. Nuclear war may be. If mankind is to live on, the urban pattern he occupies will require major unravelling and reweaving. Much understanding will be required, and the nature of the metropolis will undergo severe examination.

Men in all walks of life have raised their voices against the inequities, the ugliness, and the congestion of the city. John Ruskin and William Morris pleaded for craftsmanship, Charles Dickens portrayed the evils of the workhouses, Edward Bellamy in *Looking Backward* warned and predicted, Patrick Geddes in his *Outlook Tower* urged a broader vision, Karl Marx threatened, Robert Owen experimented, Ebenezer Howard reasoned, Jacob Riis exposed. Many turned the light of critical analysis upon the city, tested the forces of disintegration in the laboratories of their keen minds, and some dared to describe cities men could build when they acquired the will.

Nor were they all cries in the wilderness. Housing, the most appalling testimony to neglect in the urban scene, received attention. Planning agencies were formed, zoning and building laws were enacted. But these efforts remained a step behind the improvement of which society was capable; they never quite caught up with technological and scientific progress. The overgrown metropolis fed upon its inhabitants, gnawing at the physical, mental, and spiritual fabric of the people. No inhabitant could escape the heavy weight of urban living, regardless of fortune or social status. The insidious course of urban disintegration has forced an examination of the basic nature of the urban structure, and it has been to this task that the new utopians set themselves.

THE SEARCH FOR SPACE

The driving urge has been for release from the cruel congestion that degrades individual dignity. It has been a search for space in which man may recapture his identity as a person. This quest lends unity to otherwise apparently divergent views on the future urban structure.

The persistent expansion about the periphery of the great cities has removed the countryside farther and farther from the urban population. Abandoning the concentric form of the crowded city, Soria y Mata, in 1882, propounded the theory of the linear city—*La Ciudad Linear*. He sought to expand the city along the spine of communication—the highway. Stretching along the roadway, housing and industry bordered a continuous artery linking the existing cities. In the tradition of the garden city, Raymond Unwin, a pioneer in housing in England, espoused the cause of satellite communities about the periphery of the city. Each of the communities would range in population between 12,000 and 18,000 and be small enough to require no vehicular transport within them. They would have some industry, but be connected to the central city by rapid transportation.

The garden city and satellite town rely upon their relatively small size to maintain a balance between urban development and surrounding open space. The linear city employs the countryside to contain urbanization along the highway. Integrating these elements, Tony Garnier presented his ideas in 1917 for *La Cité Industrielle*. These inspiring plans for a modern industrial city separated the civic center and residential sections from the factory district by a "greenbelt," and the highway and railroad traversed this broad buffer space.

Another utopian expression among the variety of protests against the dull environment of the industrial metropolis was the swan song of Victorian grandeur—"The City Beautiful." Absorbed in the monumental splendor of avenue and plaza, Daniel Burnham reflected the fading era with his famous words:

> Make no little plans; they have no magic to stir men's blood and probably will not be realized. Make big plans; aim high in hope and work, remembering that a noble, logical diagram once recorded will never die, but long after we are gone will be a living thing, asserting itself with ever-growing insistency. Remember that our sons and grandsons are going to do things that would stagger us. Let your watchword be order and your beacon beauty.[1]

As the twentieth century drew on, many opportunists became articulate. Congestion inspired a variety of panaceas, and some fantastic proposals were suggested by otherwise practical men. Probably the most popular theme was the double-and triple-deck street. High land cost was so firmly rooted in the urban state of mind that its effect was accepted as the normal course of "land economics." Nevertheless the traffic problem had to be solved, and piling layers

[1] *Daniel Burnham: Architect, Planner of Cities*, Charles Moore, Boston, 1921.

of streets upon each other had the appearance of plausibility. As the roofs of skyscrapers moved upward so did proposals for multiple-level streets.

Beneath, on the surface of the earth, darkness pervaded man's environment. A growing apprehension of the light gripped the people. Man was building so broad and so high that the more there was light the deeper were the shadows. They engulfed humanity. People cultivated a preference for the darkness; it veiled the contrasts of their daily existence. The artificial glow of night-life became popular, and the people found release from the realities about them. With the dawn they scurried into their shells of office cubicles or apartment cells.

The art of walking was all but discarded. A subway train brought the people to the heart of the city; the less time in the open air and daylight, the more readily was the conscience of man assuaged. Escape from reality was sought in the brilliant shadows of the motion pictures and TV; into this world of fantasy and make-believe all could retreat momentarily.

The metropolis lay heavily upon its inhabitants. The problem of the underprivileged increased, social welfare expanded, and more and more of the tax income was directed to charity.

The great industrialist Henry Ford said what was in the minds of many people: "Nothing will finally work more effectively to undo the fateful grip which the city has taken upon the people than the destruction of the fictitious land values which the city traditions have set up and maintained."[2] Since these words came from a leader of industry, it is rather perplexing that he did not suggest how land values might be "destroyed," but he pointed his words at a major obstacle to the improvement of the urban environment.

All who have protested the congestion and ugliness of the city reveal the anachronism of our industrial age—the inability of society to muster the forces of technological progress in the cause of urban organization. Directed toward the same objective—improvement of the urban environment—theories conflict and opinions vary. It is inevitable and it reflects the enigma of the age. The tremendous advance of science and invention thrusts forward the horns of a dilemma and civilization is perched upon them.

In 1922 there was displayed in a Paris exposition a vision of *La Ville Contemporaine* by the architect Le Corbusier. His utopian scheme was a city of magnificent skyscraper towers surrounded by a broad and sweeping open space. The city was a huge park. Sixty-story office buildings accommodating 1,200 people per acre and covering only 5 per cent of the ground area were grouped in the heart of the city. The transportation center, rail and airfield, was the hub. Surrounding the skyscrapers was the apartment district, eight-story buildings arranged in zigzag rows with broad open spaces about them, the density of population being 120 persons per acre. Lying about the outskirts were the *cité jardins*, the garden cities of single houses. The city was designed for a population of 3,000,000.

The beautifully delineated plans and succinct reasoning with which they

---

[2] From "Mr. Ford's Page" in the *Dearborn Independent,* Dearborn, Michigan, 1922.

were described created a sensation, and in 1925 Le Corbusier adapted his "City of Tomorrow" to the *Plan Voisin* for the center of Paris. The contrast with the old city was dramatic and the architect hammered at his theme, pointing his finger of scorn at the feeble but still undesirable population density in Paris—an average of 146 persons per acre, and 213 persons in the overcrowded sections—spread thin over the city.

Le Corbusier followed this conception with his *Ville Radieuse*, the Radiant City, a city of continuous rows of tall buildings woven in zigzag form across landscaped space. A prolific writer and indefatigable reformist, he prepared his visonary schemes for Algiers, Nemours, Antwerp, and Stockholm. He was enamored of the skyscrapers of America and the energy of the industrial processes. His "shock" value was tremendous, and those who waved aside his proposals as another wild dream were themselves quite blind to the wilderness which had overtaken the city in which they themselves were trapped.

THE SEARCH FOR FORM

A brutal quality of the great city is the absence of human scale. The sense of community is obscured by the common grayness of the industrial metropolis. Despite the durability of great cities, they are caving in beneath the mammoth weight piled up at the cneter. As they spiral upward and outward the people are forsaking the centers for the suburbs. Satellite dormitory communities cling to the economic lifeline of the city, and regions of greatest urban settlement have actually become continuous linear cities. But expanding suburbanization is exhausting the space it was intended to preserve and overextending the lines of communications.

The basic yearning for harmony between the individual and the scale of the community is no less reflected in the suburban sprawl about great cities than in the garden city, the greenbelt, the towers of Le Corbusier, or the British New Towns. Movement to the suburbs is essentially motivated by the search for a desirable environment. The contrast between worn-out, second-hand residential districts and neighborhoods in new subdivisions; between shopping centers and stores without parking on traffic-ridden streets; or the advantages of an industrial park over the disorderly factory district: all suggest the same aspirations which appear in the models of the new utopians. The search is for an organic structure for the city of the industrial and scientific age in which we are destined to live. As we move toward an integration of the urban components, these emerges the form of a *regional* city.

The International Congress of Modern Architects (CIAM) subjected the city to re-examination and posed four basic elements of the urban biology: (1) *sun*, (2) *space*, (3) *vegetation*, (4) *steel and concrete*. Le Corbusier assumed a leading role in CIAM and organized the Assembly of Constructors for an Architectural Renovation (ASCORAL) to extend the investigations into the character of the city.

ASCORAL set forth the "Three Human Establishments": the *farming unit*, the *radioconcentric city*, and the *linear industrial city*. The farming unit is the space for agriculture and the villages that serve it; the radioconcentric city is the existing urban area in which the theory of concentration evolved. Although the third "human establishment"—the linear industrial city—stems from earlier utopians, it is a new element in the theories espoused by Le Corbusier. Leaving the "evils of the sprawling town," the studies of ASCORAL move into the country, and new industrial communities are located along the main arteries of transportation—water, rail, and highway—connecting the existing cities. Factories—the "green" factories—are placed along the main transportation routes, separated from the residential section by the auto highway and green strips. The residential area includes the "horizontal garden town" of single houses and a vertical apartment building with its complement of communal

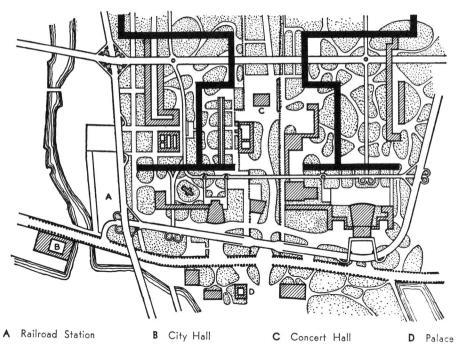

A   Railroad Station   B   City Hall   C   Concert Hall   D   Palace

"LA VILLE RADIEUSE" by Le Corbusier

The plan submitted in the international competition of 1933 for the replanning of Nedre Normalm in Stockholm was an adaptation of Le Corbusier's scheme for continuous "staggered" rows of high buildings (shown in black) set upon piers with broad open space. This plan also shows the distinction between the various types of roadways: the encircling "freeway" raised above the ground level, the secondary traffic ways uninterrupted by the building forms, and the informal system of local traffic and pedestrian ways which likewise circulate beneath the buildings open at the ground level. The existing or new proposed low buildings (cross-hatched) are provided settings within landscaped open space.

facilities. Sports, entertainment, shopping, and office facilities are distributed in this district, and all the facilities of the community are placed within ample open space enhanced with natural verdure. These industrial groups are placed at intervals along the highway and railway linking the existing cities, the latter remaining as administrative, commercial, and cultural centers.[3]

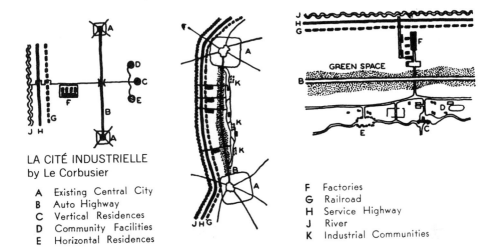

LA CITÉ INDUSTRIELLE
by Le Corbusier

A   Existing Central City
B   Auto Highway
C   Vertical Residences
D   Community Facilities
E   Horizontal Residences

F   Factories
G   Railroad
H   Service Highway
J   River
K   Industrial Communities

In 1945 ASCORAL, under the leadership of Le Corbusier, shifted attention from the existing urban center to a consideration of the basic organization of urban settlement in this industrial age. In the studies by this group, we find a fusion between the concentric form of the "garden city" and the ribbon form of the "linear city." The principal forms of circulation—water, rail, air and highway—become the arteries along which self-contained industrial cities are distributed. Although it is assumed that open space surrounding these industrial clusters would be maintained, the "greenbelt" is here used as a buffer between the various and separate land uses: housing, highway, and factories.

The basic organization is shown in the left-hand sketch, the passenger highway connecting the great existing cities, and between it and the river, rail line, and service highway are the groups of "green factories." Opposite are the housing areas which contain the administrative, shipping, sports, and educational facilities for the immediate population. The existing metropolis remains the principal administrative, commercial, and cultural center.

The sketch at the center indicates the distribution of industrial "cities" between the great cities, and the one on the right indicates the separation of traffic forms: the distinction between through traffic and local traffic, and the separation between them. Le Corbusier retains the tall building—the vertical residence—for apartments near the civic center and places the community of single-family homes away from this center for the greater freedom for families.

[3] *Les Trois Etablissements Humains*, ASCORAL, Denoël, Paris, 1945.

Thus the image of a regional city unfolds and, with it, the exposure of conventions which dominate our concept of urban practices today.

Implicit in the planning postulates of the new utopians is the assumption that land zoned for specific uses will be reserved for those uses. This is the reason, presumably, for planning, and it is apparent that the effective reorganization of the urban structure depends upon acceptance of this assumption. Our present practice of zoning, however, runs quite counter to this; any use is permitted in an industrial zone, while only industry is excluded from a commercial zone and all types of residential uses are permitted therein. As a consequence of this zoning practice, the only zone actually reserved for its planned use is the single-family district. This indiscriminate mixture of land uses is inconsistent with planning, and means by which it may be corrected are essential to the effective relationship between land uses in the future. The distinction between present trends and the theories of the new utopians would appear less sharp were the chaotic mingling of incompatible uses replaced by the principle that urban land uses shall conform to the classifications for which they are planned and zoned. This is a rather disarming thesis, since it would reveal excessive over-zoning and materially alter prevailing attitudes toward zoned uses for which there is inadequate economic support.

As the future decentralized city form emerges, some land will necessarily be withdrawn from intense use, while the intensity of use for other land will increase. The changes should result from planning decisions rather than for-tuitous speculation. Under the system of zoning for public control of land use, the potential capacity of land is thereby a function of community determina-tion. Land values thus created by the community should be retained by the community; by the same token; losses in value imposed by the community should be compensated by the community.[4]

THE DENSITY EQUATION

The extreme population density to which we have become accustomed is due for critical review. The density equation is compounded by the introduction of factors which serve the mental and spiritual needs of man, the environmental features which enrich the process of living. Such an environment, to be sure, should be the overriding aim of planning in an advanced civilization, but the practical issues alone compel attention to the density equation.

The balance between floor space occupied by people and the ground space for circulation is among these practical factors. Many cities in the industrial nations must accommodate the vehicles of transportation on the streets and provide space for their storage. It might be possible to so regiment people's lives that the freedom of movement afforded by modern motor vehicles could be rigidly curtailed, but the means for such control would hardly be consistent with

---

[4] See the discussion of compensation and betterment in Chapter 21.

the doctrine of liberty upon which our institutions are founded. The density equation must therefore embrace three practical elements: population in buildings, space for the movement of vehicles on streets, and parking space for the vehicles. A workable urban pattern requires a balance between these elements.

Man has demonstrated consummate ability to build tremendous structures. The construction of a skyscraper is a remarkable feat, but the "high-rise" has struck a popular chord by default rather than by design. It is presumed to compensate for high land cost and thus maintain a semblance of economic balance. In reality it induces ever-mounting land prices. Every urban dweller is familiar with the consequences—intolerable congestion.

The attraction of the skyscraper is undeniable. The drama has been eloquently expressed by Le Corbusier. With boundless enthusiasm for the

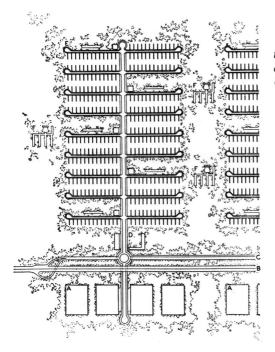

Relationship of residential areas to light industrial and commercial areas, as proposed by Ludwig Hilberseimer.

A Industry
B Main Highway
C Local Highway
D Commercial Area
E Residential Area
F Schools in Park Area

URBAN REORGANIZATION

Searching for an urban form appropriate to the metropolis of the industrial age, the new utopians have produced some principles which may guide a reorganization of the city of tomorrow. These principles merge the common characteristics of the "linear" and the "concentric" city forms; they accept the physical properties of the neighborhood unit in favor of the basic needs of the family and regain the prospect for identity of the individual parts of the great city now lost within the dreary grayness of the present metropolis. Because the city form must change if it is to survive and because it must survive as an integral element of the industrial age, the proposals of the new utopians are essential ingredients of urban thought and action.

A	County Seat Administration	H	Small Industry	R	Orchards
B	Airport	J	Small Farms	S	Homes and Apartments
C	Sports	K	Park		
D	Professional Offices	L	Motor Inn	T	Temple and Cemetery
E	Stadium	M	Industry	U	Research
F	Hotel	N	Merchandising	V	Zoo
G	Sanitarium	P	Railroad	W	Schools

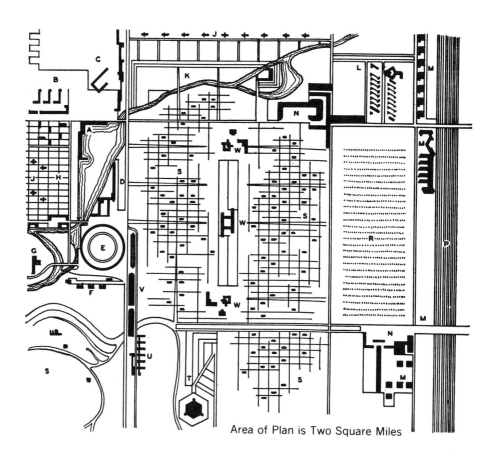

Area of Plan is Two Square Miles

BROADACRES by Frank Lloyd Wright

Essentially a "linear" city form, Frank Lloyd Wright's proposal distributes industry, commerce, housing, social facilities, and agriculture along the railroad artery and has access to highways. The unit which dominates this plan is the minimum of one acre of land for each family rather than the neighborhood unit, although the various neighborhood facilities are provided.

ingenuity, the daring, and the skill of those who made the tall building possible, his desire for the machine, conditioned air, push-buttons, and swift elevators is like a romance with science. Dreaming of his future city from within the medieval context of the European city, he sees the "tonic spectacle, stimulating, cheering, radiant, which from each office appears through the transparent glass walls leading into space. Space! That response to the aspiration of the human being, that relaxation for breathing and for the beating heart, that outpouring of self in looking far, from a height, over a vast, infinite, unlimited expanse. Every bit of sun and fresh, pure air furnished mechanically. Do you try to maintain the fraud of hypocritical affirmations, to throw discredit on these radiant facts, to argue, to demand the 'good old window,' open on the stenches of the city and street, the noise, air currents, and the company of flies and mosquitoes? For thirty years I have known the offices of Paris: conversations cut to pieces by the uproar, suffocating atmosphere, the view broken thirty feet away by the wall of houses, dark corners, half-light, etc. . . . Impostors should no longer deny the gains of our period and by their fright prevent changing from one thing to another, keeping the city or cities in general from going their joyously destined way."[5]

The towers of Manhattan and the gridiron plan are straight and clear to the European eye, the hygiene of plumbing so inviting, the illuminated brilliance by night so thrilling. It is a fascination not reserved to Europeans alone; Americans find it appealing too. Le Corbusier argues concentration versus congestion. He demonstrates that his city will concentrate the people, conserve the daily hours they consume in horizontal travel, and direct this time into productive effort and leisure. He contends the American skyscraper is *too small* and proposes a residential population of 6,000,000 on Manhattan, with a density of 400 persons per acre and 88 per cent of the ground left free and open. In his *City of Tomorrow* the density is 1,200 per acre in 60-story office towers with 95 per cent of the land in open space, a "green" city. The concept is magnificent, but it reflects the deception of high density, high buildings, and open space.

Structures permitting such densities are not unusual. Several times the density proposed by Le Corbusier is found in huge apartment buildings of America. The density in his proposed office towers is less than half that of Radio City, and the Empire State Building can accommodate nearly 10,000 people per acre. Concentration is an accomplished fact in the cities of America. The drama of the "high-rise" building is heightened by the space about it and the prospect it offers for trees and landscaped gardens. Such space, in which the tensions of the day may be dispelled, has strong appeal in contrast to the cluttered surroundings of the congested city.

But here enters the delusion of high density and open space. When the automobile is reckoned with, a site housing 400 persons per acre becomes *not* a lovely garden, but a *parking lot.* And the open space for an office building with a density of 1,200 per acre would be a *roof* garden atop a three-or four-story

[5] Le Corbusier, *When the Cathedrals Were White,* Reynal and Hitchcock, New York, 1947.

garage. The balance of the "open" space, is in the streets that carry the cars into and out of these storage places. The "green" space, to which we aspire and which offers much promise, actually becomes a pavement for the vehicles of transportation. Complicating the situation further is the fact that preservation of the air space above the ground could be assured only by restricting *all* buildings to "high-rise"; low buildings with high density would cover the ground as it is now covered.

The desirability of low density for a residential environment is obvious; it has been demonstrated in all places and for all people on the face of the earth. Low density does not forestall blight, but with the exception of apartment developments with commodious space and enriched facilities, high density has induced blight. A protest against the density of population that our gigantic buildings can accommodate does not deprecate the ingenuity of the builders, but some direct questions require deliberation if concentration is an organic necessity of the future metropolis.

Is every man destined to live in an apartment cubicle in high-rise buildings? Is this the way every man desires to live? Is man to be conditioned by science and economics? Or are these the servants of man? Are they creatures of man or is man their slave? Does not man so mold his economics that it may distribute the goods of this world for his use, and does he not invent so that his wants may be better served? If these be true, are we not obliged to evaluate first our desires and define our wants so as to employ science and economics to our advantage?

The city performs a far greater variety of services today than ever before. Its functions are more complex. Yet the same forces that have made this so are those which now render congestion unnecessary. Science, commerce, and industry have intensified the functions of the city. They have also created the instruments to neutralize its effect. The heavy concentration of people is no longer necessary for the conduct of business or for convenient and comfortable living. Methods of transportation, power, and communications invalidate the crowded concentration we unwittingly accept as a necessary evil of urban existence. Crowding of people and buildings is a negation of every contemporary means of communication and transportation at our command. Congestion denies them the chance to serve to their full capacity.

There is stimulation in great distances seen from the skyscraper. Conditioned air has its advantages. The elevator rising 1,000 feet a minute is rapid vertical transit. But do these render the human desire for a house on its land a phenomenon or a whim? Horizontal space means much to the human being. Contact with the earth is not a choice reserved to the agrarian, the tiller of the soil, alone. There is a sense of freedom, human freedom, in traversing the space of the earth under one's own power—on foot. There is a healthy sensation when interior and exterior living space merge into unity, with no more visual separation than a crystal sheet of glass. There is mental freedom and a quiet repose in horizontal space.

Because the "economy" of ownership is often a fiction or because the people are frequently tenants does not alter the essential desire for the horizontal space

Radio City

Paul J. Woolf Photo

Setbacks that begin too late and too far above the street

American Airlines

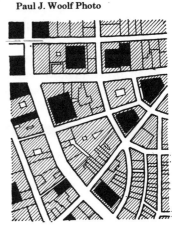

The spacing of skyscraper towers in the Wall Street district

THE DENSITY EQUATION—NEW YORK CITY

Congestion in the city is not new. It has occurred in all civilizations from the beginning of urbanized existence. The gregarious instincts of man are satisfied by the agglomeration of people. Crowds have a natural attraction. The density equation does not turn about this issue; it hinges upon the necessity to maintain a balance between enclosed and open space to accommodate the functions of both.

The drama of the city by day and by night will be enhanced when this balance is achieved. There will be room for people to circulate with convenience and pleasure. The ground level will not be reserved solely as conduits for moving vehicles or storage places for them. The spectacle of the city will be a visual experience from all about—from below as well as from above—when interior and exterior space are in balance.

111

for living. This is not a question of politics, economics, or social reform. It is a matter of human aims, aspirations, desires, and the mental repose in physical reality. It is not a theory of esthetics, nor is it romantic nonsense that people desire a home and garden. It is not enough to substitute air-conditioned cells in multistory buildings because we have the technical know-how to create them.

It is the fundamental desires that beat in the human breast which must shape the city. The skyscraper holds its head aloft with an air of plausibility; it can absorb high land cost and save utilities and transportation time. But it also can create congestion and high land values that nullify its advantages and remove all choice for another form of habitation from the hope of the urban dweller. If we are concerned with economy, it is not the skyscraper that produces it; the skyscraper is not built because it is economical—it is not so. It is built because the cost of land is *extravagant*, and continuing this process without restraint only adds fuel to the flames of urban congestion, blight, and disintegration.

ON COMMON GROUND

It is significant that whatever may be the direction taken in the search for a new urban form and however persistent the trend of decentralization, the idea of the *City* is not forsaken. The complex and diverse functions are reshaped, regrouped, reorganized, but the constituent elements of the city are not abandoned. The commerce, the industry, the cultural institutions upon which our society depends for its spiritual and material enrichment are retained. That the inherent advantages of the city have been abused, misused, exploited, or simply allowed to lie dormant, does not deny their necessity.

There is a wavering line of continuity springing from the dismal factory town of the nineteenth century through the garden city and the New Towns, the urban "biology" of ASCORAL, and the reorganization of industrial community clusters in the future regional city. The line moves at a tangent to the city we know today, but there is a strong affinity with the decentralization and sprawling suburbs that are drawing the life-blood from the overgrown, over-zoned, and congested metropolis. A comparable liberation of space appears in the greenbelt of the New Towns and the London plan by Abercrombie, Frank Lloyd Wright's Broadacre City, and Le Corbusier's towers in green space. It is likewise present in the standards for flexible zoning in modern subdivision practice.

A human scale is recovered in the statements by the new utopians for a planned integration of land uses. The assumption that the metropolis should absorb an unlimited population is challenged, and density standards are related to the organic functions of the city. The natural forces operating the great city are forcing the re-evaluation of form and structure, a development the new utopias anticipated. Advances in transportation and communication can release us from the previously inexorable destiny of large cities. We can have tall and low buildings, open space, and convenient communication, as well as the amenities consistent with good living. All of this will take place when the density equation and the relation between planning and zoning for land use are taken into account.

In the Orient, due to the age of the cities, the design of the buildings and the life styles of the people, we find housing densities that have few parallels to those in the United States and Canada. Hong Kong, since the 1960's, has raised its square feet per person from 35 to 50. In China, the current average living space per person is 2 square meters (22 square feet). The goal there is to achieve 5 square meters (54 square feet) by 1985. Such a density would be the same as the typical American two-car garage housing about 10 persons. This "living space" would not necessarily include kitchens or toilet facilities.

10

Rebuilding Our Cities

THE PENALTY FOR NEGLECT

Physical decay has eaten deeply into the urban community. Unchecked obsolescence stretches its withering fingers over the environment and brings degeneration to the city. Irresponsible civic management invites it, and negligent urban housekeeping permits it to spread. It menaces health, breeds crime and delinquency, and brings traffic death and injury. It undermines civic pride, threatens municipal bankruptcy, and gnaws at the human mind and nerves.

Blight casts its sinister shadow across the face of the city. It decays the core of the business and industrial districts, and it disintegrates the outskirts. It is not confined to the slums, but it is most apparent there; it is there we have failed to maintain the oft-quoted "American standard of living." Harold Buttenheim once said: "We not only need to defend our standard of living, we need to achieve it."[1]

The housing problem remains unsolved, but certain policies have taken shape during the past few decades. The necessity for government to render assistance in some form has been recognized. It is apparent that private enterprise, unaided, is not able to provide an adequate supply of housing of satisfactory standards to meet the wide variations in the income levels of all the people. This is evident in the mortgage insurance program of the Federal Housing Administration. Initiated as a "pump-priming" measure during the depression of the thirties, it has continued to be popular through periods of high economic prosperity. Acceptance of public assistance through public housing for the low wage earners persists as an issue before the people, but the history of housing in Europe and the situation in the United States indicate that the issue revolves about the extent to which public housing shall become an integral part

[1] "The American City," *Architectural Forum,* January 1945.

114

of our economic and social machinery, rather than whether or not such a program should be instituted.

Practically every city is vested with the police power to require maintenance of adequate housing standards. Not only has the enforcement of these powers been ineffective, but the nature of the problem has moved beyond the scope of this device. Lack of planning, poor subdivision practices, excessive land values, ineffectual zoning, archaic streets, and inadequate transportation have created a condition of congestion, mixed land uses, and economic distortions that render whole sections of the city in a process of built-in physical decay and social disintegration. The problem has transcended piecemeal treatment for improvement and has reached the stage of large-scale rehabilitation as the only feasible procedure. Such a procedure implies the coordination and participation of all forces at the command of the urban population.

Sound business thrives on production and distribution; they create investment opportunities. Speculation travels in its wake, clinging like a leech and eating away its solvency. The effect is evident in the urban pattern. Industrial and commercial growth was expected to continue horizontally and outward from the center. As speculation set in, land prices boomed and industrial enterprise eluded the trap by hurdling to the outskirts. Commercial enterprise expanded vertically via the skyscraper or skipped to the expanding market in the suburbs.

What havoc has been wrought by this economic warfare! In its wake lies a mass of industrial, commercial and residential derelicts, hemmed in by a network of obsolete streets and alleys. It has left land values so inflated they defy self-improvement through normal channels of enterprise. It has heaped a relentless burden of taxation upon the people, and it encourages the persistent exodus of the population to the periphery of cities and beyond.

City government is in partnership with this process. As the city deteriorates the cost of upkeep increases. Lip service is given to local responsibility, but it has been customary for city and state governments to avoid the issue of subsidy by transferring that responsibility to the federal government. The cost of maintaining obsolete cities has exacted heavy demands upon the taxpayer. Only some 6 per cent of the city's revenue comes from slums, but these areas cost 45 per cent of the total expenditures for urban services.[2] To meet these demands high land values have been promoted as a foundation for high tax revenue and extended bond issues. Yet the local community has been receiving less and less of the total tax dollar. Four decades ago as much as three-quarters of the total tax revenue went to the states and 25 per cent went to the federal government. The situation is now reversed; 75 per cent goes to the federal government and only 25 per cent is retained by the states. Local government must look to the federal government for financial assistance.

Although concern over the deterioration of cities was confined for a time to social reformers and a few utopians, leadership in all phases of urban enterprise

[2] Urban Renewal Division, Sears, Roebuck & Co., ABC's of Urban Renewal 7, 1957.

has awakened to the hazards to the people and institutions whose roots are in the city, its life, and its economy. Some persons have been stimulated to action by an aversion to the sole role of public housing as an instrument for rebuilding, and others by their outright opposition to public housing in any form. Still others were genuinely disturbed by the downward trend in the physical environment and were convinced that broad steps were necessary to stem the tide. Emotions and reason have been mixed among those who, comprehending the social and economic evils rooted in our cities, recoil at the prospect of saving the financial souls of those allegedly responsible for and profiting from the slums, and those who, confessing the evils, were reluctant to admit the inability of conventional enterprise to cope with them. As these forces moved toward the center, the issues gradually came into clearer focus. In the absence of concerted willingness or ability on the part of those who own urban property to check disintegration, it falls to the lot of the public through the instrument of government. "The legitimate object of government," said Abraham Lincoln, "is to do for a community of people whatever they need to have done but cannot do at all or cannot do so well for themselves in their separate and individual capacities."

The central problem of urban rebuilding is the cost of land. Measured by any standard of appropriate land use the land will cost too much; it will be out of all proportion to the economic value for redevelopment on acceptable terms, and any other terms will make the venture worthless. If we are to restore decency to the urban scene, the excess cost of land must be liquidated—written off the books as a loss. No magic will make it vanish. The cost of rebuilding our cities is the price that must be paid to restore a decent standard of city building. It is the penalty for permitting such congestion that rebuilding is not an economic possibility. Responsibility for this error rests with every community in which it has occurred.

THE HOUSING ACT OF 1949

Recognizing the necessity for action on the public front, various states enacted legislation during the forties to implement urban redevelopment in anticipation of federal financial assistance. The Wagner-Ellender-Taft Bill (S1592) was introduced to the Congress of the United States in 1946. Known as the General Housing Bill, it provided a broad legislative base for a national housing and redevelopment program. It failed to pass the 79th Congress, and a similar bill, identified as the Taft-Ellender-Wagner Bill (S866), was introduced in the 80th Congress. It extended and broadened the private housing program of the Federal Housing Administration, continued the public housing program, and implemented urban redevelopment through loans to local agencies for land acquisition and subsidies to assist in writing off the excess land costs. It provided a basis for a national policy on urban redevelopment but did not receive favorable action during that session of the Congress. During the 81st Congress, however, this position was reversed and the Housing Act of 1949 became law. Since then the act has frequently been amended.

URBAN RENEWAL

Among the deficiencies in our national well-being, disclosed during the depression decade of the thirties, was the accelerated rate of physical deterioration in our cities. It was then estimated that urban housing was becoming obsolete five times as fast as it was being replaced. Despite the high level of economic prosperity and production since World War II, the President's Advisory Committee on Government Housing Policies and Programs reported in 1953 that slums were still growing at a more rapid rate than they were being cleared and strongly urged that the attack be extended along a wider front. The Committee recommended that "the Program of Federal Loans and grants established by Title 1 of the Housing Act of 1949 should be broadened. It should provide assistance to communities for rehabilitation and conservation of areas worth saving as well as for the clearance and redevelopment of wornout areas." As a consequence, the Housing Act of 1954 extended the role of the federal government to include rehabilitation and conservation, and the program was expanded from redevelopment to urban renewal.

Fanning out from the center of the city, extensive sections have been caught in the cross-fire of traffic, transition, and neglect. Their energy has been sapped and their quality drained away. They are the twilight zones in the urban pattern. Block after block of old houses and apartments, laced with traffic streets, have been reduced to a dull order of mediocrity. Into this urbanized vacuum a haphazard and indiscriminate mixture of commercial uses has been drawn. They have not entirely deteriorated into slums but have lost their vitality as residential neighborhoods. Obsolescence in overall character has overtaken them but the physical resources—buildings, streets, utilities—might be saved if aggressive planning measures were applied to them.

A prototype for the conservation of such areas was initiated by the Health Department of Baltimore, Maryland, in 1939. An ordinance in 1942 empowered the Health Department to enforce the health requirements for housing and, in 1947, a special court was established to give regular attention to the adjudication of alleged violations. Enforcement was applied to whole blocks rather than individual buildings and, with the vigorous support of a Citizens Advisory Committee in 1951, the program enjoyed considerable success in the abatement of nuisances and some remodelling of substandard housing.

Aggressive enforcement of the building codes to maintain housing standards must be pursued, but the limitations of such piecemeal renewal should be recognized. The physical improvement of old buildings is but one aspect of effective renewal and may result in postponement of the necessary corrections in planning for traffic conditions and undesirable mixture of incompatible uses which also contribute to community blight.

The wasteful neglect of the resources within the broad belt of blight about our city centers has been underscored by the shift in emphasis from redevelopment to renewal. In the 1960 Housing Act, provision was made for pilot rehabilitation projects. Under this provision local agencies could purchase individual dwelling units, remodel, and sell them to private owners. Each such project was limited to 50 units or not more than two per cent of the total units in any renewal project. Rehabilitation will demand unusually sensitive planning or it may become a deterrent to genuine improvement; the physical condition of individual buildings is but one of the elements in the creation of a living environment.

The requirement in the 1949 Housing Act that a project be "predominately housing" reflected the general assumption that the low cost housing program was being transferred, with "slum clearance," from public to private auspices. Public housing had grown in disfavor, and political resistance to its continuation accounts for some of the reluctance to adopt the redevelopment provisions of the Act at an earlier date. It was consequently assumed that the redevelopment program would shift the emphasis from public housing as the means by which slums and blight could be overcome. It was overlooked that the physical deterioration is not confined to housing areas alone. It is the result of general neglect for the basic standards which guide the building and the maintenance of the whole physical environment. The restriction therefore interfered with a comprehensive approach to redevelopment until the Housing Act of 1954 was amended to permit 10 per cent of the federal grants for nonresidential sections of a redevelopment project.

Congress has been slow to acknowledge the responsibility of the Federal government in the total problem of urban blight, persistently inclining to the position that housing is the primary concern. Nevertheless, relaxation from this firm position has been demonstrated. In 1959 the restriction was again modified to permit 20 per cent nonresidential uses in redevelopment projects and it has since been increased to 30 per cent. By the mid-sixties concern about the displacement of families from renewal areas and the destruction of socially viable communities led to a new emphasis on rehabilitation rather than wholesale clearance. To expand the effectiveness of the program, use of funds for non-residential purposes was increased to 35 per cent. Steps have thus been taken toward a comprehensive attack on the physical decay of the urban community.

THE WORKABLE PROGRAM

An innovation in the 1954 Housing Act placed a responsibility upon the local agencies to develop an action plan for renewal—an overall community program for the removal of slums and blight. Known as the *Workable Program*, this important requirement deserved a more imaginative title.

"There is no justification for Federal Assistance except to cities which will face up to the whole process of urban decay and undertake long-range programs."

That statement from the report of 1953 by the President's Advisory Committee on Government Housing Policies and Programs is the challenge to cities laid down by the Workable Program.

The Workable Program has been accorded rather casual attention; it entails planning discipline which is not customarily practiced. For that reason it is included here as a check-list for urban renewal by responsible public officials:[3]

1. *Codes and Ordinances.* Adequate codes and ordinances, vigorously enforced, are all-important means of preventing the occurrence and spread of slums and blight and are one of the most valuable achievements, in the long run, for the entire program. Without adequate codes and enforcement a community may be permitting shoddy construction below minimum levels of health and safety. By enforcing antiquated, restrictive regulations a community is increasing the cost of housing. Codes need periodic review and revision to permit the use of improved building methods and materials.

Two principal types of regulations, essential to every community, establish:

Standards for construction, assuring structural strength, reasonable safety from fire, and proper plumbing, electrical and heating installations. These include a Building, Plumbing, Electrical and Fire Prevention Code. These codes normally apply to all new construction, including alterations and major repairs.

Standards for housing, which prescribe the minimum conditions under which a building, or parts of it, may be lawfully occupied as a dwelling. Housing regulations set standards for occupancy to prevent overcrowding, for basic sanitary facilities, for light and ventilation, for maintenance, and for heating where climatic conditions warrant. These standards should apply to all existing, as well as new, dwellings and dwelling units. They may be enacted as a separate code or may be contained in other codes, ordinances or regulations. The broad and general nature of many of these standards are more clearly defined and amplified in the construction codes.

While the two types of standards required mention specific codes, they are not intended to limit a community's responsibility to adopt and enforce other codes and regulations necessary to eliminate or prevent conditions of blight in the particular area. For example, regulations may be required for gas installations, air conditioning, air pollution, fire prevention and other hazards applicable not only to dwellings but to public, commercial, and industrial buildings.

The codes that are adopted and enforced will affect every family and every piece of improved property in the community. It is essential that the regulations developed be workable in the local situation and effective as minimum standards of health and safety.

[3] Workable Program for Community Improvement, Housing and Home Finance Agency, Washington, D.C. Revised February 1962.

2. *Comprehensive Community Plan.* The purpose of community planning is
to anticipate the physical environment that will best serve the needs of the
people living and working in an urban area, and then to make plans for
achieving this environment. It is a continuing process of developing a
comprehensive program to guide urban growth and renewal.

   A planning program which meets the needs of one community may not
be adequate for another; the complexities of a large city call for details and
studies not applicable to small communities; and the emphasis on some
elements of a plan for a built-up community will vary for a newer, more
rapidly growing community. Nevertheless, there are six minimum planning requirements which are the backbone of any program.

   The Land Use Plan—projects future community land needs, showing by
   location and extent, areas to be used for residential, commercial,
   industrial, and public purposes.

   The Thoroughfare Plan—provides a system of major streets, existing and
   proposed, distinguishing between limited access, primary, and secondary
   thoroughfares.

   The Community Facilities Plan—shows location and type of present and
   proposed schools, recreation areas, and other significant public facilities.

   The Public Improvements Program—identifies and recommends priorities for future public improvements needed to meet objectives established in other plan elements.

   The Zoning Ordinance and Map—establish regulations and zone
   districts which govern the use of land and the location, height, use, and
   land coverage of buildings.

   The Subdivision Regulations—provide standards for land development
   by requiring adequate lot sizes and arrangement, utilities, and street
   improvements; guide development to conform with the comprehensive
   plan.

3. *Neighborhood Analysis.* Only through a thorough, overall examination of
the entire community and an analysis of individual neighborhoods can
blight be found and measured, its causes diagnosed, and a sound course of
treatment prescribed. This process is essential to knowing the magnitude
of the job and to planning an all-out attack on existing blight and
preventing its spread. It involves the following basic steps:

   (a) Delineation of the residential areas of the community by neighbor-
       hoods for study and planning purposes.

   (b) Determination of the location, extent and intensity of blight in each
       neighborhood.

   (c) The analysis of each neighborhood in terms of its condition and need for
       treatment.

   (d) The making of recommendations for programming action required to
       meet neighborhood needs—code enforcement, public improvements,
       conservation, reconditioning, clearance and redevelopment.

   Neighborhoods must be analyzed by condition of housing and also in
terms of environmental conditions—the pattern of land use, traffic flow and

street arrangement, neighborhood facilities and services. The type of treatment needed for any area can be prescribed only after its total deficiencies have been determined and the causes of blight pinned down.

In developing recommendations for programming renewal action, a community can take advantage of its opportunities:

(a) To remove sore spots of blight affecting surrounding areas.
(b) To save declining areas and restore them to sound condition by early action.
(c) To plan renewal in conjunction with schedules for public improvements.
(d) To take advantage of a market for cleared land.

4. *Administrative Organization.* Each of the other program elements provides the tools for community improvement. Administrative organization is the means of putting the tools to work. No matter how good the tools themselves may be, their ultimate effectiveness will depend on whether the community's administrative machinery works efficiently.

For a community with little previous experience in Workable Program activities, the first task should be that of developing the administrative organization to handle these activities. Communities with previous experience may find that existing administration should be reorganized to meet new objectives.

Take a cold, clear look at the community's administrative machinery to see how it can be organized and put into action to meet the challenge of an effective Workable Program for broad-scale community improvement:

(a) Decide on and establish the organization needed.
(b) Find the right people for the jobs to be done.
(c) Give them clear-cut authority and responsibility.

Program activities cut across organizational lines. Most local government departments and agencies will be involved, directly or indirectly, to some extent. Without coordination of these activities, there will be lost motion, poor timing, and waste of funds.

A total attack on slums and blight and community-wide action for improvement require the strength that comes from overall coordination. Assign the responsibility for coordination to some appropriate local official or interdepartmental committee. This will provide the means of

(a) Keeping a regular check on progress and timing.
(b) Achieving balanced action so that all seven elements move forward together.

5. *Financing.* An effective Workable Program can save a community infinitely more than it costs. Some examples of financial benefits are as follows:

(a) Protection of property values through enforcement of codes and planning measures.
(b) Savings resulting from the proper planning of public works.
(c) Reduction of the drain on municipal services from slum areas which

require more fire and police protection, more health and welfare services.
(d) Increases in tax base through conservation, reconditioning or redevelopment; through stimulation of new commercial and industrial construction.

As the program gets underway, most communities will find that they need to initiate or increase appropriations for the following types of activities:
(a) Enforcement of codes.
(b) Technical assistance for comprehensive planning and neighborhood analyses.
(c) Administration of zoning and subdivision regulations.
(d) Overall coordination of the program when this is a full or part-time assignment.

As definite plans for community facilities, public works and renewal projects are developed, the community can plan and coordinate its capital outlays expenditures. By projecting them for a five-or six-year period into the future, a sound fiscal program for improvement can be developed. Advance scheduling of expenditures provides the opportunity to market obligations at better terms. Through coordination of urban renewal activities with expenditures for public improvements, a community can make local dollars do double duty.

6. *Housing for Displaced Families.* As a community goes into action on its Workable Program—enforcing codes, eliminating slums and blight, constructing public improvements—some families will be displaced from housing they now occupy. Many of the families will need substantial assistance in finding suitable relocation housing. Many communities will find that existing local housing will not meet relocation needs. This is often true in regard to the limited number of sales and rental units available to displaced minority group families.

The community must accept the responsibility of providing relocation assistance to all families displaced as a result of governmental action. It must make every effort to assure that these families have the opportunity to relocate in decent, safe and sanitary housing that is within their means. With the housing resources that exist in the community and with action to augment them, the needs of displaced families can be met—but not without advance preparation and planning.

Those responsible for relocation assistance must work with officials of agencies likely to cause displacement through activities such as
(a) Code enforcement.
(b) Construction of local public improvements, state or federal installations.
(c) Urban renewal.
(d) Expressway or street-widening projects.

By determining both immediate and long-range relocation needs in advance of displacement, a community will be in a position to remedy any shortage of housing. There will be opportunity to organize relocation services, to let people know that they are going to have help in finding a new place to live, to work with private housing developers, and to obtain federal relocation aids if they are needed.

Before a family is displaced, suitable relocation housing must be available. Hardships are created and community improvement plans and projects are delayed when a community's relocation responsibilities are neglected.

7. *Citizen Participation.* There is some degree of citizen participation in any program a community undertakes. It is evident in expressions of support or opposition in newspapers, in meetings, in conferences, at public hearings, at the ballot box. Ultimate success for the other six elements of a Workable Program depends on the kind of citizen participation a community is able to achieve.

Citizen support and concern for community improvement can be a powerful force. Enlist the finest leadership of every sphere of community life and action—industrial, professional, labor, welfare, religious and educational interests; civic clubs and women's groups. The active support of the business community will be a major asset. Special emphasis should be placed on minority group participation, for minorities are often most adversely affected by lack of housing opportunities.

A basic approach to building the kind of citizen participation a program needs is three-pronged. It must be planned to inform and to involve the following:
(a) The community as a whole.
(b) Special interest groups, enlisting their assistance in solving particular problems.
(c) Residents of areas to be directly affected by various program activities.

People need to know what is happening to their community, what neighborhoods are going downhill, what is causing blight, what is being done to fight deterioration, and what more can be done. They must have every opportunity to take constructive action.

Each community will know from its own experience what means of enlisting citizen participation have proven most successful; what groups and local leaders can provide effective support; the type of information that will promote the understanding and interest of local citizens. Work to build the kind of participation that is ready to take action and share responsibility in developing and carrying out a Workable Program for Community Improvement which utilizes the full range of private as well as public resources.

Aggressive public action against the slums in American cities was initiated in 1933 when the National Recovery Act launched the low-rent housing program of the Public Works Administration. The economy of the nation had collapsed and the times were troubled. There were those who viewed the housing program as a means to improve the standard of housing for the lower-income families in our cities, but the overriding incentive was general economic recovery. A pervasive air of emergency has attended all activities of the Federal government since then. The anachronism is apparent. Slums have grown as a natural consequence of neglect. Voices raised in protest have had effect in isolated quarters, but the national disposition has been apathetic. The deterioration of cities has been a *process*, not a wilful act which may be corrected on command. Rebuilding our cities to standards appropriate to our times is also a process, and calls for effective action along a broad front. The Workable Program gives articulation to this process as a matter of public policy, and it is not a program which, having begun, will reach an end.

The sense of urgency to produce "results" leads inevitably to compromises in administration of a public program. It is regrettable that patience cannot be applied to the renewal program, the patience to wait for cities "to face up to the whole process of urban decay and undertake long-range programs" (President's Advisory Committee on Government Housing Policies and Programs, 1953). This is the urgent need and less than adequate planning and action at the local level reduces the program to a process of "getting federal money" rather than a process of genuine urban renewal.

The formulation and diligent enforcement of ordinances to maintain adequate housing standards, zoning ordinances, and subdivision regulations which prescribe adequate standards for future building, self-analysis of local deficiencies, and action programs for correction—all require the persistent will of the people of a community. They cannot "go it alone," and Federal assistance necessary, but the Workable Program offers the opportunity to wait long enough for the treatment to take effect.

In 1965 all housing agencies were consolidated within the Department of Housing and Urban Development, a new post in the President's cabinet. The following year the Demonstration Cities and Metropolitan Development Act introduced the "Model Cities" program to coordinate federal programs related to social services, education, open land, employment, and physical development. A galaxy of amendments to the Housing Act were directed to more participation by private enterprise in the production of low cost housing. Sections 235 and 236 subsidized interest rates on housing loans to reach an equivalent of a 1 per cent rate for both home ownership and apartment rental. With much fanfare, experimental projects were financed by Housing and Urban Development to demonstrate efficient housing prototypes and new construction technology. Begun in 1969, this "Operation Breakthrough" was elaborately organized, but the practical results were inconclusive.

By 1970 inflation overtook the nation, and Federal assistance to low-cost housing was cut back. The principle of revenue sharing was proposed to enlarge the initiative of local governments in the allocation of Federal aid.

The "great" cities of America are distinguished by the concentration of huge economic institutions which dominate the affairs of the nation and the vast multitude of people attracted to them in search for survival. While cities such as New York, Chicago, Philadelphia, Boston, and Los Angeles serve the national interest as centers of enterprise, they have themselves become socially and economically unmanageable

Confronted with uncontrolled physical deterioration, a concentration of low income families in ghettos with their loss of individual identity, the flight of the affluent population to the suburbs and the extension of highways to implement that decentralization, the promotion of excessive property values in core areas to compensate for an imbalanced tax base has contributed to a condition of institutional decay.

Revitalization through federally assisted redevelopment has been undertaken with a program of piece-meal "projects" of publicly and privately financed housing. Handicapped by exorbitant costs for site acquisition in congested areas, new developments of high-rise apartments are either alien to the life-style of low income families or beyond their economic means. The social and economic plight of the underprivileged urban population continues to fester and, on occasion, to explode from intense pressure.

Reflecting the bloated character of very large cities, programs have been instituted to recover community participation in the decision-making process. New York has been divided into areas of common interest in which individuals may relate to government institutions. Los Angeles has attempted to cope with its huge land mass by delineating geographical areas in which citizen committees may participate in planning. The paradox of this urban balkanization is the fact that a city, or regional, government is necessary to assure a variety of essential urban services and coordinate basic elements of growth and development.

TO SELL OR LEASE

Congestion created high land values and congestion now threatens to destroy them. To ward off this imminent disaster, a compelling motive for improvement of the environment is protection of land values. Land is a natural resource; it is not a product of men's toil. Value which may be attached to it is essentially a by-product, a value not of the land itself but of the way in which it may be used. Stable values for land can be maintained only through social controls cast in the form of laws prescribing the limits within which it may be used. Because the laws have failed to establish reasonable limitations, restraint upon speculation has been absent from the urban scene. Stimulated by the almost anarchic nature of laws governing urban development, speculation has enjoyed a violent career. Inflation bubbles blow up, then burst; land prices quiver but rise again to unprecedented heights. Harland Bartholomew has said: "Too often is the American city considered an unlimited speculation in real estate."[4]

Negligence and abuse have sapped some of the vitality of our traditional

[4] Harland Bartholomew, *Urban Land Uses*, Harvard City Planning Series, Harvard University Press, Cambridge, Mass., 1932, Introduction.

practices. The public power of eminent domain is summoned to force adjustment, and public funds are drawn upon to aid in purging the economic congestion. The power of condemnation and public credit now receive general acceptance as necessary instruments for urban rebuilding. These are not measures to be taken as temporary sedatives. The high cost should produce a cure; it is reasonable to expect them to prevent a recurrence of the same ills.

State laws for urban redevelopment provide that land acquired by condemnation may be resold. It is generally provided that the new use to which the land is put shall comply with standards of use which conform to a Comprehensive Plan for redevelopment.

Public financial assistance for urban rehabilitation serves a dual purpose. It implements rebuilding at standards of land use that will restore a decent environment, and it provides unlimited opportunities for sound and profitable investment by private enterprise. The investment of public funds, as subsidies, is warranted on the condition that the resulting improvement is permanent, and there must be assurance that the same investment to cure the same ills will not be repeated every generation. It is of vital importance, therefore, to ascertain that the new standards of land use are of a permanent nature.

To determine this, it is necessary to refer to the laws that apply to urban building. A Comprehensive Plan is not a permanent document, nor are the "administrative decisions" which emanate from a planning agency preparing that document. A Comprehensive Plan is only part of a series of legislative acts controlling the development of cities. An immediate improvement may conform to the new standards administratively determined within the scope of a Comprehensive Plan, but subsequent use of land will depend entirely upon later revisions and modifications which may emerge. To rely upon administrative policy, no matter how inspired, is to invite inevitable chaos and abuse.

Adequate protection is afforded only by the laws that set the standards, and there is little evidence that reasonable legal standards are yet remotely intended. This raises a question as to the advisability of delivering land, acquired by the public power of condemnation, back to the same abuses that have made it necessary to exercise that power. The question may be elaborated by inquiring if justice is served by taking land from some private owners and selling it to other private interests at a reduced price. The use of public funds is for the purpose of bringing land costs down to an economic value for redevelopment at standards of decent land use. To that extent the public interest is served and to that extent it must be protected. To sell land at a subsidized price is to make a gift of public funds as an inducement to engage in urban rebuilding for a profit. Such a policy is somewhat a distortion of the high purpose for which it is designed.

In 1942 a Royal Commission reported its recommendations for a reconstruction program in England. The chairman was the Honorable Augustus Andrewe Uthwatt, a member of the House of Lords. That report said, in part,

We recommend, therefore, that once any interest in land has passed into public ownership it should be disposed of by way of lease only and not by way of sale, and that the authority should have the power to impose such covenants in the lease as planning requirements make desirable, breach of such covenants to be enforceable by re-entry.[5]

Building on leased land is by no means novel. It is common practice in commercial enterprise and offers no deterrent to sound investment. It need offer no obstruction to the sale of improvements on the land. Nor would tax revenue be affected, since a lease value would return revenue to the city and the usual taxes could be assessed against the improvement. Objection to local bureaucracy could be avoided by obtaining the services of competent and established firms in property management.

We are confronted with a situation in which public powers must be called into action to restore the productive enterprise of our cities and the initiative of private enterprise in our urban economy, and, in so doing, create an urban environment consistent with our contemporary capacities and skills. The fact that land values obstruct the path to this goal becomes a matter of concern to the people—a public responsibility—and the gains made at the expense of the people must be retained by them.

CONTROL OF OBSOLESCENCE

There is not yet available to us an effective method to control the spread of obsolescence. The police power to restrain the "nuisance" of blight has limitations. Obsolescence is an obstruction to full production of housing. Normal competitive enterprise does not and cannot cope with it, as the accumulation of huge areas of blighted districts testifies.

When blight sets in, the land is deemed ripe for more intensive land use. As single-family districts, some being the "fine old sections," begin to run down, their only salvation seems to be a change to apartment development. Intensity of land use moves relentlessly from the city center, and the "old" areas are drawn into this ever-widening vortex. The greater density permitted in apartment zoning then swiftly moves to reinforce a claim to higher land values. Thenceforth only multiple-dwelling development can be afforded. Old residences are converted to apartments and the district further declines. Strip zoning for business use is soon permitted, and stores are spotted in the neighborhood. After that, "light" industrial uses seep in. The "salvation" of revised zoning is dissipated among mixed land uses, and the community environment decays.

Pressure is ever present to "save" obsolescent areas of our cities by permitting a greater intensity of land use. There are few instances where this insidious process has restored to blighted areas a decent standard of residential

---

[5] Report of the Expert Committee on Compensation and Betterment presented to Parliament by Minister of Works and Planning, September 1942.

or commercial development. The mixture of land uses leaves a series of derelicts in its wake. Land values increase rather than decrease as blight eats its way from the central core of the city, and they defy recovery of neighborhood values. Good development retreats from these damaging blows and seeks protection of "new" and more economical land at a safe distance. Disorderly expansion continues. Self-maintenance is the urgent need—a form of preventive treatment that will build resistance to decay and render major operations less necessary.

TAXATION IN REVERSE

Buildings are built to provide space in which to live or conduct business. Taxes are collected to support the public services that make these building ventures possible and profitable. Today taxes are measured by the assessed value of land and buildings. The value of land may increase. The value of physical improvements, on the other hand, depreciates with age and use. At the same time the cost of public services increases as physical deterioration continues. Yet the present assessment of taxation actually works in reverse of this: *tax revenue goes down as the cost of urban maintenance goes up.*

There is little inducement for an owner to remove obsolete buildings so long as it is possible to derive a profit from them. The present order of real property taxation penalizes new construction and encourages the retention of old buildings until they have reached the last stages of decay. It retards sound real estate development and management, makes unhealthy communities, and adds to the burden of the taxpayer. This trend must be checked and reversed.

Taxation is our traditional instrument for maintaining economic and social equilibrium. Our system of enterprise is intended to give the individual full freedom of choice and initiative. Devices employed by government to reinforce the public welfare should remain consistent with this pattern. It is up to the individual to measure his opportunity for investment; he must determine the extent to which he, in his own interest, will take part in the building of a community. But his interest cannot be served when a system of taxation imposes the penalty of high taxes on new building while it encourages competition from old buildings. Yet that is our current method of *ad valorem* taxation, and it is inimical to the full use of our productive resources.

Take a leaf from the experience with income taxation. In computing the tax base on business enterprise the cost of improvements to carry on the business may be deducted from gross income. Application of this principle to real property taxation would establish a logical order: as buildings deteriorate with age, contribute to the spread of blight, and retard the production of new building, taxes would increase rather than decrease. Taxation would assume an effective role as an instrument for encouragement of expanding production, protection against blight, and revenue to the community for public services. This instrument is the more effective because real property taxes are levied primarily by local government and are thereby readily subject to such periodic adjustments as changing local conditions may warrant.

"ECONOMIC LIFE" RECOGNIZED

Control of obsolescence has a twofold purpose: we are concerned with the maintenance of both a stable economy through continuing full production and adequate standards through continuous improvement. The FHA program introduced the repayment of loans for urban construction in regular installments over a predetermined period—amortization. This helped to stabilize financing, but more than that it recognizes the vital part that *time* plays in our economic machinery. It acknowledges that buildings have an "economic life," a period of economic usefulness in our system. The wheels of the system are kept turning by the circulation of money, and the time required to pay for buildings marks the frequency of the circulation of money. Unless the demand for building continues to exceed the existing supply, circulation of building money diminishes or ceases. The building industry then subsides or stops.

If the physical life of buildings were linked to the economic life, building money would continue to flow into the production of new buildings. Improved methods would find normal reception and application. But so long as old and obsolete buildings remain on the market they suffocate new building production. Run-down and worn-out buildings sustain themselves too long on no maintenance and low rents. It is that type of competition that sucks the lifeblood from productive enterprise; it is that type of competition that must be weeded out. Control of obsolescence would maintain the economic flow of goods and services, and a higher level of decency in the urban environment. Taxation could be effectively used to establish this control if the rate were related to the economic life of buildings.

In *Building Height, Bulk and Form,*[6] George B. Ford pointed out that the average life of skyscraper buildings was calculated at between 25 and 30 years. The period of residential financing ranges between 15 and 25 years. Except for commercial and dwelling structures that have become a sordid blight on a community, few acceptable buildings remain in use for more than 35 years, without such major alterations that they become the equivalent of new buildings. It is the obsolete buildings which need to be weeded out of the urban environment.

It would be possible to establish a low tax base for new buildings and thereafter increase the tax rate from year to year. During the early life of a building—about 10 years—the increase would be moderate. Thereafter it would gradually accelerate for the succeeding 15 to 20 years. After that the increase would move rapidly upward at such a rate that a major improvement to sustain a profitable income on the building or a complete removal to make way for a new structure more suitable to the market and the community would be induced by the time the age of the structure had reached 35 years. A major improvement would cause a building to revert to a proportionately lower tax bracket rather than be penalized by an increased assessment according to current policy.

---

[6] Harvard City Planning Series, Vol. II.

Improved construction standards would be encouraged because they would benefit by lower tax brackets rather than be discouraged by the present *ad valorem* system.[7]

This suggestion rejects the traditional supposition that a building may remain so long as it produces a revenue satisfactory to its owner. It may seem to be bitter medicine, but the accelerating degeneration of our cities has amply demonstrated that neither the public welfare nor sound private enterprise is served by current methods. This proposal does not presume to solve the broad problem of taxation, but it would place our current tax system in a logical order without which regulations accepted today offer no prospect for correcting the insidious evil of obsolescence.

No surgeon ever performed an operation without destroying some live tissue. His aim is to save the patient, knowing that time will heal the wounds and restore the living cells. Our economy as well as our social well-being depends upon our capacity to carve out the parasite of decay with the destruction of as little useful tissue as practically possible. But we cannot continue to rely upon the vagaries of chance. It must become a matter of law in an organized society.

This proposition presents problems, to be sure. Not the least of these is the one faced by home-owners of low income who depend solely upon their dwelling as a place to live. It may be alleged that this order of taxation would impose an undue hardship on these families. While the most articulate protests to this apparent injustice will undoubtedly come from those who profit most from blighted property, each community will have to face, sooner or later, this question: How long can the accumulation of obsolete buildings and improvements that deface the environment and eat away the civic solvency be tolerated? Each community is obliged to address itself to that question and deliberate the problems—all the problems—it poses. When the answer has been decided, and only then, will cities begin the long road out of the sordid morass that the anarchy of urban development has wrought.

All things grow obsolete with time and change. That is inevitable. But obsolescence must be brought under control, as weeds are kept out of a prosperous garden. Degeneration of the urban environment is an epidemic feeding upon lack of attention. Absence of public control and treatment is like the underwriting of obsolescence by law. It has become a public liability. It is consequently a public responsibility to devise machinery to put its house in order, and keep it in order by progressive regulation of obsolescence.

RENEWAL SHOULD BE FOR PEOPLE

There is little doubt that slums must be eradicated and the families from them must have decent housing. Blight must be removed and further spread

---

[7] This approach to the application of taxation on *improvements* could be coordinated with some form of taxation on *land,* such as that referred to in Chapter 22.

prevented. Run-down business sections need rehabilitation and industrial areas must be cleaned up. The decay must be carved out, and renewal can serve that purpose.

But there are some related issues from which the program cannot be dissociated. As the program progresses there is evidence that money, buildings, and bulldozers are receiving somewhat more attention than people. Bright new projects replace the old and run-down slums. Buildings rise high and open space appears where there was none before. Efficiency and convenience replace the drudgery of a house and yard; services are performed by management. The apartments all have a view. The great new buildings are quite urbane, the parking garages and traffic circulation ingenious. But what of the people for whom these giant developments are intended?

Are these projects an expression of the environment we really seek? Is the agglomeration of cells in huge building blocks the design for future family life? Is relief from responsibility for a "home" the objective of the urban family? Is urbanity more genuinely expressed by Park Avenue or Nob Hill than George-town? Have we become infected with the "safe and sanitary" code of public housing and become incapable of distinguishing between "habitable" and "livable"? Are we not rendering prohibitive the prospect for the color, vitality and animation which is the life of a city? Do we not, from the vantage point of a high-rise "view" apartment, see much, but nothing very clearly?

The frequency with which these questions are being asked is reason enough to ponder them. It is the human spirit of the city, rather than the land price, which renewal is presumed to sustain. As the prospects for orderly rebuilding of our cities loom brighter, we cannot be unmindful of its underlying purpose: re-creation of an urban environment in which the functions of the contemporary city can be performed with order. Other advantages will accrue, but we may be guided by Aristotle's advice: " A city should be built to give its inhabitants security and happiness."

Urban renewal is not for the purpose of restoring stability to real estate values, although this will result. It is not for the purpose of bailing out the investments of landed gentry, since much of the decaying city pays dividends to its absentee owners. It is not intended to recover speculative losses, since the curse of blight has fallen upon the property of those who cannot afford to join the flight to better places. It is not for the purpose of reinforcing government bureaucracy, although the public that these bureaus represent has a heavy stake in the problem. It is not for the purpose of providing ripe opportunities for investment for profit, although it will open this fertile field. It is not for the purpose of providing employment, although it will create unlimited oppor-tunities for labor in field and factory. Urban renewal is for none of these specifically, but each is a part serving the main objective: building a decent city for people.

Cities are for people. They are not objects to be coddled by zealots nor commodities to satisfy speculative greed. The philosophy of escape from the city is a retreat from reality; within this philosophy are the seeds of our own destruction. To deny the place of the city in our industrial age is to invite economic slavery and social suicide. Our proper course is not the destruction of urban life; it is the building of a better one.

"Building a city is a sacramental act on the part of the whole people. For a city is the physical manifestation of an invisible reality: the soul of its people. Ancient cities were worshipped by their citizens. Americans appear to hate their cities. We do all we can to demean and disgrace them.

"But there is an intangible spirit at the heart of a contemporary commercial city that must find its expression in and give purpose to the city building of its people. We should endeavor to make an art out of our town building.

"The citizens of a city must discover the character of the city if they are to build an image of its soul. They must understand its nature and its function before they can design it. For the design of a city is not to be found on the drawing board of the city planner. The forms of the city live in its people. They emerge out of the mind and spirit of its citizens. They reside in the very history of 'the place'. . . ."[8]

It is well to think about that counsel as we consider the confused maze of housing "programs" intended to improve the lot of the poor while rebuilding run-down areas in our cities. Civic and political leaders, disenchanted with the public housing programs after World War II, decided private enterprise should clear slums and build decent housing for low income families. Urban renewal programs failed to take into account the plight of families who, for economic, ethnic, or social reasons, were not eligible for or could not afford the new high-rise apartments that replaced the blight. Where the new buildings were intended for underprivileged families, it was discovered that high-rise cell blocks were incompatible with the living mores of their intended occupants.

The bizarre example of the Pruitt-Igoe public housing development in St. Louis should alert our attention to the human element in the housing equation. The drama of high-rise buildings appeals not only to architects and engineers who design them; they also satisfy the land-economists and government officials who consider land prices more than the basic needs of people for a compatible living environment. Because the development had such an oppressive atmosphere for low-income occupants, less than a quarter of the dwellings were occupied, and the government ordered two of the eleven story towers destroyed by dynamite in 1972; the remaining towers were reduced to less than half their original height. Despite such an incredible experience, the housing is seldom designed for compatible living patterns; urban renewal drifts toward apartments designed for, and acceptable to, upper income groups who want to return to city-life and the amenities if offers, or accommodations for commercial institutions are promoted to replace blight.

With the drifting course of government assistance to housing, the fact that many low-income families in the nation cannot afford the full costs of decent housing—the property taxes, insurance, and maintenance—has been

---

[8] John Osman, Vice-President, Ford Foundation Fund for Adult Education, *Architectural Forum*, August 1957.

obscured in the enthusiasm to subsidize the private sector in real estate and development. It is quite possible that when the ambition for large projects attractive to planners, architects, and government officials has abated, public housing may be integrated within neighborhoods where the less economically privileged may find a compatible environment.

It would be well to heed the observations of Paul Gaff, urban affairs editor of the *Chicago Tribune,* on the sweeping plans for renewal of "Chicago 21." Despite new Neanderthal monsters in the heart of the city, such as the Prudential Building, the Marina City Towers, the John Hancock Building, the Standard Oil Building and the Sears Tower, Chicago "is losing its battle with the suburbs." Confronted with the lethargy of the City Planning Department, privately financed plans by architects Skidmore, Owings, and Merrill in 1966 envisioned a restructuring of the "loop" and lake front, and a leviathan "new town in town" on 600 acres along the river for a population of 120,000. But Gaff suggests: "Perhaps it is already too late . . . the nature of the growth points to a day when the last middle class white family has fled the city—when only the wealthy remain within their fortified apartment towers along the lake and the rest of Chicago is populated by the poor. This is no doomsday fantasy . . . Chicago, which keeps telling itself to 'make no little plans,' continues to move toward the time when it will have little left to plan for."[9]

[9] *Architectural Forum,* January-February, 1974.

11

Real Estate Practices

THE SPECULATIVE INSTINCT

The development of real estate in the United States has not been distinguished for its attention to the amenities of a living environment. Speculation was the moving spirit as the frontiers widened and pushed forward. This was not a singular characteristic reserved to enterprising Americans alone. It rather points a difference between the opportunities open to the people of this land and those of countries elsewhere. It reflects the desires that caused the people to seek this land. Freedom from oppression and tyranny implied certain rights, and among them was the right for a man to have a piece of land upon which to build a home for his family. The search for that right was itself something of a speculation and abuse of the privilege was not a newly cultivated characteristic of mankind.

During the colonial period it was customary to obtain grants of land from the mother country, and it was considered a just reward due the leaders of colonization. The subdivision and sale of the land so acquired were common practice. However, it was not always a lucrative one, and some of the heaviest dealers in land met with financial failure. Some of the large land-estates were preserved through the English system of long-term leases rather than sale.

Speculation in land offered strong temptation in the latter half of the nineteenth century. Whole towns were used as a speculative medium, and they sprung up almost at random along the railroads that stretched across the land. Some of these towns have become cities, many have vanished, and others remain as ghosts of the speculative orgy in gold and silver.

THE SUBURBAN COMMUNITY

Although the history of speculation in land has not been of the most savory variety, there were those who chose this medium as an instrument for the improvement of land development. This choice was not motivated by the high purpose of the Garden City movement in England, for instance, nor was it prompted by deep concern for the nature of the city or its social and economic welfare. It was rather the natural result of competitive necessity prodded, no doubt, by that satisfaction of the creative impulse which achievement invariably delivers. There were accomplishments, and they altered the future prospects for our cities in a manner hardly suggested by the subdivision practices employed then and, still too frequently, now.

With the dawn of the twentieth century high land costs squeezed the single-family dwelling farther and farther to the outskirts. The swelling city forced these outskirts to such distances that community facilities which one time served the urban population were no longer readily accessible. The development of extensive facilities in the suburbs gave to them the character of satellite communities. Decentralization was in progress.

Only the surveyor had been associated in the layout of subdivisions. With the development of independent residential communities, however, the planner become a more active participant. One of the earliest large-scale residential subdivisions was a 1,600-acre tract to be known as Riverside, near Chicago. It was designed by Frederick Law Olmsted and Calvert Vaux in 1869. Garden City, Long Island, was another such development and it has since become substantially a self-contained community.

The gridiron street system offered the subdivider the most convenient pattern for surveying and recording deeds. It was typical of real estate development but offered little in return as a living environment. The exceptions are, therefore, the more noteworthy for the progress in planning they demonstrated.

Roland Park, in Baltimore, was a subdivision begun in 1891. It was distinguished for singularly high standards of physical development. It was designed for fine residences, but there were few suburbs not so intended. Another pioneer development was Forest Hills, Long Island. It was one of the earliest planned residential suburbs, started in 1913, and the development company undertook the construction of many of the homes, apartments, and shopping facilities.

After World War I a number of well-planned communities were initiated. Mariemont, Ohio, designed by John Nolen in 1921, became a satellite of Cincinnati. It was devoted primarily to single-family homes with a density of six or seven units per acre, although apartments were included in connection with the principal shopping center.

About this time two other distinguished developments were begun in widely different sections of the country. River Oaks in Houston, Texas, occupies an area of 1,000 acres and was planned with a full complement of community facilities including a golf course and market center. In 1923 the Palos Verdes Estates was planned on a dramatic site overlooking the Pacific Ocean south of Los Angeles. The site covered 3,000 acres, and residential lots ranged in size from one-half acre to 30 acres. About one-quarter of the total area was allocated to schools, parks, houses of worship, libraries, shopping, and recreation. A few apartment areas were proposed about the various shopping centers, but one-half of the area was given over to residences restricted to single-family dwellings. The remainder was in roads and landscaped parkways.

Numbered among other notable subdivisions in this country are Shaker Heights in Cleveland, the Country Club District in Kansas City, St. Francis Woods in San Francisco, Nassau Shores, Long Island, and Westwood Village in Los Angeles. Each of these developments marks a high level of planning in living environment. There was no serious intention on the part of subdividers to cope with adequate housing for families of low income in these communities. They were intended for the upper income group and were promoted accordingly.

The contrast between these developments and the average subdivision is the more apparent when we observe the rank and file of urban expansion. It was not planned; it simply oozed over the edges of the growing metropolis. A minimum of improvements in streets, walks, sewers, water, electricity, and gas distribution was installed. The unaware purchaser was left to foot the bill at some later date or shift the burden to the urban taxpayer.

Local governments gradually awoke to the havoc being wrought in the suburbs, and legislation was enacted to require subdividers to make certain improvements as a condition to approval of the development. These early regulations were feeble, but they were an acknowledgment that some measure of control was necessary to protect the city for the people who live in it.

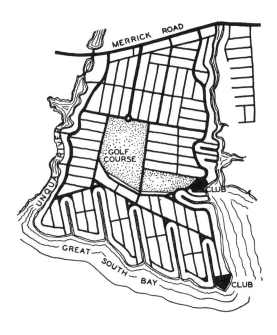

**NASSAU SHORES,
Long Island**

Nassau Shores was started in about 1926 on approximately 500 acres and designed for full advantage of the waterfront location. Subdivided in lots 20 X 100 feet, it was customary to require two lots for each dwelling.

THE MOBILE POPULATION

Suburban expansion was encouraged by the growing urban population but it did not drain off the excess population from the center of cities. People responded to their natural desire to live near their work, and employment opportunities were concentrated in the city center. Then the nature of these opportunities changed from the pre-factory system. Stable industrial employment was uncertain. With expanding commercial enterprise, the tendency to shift from job to job extended to movement from city to city. Mobility of the family offered advantages over fixed tenure.

The urban population thus became transient in character. Freedom to move was not desirable but it was necessary. The rental apartment satisfied this requirement and it became popular. The familiar tenement of the nineteenth century remained for the poor, but the multi-family building was no longer confined to the low-income family. It achieved a new dignity as a form of urban living. Park Avenue, the Gold Coast, and Nob Hill were as popular among the well-to-do as the Lower East Side for the immigrant family.

Oddly enough, the standards of planning did not change with the range of income groups who found the apartment popular. Lots of 40 and 50 feet in width were more common than the 25-foot lot of the nineteenth century and the "dumbell" tenement of New York was outlawed, but the internal planning, the size and number of rooms in "high-class" apartments made up for much of the additional lot area. There was little difference between the open space about the building, whether for the "swank" trade, the "efficiency-apartment" for the middle-income white collar clerk, or the low-income industrial worker. Narrow interior courts and side yards and little or no set-backs at front or rear prevailed as standard practice.

The city was having growing pains. The industrial economy had thrown out of gear all previous concepts of what a city should be. The traditional dwelling for the average American family was the single-family house. It had fulfilled the desires and living habits since early colonial times. Then the village of homes was engulfed by the industrial metropolis. Instead of a place to live, the city became a place to make a living. The family no longer dwelt in its home; it hired apartment space for temporary occupancy. The speculative opportunities for profit in this form of building enterprise were obvious, and full advantage was taken of them, but the apartment as a form of *investment* for capital was not yet fully realized. Adjustment to the new kind of city was, and still is, slow. But there were signs of improvements.

RECENT TRENDS

From 1975 to 1979 the land values in all parts of the country spiraled to new heights. This sharp increase reflected *inflation* as well as a basic housing shortage. In the Los Angeles-Orange County areas of California a modest home might cost a hundred thousand dollars. Jerry-built homes with less than 1000 square feet of space were selling in the fifty-thousand-dollar range. In some locations the demand was so great that lotteries were held to award homes, which were often bought by speculators seeking to take advantage of the soaring land values.

Desert land, subject to wind and erosion damage was being sold for $50,000 an acre in the areas around Palm Springs. Foreign capital from many nations was pouring into the land market, not only from the oil rich countries but from Canada and Europe as well.

Professor Robert A. Brady, once a member of the Economics faculty at the University of California at Berkeley, stated a law of physics that the depression of the 1930's confirmed held true for economics as well: "that which goes up will eventually come down."

Perhaps we will soon see a repetition of the 1930's phenomenon.

In the meantime these land costs are reflected in the cost of housing—whether as rentals or the price of a home. Because of the high cost of land, one can readily understand why developers often ask to be allowed to build housing of higher densities than that permitted by comprehensive plans and the zoning ordinances. Such requests are difficult to deny when it is realized that low density housing prevents poor people from purchasing decent housing.

12

Modern Social Trends

WORLD WAR I

During World War I it fell to the lot of the Federal government in the United States to assume responsibility for the housing of workers in war industries. Two agencies were created to implement this program: The Housing Division of the Emergency Fleet Corporation, and the United States Housing Corporation. The Emergency Fleet Corporation, through loans to shipbuilding companies, completed some 9,000 family dwellings and 7,500 single-person accommodations. The United States Housing Corporation had planned some 25,000 units in 60 projects, but completed about 6,000 family units in 27 projects, none of which were ready before the war came to an end.

Services of the most talented professional men in architecture and planning were enlisted for the program. Among the large-scale projects were Yorkship Village at Camden, New Jersey, Atlantic Heights in Portsmouth, NewHampshire, Buchman in Chester, Pennsylvania, Union Gardens at Wilmington, Delware, and a number of developments at Bridgeport, Connecticut. It was a statutory requirement that projects built by these war agencies be sold immediately upon termination of the war. To implement this provision of the law the projects followed the general pattern of subdivision practice. Superblocks and common open spaces for recreation were absent, but the studied layout of residential streets and design of shopping centers offered a decided contrast with the practices to which most people had grown accustomed in their living environment. A distinct characteristic of the planning of all dwellings was a unit only two rooms in depth in contrast with the narrow, deep building typical of the usual restricted lot in the ordinary urban subdivision. The planning of these projects exerted a strong influence in the decade following the war.

THE GARDEN APARTMENT

Mr. Andrew J. Thomas, an architect who participated in the war program, was active in the postwar period. One of the early projects designed by him was a

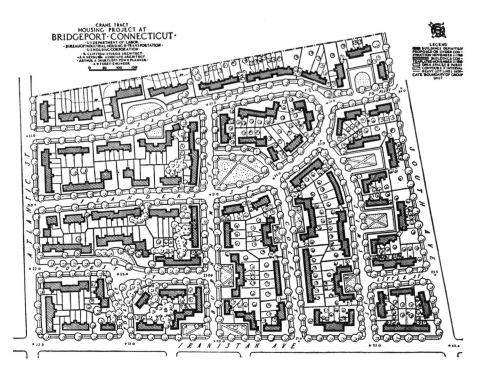

CRANE TRACT
HOUSING PROJECT AT
BRIDGEPORT·CONNECTICUT·
·U·S·DEPARTMENT·OF·LABOR·
·BUREAU·OF·INDUSTRIAL·HOUSING·&·TRANSPORTATION·
·U·S·HOUSING·CORPORATION·
·R·CLIPSTON·STURGIS·ARCHITECT·
·A·H·HEPBURN·ASSOCIATE·ARCHITECT·
·ARTHUR·A·SHURTLEFF·TOWN·PLANNER·
·A·N·TERRY·ENGINEER·

SEASIDE, Bridgeport, Connecticut

One of the World War I housing developments undertaken by the Federal Government, it included flats and single family residences at a density of about seventeen dwellings per acre and demonstrated the advantage of large-scale planning.

METROPOLITAN PROJECT, New York City
Andrew J. Thomas, Architect

One of the earliest large-scale apartment projects in this country. The strong habit of the single lot is revealed in the series of individual buildings repeated upon the large site.

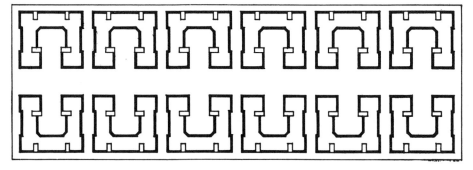

140

large-scale development built by the Metropolitan Life Insurance Company in Long Island City. In this project Mr. Thomas applied the simple principle of "two-room" deep dwelling units, with stairways serving two dwellings per floor. The units were grouped in a series of U-shaped buildings with a ground coverage of about 50 per cent of the lot area. The open courts faced the garden. It was a vast improvement over the small, enclosed light courts of the single lot but retained the characteristic narrow space between buildings.

Thomas carried this simple planning technique further in the development of buildings with various forms, using a basic unit of two and three dwelling units per stair. The essential contrast with previous planning was the relation of the buildings to the streets. Planning on the single narrow lot under the Tenement House Act of 1901 and before caused the building to be placed at right angles to the street—a narrow front and long depth. This forced all but the dwellings on the street front to face into a small courtyard, light-well, or narrow rear yard. With removal of the restrictions imposed by the narrow lot, large-scale planning permitted the arrangement of buildings with a broad front and shallow depth. The interior of the lot was opened up with improved exposure of all dwelling units toward the street and expanded interior court. This planning was hence-forth known as the "garden apartment."

HENRY WRIGHT

In 1926 the City Housing Corporation built Sunnyside Gardens, a large project planned by Henry Wright and Clarence Stein, on a 10-block site in Long Island. The architects applied the "garden apartment" in a simple perimeter form surrounding the interior garden. They also introduced the row, or group, house and the two-story flat—one dwelling above another with separate private entrances. The ground coverage was less than 30 per cent of the lot area.

Studies by Henry Wright about this time demonstrated the importance of comparative analysis in planning. He emphasized the necessity for a complete analysis of the costs that enter into housing. The planner and architect had been prone to detach their functions from that of management. Wright made clear that these functions could not be isolated and produce satisfactory housing; that improvement could not be expected unless plan-analysis was merged with experience in the management and maintenance of housing.

During this period much speculative building was producing the dreary, monotonous rows of cheap and poorly planned single-family and flat buildings that still curse so many of our cities. Henry Wright insisted upon the advantages of the group house, used at Sunnyside, to improve the planning of both dwellings and the space about them. The row, or group, house was not a revolutionary dwelling type. It was prevalent in all eastern cities. Baltimore and Philadelphia are famous for their row houses with clean, stone entrance stoops. But Wright demonstrated the principle of planning dwellings two rooms in depth rather than the tandem arrangement of rooms to which the usual row house had degenerated. He showed the improvement in land planning with the group house in comparison with detached units and their wasteful and useless side yards. Wright contributed much to the enlightenment that emerged in the 1920 decade and early thirties.

RADBURN

Inspired by the"garden city" idea, the City Housing Corporation acquired a vacant site in New Jersey within commuting distance of New York City. On this site Henry Wright and Clarence Stein planned the community of Radburn. This plan introduced the"super-block." In these blocks, ranging from 30 to 50 acres in size, through traffic was eliminated. Traffic streets surrounded rather than traversed the areas. Within them, single-family dwellings were grouped about cul-de-sac roads.

The houses were oriented in reverse of the conventional placement on the lot. Kitchens and garages faced the road, and living rooms turned toward the garden. Pathways provided uninterrupted pedestrian access to a continuous park strip, leading to large, common open spaces within the center of the super-block. Underpasses separated pedestrian walks from traffic roadways. The community earned the name of "The Town for the Motor Age."

Radburn allocated space for industry, shopping, and apartments, but permanent green space surrounding the town, typical of the English garden cities, was not incorporated. The residential character has been a prototype of sound community planning ever since.

HOUSING—AN INVESTMENT

Subsidy was a means to encourage the colonial expansion of this country, push railroads across the land, and smooth out the peaks and valleys of economic inequalities. It was used whenever necessity dictated. In 1926 it was introduced to housing with passage of the New York Housing Law, which established the State Board of Housing. This Act granted the privilege of tax exemption for a twenty-year period to limited-dividend companies engaged in housing within reach of the lower middle-class. The statutory ceiling on rents was $12.50 per room per month in the borough of Manhattan and $11.00 per room elsewhere. Investment in apartment development was encouraged by this legislation.

Fourteen projects, providing a total of nearly 6,000 dwellings, were undertaken in this program. The best known were three co-operative developments of the Amalgamated Clothing Workers, providing 625 apartments. In addition to the Housing Board projects in New York City, other limited-dividend and semi-philanthropic developments were undertaken. Phipps Houses, Inc., a veteran housing organization, built 344 apartments in four- and six-story walk-up and elevator buildings near Sunnyside Gardens in New York. In 1930 John D. Rockefeller, Jr., built the Paul Laurence Dunbar apartments in Harlem, 513 apartments designed for acquisition of the dwellings by the tenants.

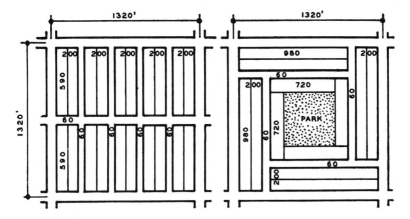

Above is a comparative study by Henry Wright to demonstrate the improvement which a modification in the typical gridiron street and block layout might provide. The sketch on the left is the usual street plan, that on the right the proposed replanning. With but slight loss of street frontage for subdivision of residential lots (the usual plan has 11,800 lineal feet of streets while the modified plan has 10,720 lineal feet), an interior park is gained and through traffic on all interior streets is eliminated.

Wright developed his "Case for the Row House" with studies like the one illustrated below. In this study the typical block layout with two-story flat buildings facing the street is compared with a revised plan using continuous rows of two-story flat units; the alley is eliminated, garage courts are consolidated at the end of each block, and a park space is gained in the center of the block accessible from all dwellings.

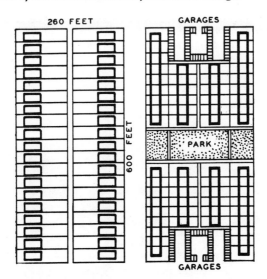

About this time the Julius Rosenwald Foundation built the Michigan Boulevard Gardens, also for blacks, on the south side of Chicago, and the Marshall Field Estate built Marshall Field Apartments on the near north side of Chicago. Chatham Village in Pittsburgh, built by the Buhl Foundation, was a two-story group house development planned by Henry Wright.

A Shopping Center
B Apartment Groups
C School
D Park Space

RADBURN, New Jersey
Clarence Stein and Henry Wright, Planners

The Radburn plan became synonymous with "the town of the motor age." In this plan the cul-de-sac (dead-end) residential streets became service roads rather than traffic ways, the house being reversed so that the living rooms face on the rear gardens with pedestrian paths leading to the continuous park space.

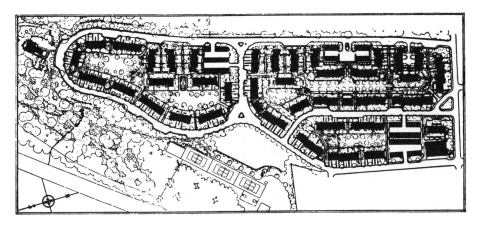

CHATHAM VILLAGE, Pittsburgh
Ingham and Boyd, Architects

A limited-divided project originally planned for 300 units within reach of the
$2,200–3,600 per year income group. The first stage of development was 128 dwellings.
The density is about 12 families per acre in two-story group houses, demonstrating the
theory of Henry Wright who espoused the cause of the group house on urban land which
had not yet reached the high levels of many areas. This project was built as an investment
by the Buhl Foundation.

These projects did not produce speculative profits but were sound investments that served a high social purpose. This purpose is not nourished by
irresponsible interests concerned with quick turnover of capital and unlimited
profits, nor does it thrive on exploitation and speculation in land, buildings, and
people.

During this period good planning was demonstrated to be economical
planning. Twenty-five years prior, the typical tenement covered 85 per cent of
a narrow, deep lot. More than half the rooms either had no light or peered into
dingy light-wells. Open space about the dwelling was either the paved traffic
street or a shabby refuse-ridden rear yard. The energetic talents of such architects as Ernest Flagg, Grosvenor Atterbury, Andrew Thomas, Henry Wright,
Clarence Stein, and Frederick Ackerman served to bring a vast change in all this.
Land coverage was reduced to 50 per cent or less, and space was planned to
enhance the environment and provide room for recreation. Careful planning and
better interior arrangement of rooms reduced waste space within buildings and
eliminated unnecessary corridors and halls. Attention was given to appropriate
size and use of rooms rather than the greatest number of people that could be
loaded on a given site.

The importance of the period we have been discussing is not the quality of
planning as a standard to which we aspire today, but rather as a comparison with
the unwholesome planning it replaced and the processes which brought it about.

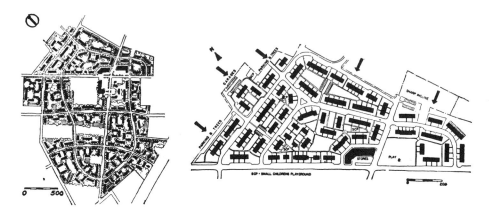

BUCKINGHAM, Virginia

One of the earliest large-scale rental developments undertaken in the FHA program, Buckingham is located just outside Washington D.C., for "white collar" workers in the nation's crowded capital. Designed by Henry Wright, Allen Kamstra, and Albert Lueders, it was planned for 2,000 units on a 100-acre site. The first stage (shown in detail) comprised 622 dwellings on 30 acres. The land cost was 25 cents per square foot and permitted low density—about 20 families per acre—with a building coverage of about 20 per cent of the land area. Approximately 13% of the area is in streets. Dwellings are two-story group houses and flats.

Complete disregard for housing standards and the desire for profit regardless of the exploitation it entailed had produced high density, excessive land coverage, and decidedly bad housing. The theory that these evils were essentially good business was exploded. Good planning was discovered to be an effective instrument to compete with bad planning. When laws were enacted to curb irresponsible building of slums, the road was cleared for good planning with financial benefits as well as the restoration of social values.

The period of activity during the twenties and early thirties did not solve our urban housing ills but it did provide a foundation upon which future progress could be continued. Building companies became conscious of the advantages of investment in housing. Large-scale planning opened the opportunity for arranging buildings on land so that all dwellings were well located on the site. As a permanent investment such factors were important. Good planning was becoming a good investment. Release from the long, narrow lot permitted greater efficiency in planning, lower land coverage, better dwelling units, more space for light, air, and recreation, and safer investment. Permanent values were built in by good planning.

Mr. Charles F. Lewis, Director of the Buhl Foundation which built and is managing Chatham Village in Pittsburgh, said in 1937:

Capital is frankly challenged by this unusal opportunity for sound and productive use of its funds.

Essentially this will be an investment and not a speculative use of capital. . .

No less has it been demonstrated by the so-called limited dividend companies, from Boston in 1871 to Pittsburgh in 1934, that limited dividends pay. I refer you specifically to the remarkable success of the City and Surburban Homes Company of New York, founded in 1896 by Mr. R. Fulton Cutting and associates. After years of operation, in 1933 in the midst of the depression, this company could boast assets of nearly $10,000,000, a surplus of more than $1,380,000, and net earnings of from $263,000 to $445,000 per year through four depression years. Its average annual dividend rate, from 1899 to 1939, was 4.65 per cent. Or let us take six non-co-operative apartment projects built in New York City under the New York State Housing Board. All have been consistent dividend payers in good times and bad. Or let us take, in the city of Washington, the Washington Sanitary Improvement Company, which with assets of nearly $1,500,000 can boast that from 1897 to 1923 it paid an annual dividend of 5 per cent, and from then on straight through the depression, of 6 per cent. Or the Washington Sanitary Housing Company which has paid 5 per cent per annum without interruption since 1927. While Chatham Village in Pittsburgh has not yet published earnings statements, those statements when released will give further evidence of the investment soundness of the large-scale housing enterprise on the limited-dividend basis.[1]

Every individual in the city has a home. Some may be rooms in a lodging-house or a hotel, others fine houses on large estates. Some are slums. Whether the home is a hovel or a mansion, every person has one. Dwellings of the people occupy nearly three-quarters of the urban area. The economic equation by which the people acquire and maintain a place to live measures the social and physical health of a community. The economics of housing is the base upon which cities rest. It is the foundation on which the social superstructure is built.

If we want to see the real city, we do not confine our view to the great skyscrapers, the shopping promenade, or the park and boulevard. To see the city, we look at the dwellings of the people. We see how people live, their streets of homes, the environment in which they raise their families, the children who will be the fellow-countrymen and neighbors of our children a generation hence.

It is this view that gives us direction toward the city of the future. When we comprehend this aspect of the city, we can guide more accurately the tools with which we shape the urban environment.

THE GREAT DEPRESSION

On the heels of the building boom during the prosperity decade of the twenties came the crash of 1929 and the decade of depression that followed. Financial credit dried up, building stopped abruptly, and unemployment brought

[1] *Opportunities for Building Rental Properties*.Conference on local residential Construction, Chamber of Commerce of U.S., Washington, D.C., November 17, 1937.

widespread privation to millions of families. As the depression gained momentum, economic and social chaos followed in its wake. Marginal investments in stocks evaporated into thin air. The "water" that had been poured into building investments during the craze of the boom was drained off, and "ownership" changed hands in rapid succession as the level lowered. Homes on farms and in the cities were foreclosed at an alarming rate. Real estate foreclosures jumped from 68,100 in 1926 to 248,700 in 1932.

The complete state of despair made it imperative for the government to act. In an effort to stem the tide, President Hoover called his Conference of Home Building and Home Owership in 1931. This conference revealed many of the problems that beset the nation and laid the groundwork for action which ensued in subsequent years. Some 28 states enacted moratoria on mortgage foreclosures in 1931 and 1932. This device relieved the hysteria but only postponed the solution. The Emergency Relief and Construction Act of 1932 created the Reconstruction Finance Corporation. This agency was empowered to loan government funds to bolster the faltering economy.

The tide of national collapse forced the government to assume increased responsibility for the helpless economy, and, beginning in 1933, the Congress created a series of agencies in rapid succession. These acts brought into focus a fact that had been almost unwittingly overlooked: the people of the United States had no inventory of the national welfare, the assets and liabilities of a going concern dealing in democratic enterprise. The blessing of abundant natural resources, the accident of favorable geographic location, and the aggressive enterprise of a free people had brought fortune and a position of world leadership to this country. This achievement had blinded the people to the corollary of great industrial and financial empires—the precipitation of social and economic hardships that filter into the lives of many in society. The Great Depression lifted the veil on this scene and disclosed the gap which had formed between fortune and stability. It was apparent that the country must take stock of its resources in order to measure the future prospects for its enterprise.

THE PLANNING DILEMMA

At no other time had there been a more pressing need for the benefit of city planning that the years of the Great Depression. Nor could there have been more convincing evidence of its absence. Much lip-service had been rendered the cause of planning in previous years, and a small but vocal profession had grown up around this theme. Yet cities were unprepared for action when the time was ripe.

The state of the Union was desperate at the beginning of the thirties. A program for action was imperative. There was encouragement when the Administrator of Public Works appointed in National Planning Board in July, 1933. For the first time in the history of this country the advantages of research and analysis of our great natural resources were available for the general welfare. Prior to this time it was customary for separate offices of the government to collect facts; it was now provided that these facts should be correlated and thus become the pattern for appropriate action by the respective agencies of government.

The National Planning Board became the National Resources Board by executive order of President Roosevelt in June 1934. It was the purpose of the Board "to prepare and present to the President a program and plan of procedure dealing with the physical, social, governmental, and economic aspects of public policies for the development and use of land, water, and other national resources and such related subjects as may from time to time be referred to the Board by the President." The National Resources Committee succeeded the Board in 1935, and in July 1939 all these functions were transferred to the National Resources Planning Board.

The Board and its predecessors were organized on a regional basis. Probably the most significant work was performed by way of encouragement of planning at local levels and technical assistance to local planning agencies. Regional, state, and city planning were reviewed and organized, comprehensive reports on the state of natural resources and recommended plans for appropriate conservation and use were made, developments and the relative importance of technological changes were recorded, and valuable data were assembled on urban growth and population.[2]

In 1943 the National Resources Planning Board was discontinued and its functions have since been performed by various committees of Congress.

The work of the National Resources Planning Board and its predecessors was directed at issues of national scope. The resistance to planning these agencies confronted was reflected at the local level. Cities were unprepared when the depression struck, the few exceptions emphasizing the general absence of plans. Faced with an immediate opportunity to establish permanent improvements in their environment, there was little evidence that the prople had concerned themselves with the question of their future urban development.

The issues of emergency and sound planning were confused. Building and maintaining the city constitute a complex and a vital problem. It requires planning to cope with this problem. The housing program during the depression demonstrated the tragic results of its absence. Subdivisions sprawled across the city without consideration of a plan into which the urban development could be integrated with the future use of land and become an effective means for improvement of community welfare. The public housing program was too frequently interpreted as an opportunity to get rid of some isolated eyesore or festering slum that pricked the civic pride.

By the time that cities had become aware of their plight, the economic cost of blight, and the social hazard of slums, there was no time to plan. That would have to wait until the depression had spent itself and prosperity had returned. Had civic leadership glanced back upon the history of city development it would have been abundantly clear that planning can never wait. The course of human

---

[2] See Bibliography, Part 2, for partial list of publications.

BALDWIN HILLS VILLAGE, Los Angeles

An attractive large-scale rental development of the early 1940's, Baldwin Hills Village, consisted of 627 dwellings in one-and two-story group houses and flats on an outlying 80-acre tract. The low land price $2,300 per acre, permits low density, about 8 families per acre, and a coverage of only 7.3 per cent of the land. A feature of this project is the private patio for about two-thirds of all the dwellings. It will be noticed in the plan that the boulevard along the north boundary (botton of plan) is separated from the project by a park-strip and a service road from which the various garage courts are accessible. Additional parking space is provided by indented parking areas along the service drive and along minor boundary streets. Small playgrounds for children are distributed about the development in addition to the "village green" in the center.

The aerial view below reveals that the standards of planning and space in Baldwin Hills Village did not influence the later conventional subdivision of land about the periphery.

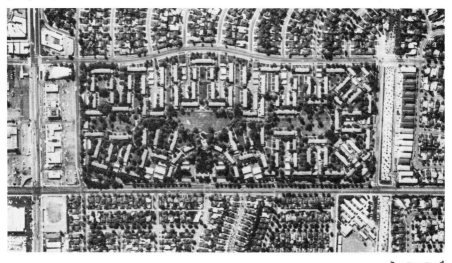

Designed by Reginald Johnson, Lewis Wilson, Edwin E. Merrill, and Robert Alexander, Architects

150

affairs marches steadily on and the direction of its course is determined by the degree of planning which precedes. it. When goals are set, they can be reached; when they are absent, the urban community drifts like a ship without a compass. The goals have not yet been considered, and our cities are still adrift.

THE GREENBELT TOWNS

As a component part of the Federal government's search for ways and means to cope with the modern city and its living environment, the Resettlement Administration planned four "greenbelt towns" beginning in 1935. They were satellite communities near large cities. The designs were inspired by Howard's Garden City idea, but they were not planned as self-contained towns; they were more like dormitory villages, the sources of employment for the residents being in the near-by cities. Each was surrounded by a belt of permanent open space part of which could be farmed or gardened. A full complement of community facilities was included in each town—shopping, schools, and recreation space.

GREENBELT, MARYLAND

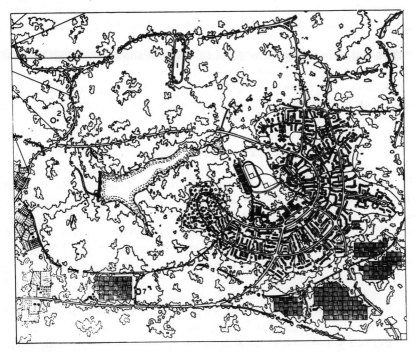

1	Water Tower	3	Picnic Center and Lake	6	Rural Homesteads
2	Disposal Plant and In-cinerator	4	Community Center	7	Allotment Gardens
		5	Store Group		

Greenbelt, Maryland. Greenbelt, Maryland, a development on a 2,100-acre site about 25 minutes' drive by automobile from Washington, D.C., includes 712 dwellings in group houses and 288 in apartments, a total of 1,000 units occupying an area of 250 acres. There are 500 garages. The sixteen-room elementary school is jointly used as a community center, and the shopping center includes space for post office, food stores, a drug store, a dentist's and a doctor's office, a 600-seat theater, and such service shops as shoe repair, laundry, tailor, barber, and beauty shops. There are a bus terminal, a garage and repair shop, a fire station, and a gas station. The recreation facilities include an athletic field, picnic grounds, and an artificial lake. The super-block is used, each block containing about 120 dwellings with interior play areas. Underpasses provide continuous pedestrian circulation without crossing main roads. The commercial and community center, in the approximate center of the plan, reduces to a minimum the walking distance from all dwellings.

WORLD WAR II BEGINS A NEW DECADE

Then came another war, and a stroke of irony marked the affairs of human conduct. Planning assumed proportions never before conceived in history. With destruction of civilization a grim prospect, the scale of planning was gargantuan, staggering the imagination, even in retrospect. However, it was military planning.

When the ominous spread of Nazi domination engulfed central Europe and threatened another world war, Congress enacted the National Defense Bill of June 1940. Industry turned its attention to production of war materials, and the Lanham Act authorized funds for housing workers in the defense plants. Numerous government agencies entered the housing program. In July 1940, the Office of Housing Co-ordinator was established to determine the need in places of acute shortage and allocate Federal funds to the various agencies.

New construction by private enterprise insured by FHA was stepped up, HOLC assisted the conversion of existing facilities, the low-rent program under USHA was stopped, and 100 per cent loans were extended to local housing authorities to build defense housing. The Public Buildings Administration, Defense Homes Corporation, and Martime Commission undertook construction of large-scale permanent government housing, and the Federal Works Agency launched a large program of prefabricated temporary dwellings.

With the attack on Pearl Harbor on December 7, 1941, all the energy of the nation was directed to the successful prosecution of the war. Peacetime and defense housing were supplanted by a vast program of war housing, and huge plants were constructed to build ships, airplanes, and armaments.

In February 1942, all Federal housing agencies were consolidated in the National Housing Agency. The National Housing Act was amended to include Title VI, providing insurance by FHA of 90 per cent loans, amortized in 25 years, for housing built by "operative" builders for sale or rent to war workers. The necessity to conserve materials was critical. The floor area of dwellings and the critical materials used in them were rigidly restricted. The Lanham Act was amended to provide for the construction of temporary dwellings by the Federal government.

More than 800,000 new dwellings were built and about 200,000 existing units converted by private enterprise, for a total estimated cost of $4,000,000,000. Nearly 550,000 family dwellings and 170,000 dormitory units were built, and 50,000 existing structures converted into family dwellings, through the direct operations of the Federal government. There were, in addition, about 80,000 "stop-gap" shelters provided in the form of trailers to permit mobility for shifts as changing needs dictated. The cost of this program was some $2,300,000,000 for a total of 850,000 living units.

It has been estimated that migration of industrial workers to war jobs created a need for housing some 9,000,000 families. War work was distributed in all parts of the country, but the most pressing need was in large centers for the tremendous new industrial plants. Individual projects of 5,000 units were built in such places as Willow Run near Detroit; Norfolk, Virginia; Vancouver, Washington; and San Diego and San Francisco, California. The largest single operation was 10,000 dwellings for the Kaiser shipyards at Portland, Oregon.

The influx of great numbers of workers and their families strained every urban service. Housing was not complete without new streets, utility systems, parks and playgrounds, theaters, shops and markets, and restaurants. Whole new communities were created in a few months, and war production was sustained.

The war was won. The goal had been clear—the survival of freedom. Planning guided the campaign. The production and distribution of goods, materials, food, weapons, and manpower were planned. It was necessary, and well done.

Thus ended another paradox in the course of human events. While military planning was winning a great campaign, planning for the peace to come was abandoned. It will be remembered that the National Resources Planning Board died during the conflict, and the planning process, with which our institutions were saved in war, was denounced as an enemy of freedom. We have need to learn from yesterday so as to prepare today for a better tomorrow.

RECENT HUD PROGRAMS

Congressional actions affecting HUD have changed over the years. Whereas under the old system, Federal grants were used for urban renewal, such funding is now part of the "Community Block Grants" allocated to local communities. For instance, in the area of housing the builders are granted funds if they produce housing for the low and middle income groups. This is a form of subsidy that is supposed to permit the builders to charge a lesser rent. Title 8, most used for the development of housing for elderly persons, provides for rent subsidies more directly. Funds are issued either to the local Housing Authority or to a private landlord when the rent is greater than 25 percent of the tenant's income.

Finanacial assistance is also given to local building officials to assist in the rehabilitation of deteriorating buildings. Costs for much of the work, if the residents are paying rent that exceeds a quarter of their income, is paid for by the city with funds provided by HUD.

Some states, such as California, have enacted "tax increment" financing to assist cities to pay for their own programs. This method freezes taxes paid to all local governmental agencies, including the counties, school districts, and all other special districts. The improved facilities on the land thereafter are assessed at the newly appraised value, which is usually much above the tax charged formerly. The difference between the old tax and the new tax defrays the cost of the bonds (tax allocation bonds) which are issued by the local agency to cover the cost of the renewal. The districts defined for the tax freeze are often much larger than the area within which the improvements are made.

As a result of Proposition 13 in California the renewal program is virtually a dead issue there since taxes have been fixed at a 1975 level and are limited to 1 percent of the appraised value of the land and improvements. New techniques will have to be devised if the California's cities are to maintain their physical structures. The private sector may have to be enlisted toward this end.

The Housing and Community Development Act of 1977

Purpose.   This Act provides for alleviation of physical and economic distress through the stimulation of private investment and community revitalization in areas with population outmigration or a stagnating or declining tax base. The money must be spent on programs that would give maximum benefits to low or moderate income families or aid in the prevention or elimination of blight.

The Act extends the Community Development Block Grant Program (created by the Housing and Community Development Act of 1974) and authorizes up to $3.5 billion in fiscal 1978, $3.65 billion in fiscal 1979, and $3.8 billion in fiscal 1980. Up to $400 million is authorized during each of the three years to assist severely distressed cities and urban counties through neighborhood reclamation. Twenty-five percent of the funds available for action grants is designated for cities under 50,000 population that are not central cities of a standard metropolitan area.

One primary goal of the Act was to provide 400,000 units of housing for low and moderate income persons in fiscal 1978, including 350,000 new and rehabilitated units under Section 8 of the rental subsidy program and 20,000 units under the state housing finance agencies. The remaining 30,000 units were to be conventional housing. Thirty-five million dollars was set aside for public housing modernization. These funds were targeted primarily for capital projects that will promote energy conservation and correct health and safety code violations. Six hundred and sixty-five million dollars was for public housing operating subsidies. About thirteen million dollars of this will defray the exceptionally high utility costs that were incurred in the winter of 1977.

The community development block grant replaced a consolidation of the previously existing narrow categorical grant programs for aid to urban areas (e.g., open space, water and sewer, beautification and model cities programs). One hundred million dollars has been appropriated for each of the three years (1978, 1979, 1980) for phasing out programs begun under the old categorical grant programs.

Cities now can choose how the amount of funds they receive under the community development block grant program will be determined: under the old formula or a new one. The old formula weighs population twice, while amount of housing, overcrowding, and poverty, are counted once. It favors western and southern regions which have growing populations. The new formula counts age of housing 2½ times, poverty 1½ times, and growth lag once. Age of housing refers to pre-1940 housing stock, and growth lag is defined as the extent to which a locality has fallen below the average population growth rate of all metropolitan cities; this formula would most benefit older cities, many of which are in the northwest and midwest.

Application Requirements.   Communities are required to include in their application for block grants a summary of housing as well as community development needs, and a program to improve conditions for low and moderate income persons to remain in or return to their community. (The HUD Secretary is allowed to waive some application requirements for some small communities where the application does not involve a comprehensive community development program.) Citizen participation is required in the formulation of the block grant proposals.

Section 8.   Section 8 provides for government rent subsidies to low-income persons. Eligiblity is limited to families with incomes up to 80% of the median income of a particular area. The law also requires that at least 30% of the families have incomes not exceeding 50% of an area's median family income. Participating families are required to contribute not less than 15% nor more than 25% of their total income to rent, which is not to exceed by more than 10% the fair market rent as established by HUD. The government makes up the difference between the family's required rental share and the actual rental price.

HUD enters into a 40-years contract with public housing agencies or a 30-year contract with private developers who provide newly constructed, rehabilitated, or adequate existing housing. Public housing agencies are required to establish 1) tenant selection, 2) procedures for prompt payment of rents and evictions for non-payment, 3) effective tenant-management relations to assure safety and adequate project maintenance, and 4) viable homeownership opportunities.

Section 312 provides 3% loans for rehabilitation of residental and business properties to residents of areas designated in an area's community block grant application. There were no new applications for 1978 because $70 million was available in carryover funds. (This program supplements and supports block grant housing rehabilitation efforts.)

Miscellaneous Relevant Items Under Title II

Mobile Homes.   Increases to $15,000 from $12,500 the ceiling on FHA Mortgage insurance for mobile homes.

Urban Homesteading.   Increases to $15 million from $5 million the authorization for fiscal 1978 for the urban homesteading demonstration program

Property Improvements.   Increases to $15,000 from $10,000 the maximum loan or advance credit for home improvements insurable under the Title I property improvements and mobile home loan insurance program.

Title I Amendment.   Authorizes the HUD secretary to make a lump sum payment of a community's grant allotment to allow the community to establish a revolving loan fund at a private financial institution.

The following private housing programs are included in this section because there is evidence that such housing programs can be very successfully implemented in smaller cities.

Neighborhood Housing Services Program.   Organizing citizens, city government, and private lenders in a team effort for neighborhood preservation, the Neighborhood Housing Services program offers a revolving loan fund for home improvements in sound but deteriorating neighborhoods. The Urban Reinvestment Task Force, a partnership between the Federal Home Loan Bank Board and the Department of Housing and Urban Development provides technical assistance to local governments interested in establishing an NHS. Once the program is operational the Task Force involvement ceases except when additional aid is requested.

Systematic code enforcement programs are used in most NHS programs. Capital improvements of code enforcement are funded by the city. NHS operating costs are funded entirely through local sources and local contributions supply much of the high risk fund. A local commitment of $25,000 is required from financial institutions to fund the development process.

Neighborhood residents control the program. Financial institutions participate in order to protect existing investments in the neighborhood, to lessen redlining allegations, to increase deposits. Thus, because of a strong city and neighborhood commitment to the area, they perceive less of a risk in investing in it. Local government paricipates because the program provides the opportunity to leverage public investment in older neighborhoods by stimulating private lending in these areas.

Control is vested in a board of directors of a private, non-profit corporation that consists primarily of citizens and financial institutions. Governmental representation is usually limited to one member from the local city government.

Each NHB office is staffed by three persons: a director, an associate director, and a clerical-administrative assistant. Each program develops its own priorities and policies. Although the Task Force may provide technical assistance in helping to establish operating procedures, important decisions that affect the loan fund are made by the NHS board.

Section 235—Mortgage Subsidy.   This is a program designed to provide financial assistance to low-and moderate-income families in achieving home ownership. The assistance is provided in the form of monthly payments made by the Federal government to the mortgagee, whose interest is reduced to as low as five percent. The homeowner must contribute at least 20% of his adjusted gross monthly income to the monthly mortgage payment. To be eligible for assistance payments, a family must have an adjusted family income that does not exceed 100% of the median income for an area, with appropriate adjustments for smaller or larger families.

Section 8-515—Renter Subsidy.   This program is administered by the Farmers Home Administration. It provides permanent financing at market or subsidized interest rates to eligible borrowers for building low and moderate income multi-family housing in non-metropolitan areas. Sponsors may be a public or private entity and must meet certain criteria. Recently the 515 program has been coupled with the Department of Housing and Urban Developments Section 8 program to obtain greater subsidies for Section 515 tenants. Under the Section 8 program, tenants pay no more than 25% of family income toward rent (in special cases, 15%). The remainder of the rent is paid through a housing assistance payment by HUD or a local Public Housing Agency.

Conventional Public Housing.   This is a program to help public agencies provide decent, safe, and sanitary housing for low-income families at rents the tenants can afford. HUD provides financial and technical assistance to local housing authorities to help them plan, build, and operate low-rent public housing projects. Federal annual contributions cover the debt service on local authority bonds sold to pay for the development or acquisition of public housing. HUD also grants preliminary loans to the local authority for planning and temporary loans for building low-rent housing.

HOUSING IN OTHER LANDS

While much of the material presented in this chapter deals with housing programs in the United States, it is important to realize that the same problems that face Americans also confront people in other parts of the world.

Densities are high in parts of the United States, mainly in some of the eastern seaboard cities. But, compared with Kowloon (Hong Kong) the densities pale greatly. There is one portion of Kowloon that may be the most densely populated place on earth, having 4,000 persons per acre. This equals approximately 10.5 square feet of land per person.

The authorities in Hong Kong are meeting the problems of their area with vast public housing programs. There is an extensive drive to provide decent shelter as a substitute for the many squatter settlements that dot public land throughout the colony. The government is expending great effort to meet the rapidly growing population, which seems to require a new town every year.

Brazil, faced with the flight of people from the rural areas to the cities, has had to deal with "favellas," slums that occupy public land both on the barren hillsides and over the tidal areas of the waterfronts. Efforts to keep people from coming to the already overcrowded cities by improving living conditions in the rural areas have not as yet had any impact. The development of the Amazon River Basin by a vast road building program and improved rural housing have not stabilized the population.

People's Republic of China.   Cities in all underdeveloped countries face the same problem. The People's Republic of China has a history of both rural and urban slums. The need for minimal housing is so great that it will take years to meet even basic housing needs. In the cities, a great effort is being made to limit family size to two children. In rural areas where the need for labor is still great, the government has made no effort to limit family size. In addition the government discourages emigration to the cities.

The housing program in Peking is integrally related to the new subway system that has been constructed under the old city wall. The high rise buildings under construction when completed will form another type of city wall. Replacing the substandard dwellings in the area, these edifices will have the same visual impact on the city that Tien En Men Square now has: both are dedicated to monumentality.

Financing the hosing in the People's Republic is accomplished through grants from the Central Government (in Peking); by grants from the local Regional Governments; through the profits made by industry or commerce, including agriculture; and finally by individual savings. The latter approach is, in general, discouraged since it places a drain on the efficient utilization of material and labor resources.

Before any building program can be initiated there must be a General Plan to assure efficient development. The housing and employment centers must be carefully linked so that employees do not have to travel by bicycle more than 30 minutes from home to work.

Hong Kong.   Public housing in Hong Kong is constructed and managed by the Housing Authority. The authority was set up in 1973 to bring together various departments that had previously been responsible for different facets of the task. It is a statutory body whose executive arm, the Housing Department, has a staff of about 6,000.

Besides having responsibility for planning and constructing new estates, the authority is responsible for controlling squatters, and clearing land required for development. It also advises the Governor on all matters of housing policy.

New Housing in Peking

More recently, the authority accepted the task of over-seeing the government's widely welcomed Home Ownership Scheme, under which 42,000 flats will be built over from 1978 to 1986. These will be sold at cost price to tenants of public housing or less well-to-do families in the private sector. Interest rates will be between 7½ and 9 per cent, with a standard repayment period of 15 years and a minimum of 10 percent of the purchase price required as a down payment.

By the end of 1977, the authority was managing 64 public housing estates that had been built during the last 24 years. They are mainly in the urban areas of Hong Kong Island, Kowloon, and Tsuen Wan and house nearly 1.9 million people—about 43 per cent of the population. A further 20 estates were under construction to provide about 30,000 flats for 200,000 people by 1978-9. Because of the shortage of land in Hong Kong and the large population, most public housing has had to be built in multi-story blocks. Current construction is designed to provide by the mid-1980's permanent self-contained homes with amenities to virtually every eligible family in Hong Kong.

PLANNING FOR THE ELDERLY[3]

One of the most pressing problems has always been the housing of the elderly. This is a world-wide problem and many nations have taken steps in one way or

[3] Based in part on an unpublished paper by Sylvia Stern, U.C.L.A., 1978.

another to meet this need. The needs of the elderly vary greatly. Some elderly persons are ambulatory, while others are infirm, and a wide range exists in between. Sometimes, special care is required in addition to a decent living environment. Both public and private solutions have been suggested to meet the housing needs of the elderly. The quality of the care at private facilities varies greatly, as does the cost.

The ambulatory aged have numerous resources at their disposal. While many have grown children with whom they could live, age and interest differences often make it impossible for the two generations to live together harmoniously.

Some elderly have joined large retirement communities. These communities serve a limited age group, mostly persons over 50 who have relatively large financial resources.

The housing of healthy ambulatory persons constitutes today's main challenge in planning for the elderly. The infirm, in general, are confined to institutional care facilities of one type or another. But decent housing for the ever increasing number of persons who have contributed to the social and economic well-being of their communities during most of their lives has yet to be accomplished. Our civilization may well be judged by how sympathetically we respond to this segment of the population.

Until the early part of the twentieth century most of the countries of the world relegated the indigent aged to "poor farms." Certainly little money was spent on resolving the problems of the aged. Further, there was no differentiation of the problems of the aged from those of the poor. It was only after 1920 that there began to be recognition of the special needs of the elderly.

The patterns and problems of the aged are similar throughout the industrialized world. The breakup of families for various reasons, whether in rural or urban areas, has left the elderly without any anchor. With the advent of social security, retirement pensions, and welfare programs, families feel even less responsibility for their elders. The elders share this attitude, not wanting to be a burden on their children, opting, insofar as possible, for the maintenance of their independence.

Since World War II there has been a growing concern for the needs of the elderly, not the least aspect of which has involved their housing. There is currently, in almost all of the nations of the world, an acceptance of some responsibility for ensuring the welfare of the aging population, especially for that portion of the population that can not afford decent housing. During the past 30 years national governments have passed considerable legislation in behalf of the housing needs of poor elderly persons.

The United States Approach.   In 1950 the first National Conference on Aging was held in Washington D.C. In that year the problems of the elderly began to assume national importance. In 1961, President Eisenhower called for another national conference. Over 2,500 delegates met to define the circumstances, needs, and opportunities of elderly citizens and to find means to improve living conditions for them. The most important conclusion of this conference was that the problems of housing for the aged is everybody's problem.

In 1976, President Ford asked Congress to join him in improving government programs servicing the elderly. There was no doubt that the over eleven percent of the total population that constituted the elderly then needed assistance and that the greatest part of the problem was economic. In 1977, six out of ten older Americans had incomes near or below the poverty level. More than twenty percent lived in substandard housing. These same persons are faced with double-digit inflation and fixed income that cannot adjust to the increases in the cost of living.

American fascination with "bigness" runs over into the provision of housing for the elderly. It seems, public or private, the ensemble must be large to be "efficient," even though this so-called efficiency often translates into endless mediocrity. The public housing facilities for the elderly, with some exceptions, are in high-rise buildings. These complexes are large enough to make the cost of operating them manageable. The clients are normally persons in the same age and health category.

Current U.S. Housing Programs for the Elderly.   The Older Americans Act of 1965 was the basis of all housing legislation for the elderly. It stated that all older people are entitled to suitable housing independently selected, designed and located in accordance with their special needs, "and available at costs they can afford."

   1.   *Federal Housing and Community Development Programs*
   a. Housing and Community Development Act of 1974: This Act created the Title I Block Grant Program for community development that places emphasis on local or community decision-making with regard to the expenditure of Block Grant funds.
   b. Senior Citizen Housing Programs: Section 8—Housing Assistance Payments Program (HAPP) is the counterpart of the European consumer subsidy, and is the nation's principal housing program.
       Section 202—Senior Citizen Direct Housing Loan—provides long-term direct, Federal construction and permanent mortgagage loans at below market interest rates for construction or substantial rehabilitation of rental housing for the elderly and handicapped.

Foster Homes for the Elderly.   A specialized service is provided by the Foster Home Program in Bucks County, Pennsylvania.[4] The program is designed for people over 60 who do not need the skilled care of a nursing home but who cannot or should not live alone. It was begun in 1961 by Peggy O'Neill, who developed the program after trying to cope with the problems of a long waiting list for an

---

[4] Denise P. Frank and Michael J. Frank, "Planning," publication of the American Society of Planning Officials, Sept., 1978, p. 340.

overcrowded county home for the aged. Many of those in the home already had been institutionalized unnecessarily. They needed only minimal care and supervision.

The service, known as the Foster Home Program, started with a grant from the Pennsylvania Department of Labor and Industry. Originally conceived as a way to provide housing for the elderly in a family setting, the program has become an interim care arrangement as much as a housing arrangement.

Unlike house-sharing programs, the Bucks County program is supported by casework services and backup facilities, which are the primary reasons for its success. Caseworkers help their elderly clients with financial matters, make sure they receive any necessary medical and psychiatric attention, and provide ongoing counseling. Foster home residents who need skilled care and are financially eligible have priority for admission to the county nursing home.

The Bucks County program benefits not only the elderly but also the proprietors of the foster homes and the community as well. The elderly benefit because they remain in the community rather than being institutionalized and segregated. Follow-up contact by caseworkers assures that their arrangements are suitable. A different home is usually found within two weeks if conflicts arise or the elderly person is being given improper care.

Foster home proprietors benefit, too. Often these individuals are themselves retired or elderly. Some of them are "empty-nesters" who provide adult foster care rather than entering the labor market. In addition to the companionship they provide, they receive supplemental income to help them with home maintenance costs and rising taxes. The fact that the proprietors know that they are not responsible for all their residents' needs help make the program work. Their contract requires that they provide only room, board, laundry, and basic supervision.

Last, the Foster Home Program has advantages for the community or the agency that provides elderly care. The county nursing home is free to serve the elderly who need skilled care. Furthermore, it is much less expensive to shelter a person in a foster home than in a nursing home.

International Efforts.   European experience yields several major findings relevant to the United States.[5]

First, consumer housing subsidies in the form of housing allowances, rent rebates, and rent differentials have been an integral part of the European solution of the housing problem of the elderly. They cope *directly* with the special hardships of the elderly poor. They provide accommodation for the elderly not only through new construction, which is necessarily limited, but also by using existing housing.

Second, production housing subsidies, amounting to roughly two-thirds of total West European housings subsidies, constitute the main financial thrust of

[5] Excerpts from an unpublished paper by Sylvia Stern U.C.L.A., 1978.

government policy. Some form of production subsidies or incentives is considered essential as long as critical housing shortages exist. They also ensure the construction of an adequate supply of cluster housing designed for the elderly that is integrated with neighborhoods having a normal cross section of the population. Effective land use planning on the part of the local government has been a further important ingredient in the production approach.

Warm Climate and Beautiful Environment. Côte d' Azur is a very popular retirement area. In towns like Nice more than a quarter of the population is of pensionable age. In Portugal, Spain, Malta, and Cyprus there are flourishing residential developments aimed specifically at attracting retired people from northern Europe. This migration, which includes people from many nations, has taken similar forms wherever it has emerged despite the cultural differences of the retired individuals. It is mainly attracting people who had live most of their lives in cities. Since indications are that the popularity of the movement will continue for years; the involved must prepare themselves for coping with the special health and social needs resulting from the increasing migration.

Canada.   Since 1946 an estimated 90 percent of all new housing produced specifically for Canada's elderly has been built with the assistance provided by the Federal Government's National Housing Act.

The majority of this accommodation has been provided in just the past ten years, reflecting vastly increased Federal funding allocations for housing and new legislative incentives to stimulate the sponsorship of developments to serve elderly persons and low-income families.

The United Kingdom.   In the U.K. the local authority has a statutory duty to review the housing needs of its area from time to time and to provide housing when it is not being provided by private enterprise. Local councils initiate new ideas about housing and often press the Minister of Housing for supporting legislation. This initiative and pressure from below is a common feature of politics in the U.K. For example, the City of Birmingham promoted a private Act of Parliament to obtain powers to pay rent allowances to private tenants long before this idea became part of national policy.

In England there are no income limits on admission to public housing projects, thus there are no income tests that can force a tenant to leave subsequently. The words "the Working Classes" were deleted from the titles and texts of all housing statues in 1949. The result is that the tenants of the public housing stock represent a much wider spectrum of the population than is the case in the U.S.

Looking for a Better Way.   Some lessons can be learned from the British approach. One of them may be found at Roehampton, a housing estate within the county of London but outside of the central city. There the housing for the elderly is in small groups of one story row houses. There are about 20 units in each

ROEHAMPTON ESTATES, London
Housing for the aged is in the foreground.

of the complexes. They are situated in a garden environment close to an elementary school and the neighborhoods shopping facilities. At the estate, the residents enjoy the friendships that can only be established in small groups.

Because they are near an elementary school the residents feel the activity of children. Thus they are near enough, yet far enough away from activity. Whenever they wish they can return to the quiet of their homes. In addition, there are jobs as baby sitters so that they can continue to feel they are useful human beings; the conveniently located stores give them a place for social contact. All of these aspects contribute to a pleasant and fruitful life.

France.   In 1971, the French Government set up housing allowances for those over 65, or over 60 for those unable to work, with the idea of reducing the rent of a principal home to a level compatible with income. This housing allowance takes the place of the former rental allowance and is no longer subject to the rules of welfare aid. It should result in the elderly being able to remain as long as possible in an independent dwelling adapted to their needs.

Sweden.   The Swedish government has an outstanding record in caring for its elderly. This country is ahead of other nations in dealing with this problem because it was recognized early and remedies have been attempted in conjunction with other social problems. Sweden has the most extensively organized programs in social service of any of the Scandinavian countries. Their goal is that each person handicapped by age or illness should have a chance to improve within the limits of his or her capacity in order to lead as independent a life as possible. The Swedes are acutely aware of and responsive to the developing needs of their growing aged population.

The national government provides for financial support to the aged. A person reaching 65 is entitled to an old-age pension, which is a basic benefit paid to all persons. The sum is index-adjusted and rises with the general cost of living. In addition, approximately half of all pensioners receive supplementary housing allowances. Social services account for 40% of Sweden's national budget. Total welfare expenditure amounts to about 20% of Sweden's national income. In comparison with other countries, this is a little above the proportion in other Scandinavian countries and considerably higher than in the U.S. Roughly 85% of the central government's and 75% of the local governments' expenditures for social benefits are distributed without a means test. [6]

The Swedes put great emphasis on home care. Pensioners live in their own homes or apartments until they can no longer care for themselves or their quarters. The support given by local authorities to the elderly covers a broad range. Apart from institutional care and old age centers, where pensioners live in a hotel environment and enjoy various facilities for recreation and occupation, there is an extensive home care system. The country has about 10,000 specially trained workers, 3,400 of whom are on the government's payroll, assisting with services that include visiting and nursing in the home and providing recreational and other activites arranged by the municipality or by private organizations. In 1967 a home nursing allowance was introduced for those requiring special attention and care and who would otherwise be entitled to institutional care. The same year successful experiments were begun with occupational therapy in the home. Home helpers—called Samaritans—shop and do other household jobs and try to help break through their patients' sense of loneliness and isolation.

There are numerous housing projects for the elderly in Sweden, many of which are outstanding in design and amenities. The vast majority of housing is currently being constructed by non-profit building companies. This trend developed after World War II and is found in all Scandanavian countries. The Swedish National Housing Board finances 90% of all housing construction, giving financial incentives to non-profit groups. These groups can receive a 100% loan as opposed to 85% for private companies.

People's Republic of China. The role of the elderly in the People's Republic of China follows traditional lines. The elderly are, in the words of one Chinese guide, "our treasures." The elderly live with and are part of the extended families. Since all in the family work, the elders are the managers of the

---

[6] John Mc Rae, "Elderly in the Environment—Northern Europe," University of Florida, Gainesville, 1975.

household, the guardians of the very young children, and the linkage that holds the home together.

Since space in the home is so limited (currently at about 22 square feet per person) one can see that the planned use of the space must be carefully arranged. As the children become older, they attend boarding schools and come into the household only on weekends.

PART 3

If we could first know where we are, and wither we are tending, we could better judge what to do, and how to do it.

—Abraham Lincoln

The Planning Process

13

The Basis for Planning

AN AGE OF URBAN ANARCHY

A century before the Golden Age of Athens, a Greek philosopher, Heraclitus, said the problem of human society is to combine that degree of liberty without which law is tyranny with that degree of law without which liberty becomes license. The democracy of Athens and the Constitution of the United States were wrought from the same precepts. An organized society was formed about a group of laws, a set of rules to guide the people in their conduct. The purpose was to guarantee liberty and justice for all.

Inspired by this freedom the people of America created a vast domain of commercial and industrial enterprise. And they built great cities.

Today we see these cities scarred by congestion and decay, speculation and ugliness. We see the science and invention of our remarkable age snarled in a tangle of the urban network. The mediocrity of our cities is a travesty on the productive genius and creative energy of America.

It is not the desire of the people that their cities should be so built. It is rather their ambition to create fine cities, else the forward strides that have been taken would not have been attempted. It is the essence of democracy that the people shall be masters of their destiny, that their behavior shall be guided by the precepts of law and order. Yet our cities suffer disorder and confusion as though born of anarchy. The most frantic antidotes of regulation appear inept and futile. The reasons for this state of urban affairs may be apparent upon examination.

Who are the city builders? They are the multitude of city people who invest in urban property and improvements. All the people participate. Some share by their investments of capital in physical improvements for conduct of profitable

169

enterprise; others invest in municipal revenue bonds which pay for public improvements. All participate through their payment of taxes for the public services that make urban investment feasible.

Forty per cent of the city area is public property: the streets, parks, schools, and variety of public improvements. Within this area local government may shape the streets, traffic arteries, and open spaces according to the designs of official planners. But the bulk of city building, 60 per cent of the total urban area, proceeds parcel by parcel as industry, business, and homeseekers find opportunity for investment.

Those who invest for personal profit are guided by the "market" for improvements. The measure of this "market" is double-barreled. Investment in a city implies stability of values. By its nature the city is a permanent institution whose purpose is to shelter the continuing activities of people. It is not a natural speculative medium. An immediate "market" induces investment, but a continuing "market" makes of it a sound investment.

Stability depends upon the quality of the improvement itself. It also depends upon the quality of the other improvements that have preceded and those that will follow. It depends upon the standards at which a community maintains itself, the maintenance of existing facilities, and the standards it demands for future improvements. These standards determine the difference between environmental degeneration or stability, and upon them rests the difference between speculation and sound urban development.

Nor do the physical improvements on private land alone affect the health of urban investment. The warp of the community pattern is the network of streets, utilities, and transportation. The city functions through the circulation of goods and services; the strength of the urban pattern is measured by the adequacy and convenience of the circulatory system, the stability of investments by the level at which the community maintains itself.

Urban growth is, in some respects, analogous to processes in nature. The soil of fertile and prosperous citizenship is tilled, the seeds of investment are planted, and the garden is cultivated with urban management and maintenance, both public and private. All urban activities and functions are inseparable. The only area in which they may be isolated is that of speculation, and, for that reason, speculation is damaging.

Speculation—quick turn-over for quick profit—contributes in large measure to building a city, but the speculator assumes no responsibility for his product since he is not concerned with the use of the improvement. That responsibility and the obligation for maintaining it are shifted to others when he transfers ownership. The motive of speculation consequently induces inferior quality; it is concerned only with the least possible initial cost.

Speculative improvements are none the less an investment in the city. They are investments in which the public participates. Public services must be made available to all property, and the cost of these services is paid by taxes and public utility rates. These costs are measured to a large degree by the quality of the improvements that comprise the city. High quality holds stable values, resists spotty shifts in urban land use, and wasteful extension and duplication of public services.

What determines the physical form of the city? It emerges from the initiative and enterprise of many people, acting individually and in groups. However, the people are guided by a set of standards and not from some preconceived model of the future city, however brilliant or inspired. This set of standards is the *law*. The real plans for our cities are the standards prescribed by law—the codes and ordinances that regulate the development of urban property.

It is a cardinal point of our constitutional form of political organization that ours is a government of laws—the rules by which our democratic "game" is played. City building is guided by the maximum quantity and minimum quality the law allows. Laws form an integral part of the whole planning process, and it is appropriate to the democratic process that the people who design and invest in urban building shall find free expression and action *within the limits prescribed by law*.

That this process imposes a singular responsibility upon the citizen must be self-evident. It is the obligation of the people to determine the standards they deem appropriate for their city and translate these standards into effective rules and regulations. It can be fairly stated that this responsibility has not been discharged with the intelligence and devotion demanded of citizenship in a democracy. Our cities bear violent testimony to that fact. If we are to bring improvement to the urban environment it devolves upon the people, civic leaders in business, industry, the arts, and public office, to assume this responsibility with vision, integrity, and an unflinching will to serve the public interest. In the final analysis it is only the few who reap profitable reward through violation of the general welfare.

Urban development implies a continuing responsibility, all forces acting together and interdependently. The degree to which these forces are integrated reflects the aspirations, ambitions, and convictions of a community, and the initiative and responsibility of the citizenship in whole and in each of its parts. When the forces that contribute to city building are unbalanced, inequities develop and the city declines. The energy is sapped, the city no longer provides a field for sound and continuing business investment, and the environment degenerates.

Since the laws applying to the physical development of the city set the standards for that development, it is important to examine the effect of these regulations and the prospects for improvement in them. It is important for those who invest their capital for profitable return and for those who pay the taxes that maintain the community. The cities themselves bear testimony to the ineffective nature of many of our laws. The legal framework that molds the urban pattern provides some advantages, but cities appear to have drifted into a state approaching anarchy.

Until recently public contact with city planning has been limited; even today most people have little knowledge about planning, its practices, its limitations, or its significance to their daily living. First contact usually comes when a building permit is sought and the aspirants are either granted a permit or informed that they may not proceed with the improvement. If the permit is granted, the relationship of the individual and planning is a fleeting one and the lack of knowledge continues. If, however, the permit is denied, the citizen may inquire the reason. When informed that the *law* denies that right beause it is inconsistent with the welfare of the community, the citizen may depart from the planning office, accepting this interpretation of the law. Or he or she may have the temerity to ask: What law? How does a community come by the right to restrain me from the free exercise of my will in developing property I own? Is this not the confiscation of private property without due process of law and without just compensation, both of which are violations of the Constitution of the United States?[1]

It is in the interest of the people that they be informed on these questions; they are the foundation of planning in democracy.

WHEN OFFICIAL PLANNING BEGAN

The time when land was first allocated to specific uses is, of course, shrouded in prehistoric mystery. The failure of land to respond to cultivation demonstrated that certain land was not adapted to agricultural use but, since there were few ways of passing this information on to others, it was probably necessary for successive users to learn by trial and error that marginal areas were unfit.[2]

Tribal experience indicated that certain land was suitable for raising crops, other land was better for grazing animals, and some was unproductive. When these experiences were transmitted from generation to generation by word of mouth and tribal custom, we had the first haphazard land-use plan. Certainly enforcement was effective; struggle for survival in a not too friendly world left the line between life and death too thin for people to cultivate land a second time after it had refused to give them food the first time. Thus land was identified as either agricultural or nonagricultural and, if the latter, it had little value. Since there was much land and the people were few in number, people living a nomadic life found little need to fight for or limit themselves to any single area. In those regions where the land gave bountiful harvest from the seeds planted, the wanderers settled down and formed the first permanent agrarian communities.

The customs of land use in the earliest days defined the planting seasons, the

---

[1] Federal Constitution, 14th Amendment, 1868, Section 1: "No State shall make or enforce any law which shall abridge the privileges or immunities of citizens of the United States; nor shall any State deprive any person of life, liberty or property without due process of law, nor deny to any person within its jurisdiction the equal protection of the laws."

[2] "Because the ground is chapt, for there was no rain in the earth, the plowmen were ashamed, they covered their heads. Yea, the hind also calved in the field and forsook it, because there was no grass. And the wild asses did stand in high places, they snuffed up the wind like dragons; their eyes did fail, because there was no grass." Jeremiah 14: 4-6.

harvesting seasons, the first descriptions of crop rotation, and the idea of resting the land after a number of years of use. The priesthood wielded tremendous persuasive powers, and many codes of land use were incorporated in religious doctrines, some of which are still part of religious observations today.

With the development of civilization, the building of cities, and the growth of population, land took on other values than that attached to agricultural use. The fixed marketplace became a land use of great value, the public open space, the forum, and the commons being the important center of the town. Special places were designated for the storage of explosives, for the slaughter of animals, and for the residential developments of the aristocracy. It did not take rulers long to recognize that the relationship between land uses was of paramount importance, that the slaughter houses had no proper place on the windward side of their palaces. In our present-day cities we have taken far less care in locating smoke-and dust-producing industries. It is true, of course, that protection of a few homes from obnoxious conditions was a far simpler task than controlling industrial development in relation to the mushrooming residential areas that crowd our urban landscape today, but some application of this principle might have given us a far less objectionable environment in our urban communities.[3]

While the storage of powder in a convenient place was important to the people's defense, it was soon recognized as a menace when stored too near their homes. With these early concepts of danger and discomfiture began the first official designation of areas within which certain uses were segregated as a matter of protection to the people in a community.

In ancient cities people were themselves regulated as to where they might live. Workers were restricted to areas outside the fortress walls and were called within when required to protect the interests of rulers. As cities grew in size and power, certain minority groups were restricted to areas commonly called "ghettos." These minority groups differed in various periods and in different parts of the world, but history repeatedly records their plight, their misery, and deprivation. These ghettos were always the overcrowded slums and the center of poverty, and when disease struck the city the people in these areas suffered most. Fear of these plague-ridden spots generated hatred and conflict, and confinement of living quarters was extended to restrictions on the work the inhabitants might perform and the places they might travel. Seldom did such imposed regulations have legal foundation, but since they were enforced by the police and with public sanction they were accepted as equivalent to legal control.

To assume that such conditions are confined to history or remote places would be unrealistic since there remains today considerable regulation over minority groups; the areas in which they live are not called ghettos but they retain many historic characteristics.

---

[3] *Ex parte Shrader,* 33 California 279 (1876): "Habeas Corpus to review judgement of conviction for violating order of the Board of Supervisors of the City and County of San Francisco prohibiting the maintenance of slaughter houses, the keeping of swine, the curing of hides or the carrying on of any business or occupation 'offensive' to the senses or prejudicial to the public health or comfort, in certain portions of the city." The courts held this to be a valid use of the police power.

PLANNING POLICIES

In order for there to be an accepted structure to planning for the public welfare it has been essential to establish policy guidelines for the elements to be considered. At a national level "The President's Urban Policy Report" was prepared in August of 1978 and was thereafter submitted to the Congress as the first biennial report in accordance with the provisions of the Housing Act as amended in 1977. This report dealt with the changing urban patterns, America's old perception and new realities, assisting urban residents in distressed areas, a new partnership for conserving urban America, and finally, A National Urban Policy.

In the chapter defining America's Urban Policy, President Carter stated:

> I think that we stand at the turning point in history. If, a hundred years from now, this nation's experiment in democracy has failed, I suspect that historians will trace that failure to our own era, when a process of decay began in our inner cities and was allowed to spread unchecked throughout our society.
>
> But I do not believe that must happen. I believe that by working together, we can turn the tide, stop the decay, and set into motion a process of growth that by the end of the century can give us cities worthy of the greatest nation on earth.

The American Institute of Planners, (A.I.P.) in October, 1977, adopted a series of policies dealing with the professional aspects of urban planning. This society is devoted to the study and advancement of the art and science of city, regional, state and national planning.[4]

The A.I.P. text is organized into two parts: (1) planning functions and their role in the decision-making process, and (2) planning goals—a list of areas of interest to practicing planners.

These areas of interest are:

Growth management

Economic development

Environmental quality

Energy and other resource conservation and development

Aesthetics and historic preservation

Transportation

Health, Education and Welfare

Public safety

Leisure, recreation and cultural opportunities

The A.I.P. stated that "the planning process may be, and often is, used

---

[4] The American Institute of Planners joined with the American Society of Planning Officials in 1978 to become the American Planning Association.

within each of these areas (functional planning), as well as for coordination between them (comprehensive planning)." [5]

The recommendations of the A.I.P. were:

1. Planning should be widely practiced by the private sector and by all levels and branches of government.

2. Plans should be articulated cogently to private decision makers, the general public, and any others who may be involved.

3. The planning process should provide public and private decision makers and those seeking to influence decision makers with the best possible information, analysis of alternatives, and long range and short range impacts so that issues may be decided in the best interest of the public and conflicts and duplication among public policies may be avoided.

4. The planning process should coordinate functional and comprehensive planning among all levels of government and should integrate planning and programming with the budgetary and legislative processes.

5. The planning process should strive to involve significantly all responsible and affected parties.

6. Public agencies at all levels of government should provide the data needed to adequately support all stages of the planning process—from problem definition through implementation to subsequent program evaluation. The data should be as correct and current as would be cost effective.

In addition to these broad policies, each state, in the legislation enabling planning, sets forth the objectives of the state government with regard to the contents and practice of planning programs. For instance, the State Law on Planning in California indicates that "each planning agency shall prepare and the legislative body of each county and city shall adopt a comprehensive general plan for the physical development of the county or city and of any land outside of its boundaries which in the planning agency's judgment bears relation to its planning".[6] Thereafter the law identifies the elements that are to be included. These may differ in name with the policies of the A.I.P., but they are similar in intent. It is in these policy statements of the legislative bodies that the mandate for public planning is established.

Private corporations need no enabling legislation for their internal operation programs. The corporation's board of directors must estimate the need for their product or activity and set goals. No large corporation would remain viable without such forecasting.

[5] *Planning Policies,* 1977, American Institute of Planners, Washington, D.C.
[6] Sections 65300 California Laws related to Conservation and Planning.

VARIATIONS IN THE PROCESSES

Considerable differences in detail exist between planning processes in the United States and those practiced in other nations. Many nations of Europe and the Orient follow the British method. In many countries there is a strong national input in planning. In the United States, variation is subject only to constitutional limitations.

In general however, planning can be divided into two major categories, that of the private sector and government regulatory agencies. The right of the government to regulate the private sector is under constant challenge by those who feel that ownership of land includes the right to do with it what one wishes, provided the rights of others are not violated. As cities have grown in size and complexity and land has changed hands frequently, however, regulation is often needed. Some sense of order has to be established and accepted.

Planning takes place at all levels of government. The Federal government plans and its plans affect the everyday lives of people in many ways. In certain areas, expecially in land use planning, it has been determined that the Federal government does not have the right to regulate. While the states are invested with such a power, they usually delegate this authority to local communities either through the state constitution or law. In some states, laws related to planning are permissive, in others they are mandatory.

Local communities, cities and counties enact laws and ordinances which, under state laws or local charters, define the areas of planning that they are constitutionally allowed to carry out. In some instances, Federal laws require specific planning to be done if a given community seeks financial assistance through one of the many programs under Federal control. In passing the laws and ordinances dealing with local planning, the cities and counties are supposed to prepare comprehensive plans, for land use, circulation, health, housing, energy, safety, education, recreation, conservation and the other elements that relate to the social, economic and physical structure of the community.

The legislative bodies in most cases create planning commissions and planning departments to carry out the mandate of the laws that have been adopted. These bodies in turn are responsible to the legislative body that created them.

THE POLICE POWER

Use of the police power to carry out the official aims of a group power has always been considered proper, but abuse of the power by ruling governments in the past gave rise to actions by the people to curtail that power. Anglo-Saxon and French legal procedures are the outgrowth of the struggle of the people against the autocratic, whimsical, and sometimes frivolous use of powers by the heads of states and nations. The Constitution of the United States and the Bill of Rights were created to guarantee that there would be no punitive action by an individual or government against persons without just cause and with full and open trial in the court of law.

Today it is a widely accepted principle that the source of all power lies in the hands of the majority of the people. This implies that the people of a city or town, through the governing body, have the right to enact laws and regulations that support their ideas of what is best for their community. The distinction between this principle and the exercise of power in the past, whether by a minority or majority, is our recognition that regulations of law today apply to all the people, and no class is expected to be immune. The principal restraint upon law is that it shall not be in conflict with the Constitution of the United States nor the constitution of the state in which it is enacted.

The power to pass and enforce laws to protect the welfare of all the people, whether they be enacted at a local or a national level, is called the exercise of the police power.[7] Enforcement of the legislation enacted by the people or their representatives generally rests with the police department, which apprehends persons accused of law violation. The police department is required to explain the charges preferred and turn the accused over to the courts for a decision on innocence or guilt and the terms of punishment prescribed by the law. The United States Constitution assures that the punishment meted out shall not be cruel and unusual, or arbitrary.

It is necessary that the police power be exercised for a worthy purpose and with definitely stated objectives. In cases where police power is used to regulate or deny the use of property without compensation, it must be clearly shown that the continued use of that property would be inimical to the best interests of the community. A house that is structurally unsound or badly infested with rats may be dangerous to the public in general as well as the persons living in it, and it is thus subject to being closed under the police power without compensation to the owner. The equity for such actions rests upon the assumption that the people are obliged to maintain their property at standards which will not impose a nuisance upon the community and the necessity to exercise the police power to abate such a nuisance does not warrant compensation to the owners of the affected property.

Taking land for public purpose when the owner does not want to sell is know as exercise of *eminent domain*. Condemnation of the property is instituted in the courts which then establish a fair price based upon testimony from witnesses representing the owner, the community, and impartial appraisers. Use of the right of eminent domain is not to be confused with use of the police power: the principal difference between the two powers lies in the matter of compensation to the owner; under the police power the state does not "take" the property from its owner—it regulates the right of use on behalf of the public welfare.

The police power of a community is limited to the area within its political

---

[7] Police power was expressed in ancient law as: "Due regulation of domestic order of the kingdom where members of the state, like a family, are bound to conform their behavior in good propriety . . . to be good members and an orderly part of the community"; and later: "Police Power . . . is the name given to the inherent sovereignty which is the right and duty to exercise when the public policy demands enforcement of such regulations for the general welfare as are necessary for the regulation of economic conditions to provide for adequate community life." *Parker* v. *Otis,* 130 California 322.

boundaries. Thus the state laws may be enforced within any part of the state unless otherwise provided in the laws, the county laws only within the county, and city or township laws only within their limits. Beyond this, cooperation between governmental agencies constitutes the only effective method for coordinated action or regulation. One exception is in Texas where cities can regulate the subdivision of land in the unincorporated (county) areas within an established area of influence, a distance of five miles beyond their political boundaries. Zoning control, however, in these extended areas is not granted to the cities.

The police power was retained by the sovereign states at the time of formation of the Federal government. Only when the national welfare is involved and when the local government is unable to cope with a situation does the state deem it necessary to call for assistance from the Federal government. Federal laws, however, do affect the relationships between the states; we have an Interstate Commerce Commission to regulate rates on railroads dealing in interstate commerce, and the national labor laws regulate wages and hours of persons employed in industries which sell their products through interstate commerce. These instances are uses of the police power by the Federal government.

Some states give the police power to cities and counties by specific legislative acts; others grant this right to communities in their state constitutions. The purpose of the police power is to protect the health, safety, and general welfare of its citizens, but the manner in which the power is granted differs in the various states. The power to make laws and regulations dealing with the activities of the citizens of a community and the property they possess is a key to the planning process and particularly to that phase called zoning.

ZONING—THE FIRST STEP

The first steps in the direction of modern city planning can be traced to practices of establishing districts within which certain rights of citizens were legally curbed. King Philip of Spain,[8] in outlining the procedure for establishing communities in the New World, instructed his explorers that streets were to be oriented in such a manner as not to be windswept, and that slaughtering places for cattle were to be located on the outskirts of town so odors would not prove offensive to the townspeople. In Boston the segregation of the storage place for gunpowder from the center of the city was one of America's first recorded acts of zoning. In 1810 certain Napoleonic decrees and the Prussian codes of 1845 contained land-use regulations.

Most early laws were concerned with only those uses considered a menace to life itself, and regulations against most of these uses were based on presen-

---

[8] King Philip of Spain, Law of the Indies, 1573.

tation of evidence in court that the uses were existing and had proven themselves dangerous. This proof was possible, in the most instances, only after some great loss of life directly traceable to the specific use. In most cases, such as the tenement house fire disasters in New York City, continued construction of the dangerous buildings was prohibited but litttle was done to eliminate the danger that hung over the thousands of people who continued to live in "outlawed" fire-traps. It was considered a critical point in all legal action at the time that the establishment of dangerous uses could be prevented, but that such laws could not be retroactive.

Legal action on zoning affairs passed through two stages of development before it arrived at the place it enjoys today. The first stage included a group of court cases which actually preceded zoning and served to establish the base for zoning law and gained it recognition as a legal use of the police power. These cases dealt with "nuisance uses" which the courts treated as separate and individual matters, the court deciding in each specific case whether a use was detrimental to the health, safety, and public welfare. As time passed, the courts required more evidence as a base for reference, evidence "indicating the character of a community," before it was willing to rule upon the validity of a use. This call by the courts for a comprehensive city plan is now answered in the General Plan of land use.

In California an ordinance which prohibited a slaughter house, hog storage, and hide curing in certain districts of the city was upheld in the courts.[9] In Los Angeles, in 1895, an ordinance which prohibited the operation of a steam shoddying plant within 100 feet of a church was upheld; in this latter case the court passed not only upon the nature of the specific use but the relationship between uses.[10]

The legality of the establishment of fire zones or districts has been upheld in most courts, the structural nature of buildings and their relation to space being admitted as an important factor in determining the uses permitted within a structure. In San Francisco, because of the great number of wooden buildings with party walls, certain districts were established by ordinance within which hand laundries were prohibited; wood fires were burned in the stoves upon which the laundry was boiled and several serious fires resulted. This ordinance was taken to the state Supreme Court[11] and was held unconstitutional and invalid, not because of the regulation itself, but because it was a breach of the 14th Amendment of the United States Constitution; it empowered a person or group of people at their absolute and unrestrained discretion to give or withhold permission to carry on a lawful business in any place. It was pointed out that the washing of clothes was not opposed to good public morals nor was it subversive of public decency, but the court cited the fact that all but one of the non-Oriental

[9] *Ex parte Shrader,* San Francisco (1867).
[10] *Ex parte Lacey,* 108 California 326.
[11] *Yick Wo v. Hopkins,* 118 U.S. 356 (1895).

applicants were issued permits in a similar business in like areas and were permitted to continue in business whereas the petitioner and two hundred others of his race were denied permits. The court held that the ordinance was not unreasonable, but that its application was arbitrary class legislation discriminating against one group in favor of another. It thus violated the 14th Amendment of the United States Constitution, and the ordinance was declared to be invalid. The fair administration of a law is integral with the provisions of the law in the eyes of the courts.

One of the earliest decisions in this country upholding an ordinance in the nature of a zoning regulation was made by the courts in 1920.[12] In sustaining a town plan before it, the court stated: "It betters the health and the safety of the community; it betters the transportation facilities; and it adds to the appearance and the wholesomeness of the place, and as a consequence it reacts upon the moral and spiritual power of the people who live under such surroundings."

COMPATIBILITY

In land use planning and zoning, compatibility between uses and districts remains a major criteria in the decision-making process. When courts have viewed cases, they have almost uniformly evaluated a proposal in the context of its environment.

Compatibility, however, does not imply uniformity. Where different land uses occur in close proximity, buffers and transitional uses tend to mitigate the otherwise conflicting land use, thereby accomplishing the compatibility essential to effective planning.

Variety in a compatible sense is the criterion by which future land uses are determined in many countries. For instance, in Japan, many of the large-scale housing projects have the lower floors given to retail commercial uses. In the Netherlands, small convenience shops have been integrated into the residential structures. In the Soviet Union, the lower floors of almost all the large residential complexes are used for restaurants and other commercial uses. In each of these instances the relationship between the different uses is planned so they complement each other.

Perhaps one of the finest examples of variety in a unified development is to be observed in Brussels, where the ancient Guild Halls, which vary in architecture, result in a pleasing sight when viewed as a whole.

In San Francisco, the Embarcadero housing development also illustrates an intended mix of land uses. Here the street level is devoted to commerce and the stories above to medium and high rise apartments. This mix is achieved through a residential terrace upon which the apartments are built. The terrace completely separates the apartments from the commerce on the street level. Since all stores and apartments are fireproof, one of the great dangers of mixing residential and commercial structures is avoided.

[12] *Windsor v. Whitney,* 95 Connecticut 357, 363.

CHANGING INTERPRETATION OF THE LAW

The series of laws which establish the right to zone and enforce zoning is like a chain linking all the powers of government with the needs and desires of the people. As in all other legal procedures in a democracy, there is always available to individuals and groups of people the final recourse to the courts for determination of the reasonableness of law or the fairness with which it has been applied.

Some very significant changes have taken place in the interpretation by the courts of laws regulating the use of property. The growth of communities into large cities has necessitated detailed and involved legislation governing self-discipline in human relations. What may have passed unnoticed in a small community may be viewed as dangerous in cities. Thus the keeping of pigs, horses, and chickens would be considered as an accepted right in a farm town, but would be looked upon with horror on Manhattan Island. What may be tolerated in a small community as a necessary nuisance is contested and actively combated in a metropolis. The maintenance of open privies in backyards may be accepted practice in nonurban areas with no funds for sewage disposal, whereas the same condition in any large city would have the entire population declaring it a menace to the health and life of all the people.

There has been in the eyes of the court a necessity for recognizing the problems created by the concentration of people in our cities. The dangers of disease, crime, delinquency, fire, and injury from traffic are rapidly multiplied as the housing, commerce, and industry of the large city absorb the open space which formerly insulated people against these dangers. Thus there came into being the concept that people have the right to protect themselves against these and other hazards by planning and zoning an environment which will meet the requirements of urban living. Where we have relied in the past upon the police power to prohibit acts which the courts determined to be a violation of a law, today we enact laws which tend to discourage in advance those acts which can be prevented.

Our philosophy of urban conduct is no longer confined to the public health, safety, and general welfare but has extended to the use of the police power for the maintenance of such matters as "public convenience and comfort." The Supreme Court, of the United States has said:[13] "The police power of a state embraces regulations designed to promote the public convenience or the general prosperity as well as regulations designed to promote the public health, the public morals, or the public safety." Traffic laws which prohibit parking on certain streets are justified on the grounds that they make access to important areas a matter of greater convenience as well as assure the safety of people. Laws which prohibit dangerous or obnoxious uses from residential areas are considered to protect values from depreciation and, in this manner, protect the general prosperity.

---

[13] *Chicago B. & R. Ry. Co. v. Drainage Commissioners*, 200 U.S. 561, 592.

Some efforts have been made to incorporate in zoning laws such matters as architectural control, seeking thus to protect the esthetic feeling of people, but the courts have not yet given much comfort to the prospect for wide acceptance of the enforcement of this device through the police power.[14] Restrictive covenants to enforce discrimination against minority groups by race restrictive provisions in zoning ordinances were declared unconstitutional by the United States Supreme Court in 1927.[15]

UP ZONING—DOWN ZONING

It has been assumed by many in the public that the only direction for zone change is to increase the permissiveness of the law, to provide for those changes that would permit land owners to enjoy greater potential profits from the use of their land. Few legislative bodies have had the temerity to tell owners that their land cannot be used as intensively as had been legislated in the past.

In recent times, however, court rulings indicate that, like any other legislative act of the city or county government, zoning is subject to modification if required to protect the public health, safety, or welfare. Legislative bodies make judgments based upon data. With new facts before it, a legislative body has an obligation and responsibility to make such modifications and changes as would bring the zoning into a consistent position with the community long-range comprehensive plan and recognized professional practices.

There is no doubt that persons paying for land on the basis of existing zoning for commercial uses would believe that rezoning for residential uses would be tantamount to taking property without just compensation. However, persons who own residential land make no such complaint nor do they offer compensation to the community when the legislative body decides to rezone the land for commerce or industry. In each case, there must be careful analysis to indicate that the decision was based on sound planning and zoning principles and that no act of favoritism, prejudice, or discrimination went into the decision process.

In most instances where "down zoning " has occurred the subject property was not developed for the permitted use. Meawhile the land around it often developed a pattern that indicated that the contested area would have been incompatible with its surroundings. If development has already taken place the legislative body may enact a "nonconforming" provision that could include a

[14] *Soho Park and Land Co.,* 142 Atlantic 548.

[15] *Buchanan v. Worley,* Louisville, Kentucky, 245 U.S. 60; 62 Law Edition, 149. Ordinance regulated occupancy of blocks of city; black people could not occupy buildings in blocks where greater number of dwellings were occupied by whites and vice versa.

The United States Supreme Court, *38 Supreme Ct. Report, 16,* ruled this ordinance unconstitutional because it forbade the sale of property to a person because of his color . . . this was not a proper use of the police power, even though the City of Louisville claimed that mixing of the races would create riots. This use of the police power was a violation of the 14th Amendment of the Federal Constitution, for it prevented the use of property and deprived its owner of use without due process of law.

reasonable amortization period after which the existing use would have to conform to the surroundings.

A zoning action which merely decreases the market value of property does not violate state or federal contitutional provision forbidding uncompensated taking or damaging of property. Accordingly, an inverse condemnation action by property owners, in which it was alleged that plaintiffs purchased property zoned commercial and that thereafter the city rezoned the property to residential so that the property was worth only a fraction of its value under the commercial zoning, did not state a cause of action and the trial court correctly sustained the city's demur without leave to amend.[16]

THE PUBLIC WELFARE

The courts were called upon to rule on some mighty problems in the early days of zoning. What was the public welfare? When was public health or life endangered? What was an obnoxious use? At what point is the establishment of a district reasonable and at what point does it become arbitrary? Was it proper for the court to substitute its judgment for that of the legislative body on matters of the "substance" of a zoning ordinance? When can a community permit a use in one area and deny it in another?

A series if court decisions records the difference of opinion held within the courts themselves, but filtering through them all are decisions accepted today as a sound precedent for interpretation of the community's right to establish zoning districts and regulate the use of property. The Hadacheck case[17] in Los Angeles, 1913, cites one of the basic considerations in all zoning law. Although it preceded recognized zoning statutes, it dealt with the violation of a city ordinance prohibiting the maintenance of brickyards and kilns within a designated residental district of some three square miles. The court ruled that this use of property must cease and desist since the smoke, dust, and fumes emanating from the plant were damaging to the health of the people living near by. In this case the brickyard was located and operating in the area before it was occupied by residences, but the court did not consider the property right claimed by the owner to be as important as the health and welfare of the people. The claim of discrimination was raised by the owner since brickyards and kilns were permitted in other areas near residential developments, but it was disallowed on the grounds that "it is no objection to the validity of the ordinance that in other districts similarly situated brick kilns are not prohibited. It is for the council to say whether the prohibition should be extended to such other districts."

In another case[18] the city of South Pasadena attempted to restrict the

---

[16] Cal. Jur. 2d. Eminent Domain. #85: Am. Jur. 2d. Eminent Domain. #157 et seq.

[17] *Ex parte Hadacheck,* 165 California 416 (1913); *Hadacheck v. Sebastian,* 2390 Supreme Court, 394; 60 Law Edition, 348.

[18] *Matter of Throop,* 169 California 93 (1915).

operation of a rock-crusher in a high-class residential district. This district was then sparsely developed, whereas similar operations were permitted in other and more heavily populated residential districts. The ordinance was declared unreasonable and void. It was ruled unreasonable to prohibit such use in a sparsely settled district when the same use was permitted in a densely populated district. The court made much of the fact that the poorer class of homes surrounding the industrial district are entitled to the same protection as the fine homes. The courts held in the Throop case, and in others dealing with the mining of natural resources, that these minerals must be extracted where they are found, and if this use is denied there would be no material for construction.

Another controversy deals with the relative value of natural resources. In the Roscoe area within the limits of Los Angeles rock was quarried for many years and each pit was abandoned when the supply became exhausted; the area of mining was then extended to a new site for extraction. In this same area, because of the excellent climatic conditions, great numbers of health-seeking individuals established their homes. The expansion of rock-quarrying, it was contended, undermined the value of the climatic resource to the point that the lives of the people were jeopardized. The residents pointed out that the air was filled with dust particles, that the unfenced and abandoned pits were dangerous, and that children had been killed and injured. The Planning Commission of the community upheld the contention of the residents, whereas the City Council reversed this stand. The lower courts upheld the legislative body, refusing to substitute its judgment for that of the council on matters of "subtance."

The interpretation of the general welfare clause is fundamental to all zoning, and planning rests upon the thesis that regulation of property use will secure to the community numerous benefits. Among others it will lessen congestion on streets, secure greater safety from fire, panic, and similar dangers, promote health by requiring adequate light and air, prevent overcrowding of the land, avoid undue concentrations of population, facilitate the provision of adequate transportation, water supply, sewage disposal and other basic necessities such as schools, parks, playgrounds, and civic and cultural amenities. The preservation and stabilization of property values are also important to both individual and community; the more these values are conserved, the greater will be the city's income from taxation, and the lower will be the tax rate to supply the required services. Blight, obsolescence, and slums are discouraged, the city retains a good "character and appearance," and improvement in the physical and moral fiber of the community reduces the need for, and the cost of, many social services.

Maintenance of the "general welfare and prosperity" as a reason for imposing race restrictions by means of zoning was termed an illegal use of the police powers by the U.S. Supreme Court. The property owners sought to prove that the intrusion of "nonwhite" families into a "white" district caused a loss of property values and thus endangered the prosperity of the community. The court held that the agencies of government could not be used to enforce a law which specifically violated the 14th Amendment of the Constitution. The courts in many others cases have ruled that financial gains or losses are not, in themselves, sufficient to decide the validity or constitutionality of a law.[19]

Test of the community's right to prescribe the manner of development within its boundaries "spread-eagled" the courts during the 1920's. In these early days decisions were more likely to support the individual against the community welfare, the courts being reluctant to take acion which would infringe upon property rights. Inexperience in the framing of zoning law was reflected in some phrasing which suggested discrimination to the courts. The courts hammered at a thesis which has become a cornerstone of zoning: to be valid the law must be reasonable and fairly applied.

As zoning received wider acceptance as a proper use of the police power, a variety of features were incorporated in the ordinances. There were efforts to use the law as a device to protect the property of the few while permitting the remainder of the city to continue unprotected. Occasionally, in concert with the land speculator, property was zoned for a use which would bring the highest price at the moment; whether the use was commercial, residential, or industrial was of little concern. A weird pattern of "spot" zoning covered the land like a crazy quilt. Purchasers of vacant land were informed they could use the land for any purpose they willed, and their neighbors were helpless to protect their investments. Efforts of public officials to maintain conformance with the "character" of a neighborhood when called upon to issue building permits were hotly contested. "Interim Ordinances" were sometimes enacted to forbid encroachments upon "fine" residential districts and, although some of these were sustained, the courts generally found them invalid because of the arbitrary nature of their boundaries; the courts viewed the guarantee of a special area from detrimental uses as a discriminatory act since the same encroachments were permitted unchecked elsewhere.

In all these decisions the courts were actually leading the way toward the planning of cities; the courts were appealing for a "comprehensive plan" which would provide a foundation for zoning acts and decisions of equity in the shaping and administration of these acts.

ZONING AND COMMUNITY CHARACTER

One of the most important legal decisions in the history of zoning was the Euclid case[20] in 1926. In his decision, Justice Sutherland of the United States Supreme Court pointed out that each community had the right and the responsibility to determine its own character, and as long as that determination did not disturb the orderly growth of the region or the nation, it was a valid use of the police power. Justice Sutherland stated:

[19] *Smith v. Collison,* 119 California Appellate 180 (1931). Depreciation in value of property is not fatal to the validity of the ordinance.

[20] *Village of Euclid, Ohio v. Amber Realty Company,* 272 U.S. 365 (1962).

Point is raised by the appellees that the Village of Euclid was a mere suburb of Cleveland, and that the industrial development of the latter had extended to the village, and that in the obvious course of things would soon absorb the entire area for industrial enterprise, and that the effect of the ordinance was to divert such natural development or expansion elsewhere, to the consequent loss of increased values to the owners of land within the village. But this village, though physically a suburb of Cleveland, is a separate municipality, with powers of its own and authority to govern itself as it sees fit within the organic laws of its creation and the state and Federal constitutions. The will of its people determines, not that industrial development shall cease at its boundaries, but that such development shall proceed between fixed lines. If therefore it is proper exercise of the police power to reguate industrial establishments to localities separated from residential sections, it is not easy to find sufficient reason for denying the power because its effect would be to divert an industrial flow from a course which would result in injury to the residential public to another course where such injury would be obviated. This should not exclude the possibility of cases where the general interest so far outweighs the interest of the municipality, that the latter should not be allowed to stand in its way.

This decision made it abundantly clear that a community may determine the nature of development within its boundaries; it may plan and regulate the use of land as the people of the community may consider it to be in the public interest. Justice Sutherland also enunciated another principle: a community is obliged to relate its plans to the area outside its boundaries. Again the courts anticipate the planning process. Cities are not surrounded by walls, they are each a part of their region and each is obliged to plan the spaces within its boundaries as an integral part of the plan for spaces outside its boundaries. This suggests, for instance, that a highway plan prepared without consideration for the routes of major importance within the regional plan would constitute an improper use of the police power. A community has both the right to determine its character and the obligation to relate its plan to its regional environs.

ENABLING LEGISLATION FOR PLANNING

The grant of police power by the states to the cities and counties vests these political subdivisions with the power to regulate their affairs and enforce the regulations. It is nevertheless found necessary on occasion for the state to enact legislation for the specific use of that power and such legislation is generally termed "enabling acts." Its purpose may be twofold. It may be for the purpose of affirming the state policy in matters of vital interest to the people at any given time and thereby encourage local communities to act, or the special legislation may be for the purpose of removing doubt that the police power was intended for the specific subject of the act. Such enabling acts are drawn to establish clearly the relation between the use for which the police power is granted and the public health, safety, convenience, and general welfare, and the preamble states in detail the purposes of the legislation.

Zoning enabling acts are sometimes passed by the state even though cities and counties have been previously delegated the police power but are reluctant to exercise it until the state has specifically signified that it be so used. These special enabling acts are usually written in greater detail than the general grant of the police power. In the case of zoning they define the scope of zoning, the procedure for adoption of the ordinance, the composition of the zoning board and its powers and functions, the methods for modification or exceptions to the ordinance.

State Planning Acts are a form of special enabling legislation, although they generally establish a state agency to co-ordinate planning functions at the state level in additioon to the specification for local planning activities. Such acts describe the functions of a state planning board and prescribe the process for each city and county to acccomplish a complete planning job for itself. These laws usually call for the preparation of a general plan, list the scope of the general plan, and specify the methods for its adoption and enforcement. Power is sometimes given to the local planning commission to levy a tax upon the general public for funds to administer the law, but this power is seldom invoked; planning commissions prefer to work within the departmental family of the city government and draw their support from the general tax funds.

Another form of enabling legislation is that which creates new agencies in the state, cities, or counties to cope with problems of a particular nature. Housing and urban redevelopment acts are of this type, local agencies being created with powers conferred upon the city or county to engage in the program prescribed in the state statute.

Just as specific enabling legislation is created at the state level to cover certain fields of urban activity, so special ordinances are drawn at the local level to define in detail the manner in which city charter provisions are to be executed. In cities where there is no "freeholders' charter"[21] the state laws are in effect, whereas in cities having charters which define the exercise of the police power in stricter terms than the state, the local law takes precedence.[22] Thus, if a state speed limit in a school zone is 20 miles per hour and the city law restricts the speed to 15 miles per hour, the city law is enforceable. If, on the other hand, the city has a limit of 25 miles per hour or no regulation at all for those specific areas, the state law is then enforceable. City charters often define in terms almost identical to the state enabling legislation the functions of a planning commission, and as long as all the duties included in the state law are included in terms not less restrictive, the city charter provisions apply.

Too frequently there is no provision for a penalty for failure to abide by the requirements of state legislation. An example would be the case in which states call for all counties to have planning commissions and many small counties ignore the requirement. Since there are few ways to compel the local government to conform, great resources are sometimes dissipated without control. In some

---

[21] An act of municipal incorporation, provided for in the constitutions of the individual states.

[22] *Brougher v. Board of Public Works,* 205 California 426 (1928). A charter city need not follow the procedures of the State Zoning Enabling Act.

states the local governments are restricted from the benefits of funds appropriated by the state for public improvements until they conform with state laws. There are occasions when funds for the state highway system are withheld until the counties adopt general plans for highways which show the relationship between the state routes and local roads.

TRANSITION

Since the inception of action against the use of property deemed a menace to health and life of neighbors, zoning has passed from the state of regulating land uses for the preservation of property values to the present position of responsibility, not only for protection of the status quo, but for the creation of a better city, better state, and more prosperous nation. It is true that, as zoning becomes a more effective instrument for improvement of the good city, it becomes less like the traditional instrument called "zoning," and more like the act of planning the city, for many other factors than those usually identified with zoning enter the scene.

Recently zoning has become a means for both conservation and planning; the narrow concept of zoning is extended to the broadest interpretation of the use of the police power for the protection of the public welfare. In these instances zoning law anticipates the future and guides the development of areas through planned uses rather than waiting until the die is cast and merely fixing land uses that already exist. In the cut-over areas of Michigan, Wisconsin, and Minnesota, where erosion threatened to rip the growing heart out of the soil and create "dust-bowl" conditions, steps have been taken legally to label as submarginal the worst of the land. In this way use of rural land was discouraged until such time as the top-soil could be replaced and refertilized. Further "mining" of trees in the areas not entirely destroyed was forbidden and a reforestation program, under the guidance and with the assistance of the Federal government, now assures the people of a continuing supply of lumber for future generations. Thus the priceless possession of fertile land will not be wantonly wasted. The State Planning Act of 1961 in Hawaii encompasses more than conservation. It provides for urban, agricultural, and conservation land-use classifications, and requires that tax-assessing authorities be guided by these zoned land uses in establishing assessed values for real property.

J. H. Bradley, in his *Autobiography of Earth*, has stated: "The fabric of human life has been woven on earthen looms." We must use every device in our legal system to protect our land and devote it to its highest and best uses for we cannot escape to new frontiers after abusing and ruining what we have. Almost two centuries ago George Washington observed: "Our lands . . . were originally very good; but use and abuse have made them quite otherwise. . . . We ruin the lands that are already cleared, and either cut down more wood, if we have it, or emigrate into Western country.[23] The use of the police power—zoning—to insure

---

[23] U.S. Department of Agriculture, *To Hold This Soil,* Publication No. 321, 1938, U.S. Government Printing Office, Washington, D.C.

our future seems neither arbitrary nor in contradiction of any freedom assured to the people by the Constitution.[24]

AESTHETIC CONCERNS

The drab, uninspired appearance of our cities approaches offensive ugliness. The lack of a long tradition of the arts in society has dulled our response to the visual plunder in our surroundings. The grace and charm of a European village, a New England town, the delight of Paris, Venice and Vienna, came by way of the manners and morals of the time quite as much as by craftsmanship. Our values have undoubtedly been contorted by materialism and the sheer preoccupation with the practical chores of everyday urban housekeeping. It should not be conceivable in a democratic society with balanced cultural values, but improvement of the esthetic quality of our cities has been attempted through legislative action.

In the past, legislative bodies have been reluctant to embody esthetic considerations in legislation. Judge Swayze of New Jersey specifically expressed this sentiment:

"No case has been cited, nor are we aware of any case, which holds that a man may be deprived of his property because his tastes are not those of his neighbor. Esthetic considerations are a matter of luxury and indulgence rather than of necessity, and it is necessity alone which justifies the police power to take property without compensation."[25]

An early step toward esthetic control was directed to regulations against the use of billboards along highways. As the advertising mania spread, the extravagant use of signs and billboards along the highway reached intolerable proportions. The police power was invoked when, 1905 the metropolitan Park Commission of Massachusetts sought to prohibit signs near a parkway. This regulation was held invalid by the court, but spurred into action, restrictions against the wanton blight of the billboard rash gained momentum. In 1935 the same court in Massachusetts supported the use of the police power to regulate signs and billboards.

Although there is precedent for esthetic control in areas of particular historic importance,[26] the device of architectural control is usually avoided; the prospect of imposing a hierarchy of taste upon a community is approached with caution. Quite a different matter was presented to the Supreme Court of the United States in 1954. In the unanimous opinion set forth by Justice Douglas, it was clearly affirmed that a community need not tolerate ugliness and may take legal steps to correct it.[27]

... Public safety, public health, morality, peace and quiet, law and order—these are some of the more conspicuous examples of the traditional application of the police

---

[24] U.S. Department of Agriculture, *The Why and How of Rural Zoning,* December 1958.
[25] *Passaic v. Paterson Bill Posting Co.*
[26] 333 Mass. 773 and 783 (1955).
[27] *Berman v. Parker,* 348 U.S. 26, 75 Sup. Ct. 98, 99 L. Ed. 27 (1954).

power to municipal affairs. Yet they merely illustrate the scope of the power and do not delimit it. Miserable and disreputable housing conditions may do more than spread disease and crime and immorality. They may also suffocate the spirit by reducing the peopl who live there to the status of cattle. They may indeed make living an almost insufferable burden. They may also be an ugly sore, a blight on the community which robs it of charm, which makes it a place from which men turn. The misery of housing may despoil a community as an open sewer may ruin a river.

We do not sit to determine whether a particular housing project is or is not desirable. The concept of the public welfare is broad and inclusive. The values it represents are spirtual as well as physical, aesthetic as well as monetary. It is within the power of the legislature to determine that the community should be beautiful as well as healthy, spacious as well as clean, well-balanced as well as carefully patrolled. In the present case, the Congress and its authorized agencies have made determinations that take into account a wide variety of values. It is not for us to reappraise them. If those who govern the District of Columbia decide that the Nation's Capital should be beautiful as well as sanitary, there is nothing in the Fifth Amendment that stands in the way. . . .

. . . In the present case, Congress and its authorized agencies attack the problem of the blighted parts of the community on an area rather than on a structure-by-structure basis. That, too, is opposed by appellants. They maintain that since their building does not imperil health or safety nor contribute to the making of a slum or a blighted area, it cannot be swept into a redevelopment plan by the mere dictum of the Planning Commission or the Commissioners. The particular uses to be made of the land in the project were determined with regard to the needs of the particular community. The experts concluded that if the community were to be healthy, if it were not to revert again to a blighted or slum area, as though possessed of a congenital disease, the area must be planned as a whole. It was not enough, they believed, to remove existing buildings that were unsanitary or unsightly. It was important to redesign the whole area so as to eliminate the conditions that cause slums—the overcrowding of dwellings, the lack of parks, the lack of adequate streets and alleys, the absence of recreational areas, the lack of light and air, the presence of outmoded street patterns. It was believed that the piecemeal approach, the removal of individual structures that were offensive, would be only a palliative. The entire area needed redesigning so that a balanced, integrated plan could be developed for the region, including not only new homes but also schools, churches, parks, streets and shopping centers. In this way it was hoped that the cycle of decay of the area could be controlled and the birth of future slums prevented. Such diversification in future use is plainly relevant to the maintenance of the desired housing standards and therefore within congressional power. . . .

This decision acknowledged that the visual image of the city stands with other features which involve the public interest. It pertained, however, to conditions which existed and found that the spiritual welfare of the people was imperiled by these conditions. It provides a foundation for legislation which employs the police power to discontinue such conditions. We apparently have yet to establish means by which such conditions may not be *created*.

The public can assert its interests directly in two areas. One is in the public domain, since some 40 percent of the city area consists of streets, walks, parks and civic reserves. Herein is a broad and impressive arena for creative treatment of space arrangement, landscaping, street furniture, lighting, signs, and structures. The other is in the realm of public regulation of three-dimensional volumes related to community design. This involves integrated use of land —open space and landscape—structures, the character of building design, advertising media, and ingress and egress for pedestrians and vehicles. Sensitive attention to the formulation of these regulations may accomplish some effective results without impinging on good taste. In the final analysis, the creation of beauty is the result of a desire that it be produced as well as the talent to produce it, and this demands the cultivation of cultural values.

The importance and validity of esthetic considerations, has been upheld in a case involving the County of Santa Barbara. The County Zoning Ordinance established an amortization period for outdoor advertising structures along its main highway. The outdoor advertising company sued the County implying that zoning for esthetic purposes was unconstitutional, that beauty is matter of personal taste, that outdoor advertising was a legitimate commercial enterprise and, therefore, must be given the same rights as other commercial uses. The Court held that the scenic quality of Santa Barbara County was one of its most important economic assets in attracting tourists and visitors, and as such, must be protected for the general welfare. The billboards were therefore ordered to be removed. There was no appeal.

14

Public Planning

Public Planning is accomplished through the activities of many agencies and authorities. The number of persons involved and the process may vary with different levels of government and with different enabling legislation, but the responsibilities are largely similar in most parts of the country.

The Legislative Role. The role of the legislative body is that of decision on the character the city shall aspire to achieve. It activates the Planning Commission, provides finances for its staff, approves its membership, and supports its activities through regard for its recommendations. Except for the relatively narrow limits reserved to administrative determination by the Planning Commission, decisions on all planning policies rest with the elected representatives of the people. The legislative body, acting upon recommendations of the Commission, translates the plan into action. It may also act as a board of appeals on decisions rendered by the Commission, but this function is usually assigned to an administrative committee specifically charged with this responsibility. Policies which direct the shape of the city reflect the capacity of the Planning Commission and the stature of the legislative body.

The Planning Commission. The planning commission is the legal agency of the city through which most planning is performed. In many cities the official family is few in number and the planning commission may have no staff, the city engineer or clerk being largely responsible for the preparation of all plans. Large cities, however, usually have well-staffed organizations of qualified personnel.

The commisssion is a group of private citizens appointed by the mayor and approved by the city council. These commissioners are leaders in local enterprises, real estate, banking, chamber of commerce, or attorneys, architects, doctors, labor representatives, and social workers. It might be assumed that some commissioners, by the nature of their background and personal interests, would be devoted to preservation of property values rather than the general community welfare. Although it cannot be denied that such has been the case in some instances, it is not infrequently found that men with experience in the private business of city building are well qualified to serve the public interest and respond accordingly when given positions of genuine public responsibility.

192

New commissioners are not always adequately informed about the planning process, its purposes or objectives, and they may require some time for training and familiarity with the nature of their responsibility. Some cities appoint ex officio members to the board of the planning commission to assist the commissioners in their tasks. These members may be the heads of various departments of the local government, the city engineer, the road commissioner, the county surveyor, city attorney, the public works officer, health officer, or members of the legislative body. They advise the commission on matters in which they have special knowledge, but they seldom enjoy the privilege of voting upon the proceedings before the commission.

Exclusive of ex officio members, the commission varies between five and nine in number according to the provisions of local charter regulations or the state legislation which creates the planning commission; the civic interest and qualifications of the members are more important than the numerical quantity. Frequency of commission meetings depends upon the extent of the planning program which, in some large cities, is sufficiently active to warrant the establishment of a separate commission to administer the zoning ordinance.

The planning commission usually serves in an advisory capacity to the legislative body, the council and the mayor referring matters of planning to the commission for reports and recommendations which the legislative body may accept or reject. As a rule, the preparation of the comprehensive plan and other plans for civic development are specified in the enabling legislation which creates the commission, and in such activities the commission requires no specific instructions from the legislative body although these functions require legislative appropriation of funds for an adequate staff and unless the council is sympathetic to the planning program, it can effectively delay the commission's performance.

Being an advisory rather than an executive agency of the local government, the planning commisssion recommends plans to the legislative body after it has held public hearings to ascertain the response and opinions of citizen groups. When a plan is adopted by the legislative body, it becomes a law which governs the actions of all the people in the community including local governmental agencies. Consequently, all city departments are required to refer their plans for specific improvements to the planning commission for review and approval. The service performed in the general public interest by this coordination avoids duplication of services and cross-purposes which can readily occur in the wide range of urban activities.

Matters which generally fall within the legal responsibility of planning commissions are the comprehensive plan, zoning ordinances, and subdivision codes, but the coordinating functions are becoming a more important service as the city grows. While the planning commission administers the zoning ordinance in most small cities, some large cities have a separate zoning administrator and board of appeals. This board is responsible for interpretation of the zoning law and such variances from the ordinance as unforeseen conditions may warrant. The planning commission prepares the ordinance, and the zoning administrator, or local building and safety department, enforces it.

Relief from the requirements of the planning policies established by law is provided all citizens if the law deprives them of property without just compensation or if it is applied in a discriminatory manner. This relief may be obtained by appeal to the planning commission and the legislative body. In the event that these appeals fail to bring a satisfactory resolution of the case, it may be referred to the courts for decision. It is from such cases that the great fund of judicial opinions on the planning process have emerged.

Being an advisory body only with no legislative powers and with limited administrative authority, some persons have questioned the necessity for the planning commission. It has been suggested that a competent planning department should report directly to the administrative or executive office and the legislative body. The planning commission, however, plays a vital role as a catalyst for the variety of interests concerned with the objectives and the consequences of planning. Providing a forum for deliberation of facts and opinions, the planning commission can serve in resolving issues and offering to the legislative body a well-defined and supported foundation for policy decisions.

The Planning Department. Organized as one of the official family of government agencies, the planning commission depends for its effectiveness in large part upon the competence of the technical staff in the planning department. Whether the city charter provides for the planning director to report directly to the mayor or to the planning commission, the policies finally adopted by the legislative body are dependent upon the competence, skill and enlightenment of the staff in the planning department. It is the staff which prepares the comprehensive plan, probably the most important single action affecting the future development of the city, and it is the staff which formulates the provisions of the zoning ordinance and subdivision regulations. Implementing the comprehensive plan, it coordinates with other departments of government with respect to streets and highways; health, education, and recreation facilities; utilities; police and fire protection; and all building and engineering activities. The department cooperates in preparation of the city budget for both administration and the capital improvement program. When the staff is endowed with that rare combination of vision, technical skill and administrative talent, it becomes the heart of urban government.

Zoning Board. The variety and volume of improvements in a large city become immense and may require an independent board for administration of the zoning ordinance. This board renders interpretation of the zoning ordinance applicable to specific cases and may provide relief by variance permits when warranted. Decisions may be appealed to the planning commission, city council, appeals board, or court of competent jurisdiction.

The Appeals Board. As affairs of local government in complexity, usually proportionate with the size of cities, action on zoning interpretations and variances has encouraged the creation of an appeals board. This agency is composed and derives its authority similarly to the planning commission. It conducts hearings for appeals from decisions of the planning commission or zoning board, and offers objective attention to appeals warranting reconsideration.

PLANNING CONSULTANTS

Consultants can bring to the planning commission the advantage of particular experience, judgment, and technical knowledge, but their most vital contribution is courage, conviction, and inspiration for the staff and commission. Their role varies from that of performing in lieu of a full staff in small communities to that of expert counsel on planning problems of particular complexity. In the performance of a consultants service it is essential for the consultant to work intimately with the leaders of the community as well as with government agencies and their staffs. This may include participation in public gatherings and hearings on legislative proposals, including the adoption of general plan. This important policy statement would thereby enjoy some assurance of favorable acceptance and action in the community. It is equally important that the staff be equipped to maintain the planning process or arrange with the consultant to serve in that capacity with regularity.

PUBLIC PARTICIPATION

Public involvement in planning may be characterized by courtesy or by confrontation; public participation may be extensive or slight. The current emphasis is on public information and the participation of as broad a segment of citizens as possible in the planning process. Success has been achieved in communities where the public was asked not merely to support predetermined policies but to participate in the development of policy.

Most, if not all of the Federal programs providing financial assistance to local communities call for citizen particpation. As indicated, this has not always been the most rewarding of efforts since the persons supposed to represent the general public have, for the most part represented the positions of the group that appointed them.

The effort on the part of the Federal grant agencies to have local determination of the nature of the programs and continuous support for them has seldom been successful in spite of some heroic efforts. People tend to become involved in planning programs in a defensive manner. That is, a controversial issue seems to be required to rouse the public. Even then, interest and participation tend to disappear as soon as the issue is resolved.

There is no doubt that the concept of public participation is excellent. What must be determined is the best way to achieve it. Citizen involvement in public issues is the best way to obtain effective and responsible government.

Planning Advocate. In almost every instance the presentation of a proposal to the Planning Commission or legislative body can be considered as "advocacy" planning since the plans presented are intended to serve the special needs of the applicant. The term "advocacy" planning, however, in recent years has come to imply that planners should represent minority and poor people's interests in planning matters. This condition seldom occurs. The effect that plans will have on the least mobile elements of society is rarely taken into account.

The advocacy planner is supposed to insure that those who are not able to attend public hearings have their interests represented, so that the influential and affluent do not dominate public policy. Most cities do not employ persons whose responsibilities include involvement with these "special interest" groups. Design Centers in some cities have assumed these responsibilities.

Design Centers are organizations established by local people in a community. They are supported by Federal funds through a local University. These design centers usually serve the planning and architectural needs of the poorer areas of the community. The Design Center in San Francisco was supported through the University of California in Berkeley, the one in Kansas City, through the University of Kansas. In San Francisco they represented the residents of redevelopment areas in an effort to maintain the people's homes.

The Role of the Courts usually becomes part of the planning process when there are charges of violation of the basic community law, state law, or the state or Federal constitution. In some instances discrimination may be claimed, in others that the plan is not clear or reasonable and is therefore inapplicable. Legislative body decisions are usually final unless they are taken to a court of competent jurisdiction in such matters.

The Role of the Media is often overlooked. Most people are informed through the newspaper or through legal notices that are printed in newspapers. In areas where radio and television programs feature local news, items dealing with planning may be included, especially if they become controversial. In some instances owners of the media participate in the discussion as "citizens". Their power to influence the final decsion cannot be underestimated since their views, which are usually set forth convincingly, are not subject to an immediate counter-presentation.

THE PLANNER'S ROLE

Recognizing that planning decisions mainly rest in the hands of elected officials and business leaders, the professional planner, must find out what is the makeup of local politics and learn to deal with that reality.

The "publics" that participate in the various programs will vary. At governmental hearings, the community at large tends not to take a stand owing to its general lack of detailed information on most issues. This lack effectively prevents it from making decisions in its self-interest. Thus , as mainly special interest groups are heard from, it is they who become "the public" in the minds of the legislators. No amount of facts or reasoning not supportive of the interest of a special interest group will alter an interest group's position on a particular issue.

At times, the wishes of the local residents are made known, especially when they form into a pressure group. These groups sometimes take positions of blind opposition to any development, planned or unplanned, good or poor. They may not have the financial resources of the proponents but their voting strength gives them power in the local community.

The planning profession has made considerable progress in its advisory role as the legsilative directives have expanded the required programs and the administrative responsibilities of the staff. This position will become more potent as the public is informed of the implications of the proposals under consideration. Conversely, the planners must be open to suggestions made by members of the community even though these suggestions differ from their point of view. Their task should be to bring together diverse viewpoints for the benefit of the entire community.

THE PLANNER AND SOCIAL WELFARE

In 1974 the American Institute of Planners asserted that "our national priorities have reflected a growing concern for the fate of those individuals and groups who have not received an equitable share of the benefits of our affluent society," and "since manipulations of the physical environment inevitably affect the distribution of social and economic costs and benefits, virtually all public planning bears strong social welfare implications."[1]

If these developments project the planner into the role of advocate for social well-being, it is hardly a new role. A *good* city is the intended historical objective of the planner; it should be designed for social well-being. Awareness of urban deterioration has generated among many people a subconscious sense of guilt for neglect of fundamental human rights. Planners seek to restore cities to a favorable environment for *all* inhabitants. But such a goal cannot be achieved by remaining in the passive role of "expert technicians." Planning Commissioners. too, have an obligation to assert the public interest on all measures embraced in the planning process. Developments in the fields of social welfare and the physical environment have intensified the essentially *affirmative* role of those whose civic and professional responsibility is directed to the public interest. The creative planner is among them.

Our institutions of higher learning must generate the perception, talent, and capacity for creative contributions to the transformation of the urban structure, and instill in their students the commitment to stand up for them as advocates.

---

[1] Position Paper concening Social Welfare Planning, by a committe of the American Institute of Planners, February, 1974.

Among the social welfare issues which directly affect the quality of urban life, according to the American Institute of Planners, housing is a major priority for planners.[2] The professional planner may not be expected to present all the solutions to the housing problem, but he or she must maintain a healthy perspective.

The planner should recognize that juggling quantitative statistics of housing production does not produce adequate housing for the underprivileged. He or she should understand that ethnic discimination will not disappear, nor will social comfort and compatibility appear, simple by dispersal of "low cost" housing in affluent suburbs. The planner should know that the major financial obstacle to building better housing is the high interest rate on home mortgages, not the wages for labor, nor the materials of construction, however sensible it is to explore appropriate economies in construction. The planner must understand that so long as land owners may reap the benefits of values created, not by their own investments, but by *community* prosperity, the public will be obliged to deal with unabated rises in land costs in its subsidy of low cost housing. The planner must be aware that many families cannot afford the full cost of purchasing and maintaining their own homes, and he or she recognize the inverse logic of reducing costs for the poor with Federal subsidies designed to assure profit for private homebuilders and high interest rates for financial institutions.

The planner should realize that ghettoization is not a result of ethnic discrimination alone. People of all groups seek to maintain some vestige of social cohensiveness and economic, religious, and cultural identity: it happens in Scarsdale, Grosse Point, Palm Beach, and Beverly Hills, as well as in Harlem, Watts, and the *barrios*.

And the planner should recognize that the stain of slums and the blight of physical deterioration must be erased from the face of the city if the human dignity of any people is to be preserved. Toward this goal, the planner must encourage the general public to view problems of the less privileged as community responsibilities to be faced and resolved through the efforts of an informed public, both general and official. Housing, health, culture, and social affinities are interrelated and must be resolved by local agencies run by their peers.

---

[2] Policy Statement for the American Institute of Planners, February, 1974.

PART 4

I am vitally interested in the future, because I am going to spend the rest of my life there. . . .

—Charles F. Kettering

Planning for the Future

15

The Comprehensive Plan

A COMPREHENSIVE PLAN IS NEEDED

After the early adventures in zoning property for specific uses it became increasingly apparent that this use of the police power to safeguard the public welfare could not stand by itself. The courts had upheld the right of a community to exercise the police power in legislating regulations governing the use of land. They had granted that a community has the right to determine its own character. Conservatives such as Justice Sutherland had supported this right of the citizens, and there was a growing popular acceptance of zoning as a means to protect the interests of a community.

But the courts perceived the necessity for a community to appraise the use of all land within its political jurisdiction and give consideration to conditions in areas contiguous to it in order to determine properly the appropriate uses and provide a firm basis for the control of land use prescribed in zoning ordinances. The courts had found good reason for this view. They had observed numerous abuses of the police power to establish arbitrary and discriminatory districts. There was a tendency to establish many small districts as a means to restrain the construction of some particular improvement or deny a use deemed undesirable in some existing structure, and there were cases in which a zoning ordinance was intended to create or protect a monopoly.

In order for the courts to have assurance that zoning districts were not arbitrarily determined, they required evidence that the various districts were related to an overall evaluation of land use in the city. There was a growing insistence upon a "comprehensive plan" for land use to form a foundation for zoning ordinances, and the opinion of Justice Sutherland in the Euclid case clearly expressed the need for this evidence. In the fulfilment of this need the process of the Comprehensive Plan was evolved.

Seeking techniques with which to satisfy the requirement for a *comprehensive plan,* some communities willfully avoided the issue by employing specious devices. One of these was the zoning of all land in a community to the least restrictive use with the exception of certain limited "refined" districts. A community could thus allege in court that it had enacted a comprehensive zoning ordinance since every parcel of land in the city was within a zoning district. Although the statement was true, it was not a plan. The other technique was to zone all land not specifically zoned for other purposees, as a residential district with the provision for variances from the residential use; in the administration of the ordinance each variation was then interpreted as an act of making more "precise" the original plan. Neither of these techniques could have stood the test for long since they were evasions of the basic principles of planning.

Too frequently zoning practices resolved themselves into a process of "freezing" the existing land uses including all the misuses which had previously established themselves. In some communities, an inventory and classification of all existing land uses were adopted as the "Plan" of the city. Travesties on planning, these practices are gradually being replaced by a more enlightened concept of planning and its advantages to civic growth and development. As a means to provide a pattern for future development of the city, the General Plan has become a generally accepted instrument.[1]

The difference between "comprehensive planning" and a *comprehensive plan* should not be confused. Comprehensive planning may range from the preparation of a series of highly specialized studies to an intensive study of a development plan for an entire area. The comprehensive plan, however, must include a review of the physical structure of a city or planning area, a measurement of development trends, a definition of goals and objectives for future growth and change, and specific recommendations in the form of maps and charts which delineate the plan and establish standards of density and building intensity in support of the plan.

PURPOSE OF THE PLAN

The modern city is a complex organism. It is a great human enterprise serving the material and spiritual needs of man. It is a segment of the land on which the people have selected their places to live and to work, to learn and to trade, to play and to pray. It is a mosaic of homes and shops, factories and offices, schools and libraries, theaters and hospitals, parks and churches, meeting places and government centers, fire stations and post offices. These are woven together by a network of streets and transportation routes, water, sanitation, and communication channels, and held together by social bonds and economic conditions.

[1] Edward M. Bassett, *The Master Plan,* Russell Sage Foundation, New York, 1938.

To arrange all these facilities properly as the city develops is the function of the Comprehensive Plan. The city is a cumbersome affair, at once sensitive to the multitude of small shifts and yet capable of absorbing great shocks. A change in any part affects other parts of this structure. A new home means more traffic on the streets, extra mail in the postman's bag, another customer in the super-market, more children in the school, more water for the lawn, more picnics in the park, and it means more revenue in taxes. But growth does not always mean strength and prosperity for the community. This rests with the standards a community determines to maintain and the balanced use of its land and resources.

The term "Master Plan" has been applied to almost every scheme for property development from an individual lot to a large estate, a shopping center, or a city. The term "General Plan" identifies long-range, comprehensive plan-ning by or for a government agency as a foundation for overall land development policies within specific corporate limits. These terms were interchangeable, but "General Plan" was adopted to distinguish it from the varied nongovernmental applications associated with "Master Plan."

The term "Comprehensive Plan" was added to the planner's vocabulary in recent years to indicate that current community planning is more than "general." The planning program now includes many social and econmic elements that were not included in the earlier days of professional practice. Students graduating from the universities where urban planning degrees are offered frequently are equipped to participate in a variety of programs, many of which have little or nothing to do with the physical planning that was the basis for the early development of the profession. This should not demean the importance of physical planning; it merely adds a new dimension to it.

The Comprehensive Plan is a guide to orderly city development to promote the health, safety, welfare, and convenience of the people of a community. It organizes and coordinates the complex relationships between urban land uses and many civic activities. It charts a course for growth and change. It expresses the aims and ambitions of a community, delineating the form and character it seeks to achieve. It reflects the policies by which these goals may be reached. It is responsive to appropriate change and, to maintain its essential vitality, is subject to continual review. It directs "the physical development of the com-munity and its environs in relation to its social and economic well-being for the fulfillment of the rightful common destiny, according to a 'master plan' based on 'careful and comprehensive surveys and studies of present conditions and the prospects of future growth of the municipality,' and embodying scientific teachings and creative experience. In a word, this is an exercise of the State's inherent authority, antedating the Constitution itself, to have recourse to such measures as may serve the basic common moral and material needs. Planning to this end is as old as government itself—of the very essence of an ordered and civilized society."[2]

---

[2] *Mansfield & Sweet. Inc.* v. *Town of West Orange,* supra.

THE PLAN IS A PROCESS

State legislation usually requires the preparation of a Comprehensive Plan
and sets forth the scope. A passage from the California law reads, in part:

"Each Commisssion or planning department shall prepare and the commission shall adopt a comprehensive, long-term general plan for the physical
development of the city, county, area, or region, and of any land outside its
boundaries which in the commission's judgemnt bears relation to its planning.
The plan may be referred to as the master or general plan and shall be offically
certified by the planning commission and the legislative body.[3]

After the Comprehensive Plan has been adopted by the legislative body,
". . . no road, street, highway, square, park, or other public way, ground or
open space shall be acquired by dedication or otherwise, and no street, road,
highway or public way shall be closed or abandoned, and no public building or
structure shall be constructed or authorized in the area . . . until the location,
character, and extent thereof shall be submitted to and shall have been reported
on by the planning commission."[4] It is such statements of offical policy that
establish the planning process in our cities, and it is such statements which have
been upheld by the courts of our land because they recognize the necessity for a
city plan.

Ladislas Segoe described the Comprehensive Plan in these terms:

> The comprehensive city plan or master plan, while it must be thoroughly practical
> and sound economically, must give expression also to other than the purely
> materialistic aspirations of the people of a community. Only then will the plan
> possess—in addition to its influence toward a more convenient, efficient economical
> development—the inspiration force that will force civic interest, devotion and
> loyalty essential for building better cities.
>
>   The comprehensive city plan or master plan must therefore be—first, a
> balanced and otherwise attractive general design best suited to present and
> probable future needs; second, in scale with the population and economic pro-
> spects of the community; and third, in scale with its financial resources, present
> and prospective. The satisfying of the above criteria calls for the application of
> scientific as well as artistic effort, in order to produce a city plan of attractive form,
> pleasing balance and detail, attuned to the economic and social activities of the
> community. . . .[5]

It is probably more accurate to define a Comprehensive Plan as a process
rather than a conclusive statement. It is a pattern for the physical development
of the city, a pattern to guide the city builders in locating their investments and
measuring the prospect for success. It is a design for the physical, social,
economic, and political framework for the city; it welds the sociological, economic, and geographic properties of the city into a structure.

To suggest that the plan is a fluid process may imply that decisions are not

[3] State of California. Laws Relating to Conservation, Planning and Zoning, 1959.

[4] *Ibid.*

[5] Ladislas Segoe, *Local Planning Administration,* International City Managers' Association,
Chicago, 1941, first edition.

represented in it. The plan for a city will be modified as conditions may alter the affairs of people from time to time, but a Comprehensive Plan represents certain decisions of vital importance to the welfare of the people and their city. It represents a decision on the number of people the city may build to accommodate; it represents the standards by which the city will be developed. It represents decisions on the appropriate relation between the uses of land, the relation between the land to be developed for residential, commercial, and industrial enterprise. It calls for decisions on the lines of communication that link these areas—the circulation system. And it represents decisions on the plan for reservation of open space throughout the city.

These are broad decisions, but they are essential to the formulation of a pattern for city building. It is upon these decisions that the health of urban development rests for they express the aspirations of a community and set the goals toward which the city may advance.

The Comprehensive Plan has been sometimes regarded as only a reference guide for the Planning Commission, being subject to neither formal public hearings nor official action by the legislative body. This arrangement appears to avoid the cumbersome proceedings which accompany formal action to modify the plan, thus affording maximum flexibility at the discretion of the commisssion and staff. But it also opens the possibility for personal decision-making in response to special pressures. This status of the Plan fails to recognize the essence of the Plan itself. Affecting the future of all the people and property in the city, the Plan represents the policy which directs future growth and development of the city. It is a public policy for protection of the public welfare and investment in the urban community.

Assembly Bill 1301 adopted in California in 1974 requires that zoning be consistent with the Comprehensive General Plan, thus establishing these planning policies as the legal criteria for implementation through detailed zoning. This public document has an order of importance which demands that it be subject to public response and discussion, thorough consideration by the legislative body, and adoption as the official plan. It, and subsquent revisions to it, should be adopted by resolution of the legislative body. It serves as the basic frame of reference for all administrative and regulatory measures relating to the physical development of the city—the zoning ordinance, subdivision regulations, urban renewal, the capital improvement expenditures. The financial solvency of a city hinges upon a program of public facilities which maintains a balance between expenditure and revenue. The Plan aids in weighing this balance.

Two basic elements of the Comprehensive Plan are the *Plan for Land Use* and the *Plan for Circulation*. Each of these elements is supported by complete documentary evidence, the social, physical, and economic facts and premises, from which they were derived.

SOCIAL AND ECONOMIC CONSIDERATIONS

If the data on the nature of the physical character of the city seem to be a complicated process, the social and economic facts are even more so. People are not inclined to conceal the manner in which they use the land unless an evasion of the law is involved, but they are reluctant to divulge their ages, incomes, or personal health; such information is naturally considered to be of a personal nature. To plan for the community welfare, however, it is important to know about the people who make it and for whom it is intended.

The principal source of economic and social data is the U.S. Census; included in the census are data on family incomes, family sizes, dwelling rent, condition of structures, owner and tenant occupancy of structures, years of schooling, age composition, occupation of the wage earner, and other information. Based upon these data, the Bureau of the Census analyzes the spending habits of the various income groups which indicate the amount in each income group spent for rent, clothes, food, amusement, and other living necessities. Much of the latter data is given for the whole city and is therefore difficult to relate to the census tracts which are the units in which urban statistics are usually tabulated. Housing data in the census are listed by blocks and provide a source of information for the land-use survey.

Although most public and private local agencies normally assemble only the information on the social and economic structure of the community in which they are directly interested, the planning agency may obtain and correlate this special information to form an overall picture. Since the various agencies may interpret similar data in different ways, these differences must be resolved by the planners on the basis of the best available known facts.

It is a well-known cliché that anything can be proved with statistics; the corollary is that statistics may not prove anything. It is important that they not be misleading. As an illustration, the increase in the number of families and the number of houses built may be nearly the same and therefore indicate no shortage of dwellings. These "pure" numbers mean little as an evaluation of the housing supply in relation to the housing need. The number of families formerly "doubled-up," the cost brackets of the new residences, the absence of a normal vacancy factor, and the occupancy of substandard housing facilities are among the statistics to be evaluated with those on the number of families and the housing supply.

Juvenile delinquency and crime data in the local police and probation department files record the location of the incidents and the residences of offenders. Other social statistics support as well as guide the preparation of the Comprehensive Plan and the building of a good city. Data on disease and health can be obtained from the health departments of the cities, counties, and state, as well as the tuberculosis and health associations. Many other private agencies, such as foundations, service clubs, veterans' organizations, universities and charitable groups, have valuable data. Material on the birth rate, death rate, infant mortality, marriage, and divorce rates are other social factors; and the rate of population immigration and emigration, the years of schooling, occupations on the working force, and the cultural inclinations are among the data which the planning commission must necessarily correlate objectively.

Information on the economic development and prospects of the community is usually available through the Chamber of Commerce, and these data can be cross-referenced with reports by Dun and Bradstreet and the U.S. Department of Commerce, the U.S. Department of Labor, State Employment Offices, and local agencies and industries. Trends in industrialization and increases in the working force can be traced through the U.S. Depatment of Labor, the State Employment Services, and local industries. The trends in the industrial population will have a decided effect on the planning process. Data on the earning capacity, the average years of employment, the social security structure, types and diversification of employment, and the income groups represented in the working population are necessary to calculate the purchasing power of the community and the ability to pay rents and taxes. These statistics are important as a basis for the Comprehensive Plan.

Too frequently the social scientist has been cast in the role of historian of economic facts, reporting past trends and current conditions. The economic aspects of planning have thus been limited to an inventory of data which presents the *status quo*. Statistical techniques are employed in the projection of population and related fields of importance to planning, but the general effect is a kind of resignation by all concerned to the prospects which these projections imply. If planning means anything, it is the endeavor to *direct* future growth and development, being quite the opposite of drifting with the currents of un-regulated trends. The tools of socioeconomic analysis are therefore essential to seek a balance among the basic urban activities. And this balance may require that accepted trends be altered, diverted, or redirected—but this is planning.

The increase in population is a natural phenomenon, and the trend of population growth in cities is a consequence of broad economic and social pressures. But to be effective, urban planning cannot succumb to the weight of statistical evidence. *Survival* of the urban population is at stake and so is the prospect for building decent cities. Means may be developed to control the number of people who are born as there have been means to lengthen the life span. With the reduction of pestilence and famine, means to stabilize the population, short of war, are meager, However, we have the means, through planning and legislation, to regulate the *distribution* of the urban population, the amounts of land required for the various functions of an urban community, and the standards for the development of the land. To determine the appropriate allocation of land, in amount and location, the economic demands must be measured. The physical structure must be arranged to accommodate the facilities required for economic survival, and accommodate them in a manner that will produce good places in which to live and work.

The social scientist carries a heavy responsibility for creative analysis of the relationships between people and their employment opportunities, the production resources, and the commerce and industry needed to support an urban population, The city must be built upon a firm economic base or it cannot provide the amenities of a civilized community. The future of cities as desirable social environments will depend upon our capacity to integrate physical and economic planning. Walter Blucher has stated: "What is the responsibility of the planning agency for a determination of employment possibilities outside of

public works? You may not think the planning agency has any such responsibility. I don't see how we can do an effective planning job in any community,
however, unless we know what the population of the community will be and
what the economic possibilities for that population are."[6]

CHANGING CHARACTER OF CITIES

With the assembly of the data previously suggested—that part of the planning
process identified as research—we learn the nature of the existing city. This is the
knowledge needed for analysis of the city; from it we learn why the city was
begun, how it grew, and why it prospered.

There are reasons why cities are located where they are; they were
important reasons in the history of the city and they bear upon its future. They
may be important as a pattern for the continuous development of the city or they
may reveal what changes have overtaken the city and thus indicate the new
directions for which they city must be planned. The reasons for the founding of
a city may have multiplied, or they may have vanished. There may be entirely
new purposes for the city than those which moved its original settlement.

The sleepy village of the eighteenth century has apparently little in
common with the metropolis of today. There may remain marks of its historical
origin, but the functions may have altered completely. As the city grew in size,
as the population increased, and as new enterprises developed, the character of
the city may have altered. Perhaps the quality of community living deteriorated
as the city grew from a small, intimate town to the unfriendly metropolitan
machine it now seems to be. Much may have been lost in this process, enough to
question whether the city can recover the human values by which the living
standards of people are measured.

The changes in urban character reflected in the growth and the deterioration of neighborhood life are illustrated in all our cities. It is apparent in a
growing metropolis like Los Angeles. Hardly more than 40 years ago this
community was reputed for its climate, its recreational opportunities, its
beaches, and the grandeur of its mountains. The quality of its living environment and the pleasant mildness of its atmosphere made this city a haven for
travelers from all part of the world.

The population of Los Angeles was 500,000 in 1920; in 1977 it was more
than 2,800,000 and the city had spread over the 450 square miles of its area. From
its beginning as the center of a predominantly agricultural area it has developed
an important industrial economy. Industrial plants have sprung up with little or
no attention to their probable effect upon the living conditions of the region and
its inhabitants. Water was brought more than 250 miles to supply the growing

---

[6] Walter H. Blucher, Executive Director, American Society of Planning Officials, in *Planning,
1945*, Part 1, Chicago, May 16–17, 1945.

population. Congestion overtook this city of "open space," blight and slums are taking their toll, and smoke and fumes taint the air.

This story differs only in degree and detail in all our cities; it is the tale of the metropolis. The native advantages of our urban communities have not been respected by the people who built them; in the name of a bigger and more prosperous city, they have been desecrated and the people are retreating. The people are fleeing the city and it remains neglected, but the same indifference is guiding development on the outskirts. Rather than making capital of the native characteristics of a region, exploitation of the urban community is undermining its own investments.

The Comprehensive Plan of a city or region has two objectives: forestalling the drift into chaos in the yet undeveloped areas of the city and gradually reconstructing the developed area of the city with particular attention to blighted sections and improved circulation. The present chaotic development of the city is a trend, but this trend can be corrected and redirected to benefit all the people through planning.

The changing nature of the city must be appraised and the natural character defined. Shifts in the emphasis of the urban economy and the services and functions it performs require adjustments in the living habits of the people, the land use, and the transportation, if they are to continue as favorable environments in which to live and work. The Comprehensive Plan will reflect these adjustments and thereby become a guide for the future growth and development of the community. This demands inquiry into every facet of urban existence; it calls for the coordination of a team of trained decision makers (both public and private) and enlightened and enthusiastic citizens.

THE PLAN IS TEAMWORK

Knowledge of the physical structure of the city will reveal certain natural uses for the land and existing uses which deserve particular respect in the plan. There may be well-established industrial areas, commercial centers, residential developments, a great park, waterways, railroads, and historical and natural features. This knowledge will also indicate some apparent maladjustments in current land use for which corrective measures are obviously necessary. It will also indicate an appropriate relation between industrial and residential areas. With these broad strokes the Comprehensive Plan is begun.

The city is linked with its neighbor cities and towns and its environs by the highways, railroads, and mass transportation facilities; these form the main arteries of circulation about the city, and they will form the boundaries of the neighborhood units. The freeways, parkways, rapid transit and railroads will establish the relation between the sources of employment in commerce and industry, and the residential neighborhoods.

Laid upon this general plan will be the reservations of open spaces, the areas adapted for natural parks, or the submarginal lands unsuited for active urban development. In this process the Comprehensive Plan begins to take shape. The Comprehensive Plan will reflect the local policies on the density of population desirable and consistent wiht the character of the city in its residential areas, and it will indicate the standards for the relation of building bulk and open space in these areas and in the commercial districts. Within the broad land-use plan and guided by these standards, the precise plans for the various areas of the city may be refined as the time for their development approaches. The schools and playgrounds may be located within the neighborhood units, and requirements for the local shopping centers may be determined. Space may be reserved for the freeways and rapid transit rights-of-way. Detailed plans for the improvement of the "downtown" business center may be formulated, and the reconstruction of blighted areas in the central section of the city may be planned and executed. The Comprehensive Plan will set forth the appropriate use to which the land in the city should be devoted so that the enterprise of city building may have a tangible guide in its determinations for investment.

It takes teamwork to produce the Comprehensive Plan that contains the inspired will of a people bent upon building a decent and fine city. The decisions emerge from the coordinated teamwork of sociologists and economists, statisticians and engineers, finance advisors and lawyers, politicians and architects, health authorities and public administrators, and public-spirited businessmen and consumers. It takes boundless enthusiasm and enlightened civic interest, and it takes a competent staff of trained planners to perform the job of coordination and translation.

The preparation of the Comprehensive Plan, which represents the aims and ambitions of a community in shaping its enviroment, requires a shift in the usual roles of allied professionals on the planning team: the social scientist must set aside his role as social critic, the economist his role as statistician, the lawyer his role as legalistic obstructionist, the real estate professional his role as super-salesman, the engineer his role as computer expert. These essential participants on the planning team then become *creative urban analysts.*

Commercial centers and industrial areas may be fairly defined, and single-family suburbs readily delineated, but the process becomes complex within the twilight areas of the city which are, in planners' parlance, "transition zones." With Federal financial assistance, redevelopment in large cities may be planned as components of the city as a whole. But most cities have not become overgrown metropolises. Transition areas are older residential sections trapped between chaotic commercial and industrial development and new residential subdivisions. Although blight may have begun, and they may have become the refuge of ethnic minorities, these areas often contain vintage homes and handsome trees which represent the only vestige of urban charm.

It is standard procedure for planners to sweep these transition areas with a broad brush into land use classifications of "R-2, R-3, or R-4": apartments and a mixture of commercial zoning. With no modification of land subdivision, the intrusion of mediocre apartments on single-family lots erodes residential quality and reduces the prospect of neighborhood cohesiveness.

The city is in constant transition. The Comprehensive Plan delineates the concept of the city the people seek to achieve. Zoning is one of the instruments by which that concept is implemented, but as an instrument of transition it is suffering from atrophy. Conventional zoning regulations are obsolete. Sensitive teamwork to untangle the chaos of urban land uses and shape new instruments of regulation, while guarding the general social well-being, requires, as Jacob Crane observed, "intuition, imagination, and bold action."[7]

PLATITUDES

Planning is plagued with platitudes. Some familiar expressions have almost reached the stature of symbols, the mere mention of which presumably being sufficient to convey a significant message. It would be well to examine some of these phrases in order to recognize their meaning.

We frequently refer to the necessity for "flexibility" in city planning. It is suggested that city plans must be adjustable to changing conditions, that cities grow like "living cells." These are convenient terms and contain much truth. Unfortunately they too generally become picturesque phrases. There are some very specific limitations upon their value and application.

A city is more than buildings, streets, utilities, steel, concrete, and glass. Nevertheless, these are the materials of which the physical structure is made. They are inert. They have chemical properties, but they are not elastic. Once in place they cannot be shifted about to suit either fancy or "changing conditions." They are static. The width of a street does not pulsate with the intensity of traffic flow, nor can a building flex its beams and columns.

In these important particulars the analogy of city building to a "living organism" is literary confection. The pictorial similarity between a medieval town plan and the cross section of a tree or the veins in the human arm becomes pure poetry. Lifted out of the rarified atmosphere of romantic fantasy "flexibility" means enough space to bring the products of industrial genius into useful service in the city structure.

Cities are inflexible because they are so crowded there is no room for the various elements to "work." They are frozen into congestion, and flexibility will be attained only through the establishment of adequate standards to guide those who participate in building the city.

There comes a moment when decisions must be made. When that moment arrives, there is a degree of finality implied by the act of decision. The structure of the city does not float; it cannot be tugged or pushed about. When a building or other civic improvement is erected, it is there to stay. Flexibility in the plan of a city will be accomplished by standards for city building that preserve enough space for all improvements without overcrowding.

[7] Jacob Crane, Urban Planning—*Illusion and Reality: A New Philosophy for Planned City Building,* Vantage Pres, New York, 1973.

In nearly every kind of business enterprise there is reference to "trends." New conditions, scientific development, and social improvement require adjustments in the conduct of enterprise. They likewise require adjustments in the city. Shifts in the growth of cities prompted by such changes and accompanied by some degree of orderly direction serve as a measure of trends in healthy city development.

But these shifts are confused with quite another sort of change: the urge to escape from the contagious disease of obsolescence and unrestrained speculation. Healthy enterprise shuns association with derelict neighbors; unbridled physical deterioration repels improvement. Shifts in the urban pattern compelled by these desultory forces do not mark *trends*. They report a rout, a desparate and disorderly retreat. Diagnosing this disease as a trend is to spread the contagion further, and ignore or misinterpret the only value that observation of trends can provide: a guide to the natural and appropriate use of land in the growing city.

Economy is a familiar slogan. It is also a worthy aim. In practice, however, it has unfortunately been too frequently reduced to a fiction. Expenditures for civic improvements are generally decided upon by their budget appeal, not their adequacy. Patchwork improvements display such an appeal; they appear to be "economical." The question of whether they may actually solve any particular problem is usually overlooked or avoided. Economy may really be, and usually is, quite another matter. We have seen a street widening prove inadequate almost upon the day it was completed. We have seen the immediate need for another improvement added. We have seen the value of adjacent land enhanced with each such piecemeal improvement, and new buildings erected about it. We have then seen the public forced to pay the added increment of land and building "value" each of these improvements has induced. This process is characteristic of urban "economy," but it is not economical.

Each new or improved utility service introduced to a city crowds some equally needed service. The utility system—sewers, water, gas, electricity—distributes the energy to operate a city of a million people. Yet these vital veins are, with some rare exceptions, buried beneath, or suspended above, the arteries that carry the stream of daily traffic. The conflict between these services is experienced day in and day out. A utility line breaks down and the repair job stops the circulation of automobiles and street cars. These conflicts choke an already congested city and are not economical.

"Efficiency" is another ingrown term. Efficiency obviously has virtue; that virtue is the elimination of waste. In the name of "efficient" planning, however, there are examples of the creation of waste. We have observed acres of subdivisions, planned with alleged efficiency, which are actually a waste of the urban resources. We have seen the width of a street, the size of a house, or the lot it occupies squeezed to an efficient minimum so low it is reduced to nothing more than a cheap commodity.

In the light of the studies by Sir Raymond Unwin and Henry Wright, efficient planning is more than an obsession to save; it is also a method to *improve.* Standards are the measurements by which we must be guided rather than remain content with what Elizabeth Denby called "the intellectual pleasure which the architect got from a triumphant arrangement of inadequate space."[8]

It must be clear that space in a city must first and foremost provide for *adequacy;* it must be ample.

The measure of adequacy will be the capacity of the space to receive the buildings of a city without itself being lost completely. It means enough space so that buildings may stand alone or together without violating the sensibilities of those who see and use them. It means that cities will provide space into which the buildings are built rather than a solid mass of buildings through which the fissures we call streets are carved.

The concept of space means a relatively constant limitation on population density regardless of the heights that structures may reach. The prospect of squeezing more people into the same space creates instability, not only in land value, but in urban services. It imposes an extravagance on the installation of service facilities. Water, sewers, gas and electric distribution, telephones, streets, walks, transportation, fire, health, educational and recreational facilities cannot be estimated with any possible degree of efficiency. These services must be installed in sufficient size and quantity to meet unlimited future requirements, or be repeatedly removed, altered, and replaced as the demand may fluctuate. Either course is an extravagant venture as city budgets and utility bills attest.

Within a reasonable concept of space in the urban environment is the room for the vehicles of transportation to circulate with ease and safety. This means enough room to separate the different types of vehicles and the direction of their travel; room enough to move about on the surface of the earth rather than burrow into the ground with subways. This means the city will no longer be a maze of streets and alleys slicing through a solid bulk of buildings.

This concept means that parking space for the free-moving vehicles of our contemporary age shall be a component part of all floor space provided within or adjacent to buildings, and it means that this integration will bring the relation between open space and building floor area into some degree of balance.

There will be enough room for all the essential utility conduits, a network of vital service arteries so aligned within their respective rights-of-way that interference is avoided at all times.

This concept of space means room enough for people to walk in safety and some degree of beauty; trees would not be unwelcome. Finally it means an environment in which the human spirit can rise above mediocrity; it means relief from the din and the danger that fray the human nerves and dull the human mind.

It may be suggested that the concept of space within the city described above is not a "practical" one. The planning of cities is rather cluttered with

---

[8] Elizabeth Denby, *Europe Rehoused,* W. W. Norton, New York, 1938.

bromides, but hardly any is so overworked as "practical." Compromise is the inevitable road to satisfactory human relationships. The capacity to compromise is a requisite to accomplishment. It implies, however, that an objective is clearly defined. The objective of planning is the solution of a problem; in city planning the problem is that of an environment that is rapidly disintegrating under the spell of congestion and ugliness.

Opinions may vary as to the way in which to arrive at the objective of decent cities, but no purpose is served until some area of agreement can be reached about the nature of the objective itself. Solutions call for ideas. They deal in ideas. Ideas are the tools with which we shape an objective, and they cannot be dismissed only because they may at first appear "impractical." We see about us the results of thus being "practical"; we see these results repeated time and again: more congestion, more traffic problems, more deterioration, more expense, and boundless confusion and bewilderment. If we peer behind this scene, we may well find the reason: the process of planning began with a compromise. The ideas that are the stuff of progress never reach the surface where they may be observed and tested for their validity.

Nor is this approach really practical. The first test of practicality is whether a thing "works." Can it be claimed that our cities work? Is traffic congestion practical? Or the crowded business centers? Or the blighted areas and slums? Are the extravagant devices for parking automobiles—overhead and underground—practical? Is the mediocrity of the living and working environment, and the obsolete transportation in our cities really practical? Is it practical to spend huge sums on surveys, consultations and plans, then ignore them all? The urban malady of congestion is like the itch; scratching produces a sensation of relief. But common sense tells us the only practical treatment is a cure, not more irritation.

Must it be considered impractical to propose standards which have as their sole purpose a restoration of permanent values in the urban environment? Ample space for London was denigrated by F. J. Forty, Chief Planner for the rebuilding program, with the words, "I want it [London] to be the leading place of commerce in the world and not—as some planners suggest—a park."[9] Must this be the interpretation of the need for adequate space within our cities? The original plan proposed for the City of London, a plan that offered little improvement over the city that was destroyed, was commented upon by Donald Tyerman in the *Observer* as "timid rebuilding proposals." He said "The makers of this plan are not planners but pessimists."[10]

We might hark to the words of Lewis Mumford:

"As so often has happened during the last quarter century, the self-styled practical men turned out to be the weak, irresponsible dreamers, afraid to face

[9] *Architectural Forum,* September 1944.

[10] *Ibid.* The plan to which Mr. Tyermann referred was that proposed for the mile-square "City" of London by the Improvement and Town Planning Committee.

unpleasant facts, while those of us who were called dreamers have, perhaps, some little right now to be accepted—at least belatedly—as practical men. By now history has caught up with our more dire prophecies. That is at once the justification of our thinking and the proof of its tragic failure to influence our contemporaries."[11]

THE PHYSICAL STRUCTURE

Before any land use plan can be made, the physical structure of the community must be known and understood—its rivers, its mountains, its plains and prairies, its hills, its climate, the direction of its winds. Is the land suited for agriculture, is it good for grazing? Are there oil or mineral deposits, is it subject to floods, are there natural or historic features to be preserved? The geology, hydrography, meteorology, and geography must be rediscovered beneath the blanket of the built-up city. Thus we can comprehend the three primary elements of nature without which there is no life: land, water, and air.

The constant relationship of land, water, and air is necessary to the support of human life. One can imagine controlled air conditions, and we know that water can be transported from distant mountain sources to semi-arid regions, but the land is where you find it. Perhaps it can be built up, the marshes drained, fertility improved, and water can increase its growing yield, but land itself must have the basic capacity for response to man's treatment and we classify it as good or bad according to its fitness to provide life for humankind.

Because a parcel of land may be suitable for a variety of uses, it is the relationship between these uses which becomes the problem of planning. Some uses are favorable to each other, whereas some are not only detrimental but dangerous. Recognizing that land may have many uses and that the relationship between them is the most important consideration, the plan begins with a definition of land uses and the appropriate location within the topographic, geologic, and geographic structure of the city. Upon these the city pattern should be developed.

INVENTORY AND CLASSIFICATION OF EXISTING LAND USE

Regardless of the high aspirations a people may share for the future of their city or the distant range over which they prepare their plans for its development, the planning process must obviously begin with the city as it exists. It is consequently necessary to know the way in which the land is used and maintain the inventory as a current record. From this inventory the physical characteristics of the city are discernible, those which warrant change or necessitate retention

[11] *Architectural Forum,* May 1945.

in the Comprehensive Plan may be determined, and some existing uses may become key controls over the pattern of future land use.

This prospect is particularly marked by the fact that zoning laws are not retroactive, and the transition from an existing land use to another classification may span a great number of years. According to Anglo-Saxon theory, if land has never been used for a particular purpose it does not constitue a deprivation of property rights to deny the right to so use it in the future. On the other hand, it is assumed that zoning ordinances must not restrict property to uses considered less liberal than the existing use. The courts have held that zoning may not be retroactive, that existing land uses may not be "zoning out of existence." They must be permitted to continue as "nonconforming" uses if they are inconsistent with the use the zoning ordinance prescribes.

This may appear to permit the continuation of a nonconforming use which would prove to be a detriment to the surrounding development, like an obnoxious industry in a residential zone. The courts have pointed out that other means are available for relief from such intrusions; proof that a nonconforming use is a

Actual Land Uses[1]

Use	CENTRAL CITIES	
	Per Cent of Total Developed Area	Acres per 100 Persons
Single-family dwellings	31.81	2.19
Two-family dwellings	4.79	0.33
Multifamily dwellings	3.01	0.21
Commercial areas	3.32	0.23
Light industry ⎫ Heavy industry ⎬ Railroad property ⎭	11.30	0.78
Parks and playgrounds	6.74	0.46
Public and semipublic property	10.93	0.75
Streets	28.10	1.94
Total	100.00	6.89

[1] Harland Bartholomew, *Land Uses in American Cities*, Harvard University Press, Cambridge, 1955.

Studies by Harland Bartholomew revealed the actual land uses in a number of survey cities. Three types of urban communities were included. The "Central Cities" are self-contained cities which perform the major social and economic functions of an urbanized area. They include 53 cities ranging in population from 1,740 to 821,960. The "Satellite Cities" are incorporated cities which are economically dependent upon an adjacent central city. They include 33 cities ranging in population from 900 to 74,347. The "Urban Areas" are metropolitan areas embracing a central city, and an urbanized fringe. The 11 urban areas in the survey range in population from 7,150 to 119,825. The study does not include the largest metropolitan areas but presents a fair cross section of nuisance and dangerous to the life and health of the inhabitants and the public welfare may be sufficient reason for the courts to deny a use to continue.

Nonconforming uses may not be renewed if destroyed by fire or act of God. In such cases the new structure must conform to the provisions of the current zoning. In some ordinances a nonconforming structure may be repaired or slightly altered, but it may not be modified to the extent that the space or facilities are enlarged, nor may a different nonconforming use replace that which is removed.

Some zoning ordinances specify a period during which a nonconforming use shall be retired. This time is equivalent to an amortization period with an established date for removal of the structure, the period being related to the years of use already experienced in the structure and the investment in it. In this way property values and human values may be reasonably balanced, and intruding uses gradually removed to be replaced by conforming uses. The logic and equity of such a method would seem to impel cities to adopt it in the public interest.

Most cities classify their land in four major categories: agricultural, residential, commercial, and industrial. Each of these broad groups is subdivided into uses ranging from the most to the least obnoxious, from the most to the least

SATELLITE CITIES		URBAN AREAS	
Per Cent of Total Developed Area	Acres per 100 Persons	Per Cent of Total Developed Area	Acres per 100 Persons
36.18	3.14	25.05	3.72
3.31	0.29	1.63	0.24
2.49	0.22	1.31	0.20
2.54	0.22	2.65	0.39
		1.87	0.28
12.51	1.09	3.77	0.56
		6.22	0.92
4.37	0.38	4.59	0.68
10.93	0.95	25.30	3.75
27.67	2.40	27.61	4.10
100.00	8.69	100.00	14.84

urban land-use characteristics. (Each community is unique, and the land uses in each should reflect its special qualities.)

In evaluating the space requirements for the various land uses in the Comprehensive Plan, the standards of development—population density and character of the physical environment appropriate to the region—introduce an additional factor: the building bulk and floor space which will occupy the land. This factor may be expressed as a ratio of building floor area to lot area and should be considered in formulating the basic concept of the Comprehensive Plan (see Chapter 21, The Zoning Plan, and Chapter 17, Commerce and Industry).

restricted, from the most concentrated to the most open. This is generally identified as "step-down" classification as it is applied within each of the four broad groups. Thus the general industrial classification contains heavy industry and light industry, expressing the difference between a boiler works and a tin shop, for example. A large department store would be classified in heavy commercial, whereas a neighborhood grocery store would be placed in the lightest commercial zone. Likewise, a multistory apartment building would be in the least restricted residential zone, whereas a single-family detached house is in the restricted area.

The number of intermediate steps between the most intense use and the least intense will vary in different communities as the complexity of the community may warrant. In a very large city there may be as many as fifty classes of land use, whereas in a small town there may only be nine. This difference in the number of classifications does not suggest less accuracy in determining the classifications; it indicates that the manner in which the land is used in a small town is less complex than in a large city. The number of classifications should be as few as possible consistent with a complete coverage of the various uses of land and an accurate description of each.

A city should have a record of the way in which the land within its boundaries is used, as well as the quantity of space and structures which comprise it. A periodic inventory of these assets should be undertaken just as a well-organized and well-administered business maintains an inventory of its stock and the value of it. During the depression of 1930–40, land-use surveys in a number of cities were conducted under auspices of the Works Progress Administration of the Federal government. These data were of immeasurable value to the planning commissions in the respective cities, and yet there are few instances in which the records were subsequently maintained in current form.

A continuous record may be maintained by reference to building permits and the tax assessor of the city. Other sources of reference are The Sanborn Insurance Atlas; the Building and Safety Department of the city, which records changes in building occupancy and alterations that indicate a change in the use of existing structures; the Health department, which maintains data on substandard structures, pest infestation, lack of sanitation facilities; and the local housing authority from which information may generally be obtained on the physical condition of housing. Banking and lending institutions frequently maintain valid information on new building activity.

The record of urban land use is not for the purpose of only ascertaining the condition of the physical structure. It provides the information necessary to observe the rate at which the city is increasing or decreasing its physical plant in the various classifications of land use. It offers a basis for measuring the amount of land to be reserved in zoning for future developments of the city, the quantity of land, and the most appropriate location for the various uses.

The land-use inventory is good urban business and should be maintained as a current record. It is not a plan; it is part of the vital data from which plans may be made.

16

The Land Use Plan

The land use plan is intended as an important means of reaching physical, economic, and social community goals. The plan, through its effects on public and private decisions and investments, can be a powerful influence on the growth rate, character, quality, and pattern of the city's physical environment.

The land use plan sets forth policies intended to encurage the upgrading and preservation of the existing city and to provide for an orderly efficient, and logical extension of urban development in the predominantly undeveloped area surrounding the city. A central issue in deciding the future pattern of development is the manner in which future growth is to be accommodated. Already-developed areas can be used more intensively (higher average densitites) or undeveloped land can be brought into use. A range of choices exists between these two extremes.

Until recently, many cities have emphasized expansion into new areas rather than the recycling and more intense use of existing areas. However, over the years, experience and analysis have brought about a general acceptance that such an approach toward growth can raise the cost of city services and add to the severity of a number of environmental, social, and economic problems.

Many cities are now attempting to define a "balanced" program of expansion and increased utilization. In large measure, each community's proper balance is unique. The balance is a function of the scale of priorities that a community attaches to its goals.

Another important factor affecting the community's choice is the existing pattern of development. The face of the city changes very slowly and some choices may be feasible only in the long run. For example, an already intensely-developed city may have little choice but to expand into new areas. Alternatively, a city "land locked" by external development or jurisdictions can only accommodate growth internally.

The land use considerations in planning can be divided into five parts. The first part identifies objectives and priciples pertaining to residential, commerical, recreational, educational and industrial uses of land and enumerates existing standards for such uses.

219

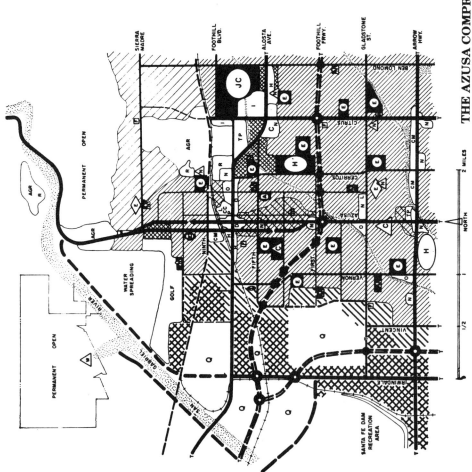

THE AZUSA COMPREHENSIVE PLAN (Azusa, Calif.)

The second part focuses on the nature and pattern of development within the existing city boundaries. Descriptive data in this section provides the basis for answering, in part, questions as to what changes in the pattern of land use are needed and how much growth can be accommodated within the existing area of urban development.

The third part looks in detail at the area of predominantly undeveloped land surrounding the city, the city's "area of influence." Existing uses of land are identified, and factors affecting the land's suitability for future development are discussed. Standards for new development are proposed.

The fourth part brings together the analysis and results of the preceding sections and proposes a coordinated, comprehensive land use plan for both the city and its area of influence, including all recreational, educational and other necessities and amenities required to serve the people under the planning program. This plan is an important element in efforts to "manage" growth and is based upon current expectations of future growth, the existing pattern of development, and community desires as to how growth can be physically and financially, accommodated.

The fifth part of the land use element explores and identifies tools that could be used to implement the proposed plan.

The land use plan establishes the allocation of neighborhood units with their several facilities, schools, parks, playgrounds, and shopping. It is the plan which sets the standards to guide the city builders in their various enterprises, and a complete plan will be more than a single map of the city. It will be a compilation of all the data from which the estimates of required areas were calculated and the standards determined. It will become a reference for all who are engaged in urban development.

This plan will chart the relation of the city to the region and indicate its integration with its satellite communities, and will define the areas and standards for subdivision of new land. This is the plan which forms the foundation for the precise plans for zoning, parks and recreation, schools and other public buildings, the civic center, cultural and sports centers. It is the plan which will guide the city and public utility corporations in the design of utilities—sewers, gas, water, electric distribution, and street lighting. And this is the plan to which all can refer for guidance in determining their investments in the city.

MISUSE OF THE PLAN

The importance of the Comprehensive Plan has been emphasized as much by the abuses to which it has been subjected as by the uses to which it has been put. Adoption of a plan has often been treated as a spurious political gesture; the less specific the plan, the more adaptable it is to political manipulation. Diagrams of existing land uses have been accepted as a plan; unrealistic agricultural or single family zoning has been adopted for underdeveloped areas to avoid decisions on growth and development policies. Environmental Impact Statements for separate developments have become a convenient substitute for planning.

These irresponsible tactics have been politically expedient for incompetent civic leaders, and have cast grave doubt on the social and economic usefulness of planning. The doubts are well founded; much of the planning has not been demonstrably effective in improving the urban environment. City and rural land has become an inviting source for commercial exploitation and speculation. The extension of existing zoning, the legal regulation of land use, has also been misused as a substitute for the Comprehensive Plan in making decisions about changes in land uses.

Due to the failure or reluctance of local communities to prepare and adopt significant long range plans for community betterment, some states have found it necessary to require not only that these plans be prepared, but that they contain specific elements, and have further mandated that zoning conform to the plan. Besides the land use and circulation elements, these specific new elements include open space, conservation, noise control, seismic safety, and—to underscore local responsibility for a commitment to the social and economic well-being of *all* citizens—a housing element.

UNIT OF URBAN PLANNING

As the city grows in size, some areas within it assume homogeneous qualities which we have identified as neighborhoods. People who came to America frequently grouped together with those who spoke their common language, shared their particular religious tenets, or stemmed from similar racial backgrounds. When some of their number became richer than the rest and enjoyed the greater mobility provided by a fine brace of horses and a carriage they moved their residences to near-by hills and formed more exclusive neighborhoods founded on differences in social and economic status. Different environmental standards were established and people who desired and could afford them gathered there to secure these amenities.

Some neighborhoods developed, as in ancient times, more from compulsion than native choice; restrictions of prejudice, limitations of language, or economic pressures often forced the cultivation of neighborhoods identified by class distinctions.

As open space in the growing city was built up, some neighborhoods were unable to retain their original identity, the economic level of the people living within them being inadequate to maintain a standard of physical maintenance or community services. Decay set in and slums were on the way toward formation. Residents of formerly exclusive areas moved to new districts beyond the reach of this influence. The metropolis created by the industiral revolution completely dissipated whatever urban unity remained from the medieval town and, except for exclusive residential districts which escaped from the sprawling industrial city, the distinctions between neighborhoods gradually merged into a common mediocrity. It was necessary to restore some semblance of human identity to the urban scene and, prodded by the social evils that enveloped the factory town, social workers emerged with the settlement house. Probably the settlement house movement which began in London about 1885 was the first conscious recognition of the neighborhood as a basic element in the urban structure; it served as a nucleus for the restoration of human values which had dissolved within the indistinguishable mass of the industrial metropolis.

The dissolution of these values has created among urban dwellers a detachment from each other. Opinions among social scientists differ on the effectiveness of the neighborhood principle as a means to overcome this detachment. Some contend it is imperative to re-establish a "face-to-face" relationship through neighborhood association, others expect that people will seek their friends no matter what distances may separate them, even while they remain only chance acquaintances and even strangers with their next door neighbors, and some oppose the neighborhood with the claim that it leads to a grouping of people that inevitably results in compulsory class distinctions.

These conflicting opinions notwithstanding, it has become a practical necessity to employ the neighborhood unit, or its counterpart, as a means to restore a recognizable form in the physical organization of the city. However large or small the city may be, there must be a workable unit of human scale with which to weave the urban pattern into a workable whole. Dissolution of human scale has allowed the industrial and commercial metropolis to become socially stagnant and physically flabby. As Benton McKaye said, "Mankind has cleared the jungle and replaced it with a labyrinth."[1]

THE NEIGHBORHOOD UNIT DEFINED

The neighborhood unit is not some sociological phenomenon; it embraces no particular theories of social science. It is simply a physical environment in which a mother knows that her child will have no traffic streets to cross on his way to school, a school which is within easy walking distance from home. It is an environment in which the housewife may have an easy walk to a shopping center where she may obtain the daily household goods, and employed persons may find convenient transportation to and from work. It is an environment in which a well-equipped playground is located near the home where the children may play in safety with their friends; the parents may not care to maintain intimate friendship with their neighbors, but children are so inclined and they need the facilities of recreation for the healthy development of their minds and spirit.

The unit measurement for space in urban society is the individual; the common denominator for the arrangement of that space is the family. To satisfy their relatively simple social wants, it is natural for families to seek the advantages which appropriately planned neighborhoods provide. The functions of a neighborhood have been described by C.J. Bushnell as: maintenance, learning,

[1] Benton Mc Kaye, *The New Exploration: A Philosophy of Regional Planning*, Harcourt, Brace, & Co., New York, 1928.

control, and play.[2] One of the earliest authorities to attempt a definition of the neighborhood in fairly specific terms was Clarence A. Perry. Although opinions differ to some degree, the definition he set forth in the Regional Survey of New York and Its Environs, 1929, is still a valid statement.

Perry described the neighborhood unit as that populated area which would require and support an elementary school with an enrollment of between 1,000 and 1,200 pupils. This would mean a population of between 5,000 and 6,000 people. Developed as a low-density dwelling district with a population of 10 families per acre, the neighborhood unit would occupy about 160 acres and have a shape which would render it unnecessary for any child to walk a distance of more than one-half mile to school. About 10 per cent of the area would be allocated to recreation, and through-traffic arteries would be confined to the surrounding streets, internal streets being limited to service access for residents of the neighborhood. The unit would be served by shopping facilities, churches, a library, and a community center, the latter being located in conjunction with the school.

The neighborhood unit, or some equivalent of this unit, is repeatedly referred to in proposals for urban reorganization. The suggested form varies widely, but the essential characteristics are fairly consistent. The suggested population appropriate for a unit has ranged between 3,000 and 12,000 people. In the plans for Chicago in 1942 the range was from 4,000 to 12,000; in the Greater London Plan, 1944, by Abercrombie and Forshaw, the unit size was 6,000 to 10,000. Some authorities have expressed a desire for units of smaller size than a school district, believing the nature of the neighborhood requires a relatively small size—generally 1,000 and not to exceed 1,500 families.

In its report in 1972 on "A strategy for Building a Better America," the American Institute of Architects adopted the neighborhood unit as the recommended "Growth Unit" for future urban growth. The Growth Unit would range in size from 500 to 3,000 dwelling units (populations of between 1,700 and 10,000).[3]

Despite the variations the principle of the neighborhood unit runs through all considerations for social, physical, and political organization of the city; it represents a unit of the population with basic common needs for educational, recreational, and other service facilities, and it is the standards for these facilities from which the size and design of the neighborhood emerge.

N. L. Engelhardt, Jr. has presented a comprehensive pattern of the neighborhood as a component of the successively larger segments in a city structure. The neighborhood unit includes the elementary school, a small shopping district, and a playground. These facilities are grouped near the center of the unit so that the walking distance between them and the home does not exceed one-half mile. An elementary school with a standard enrollment of

[2] "Community Center Movement as a Moral Force," *International Journal of Ethics*, Vol. 30, April 1920.

[3] American Institute of Architects, Washington, D.C.

between 600 and 800 pupils will represent a population of about 1,700 families in the neighborhood unit.[4]

Two such units (3,400 families) will support a junior high school with a recreation center in conjunction; the walking distance does not exceed one mile from the center to the most remote home. Four units (6,800 families) will require a senior high school and a commercial center. It will also be an appropriate size for a major park and recreation area. This grouping of four neighborhood units forms a "community" with a population of about 24,000 people. The component parts of this community pattern are integrated, and such communities may be arranged in whatever combinations the sources of employment and communications to and from them may require.

DISCRIMINATION PERPETUATED

The association of families in "desirable neighborhoods" is not usually looked at as "ghettoization" since those living in the confined area are not forced by law to reside there. In fact, however, the prohibitively expensive rents or price of home ownership in some areas have made these communities ghettos, effectively excluding from them those ethnic groups unable to afford the price of housing in the area.

In a Supreme Court decision in 1964 the Court held that racial or ethnic agreements based on law could not be enforced in the courts since they violated the 14th Amendment of the U.S. Constitution. This decision, however, did not terminate "gentlemen's agreements" which limited the availability of property to certain ethnic groups.

In order to overcome some of the educational problems derived from ethnic and economic segregation the Supreme Court held that "separate and equal" educational programs were in fact unequal and thus violated the 14th Amendment. It was obvious that the poorer economic districts, black or white, obtained the poorest of facilities and least qualifed teachers.

In the mid-1970s the method developed to solve this problem was to introduce the busing of children from one area to schools in other areas in an effort to produce racial and ethnic balance. In some instances, the children are required to travel a considerable distance from their homes. Protests from both the majority and minority sectors became routine, not only in the south, but in all parts of the country. Obviously, the problem of segregation was not being solved by this effort. In fact greater alienation between whites and racial minorities often resulted.

Similarly a decision in California decreed that the tax funds that support a school system may not be levied on a neighborhood or city basis, as the children

---

[4] N.L. Engelhardt, Jr., The School-Neighborhood Nucleus, *Architectural Forum,* October 1943.

THE NEIGHBORHOOD UNIT

Clarence Stein's Conception

These sketches show Clarence Stein's determinations of the proper design of the Neighborhood Unit.

In the upper-right diagram the elementary school is the center of the unit and within a one-half mile radius of all residents in the neighborhood. A small shopping center for daily needs is located near the school. Most residential streets are suggested as cul-de-sac or "dead-end" roads to eliminate through traffic, and park space flows through the neighborhood in a manner reminiscent of the Radburn plan.

The upper-left diagram shows the grouping of three neighborhood units served by a high school and one or two major commercial centers, the radius for walking distance to these facilities being one mile.

Clarence A. Perry's Plan

Perry was one of the first to give some consideration to the physical form of the neighborhood unit. It is substantially the same as that in the diagram by Stein but suggests that the maximum radius for walking distance from the home to the community center should be only one-quarter mile. Accepting the practice which was then, and still is, generally prevalent, shopping areas are situated at intersecting traffic streets on the outside corners rather than at the center of the unit.

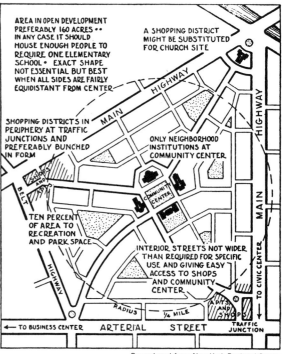

226

living in a poor community obtain only meager funds for education under such an arrangement, while students from wealthier areas obtain the advantages large amounts of money can buy.

OPEN SPACE

To suggest that American communities are deficient in recreational facilities is only to repeat what has been often said by many authorities. The reasons for the deficiency are manifold, but one of the most glaring is ill-planned land uses. Our present zoning practices provide extravagant areas for commercial and industrial uses, and the result is an urban pattern riddled with mixed land uses and an absence of stability in residential improvements. Consequently, we are faced with two predicaments: either land values render it too expensive to allot adequate open space for recreation, or existing parks are swallowed by commercial and industrial areas from which the people are trying desperately to escape to a better living environment.

A similar situation prevails with our schools. Because of unfortunate site selection, miscalculated population shifts, or lack of planning at the outset, schools are found languishing in the midst of business and factory areas, stranded between main traffic arteries, or situated in subdivisions too remote to serve the people. Recreation and education are linked with all other phases of urban development, whether they are planned or unplanned. Statistically, parks and playgrounds are deficient in amount, but the maldistribution of available facilities is even more striking. This combination of circumstances makes it imperative to establish neighborhood units in city planning.

As the machine has produced more and more with less and less manpower, and with the organization of labor, the work has been reduced from 60 hours to the 8-hour day and the 6-day week; then, during the 1930's it was further reduced to 40 hours and in some trades to 35 hours. Not only has this change made more leisure time available, but the intensified nature of modern production has rendered the necessity for relaxation and recreation the more important.

Uncontrolled spread of blight hastened the flight to the suburbs, the process we usually identify as decentralization, and the absorption of open space within the central areas of our cities was a major factor in creating this blight. The combination of mixed land uses, physical deterioration, and lack of open space has created a situation which can hardly be cured by the injection of occasional playgrounds into these areas. They will improve the amenities within the hard and bare confines of blighted areas, but such devices will not remedy the condition; replanning and rebuilding will be needed in the great areas of our blighted and congested urban core. This process of rebuilding will necessarily be predicated upon the provision of ample open space, but there is another important and urgent problem of open space which our cities are facing: the reservation of space within all the subdivisions spreading out across the urban landscape. Standards—adequate standards—of open space are urgently necessary to avoid a repetition of the identical problem presented by the blighted city centers.

Open space in the city is usually considered as the area for recreation, and appropriately so. However, this space falls into a number of categories. There is space devoted primarily to active playgrounds for children, youth, and adults; there is also space arranged for the more passive relaxation of adults. These spaces are those to which reference is generally made in a consideration of recreational facilities. Another classification should not be overlooked: the conservation of natural areas within as well as without the city. This conservation may take the form of greenbelts to serve as buffers between different land uses—residential and industrial areas—or it may become a reservation of places of particular historic or geographic interest, or spaces which are topographically unsuited for satisfactory development in other urban improvements.

The standards of open space cannot adequately specify the required areas in a city for all these classifications; part of the distinction of cities derives from the way in which the natural site is shaped and planned. The specified spaces for defined recreational uses are not the full measure of adequacy of a recreational program under any circumstances; an abstract area of land in proportion to the population is but a part of the planning for recreation space in the city. It is the distribution of this space which measures the adequacy, not the amount alone.

NEIGHBORHOOD RECREATION

There are three categories of recreation space for which the distribution as well as the amount of land is an important factor. They are identified by different terms in various localities, but the National Recreation Association has classified them as (1) the Playlot, (2) the Neighborhood Playground, and (3) the Playfield. Each type fulfills a specific function in the design of neighborhoods and groups of neighborhoods.[5]

The first category, the Playlot, is for children of preschool age. It is the equivalent of the "back-yard" of homes in sparsely settled residential districts, and in single-family districts the function is generally fulfilled by the usual open space about the homes. This is usually adequate when the street system is so designed that through traffic is discouraged or eliminated. In densely built apartment districts, however, the Playlot assumes an important function and there should by one Playlot available for each group of families ranging from 30 to 60 in number. The size of each lot should range from 1,500 to 2,500 square feet in area, and each should be located within a clear view of all the dwellings it serves. If a Playground is more distant than several blocks or is separated from the residential district by a busy traffic street, the area of the Playlots should be increased to 2,000 to 4,000 square feet. The Playlots should be equipped with such devices as low swings, slide, sand-box, jungle gyms, and space for running and circle games; a portion of the lot should be paved. All equipment should be designed and arranged for small children, and authorities have pointed out the

---

[5] George Butler, *Recreation Areas,* for National Recreation Association, 1958.

fascination of tots for objects like low walls, logs, and other common forms like shallow trenches and small hills. Some form of enclosure—a hedge or fence—about the Playlot is advisable, and a pergola and benches for mothers should be included.

The second category is the Neighborhood Playground. Designed for children whose ages range from 6 to 14, this Playground is the center of recreation activities for a neighborhood. Most authorities contend that a Playground should be within one-quarter mile walking distance of the dwelling area it serves; this distance is particularly important in densely built districts, and it should not exceed one-half mile in the most sparsely settled residential areas. A study of five large cities surveyed a total of nearly 35,000 children; of this number two-thirds went to a Playground within three blocks of their home and three-quarters lived within four blocks.

The preferable location for a Playground is adjacent to a community center or elementary school, where supervised recreation is possible. Below is a schedule of suggested space allowances.[6]

Population	Number of Children	Size in Acres
2,000	450	3.25
3,000	600	4.0
4,000	800	5.0
5,000	1,000	6.0

As a rule a playground for fewer than 200 children is impracticable for operation, and more than 1,200 children require two or more separate playgrounds. A minimum size of 3 acres for a Playground is recommended.

The Playground should provide an area for apparatus and an open space for informal play. There should be courts for various games such as soccer, softball, tennis, handball, and volleyball. Space is also needed for the quiet activities such as crafts, dramatics, and story-telling. A wading pool is desirable in warm climates, and there should be a Playlot with its facilities included. The lot should be near a shelter and rest area for adults. Lighting for evening use is desirable. Because economy in the operation and maintenance of recreation space in a community is highly important, it is impracticable to substitute a number of small play spaces throughout a residential development. The recommended sizes and design of spaces are more economical and avoid confusion between the various age groups who use the facilities.

The Playfield is intended for young people and adults and provides a variety of recreational activities. A single Playfield may serve four or five neighborhoods; the walking distance should not exceed one mile, one-half mile radius

[6] *Ibid.*

Minimal Standards for Public Recreational Areas, City Planning Department, Los Angeles, California*

Nature of Recreation	Operational Agency	Ages Served	Minimum Acres	Service Radius	1 Acre Serves	1 Site Serves	Desirable Features Minimum Facilities
1 Playlot	Group Housing	Pre-school	⅛	1 block	—	136 tots	Housing projects only
2 Neighborhood Playground With Park Facilities	Elementary or junior high school or recreation dept.	5 to 14 and aged persons	Active area—3 Passive area—2	¼ to ⅜ miles Same	218 children 2000 tot. pop.	600–800 children 3000–10,000 tot. pop.	Space for juvenile tag and athletic games, crafts bldg., table games, rest area and boundary planting
3 District Playground and Park	Senior high school or recreation dept. and park dept.	15–20 and adults	Active area—10 Passive area—5	¾ to 1½ miles Same	290 youth 2,000 to 6,000 pop.	1,000–4,000 youth 10,000 to 50,000 pop.	Swimming pool, athletic field, all-purpose building, facilities for large group activities
4 Sports Center	Recreation dept.	Youth and adults	30	5-10 miles	Variable	500,000 pop.	Multiple facilities for field games, field house
5 Urban Park	Park dept.	All	30	5 miles	2,000 tot. pop.	50,000 to 100,000 pop.	Shade, lawn and water
6 Regional Park	Park dept.	All	No limit	No limit	Variable	Variable	Outstanding scenic or recr'l attractions
7 Beach	Recreation dept.	All	No limit	No limit	Variable	Variable	Multiple recreation facilities
8 Camp	Recreation dept. or school board	Various	20	No limit	Variable	Variable	Isolated location in primitive area
9 Specialized Park	Park dept.	Various	No limit	No limit	Variable	Variable	Golf course, or other special uses

230

10 Cultural Site	Semi-public or public	All	No limit	No limit	Variable	Variable	Historical, scientific, or educational interest
11 Miscellaneous Open Spaces	Any government agency	All	No limit	Local	Variable	Variable	Planted strips, squares, public bldg. grounds
12 Preserve or Reservation	Any government agency	All	No limit	Local	Variable	Variable	Protection of primitive or scenic areas

* April 1948.

Standards for Recreational Areas*

Type of Area	Acres per 1,000 Population	SIZE OF SITE (Acres)		Radius of Area Served (miles)
		Ideal	Minimum	
Playgrounds	1.5	4	2	0.5
Neighborhood parks	2.0	10	5	0.5
Playfields	1.5	15	10	1.5
Community parks	3.5	100	40	2.0
District parks	2.0	200	100	3.0
Regional parks and reservations	15.0	500–1,000	varies	10.0

* *Urban Land*, May 1961, by George Nez, Director, Inter-County Planning Commission, Denver, Colorado.

being preferred. One acre per 800 population is a desirable space standard, with a minimum size of 15 acres. Here again the standards vary, some cities holding to a minimum average area of one-half acre per 1,000 population for this type of recreation space. The space should be designed for the same facilities as a Neighborhood Playground with addition of space for sports like football, baseball, hockey, archery, a swimming pool, outdoor theater, bandshell, and a recreation building. Night lighting should be provided.

TYPES OF URBAN RECREATION SPACE

The three types of recreation spaces—Playlot, Neighborhood Playground, and Playfield—require the greatest attention with regard to their distribution in the community, the adequacy of space allotted to them, and their relation to the traffic arteries, community facilities, and accessibility from the homes. The total space for recreation is not confined to these categories, however. There are, in addition, the large city parks which supply the main facilities for city-wide recreation, organized sports, public golf courses, open-air entertainment, and the zoological and botanical gardens. These parks usually retain or reintroduce natural surroundings to the city and, where the sites are so adapted, they maintain the native wildlife as far as possible. They vary greatly in size, but they are usually of considerable area. Fairmount Park in Philadelphia and Griffith Park in Los Angeles each contains nearly 4,000 acres; Forest Park in St Louis with its famous outdoor amphitheater has 1,380 acres, Balboa Park in San Diego has 1,100 acres, and Golden Gate Park in San Francisco contains about 1,000 acres. In addition to well-known Cental Park which has only 840 acres, New York City has five other parks ranging from 1,000 acres to nearly 2,000 acres each.

Another type closely akin to the large park is the familiar "city" park which serves as a breather in the built-up urban areas. Their frequency depends a great deal upon the degree of population density, 5 miles apart being an average distance in congested areas and 10 miles being a standard in a highly decentralized city like Los Angeles. It is preferable that these parks be not smaller than about 30 acres in size, with a standard of about one acre per 2,000 people as a minimum area. This type of park is somewhat reminiscent of the Boston Commons (44 acres), but it is not intended to resemble a village green like the diminutive 6-acre public squares located in each quadrant of the original plan by Penn for Philadelphia. Such "squares" are little more than open space upon which some buildings may front. The city park should provide a natural atmosphere which may induce relaxation and some degree of repose.

The broadest reach of open space may be identified as the regional parks or park reserves. They comprise great areas of space, most of which is maintained in its natural state. Cook County Forest Preserve near Chicago is one of the greatest of these spaces devoted to conservation; it contains more than 30,000 acres. Others are the South Mountain Park of 15,000 acres near Phoenix, Arizona, the 10,000 acre reserve near Denver, Tilden Regional Parks in Oakland, California, and the Westchester Park System in New York.

It is the great stretches of open spaces represented by these reserves or regional parks for conservation purposes, and also some of the large city parks, that stir the vision of greenbelts many of these spaces might have become had they been formed as an integral part of the city plan. These parks are frequently the transition between the urban development and the rural countryside, being situated beyond the center of population. They might have been formed as green buffers to separate the different land uses within the city and have been even more accessible to the people than their present location offers.

There are many recreational spaces of a special nature: cultural centers including the museums and art galleries, beaches, amusement parks, sports centers including athletic fields, swimming pools, and stadiums. There are also the grand sweeps of broad parkways in which recreation areas are developed; the Outer Drive along the lake front of Chicago is a magnificent illustration of this latter facility.

The over-all minimum urban space devoted to the total of the foregoing recreational spaces ranges from about 3 acres per 1,000 population in the city to a desirable standard of 10 acres per 1,000 population. It is further recommended that the urban area be planned for a reservation of about 10 per cent of the gross area of the city to accommodate the space for an increase in population growth. In the vigorous replanning of London in preparation for the rebuilding program as a result of war devastation, the standard of open space in the outlying areas of the county is 7 acres per 1,000 population, while the density of land use within the city boundaries has forced a standard of no more than 4 acres per 1,000 persons.

The absence of open space within our cities may serve as the signal for tomorrow's direction in planning. It will be a sad commentary, indeed, if 20 or 30 years hence our suburbs present the plight of the central city today. Now is the time to prepare the open space within the growing subdivisions for we cannot

forget that the slums of today were the subdivisions of yesterday. This preparation is implemented by Title VII of the Housing Act of 1961. Identified as a
provision for "Open Space Land," it made financial assistance available for
acquisition of open space in urban areas. Undeveloped or predominately undeveloped land in a comprehensive plan for parks and recreation, conservation
of natural resources, and for historic or scenic purposes may be acquired by a city
with the benefit of Federal grants to meet the partial cost.

SCHOOLS

The school board in each community has its policy for extension and design of
the public school plant, but there are a few simple standards which are being
generally adopted as a key to the allocation of space for the school system. These
standards link closely with recreational space since the elementary school is the
focal point within the neighborhood unit, and the junior and senior high schools
within the group of neighborhoods we have identified as a "community." The
open space for recreation should become therefore an integral part of the school

School Standards*
Inter-County Regional Planning Commission, Denver, Colorado

School Type	Minimum Size (pupils)	Ideal Size (pupils)	Maximum Size (pupils)	Site Size (acres)	Radius of Area Served (miles)
Elementary	230	700	900	5 + 1 per 100 pupils	0.5
Junior high	750	1,000	1,500	15 + 1 per 100 pupils	1.0
Senior high	900	1,500	2,500	25 + 1 per 100 pupils	2.0
Elementary – junior high combination				15 + 1 per 100 pupils	1.0
Junior high – senior high combination				25 + 1 per 100 pupils	2.0
Elementary – park combination				8 + 1 per 100 pupils	0.5
Elementary – junior high – park combination				20 + 1 per 100 pupils	1.0
Junior high – senior high – park combination				18 + 1 per 100 pupils	1.0
Junior high – park combination				40 + 1 per 100 pupils	
Senior high – park combination				35 + 1 per 100 pupils	

* *Urban Land*, May 1961, by George Nez, Director, Inter-County Regional Planning Commission, Denver, Colorado.

location and thereby provide the type of adult supervision and youth leadership necessary to guide the development of young people.

N. L. Engelhardt, Jr. has estimated one-half child of elementary school age (grades one through six) in the average family. The average for families among the low-income group is about 0.7 children and 0.4 children per family in the high-income group.[7] Since most communities favor elementary schools with an enrollment between 600 and 800 pupils in the first six grades, a neighborhood designed about such a school would have a population of between 1,500 and 1,700 families, or between 5,000 and 6,000 people.

Two such neighborhoods would support a junior high school with enrollments between 1,000 and 1,200, and four neighborhoods would support a senior high school of about 1,500 enrollment. The walking distance for a junior high school (grades seven through nine should not exceed one mile, and the senior high school (grades 10 through 12) should be a distance of not more than 1½ miles.

Although the public school system in most communities does not support nursery schools, it would be desirable to establish them by private means. The size recommended by Engelhardt is 25 children for each school within a radius not to exceed one-quater mile from the most distant home served. The average is 0.1 child of nursery school age per family, and a nursery school would serve about 400 families.

It has been considered necessary too frequently in the past to select a school site after the population has arrived and the land has been absorbed for other uses than education or recreation. Consequently, standards of adequate area for these facilities have been overshadowed by expedient decisions based upon the cheapest price for such land that might still be available. It is generally agreed, however, that a desirable standard for the three types of schools is elementary, 10 acres; junior high, 15 acres; and senior high, 50 acres.

NEW EDUCATIONAL CONCEPTS

In the late 1960's educational authorities tried to solve the problem of school segregation resulting from racially segregated communities. It became clear that bussing was not working and that a fresh approach was needed.

One such approach was the "educational park", a complex of three or more elementary schools located in a large recreational area. The possibilities of reduced educational costs and educational advantages made the idea attractive both to tax payers and educators.

The system consists of several related parts, serving different grade and age levels of young people within the community. For the youngest members of the community, a pre-school program with facilities closely related to the neigh-

[7] N. L. Engelhardt, Jr., "The School– Neighborhood Nucleus," *Architectural Forum,* Oct., 1943.

borhood structure is suggested. For children in the elementary and junior high age range, facilities are planned at the village level with a cluster of schools on a large, single site, bringing students with varying socio-economic, ethnic and religious backgrounds together. This new structure is called an Educational Park. High school educational facilities serve two or three villages.

The educational park concept emerged from a study done by the Bureau of Educational Research and Services for Litchfield Park, Arizona, entitled "Design for Lifetime Learning in a Dynamic Social Structure," 1968.

SCHOOL SERVICE AREAS

NURSERY—2ND GRADE
800 Families/250 Children
4"N" Schools per Village

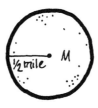

MIDDLE SCHOOLS—3—8
1066 Families/600 Children
3 "M" Schools per Village

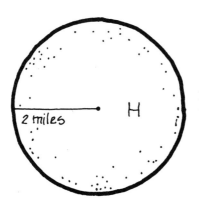

HIGH SCHOOLS—9—12
6400 Families/1500 Children
1 "H" School per 2 Villages

Parent-Child Educational Center   Each village is composed of 3 to 4 neighborhoods. Ideally, a Parent-Child Educational Center should be located in each neighborhood. The facility is intended as a social and recreational activity center for children from infancy through seven years (grades N-2) and their parents. These centers should be located within easy walking distance of the children's homes.

The Educational Park   A village, roughly one square mile in area, containing approximately 8,500 people, could support an Educational Park. The park would provide a program of education for children of elementary and junior high/high school ages. The park would contain three or four middle schools, providing instruction for children in grades 3–8.

The goals of an Educational Park should be reflected in its shape and organization. An Educational Park's goals will be unique, reflecting the cultural, educational and social values of a particular community.

The object of the Educational Park is to create an environment in which learning becomes exciting and rewarding. The use of physical space to complement educational objectives is a principal objective.

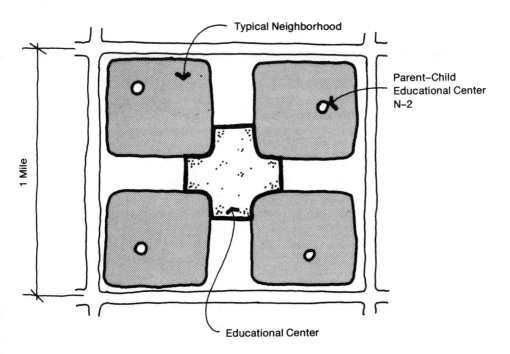

Education within the Village

17

Commerce and Industry

THE NEW MARKET PLACES

The market place has always been the focal point of the city, a center for the exchange of goods. In ancient times it was the open space to which farmers and craftsmen brought their products for barter. The development of transportation and money systems implemented the transfer of goods, and the barter system shifted to a form of retail enterprise. Expansion of commerce created a merchant class dealing in the exchange of goods produced by others than themselves. The importance of cities increased as centers of wholesale and retail trade.

As with so many other human activities, the industrial system brought more changes in the nature of the market place. Not only did the transportation of goods quicken, but the systems of communications accelerated the exchange of goods. The great cities became the trading centers in which world commerce was concentrated. With the growth of urban population the city continued its wholesale and retail functions, but emphasis in the great business centers of the city has shifted from the commodities being exchanged to the methods and processes for trading in them. The goods are replaced by pieces of paper—documents—which purport to represent them, and transactions for the transfer of commodities are consummated by an exchange of these documents. Negotiations for the sale and payment of goods transferred from a merchant in Montevideo to a merchant in Buenos Aires are transacted in a London banking house, or the exchange of grain and meat between the producer on the farm and the consumer in the city next door is arranged through the trading centers of New York or Chicago. The industrial system has introduced a variety of commercial functions to the city never present in the simple market place of the ancient town, and four recognizable types of commercial districts have emerged in the modern city.

"Downtown" of the large metropolitan city is familiar to every urban dweller. It is the financial and administrative center of its region and, in some cities, it has become the center of business for the nation. New York has its Wall Street, Chicago its LaSalle Street, Paris its Bourse and London its Exchange district, but every city has its financial center, even though it may serve as a satellite of a greater center. "Downtown" includes the wholesale and retail centers for service to the satellite districts within the city proper or its region. These centers have not been planned; they have simply crept outward and upward within the network of obsolete and confining streets as the fortune of cities and nations fluctuated. The central business district serves a vital and useful purpose as the heart of the city, and its deterioration presents a challenge to business and civic enterprise. Affected by intolerable congestion, noise, fumes, exorbitant land values, and overcrowding, business enterprise shifts restlessly away from the blight eating into the urban core.

A second type of commercial area is the small, central business distict of the satellite community. Dependent upon the metropolitan center for major administrative and wholesale functions, the small commercial center contains the chain retail stores, professional offices, service supply enterprises, motion picture theaters, branch banks, and stock exchanges. In the small, self-contained city, this district will also provide wholesale facilities and include the necessary administrative and transportation centers.

The third type is represented by the outlying shopping areas of the city. They may overlap with, or be the counterpart of, the commercial center of the satellite community, but they contain the large-scale service facilities which do not lend themselves to further subdivision and distribution. Among these facilities are large food markets, chain stores of various types, branch banks, and telegraph, telephone, and postal district offices, motion picture theaters, branch library, and medical and dental offices.

The smallest commercial unit is the neighborhood center. The modern counterpart of the "corner grocery store," the neighborhood shopping center provides the day-by-day commodities for the direct convenience of a limited population. Here, the housewife may perform her regular shopping for the staple goods. It may have an independent grocery store and meat market, radio and electric shop, shoe repair shop, hardware store, a bakery, drug and stationery store, and barber and beauty shop.

OVERZONING

When communities were small and served a vast outlying area, commercial uses were permitted along both sides of principal traffic routes. A highway passing through the center of a town became the axis for the central business district, and "strip" business developed at random along its route. As the population of the community expanded, additional traffic routes were provided and more business stretched along them. It was then presumed that business on the highway was the appropriate location for commercial enterprise and, with little further examination of the amount of business a community could support, all existing and proposed street frontage was zoned for commercial use. It is now impossible to classify almost any of these business areas as shopping "centers."

About one-quarter of the streets in our cities are used as main thoroughfare with the property fronting upon them zoned for business use. Harland Bartholomew has estimated that some 25 percent of the total area of the average city is occupied by commercial zoning, whereas the area actually used by retail business is only about 3 per cent of the total developed area of the city. This contrast gives some measure of the degree to which cities have been overzoned for business development along the traffic arteries.

The gross excess of commercial zoning weighs heavily upon the city. Despite the relatively small proportion of commercial zoning which is actually developed for business, much of this enterprise operates on a marginal basis. The mortality rate of retail business is extremely high, between 15 and 25 per cent of the retail stores going out of business each year. About one-third of all retail stores have a life-span of a year or less, one-half remain in business no longer than two years, and less that one-quarter remain as long as 10 years. Mr. Robert Dowling, a prominent real estate counsellor in New York City, estimated that four or five times as many stores are in business as the need demands.

Inducement to engage in uneconomic ventures is apparently strong, and the impact spreads far beyond the failure of an individual entrepreneur. Unstable business enterprise breeds physical blight; the "shoestring" investments in retail business are analogous to the "strip" character of zoning. In some cities fully half the property zoned for business is used for residences, and these unplanned mixtures of land uses not only create an undesirable environment but remove the prospect for consolidation of shopping facilities for convenient access.

Each community has some peculiar local conditions and practices which will bear upon estimates of the amount of land required for commercial purposes, but investigations in a number of cities shed some light upon the relation between population and the area for business as a point of departure in developing appropriate standards for the allocation of space for commercial districts. The familiar "rule of thumb" for allocating space for commercial development is 50 feet of street frontage for 100 persons in the area to be served. That the "overall" amount of space devoted to business is an inadequate measure is evident from observation of cities as well as statistics of land use. The distribution of the space is equally important, if not more vital, to the welfare and service of a city than the total area allocated for commercial development. The Bartholomew survey showed that 44 per cent of the total commercial area was in the central business district, and 56 per cent was distributed in the residential neighborhoods.

A survey by the Los Angeles Regional Planning Commission showed a further breakdown in the types of commercial districts.[1] The combined commercial uses amounted to 2.72 acres of land per 1,000 persons throughout the County of Los Angeles. Of this area 1.19 acres was in neighborhood shopping districts, while local or community business districts occupied 0.92 acre, and the balance, 0.46 acre per 1,000 persons, was in the satellite commercial centers. An additional 0.15 acre per 1,000 persons was contained in the main "downtown" business center of the city of Los Angeles. These classifications of districts

[1] *Master Plan of Land Use (Inventory and Classification),* Regional Planning Commission, County of Los Angeles, California, p. 38.

correspond to the four types described at the beginning of this chapter.The Los
Angeles County survey included a great variety of communities, ranging from
the great metropolitan area of the city of Los Angeles through the small towns
surrounding this city to semirural areas served by village centers. The land area
devoted to all commercial uses in four large urban centers in proportion to the
population is shown below:

	Acres per *1,000 Population*
Detroit	3.50
San Francisco	1.75
St. Louis	2.15
Los Angeles (City)	3.30

The amount of land area devoted to commercial uses is but a tentative guide
for planning. It may, in fact, be deceptive. It omits the primary measure of
floor space. Since the inventive genius of man produced the capability to build
structures of unlimited heights, the area of land they occupy has been reduced
to a relatively insignificant factor in calculating the capacity to accommodate
people and their manifold activities. A defect in zoning practice has been the
absence of this measurement in allocating space for the various uses in the urban
Plan. This was illustrated in the Regional Survey of New York and its Environs
of 1931. That study showed that within the 8-square-mile area between 59th
Street and the Battery, on the island of Manhattan, the average building height
was only six stories covering 60 per cent of the land, and the average in the Wall
Street district was less than eleven stories covering less than 50 per cent of the
ground area. Yet the Wall Street district bristled with the most dramatic display
of skyscrapers the world had ever seen and the tallest buildings ever built were
held in the palm of midtown Manhattan. Within the relatively limited land area
of the great city of New York, the zoning regulations permitted enough floor
space to accommodate a business population of 344,000,000 people. Fifteen
thousand people could work in the Empire State Building alone. The
significance of floor space to ground area is further illustrated in the floor area
ratio provisions of the 1957 Chicago zoning ordinance which permit floor space
ranging from seven to sixteen times the lot area.

Each community has characteristics which form the basis for determining
the appropriate relation between population and the space required for the
commercial facilities to serve it. It is the restoration of a balance between the
open space for the movement of people and the enclosed space they occupy upon
which, in large part, the health of city development depends. Although the
differences among cities are recognized, Larry Smith and Company has estimated the relative range of floor space for the principal uses in the urban
community:[2]

[2] Larry Smith. "Space for the CBD's Functions," *Journal of the American Institute of
Planners*, February 1961.

Metropolitan Per Capita Floor Area Requirements
for Selected Activities

ACTIVITIES	FLOOR AREA PER CAPITA (SQUARE FEET)
Retail	20 to 55
Office	2 to 15
Parking (on the ground floor or in structures)	4 to 16
Public	1 to 3.5
Quasi-public	1 to 3.5
Wholesale	5 to 15
Industrial	2 to 15
Residential	200 to 400

PARKING

Directly related to the amount of floor space occupied by commercial enterprise is the requirement for vehicular parking to serve it.[3] The future stability of commerical districts will depend in large measure on the adequacy and convenience of space for automobile parking available to customers, employees, and service. The effects of deficient and extravagant parking and service may be measured by the shifts in commercial space to outlying areas of the city.

The automobile is a special breed of locomotion. By far the most uneconomical mode of transportation, it continues to gain in popularity year after year. Although excessive in physical bulk, this remarkable machine carries few passengers. The phenomenon may be explained in large part by the extended freedom of movement the automobile offers to the driver. Its excessive bulk clogs the city streets, and the space it requires for parking is extravagant.

Lawson Purdy estimated sidewalk space should provide five square feet per person. Assuming that there is an average of 100 square feet of building space per occupant and that one-third of the occupants use the sidewalks at one time, he estimated that, if commercial space in New York City were built to that permitted by the zoning ordinance, pedestrians would have less than three and one-half square feet per person in the combined areas of sidewalks and streets.[4] A standing automobile requires 175 square feet.

The enigma compounds. The pedestrian has become a human jumping-jack in the struggle for a place on the sidewalk, and when streets are widened, the sidewalks are narrowed. Curb parking impedes the traffic lanes and renders the street obsolete as a channel for movement. Land prices exceed any economic

[3] See Chapter 12, The Zoning Plan.
[4] Regional Survey of New York and Its Environs, 1931.

value for surface parking, and multi-deck garages are built. Commercial enterprise is gradually forced to seek other locations in order to conduct business. Mass transportation shows little evidence of correcting the situation. The availability of economical off-street parking is a critical necessity.

SHOPPING CENTERS

In the decade between 1940 and 1950 the suburbs surrounding cities[5] increased 35 per cent, and the rate of growth between 1950 and 1960 jumped to 50 per cent. This remarkable expansion was generated, in large part, by the natural increase in total population but, also, from the large central cities by people moving to the urban fringes. Retail enterprise to serve the sprawling residential suburbs gathered in scattered clusters. The corner grocery store was transformed into the neighborhood shopping center. This "new look" suggested a strong contrast with the shabby and congested commercial streets of conventional business districts. Convenient parking, without charge was a novel and refreshing experience for the housewife. Nourished by the volume of new population, the shopping center became popular. The distinguishing feature of the new center is the positive separation between the automobile and pedestrian. Smarting under this new form of competition, the downtown business districts of the large cities and small towns made belated efforts to improve shopping conditions.

   1.   The *Neighborhood Center* is the local source for staple goods and daily services for a population of between 7,500 and 20,000 people. An average size is about 40,000 square feet, but it may range between 30,000 and 75,000 square feet of gross floor area. The site should be 4 to 10 acres in area. It is usually designed about a supermarket as the principal retail service.

   2.   The *Community Center* may serve a population of between 20,000 and 100,000, and extends the services of the Neighborhood Center by providing a variety store or small department store as the major tenant. The average size is 150,000 square feet of gross floor area, with a range of between 100,000 and 300,000 square feet, requiring a site between 10 and 30 acres in size.

   3.   The *Regional Center* is usually built about a major department store and includes a full complement and range of retail facilities usually found in a balanced small city. It could serve a population ranging from 100,000 to 250,000 people. An average size is about 400,000 square feet of gross floor area, although it may range as high as 1,000,000 square feet. A minimum site of 40 acres is required and centers of the largest size require as many as 100 acres.

   Shopping centers can be divided into three general categories:[6]

---

   [5] The 212 Standard Metropolitan Statistical Areas of the U.S. Bureau of the Census, 1960, having 50,000 or more urban population.

   [6] *Community Builders Handbook,* Executive Edition, Urban Land Institute, Washington, D.C., 1960.

Examination of the economic base for retail trade is the initial stage in planning the shopping center, and the techniques of market analysis have come into full play by authorities in their development. The steps in such an analysis follow a logical sequence:

1. The trading area involves an investigation of the population, income levels, places and direction of its growth, the existing and potential location and volume of trade in competitive establishments. This information will indicate the volume of trade in relation to the site of the new center.

2. The gross potential sales for the center is derived from estimated expenditures in the trading area. Family income data will disclose the portion devoted to living expenses for various goods and services—food, furniture, clothing, appliances, drugs, automotive equipment, restaurants, entertainment, miscellaneous merchandise.

3. The potential net sales volume for a new center is related to the sales volume in existing and potential competitive enterprise in the trading area. This requires informed judgement of the proportion of existing trade which may be attracted to the new location. The sales volume per square foot of retail floor space for the various goods will aid in estimating the gross sales in existing establishments offering comparable goods.

4. The physical space that can be supported by the net sales from the trading area may be estimated from the average annual sales per square foot of floor space in the several retail facilities.

5. Anticipated income from the center may be determined by application of the probable rental rates per square foot of retail space, less operating and management costs, taxes, insurance, interest and amortization on the loan for the capital cost for the complete development. The balance represents the net return which may be expected by the developer on his equity investment.

In formulating the program for a shopping center, the balance, or "mix" of retail facilities is important. The key facility in a Neighborhood Center is usually a supermarket. Around this may be grouped a drug store, barber shop and beauty shop, bakery, shoe repair shop, laundry and cleaning shop, and service station. The Community Center will introduce a large variety store or small department store, and augment the facilities of a Neighborhood Center with such establishments as an apparel shop, hardware store, radio shop, stationery store, restaurant and bar, bank, and branch post office. The distinction of the Regional Center is the full complement of specialty shops and the wide selection of goods and services offered to the patrons, sometimes referred to as "Noah's Ark." The key elements are major department stores, and there may be a motion picture theater and community meeting halls. Recreation facilities, such as bowling, and professional offices may be included in a center of any size, depending upon local conditions.

Space for automobile parking is a feature of the shopping center. The requirements for retail facilities vary: some specialty shops are reasonably well

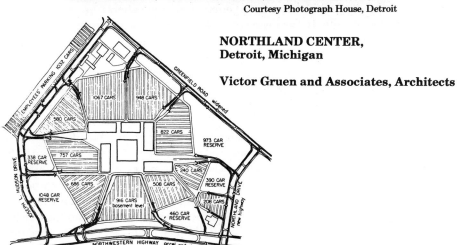

NORTHLAND CENTER,
Detroit, Michigan

Victor Gruen and Associates, Architects

A major regional center of 1,100,000 square feet in retail space, with a theater, auditorium, and community center. Parking space is available for 10,000 cars, and the center is patronized by as many as 70,000 people per day.

245

served with less than 5 car spaces for each 1,000 square feet of gross floor area, whereas supermarkets may require at least 10 spaces for each 1,000 square feet of floor area. An average may be struck at 6 spaces per 1,000 square feet of gross area in Neighborhood Centers and 8 spaces for each 1,000 square feet of gross area in Community and Regional Centers.

REGIONAL CENTERS REVIEWED

Many persons have lost their enthusiasm for regional shopping centers. Originally intended to bolster the city, shopping centers have become magnets for decentralization, hastening the decline of central cities.

One of the major proponents of large-scale shopping centers and the architect of many of them throughout the United States, Victor Gruen, recently indicated that they are far from what he had envisaged them to be. He had thought that shopping centers could combine retailing with recreational and cultural activities, thereby promoting the revitilization of central city areas. While not accomplishing all the goals initially expected of them, regional shopping centers have nevertheless been built in cental core areas in order to reestablish their retail function. Urban renweal has been the vehicle that has freed land for such centers.

DOWNTOWN

There is a romance associated with the downtown of almost any city. It represents the tradition which springs from, and clings to, a place of the beginning. It has been the place where generation after generation has witnessed the vicissitudes of time. It has been the core from which the vitality of the city has found nourishment and energy. It has been the Civic Center; the place of the City Hall, the "big" stores, the theaters. It has been the place people went to when they went to work, and the place they went to when they "went out." It has been the terminus, the hub for railroads, commuting trains, and buses. It has been the headquarters for firms and institutions. It has been the symbol of the life of the city.

But the structure of the city is undergoing major changes while downtown is not. Its future is uncertain, not because it is expected to disappear beneath the waves of change, but because of the resistance it poses to change itself—the reluctance of its response to the demands these changes are imposing upon it. Whole districts have deteriorated. Throngs of people mingle in the snarl and ugly tangle of traffic and buildings. It is suffocating under an economic oxygen tent and breath is coming in shorter and shorter gasps. Choked by obsolescent circulation, people and vehicles have too little room to move. Worn, haggard, and with shattered nerves, the urbanite bears testimony to the tensions.

The forces gnawing at downtown are manifold and the lag in positive response to the competition is hurting. Decentralization of retail shopping centers has been a natural evolution of urban expansion, and the relative

City of Miami News Bureau

LINCOLN ROAD MALL, MIAMI BEACH, FLORIDA
Morris Lapidus Associates, Architects

position of the central business district is headed for modification. Until the depression of the thirties, over 90 per cent of general merchandise trade was concentrated in the central business districts. In 1954 the amount of this trade outside the central business district had surpassed downtown in all cities with more than a million people, and by 1958 it was nearly 20 per cent higher than the central business districts in 94 of the great metropolitan areas. While the rate of this increase spirals upward, the dollar volume of trade in the central business district has been cut in half.[7] This trend will not subside automatically nor from natural causes. Aggressive and imaginative attention to the central district is necessary.

The central city was once the transportation hub. Except in a few large cities the private automobile is the primary carrier today. The central district is jammed with traffic, but one-half or more of the vehicles that crowd the streets are passing through downtown for destinations beyond. Yet the district, bulging with vehicles, resembles an endless parking lot. A striking image of the central

[7] Homer Hoyt, *Urban Land,* September 1961.

city is Los Angeles, where two-thirds of the downtown area is devoted to streets, alleys, and parking lots. It is not that this allocation of space is disproportionate when compared with modern shopping centers, but the inferior quality of the space, created by the disorderly scattering of buildings among automobile repositories and traffic-ridden streets, is spoiling the district.

Dispersion of the residential population from the environs of the central business district has altered the economic base. Those who could afford to have escaped to the outskirts, and a ring of slums chokes the central city. The flight to the suburbs has drawn with it a decentralization of consumer retail business. Perhaps more insidious in its effect, however, is the shifting of other traditional downtown activities caught in this centrifugal movement. Restaurants, department stores, theaters, civic and cultural facilities—museums, art galleries, libraries, auditoriums and sports centers, government offices—and a variety of business firms, are moving to new locations along the fingers of commerce stretching outward from the core. These shifts are sporadic, but they seem to be persistent. Consumer shopping naturally seeks proximity to its direct market, but most of the movement is not necessarily induced by improved geographic location nor compatible relationships; it is flight from the congestion of downtown.

A virtue of the central district is its compact form. The hard core of the center is of relatively limited size, rarely exceeding 160 acres. It thus becomes a natural area for ready access by pedestrian communications. The spearheads of commercial expansion spreading outward overextend these lines of communication and drain the internal energy rather than buttress the economy of the core. Property owners seek to sustain their values but the incentive to risk capital for improvement by absentee owners lags so long as property yields an acceptable return on the investment. Concerted action is thus slow in forming. Oblique maneuvers, slogans, clean-up campaigns, sidewalk twig planting, reflect a basic pessimism. Enthusiasm will be expressed by a frontal attack, a bold and imaginative plan by business leaders to revitalize the district.

It is possible that major retail commerce may not be equated with the central business district as the functions of downtown evolve. The central area of a great city usually forms into specialized districts—the financial district, theater and hotel district, business and professional offices, the large department stores and shops, offices of government. These several functions may mingle in a single district of a small city, but they form a fairly compact unit, having their own identification and supporting services.

The future of downtown demands more than piecemeal rehabilitation. The occasional bright new building, replacing some old and worn-out structure, is attractive. But the impact of increasing intensity of land use, without change in the street system and parking accommodations, only aggravates an already overburdened circulation system. Business enterprise thus excerises its option to use land more productively, but the public responsibility has not been exercised to up-date the circulation system and terminal facilities. The "golden noose" draws tighter.

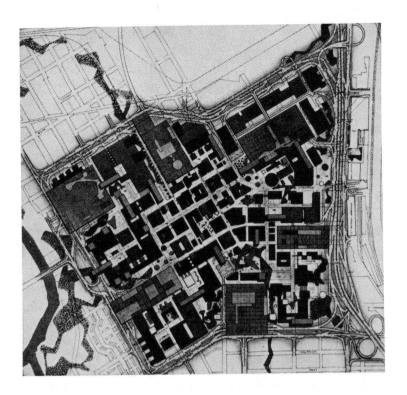

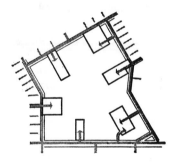

**FORT WORTH,
Texas**

**Architect:
Victor Gruen and Associates**

Courtesy Gordon Sommers

This well-known plan for reshaping the central business district of Fort Worth combines the features of the regional shopping center, which are lacking in the downtown of most cities. A circumferential highway system about the district feeds six four-story parking garages. Each garage projects into the central core, and convenient walking distance from the garages to the center encourages the closing of internal streets to serve as pedestrian shopping malls. Service to business establishments is through underground tunnels.

Vehicular and pedestrain circulation are not rehabilitation measures, nor is parking. Rebuilding the broad fringe of slums and blight encircling the city center could attract a multitude of those who have fled to the outskirts. Integrated replanning from within the central district outward and across the wide twilight zone surrounding it, may restore an enriched quality to this critical area of the city.

THE MALL

An animated, colorful scene is the attraction of city streets. The gaudy array of signs by day and night conveys a carnival spirit. The kaleidoscopic spectacle is a tasteless, even vulgar, display, but it is the asset of the street. People warm to crowds and the excitement of variety. Shouting loud to the passerby is a commercial necessity. City streets have become traffic arteries. Capturing and holding the attention of a passing motorist intensifies the pressure on advertising. Business notices must project themselves into the street with a galaxy of illuminated devices. Signs grow in size and novelty in direct ratio with the congestion of traffic. It is a grim, bizarre reality and design reform could sterilize the city street scene. Neither the shopper-driver nor the shopkeeper can forsake the nervous disorder. The anachronism is obvious. The automobile is not a natural means of locomotion for shopping; the patron of business is essentially a pedestrain, not a motorist.

It is quite possible that much of the distasteful quality of the commercial street would disappear under its own weight if the patron were readily converted from a driver to a pedestrian. The necessity for loud shouting, the raucous display, could be replaced by attention to the goods for sale. Again the shopping center makes the case; the automobile is removed from the street, the shopper returns to his natural status of a pedestrian, and the animation of the scene is *enhanced*. As though it were "proof positive," more dollar volume of business results.

The Mall has acquired a magic ring. Contrary to some impressions, it is not accomplished by the simple gesture of closing a street to vehicular traffic. It becomes a complex arrangement of traffic rerouting, parking, service for merchandise delivery and refuse collection, adjustments in utilities, illumination, fire and police protection, and maintenance. Nor is the mall a panacea for the ills that beset downtown. It may become an important element in replanning the central business district, but it is effective only to the extent that the traffic, parking and general spatial rearrangement are integrated. Not the least element in the program for a revitalized downtown is the spirit with which the property owners and tenants participate. Full cooperation may produce a metamorphosis in downtown and restore it as the heart of the city.

The tragedy of physical and economic neglect which has disfigured so many areas of cities is apparent in the futile and desperate efforts to breathe life into already dead city centers by conversion of traffic streets to pedestrian ways—malls which traverse a desert of vacant stores, empty lots and outworn advertising signs. The penalty for *no* planning or *bad* planning is underscored by this dilemma. In new shopping centers space is reserved for pedestrians separate from automobile parking, and a handsome environment is created free from ugly advertising. The unattractive "strip" commercial traffic street cannot compete with those advantages. With the deterioration of city centers and in the absence of planning foresight, retail enterprise has been allowed to disperse carelessly in new shopping centers. City centers further decline until remedies for their recovery are too little and too late.

OTHER TYPES OF COMMERCIAL DEVELOPMENT

The shopping center is just one of many elements that compose the commercial structure of a city. Legal services, building construction, real estate, and accounting are just a few of the numerous economic activities a city requires. They are as important to the urban pattern as the shopping center, often occupying more total within a city since they are not usually found in concentrated areas like shopping centers.

General business offices are also a part of the commercial structure of a city. Large office complexes in the centers of all of the major cities of the world are occupied by a great variety of businesses and corporation headquarters. Government office and courts of many types also occupy facilities in or immediately adjacent to business districts. Central city areas that have lost their retail sales attraction are often converted to office or light industrial uses such as garment manfacturing.

The medical center may be one of the exceptions to the scattering usually discerned in other services. The medical center is often located next to a major hospital. This center may include rest homes, clinics, convalescent homes, as well as doctors' offices. Such centers exist in Santa Barbara, California, and El Paso, Texas, and in many communities throughout the United States.

Industry   Some form of industrial activity is always an essential part of a community's economic structure. However, the term industry has many facets. Places of employment, research and development centers, electronic assembly plants, heavy industry, factories, and the testing of atomic bombs all come under the heading of industry. The kind of industry that a community permits within its confines will determine its quality of life.

In cities such as Santa Barbara, Miami Beach, Palm Springs, and Las Vegas major industry takes the form of tourism. There are also alternate sources of employment for the residents of these communities in commerce, real estate, and general services but they are usually in some way related to tourism and recreation.

In some communities, educational institutions are the major "industry." They bring financial support to the area through the employment of faculty and service personnel. These people in turn support the shopkeepers and the other institutions that provide housing, food, and other services. One of the purest forms of the educational community is in Davis, California. Once an agricultural college, the University of California at Davis is now a full-fledged university with approximately 17,000 students. Its influence on the surrounding community is enormous.

Industrial Parks.   The development of "industrial parks" has been due to the efforts of specialized industries to become more completely integrated with the home areas of their employees. The development of excellent architecture within a landscaped environment, the maintaining of noiseless, pollution-free operations, and service roads designed not to conflict with the residential area of the community have made the industrial park welcome in many communities, even the most restrictive ones.

Typical standards for the industrial park include architectural control through an architectural board of review, minimum setbacks of 25 feet with complete landscape treatment of the open areas, provision of adequate enclosed parking and loading spaces, exclusion of any operation that emits smoke or fumes, and limiting of noise levels. Performance standards for landscaped areas and plant operations are set forth to insure that high standards are maintained. The type of operation carried on within any plant in the industrial park is less than the effect that the operation will have on the city as a whole.

Many cities, however, are substantially developed industrially. These cities afford their residents substantial employment opportunity in manufacturing. This does not imply that the bulk of the land areas of cities like Gary, Indiana and South San Francisco, is occupied by manufacturing. In such undustrial cities, usually only about 10 to 15 percent of the land is taken up by manufacturing.

18

The Circulation System

CHANNELS OF MOVEMENT

Since people first charted the fleeting trace of a path across the landscape, routes of travel have been the vital threads in patterns of commerce, cultural exchange, and military conquest. Progressing from the path to the road, the river to the ocean, the rail to the sky, the space for movement of man and his vehicles now occupies more than a quarter of the land in the urban community. For 3,000 years his mode of transportation was by foot or horseback. Then came the industrial revolution and mechanization, steam for rail and water travel, the internal combustion engine for automobile and airplane, and the beginning of space travel.

Of all the products of a remarkable age, none have made more striking progress than the vehicles of transportation. With the variety in modes of travel came increased speed, extended lines of communication, and most important, unprecedented mobility of countless millions of people. The impact on the structure of our civilization is appalling. The industrial economy is rooted in large part on the production and circulation of vehicles of transportation. Commercial enterprise in metals, plastics, fuels, rubber, even in insurance, hospitals, and funeral parlors, depends to a large extent upon our capacity to move people and goods. Within our cities we are confronted with a paradox. On the one hand is the struggle to design a circulation system to accommodate vast changes in the speed of transportation; on the other we search desperately for a place for these vehicles to come to a halt. The freedom of movement afforded by the revolution in transportation has reached such an advanced stage of development it is now a major problem to *slow down and stop*. The automobile is trapped in the network of an archaic street system, but when the circulation routes are improved there must be a place to park at the points of destination. This paradox of conversion from vehicular speed to pedestrian tempo is

253

dramatized in airplane travel. The time consumed to and from the airport may be greater than the flight of a thousand miles.

In 1847 the Messageries Nationales coach line in France travelled at 6 miles an hour and 56 miles a day. With the introduction of asphalt about 1860 the improved roadways brought an increase in the speed of travel. The Malles-Poste coaches travelled 9 to 12 miles an hour and 75 miles a day. The automobile has the capacity for speeds several times that of the nineteenth century horse-drawn coach, but the time consumed by the fits and starts along traffic streets, the search for a place to park, and then the walk to the office reduce the average speed of the commuter to an even lesser rate.

An even greater issue than the speed of modern transportation is its safety. If urban travel were confined solely to the irritation of a traffic jam, we might withdraw to a point of vantage and view the scene as a farce. But the automobile has indeed become a weapon of murder; some 49,500 people were killed by it in 1977. Many of these tragedies are due to carelessness, but the tensions generating from the tempo and confusion of the modern city might be relieved through well-ordered street and highway design.

The function of a city's circulation system is to provide for the movement of people and goods. It ranges from the movement of an individual on foot to the daily hordes of commuters entering and leaving the city from distant points. It comprehends automobiles, buses, trucks, and railroads—on the surface, underground and overhead—ships and airplanes. It is the series of routes traversed for a variety of purposes—work, entertainment, shopping, transport of raw materials and manufactured products, education, relaxation, affairs of state, and law enforcement. The mixture of these demands for transport, and the vehicles to serve them, compounds the equation for the system. It embraces walkways, service lanes, major streets, highways, freeways, the rights-of-way for rail lines, and airway routes. Each of the elements in the circulation system we know today has been inherited from the pre-machine era. Adjustment to the mechanical vehicle has been an arduous process of wrestling some semblance of order and utility from the archaic layout.

The pioneer surveyors usually laid out towns in gridiron sections one mile square. The major highways followed these section lines in ribbons 100 feet wide. Secondary highways 80 feet in width were aligned along the quarter section lines, and within these squares the interior roads were laid in 60-foot rights-of-way. The system was adaptable to a regular division of land into lots, and people settled at strategic locations. The pattern continued as the population in-increased, and later through this network of streets, vehicles of modern transportation poured into the growing cities.

HOW SHALL WE MOVE?

Satellites in outer space make instantaneous audio-visual communication possible on a global scale. Spaceships carry men to the moon, and television is projected into our living rooms from moon-walkers. Yet this same technology only complicates the movement of earth-bound persons in cities.

The ever-increasing number of motor vehicles crowd the streets and are trapped in their own self-perpetuating traffic jams. Once associated with social status and the individual's freedom to move any time, anywhere, at any speed, the illusion of the automobile has been fleeting.

The expressway (freeway) system was conceived to relieve congestion. But the proliferation of automobiles strains them beyond their capacities. Armed with formulas for measuring "cost-benefit ratios," the limited vision of traffic experts justifies widening streets and adding more expressway lanes and extensive new routes, only to compound the congestion, multiply accidents, and increase injuries and deaths each year. Once expected to delineate the boundaries of neighborhoods, the expressways destroyed them; they became channels of escape from the congested city to the sprawling suburbs.

Automobile manufacture, with related oil, steel, and service enterprises, comprises a major element of the national economy. There are over three times as many new automobiles produced than babies born each year in the United States.

THE PLAN FOR CIRCULATION

This is the plan for major highways and streets, routes for mass transportation, railroads, airfields, and waterways. It defines the through-traffic arteries, freeways, parkways, and their intersections and interchanges. It charts the course of rail and bus routes about the city and its environs. It is in this plan that all lines of communication are integrated for the circulation of the people and goods in and about the urban area.

This system of circulation will define the boundaries of neighborhood units. The street system within this broad framework need be determined only to the extent that it impinges upon the through-traffic arteries and mass transportation routes. The internal design of the streets could remain unspecified until development is imminent and then be made precise.

As the city develops, this plan will become the reference for improvements and extensions of the circulation system. Precise plans may be made for railroad passenger and freight lines, yards, terminals and stations, air terminals and fields, and internal helicopter connections. Harbor and waterway development may be guided by this plan as improvements are proposed.

The *Plan for Circulation* and the *Plan for Land Use* require integration, and they may require occasional modification, but there is no development within one category which can remain unrelated to the other.

TRAFFIC AND AIR POLLUTION

As traffic grows, atmospheric pollution spreads across entire urban regions. Streets, expressways, parking lots, and multi-level garages consume valuable land as exhausts poison precious air. There is not, nor can there be, enough space to accommodate the moving and standing flood of automobiles. In the thirties Sir Raymond Unwin calculated that all the automobiles that enter New York

City would absorb all the space on Manhattan Island. Victor Gruen estimated in the 1960s that nine stories of garage space covering Manhattan would be necessary to store automobiles if everyone entering that island came by car.[1] The Urban Land Institute reported in 1970 that parking for the 150,000 cars entering Pittsburgh's Golden Triangle each day would require 214 garages with 700-car capacity, at a cost of $535,000,000, exclusive of land.[2] These projections may seem preposterous. Yet of the sixty stories in the twin towers of the Marina City apartment complex built in Chicago in the 1960s, nineteen stories are a garage.

The profligate waste of resources in materials and land has turned the personal freedom promised by the internal combustion engine into a frantic search for survival at the periphery of cities. Continued decentralization persists without concern for the cost of transportation or the arrangement of land uses related to economic and functional channels of mass transportation.

Therein lies a crux of the urban planning process: a structure of land uses and distribution of population within a network of mass transportation which can move people and goods with convenience, comfort, and economy. In great cities which evolved before the automobile—London, Paris, Moscow, Sao Paulo, New York, Chicago, Boston, Philadelphia, San Francisco—the concentration of land uses and the inadequate surface space have forced tunneling underground for subways. Yet building bulk in these cities continues to accelerate and the equation between the concentration of people and transportation is continuously unbalanced.

If a planned balance between building concentration and transportation service were achieved (and there is no evidence that this is about to happen), the subway would not be desirable. Man is not by nature a subterranean creature; he needs bountiful natural light and air. Since broad rights-of-way are being acquired for vast systems of expressways, comparable channels could be provided for a system of surface transportation within existing city centers, as well as outlying areas.

Such an approach to a desirable system of urban transportation will be expensive; any system of adequate transportation will require vast sums of public financing, as the massive cost of freeways and highways testifies. But it will require much more than public funds; it will require a rare commitment by public and private leaders to the transformation, the reshaping, of the city structure.

Perceptive minds since Ebenezer Howard have recognized the need to restructure the industrial city—now the commercialized city—in the image of man himself. Recovery of human scale is at the root of every enlightened concept of the city of our age. Sir Raymond Unwin applied Howard's theory of the self-contained Garden City to his own diagrams for the decentralized metropolis. The British New Towns, the planned decentralization of Stockholm, and Tapiola— near Helsinki in Finland—have pursued ths same objective.

---

[1] Victor Gruen, *The Heart Of Our Cities,* Simon and Schuster, New York, 1964.
[2] George Prytula, *Community Mobility Systems.* Urban Land Institute, Special Report, 1970.

The urban structure must be designed or redesigned as a series of physically functioning neighborhoods and communities integrated with a circulation system of mass transportation. Whatever the sociological variations, physical facilities for education, worship, trade, recreation, and work are determined by essential human needs. Special services may fit into the basic pattern of facilities which make up the areas of common interest, the neighborhoods and communities.

People are now dependent on automobiles to get to and from homes, schools, stores, and parks. Walking distances are excessive, traffic confrontations too hazardous, and the surroundings are often unpleasant or downright ugly. Poorly located schools and efforts to bring about a socio-ethnic mix have made the school bus a familiar feature in every city and town,

The family car is an anachronism in an industrial system which presumes to glorify "efficiency and economy." The family uses the car for an average of eight to ten trips each day. Most are short hauls to local facilities—shopping, school, house of worship, playground or friends; they are seldom emergencies. Yet the car is 2000 pounds of steel, powered with a 250 or more horse-power engine, transporting fewer than 1.5 persons per trip (1.1 in the west).

Stable neighborhoods and communities should have local systems of small *low*-speed mini-buses running on frequent convenient schedules; one may recall the "elephant trains" at the 1933 Century of Progress exposition in Chicago, the electric trams in Disneyland parking lots, the free bus systems in modern retirement colonies, moving sidewalks in large airports. With the resulting reduction, or elimination, of traffic accidents, both pedestrians and bicyclists could discover the joys of a relaxed tempo, as well as economy, in travelling to and from their daily activities. Having successfully created space-ships, technology, with some measure of humane ingenuity, might even produce a non-polluting mini-bus with "piggyback shopping carts."

With city planners spurred by the conviction that relief from traffic congestion would come by way of broader streets, there followed a rash of street-widening projects along the established rights-of-way, and major and secondary highways were designated. Congestion was not relieved, however. More traffic was invited onto these broader streets, slow-moving and short-haul traffic mixed with vehicles destined for more distant points, left turns occurred at all intersections, truck and passenger vehicles vied for parking and loading space along the curbs, vehicular and pedestrian traffic conflicted, unlimited ingress and egress flowed from abutting property into the traffic lanes, frequent intersections impeded movement, and the multitude of commercial distractions along the streets brought chaos to the city.

TRAFFIC ENGINEERING—A PALLIATIVE

Because the street plan of cities is insufficient to cope with traffic , there have been various methods devised to control the operation of vehicles. It might be more accurate to describe these as measures of control by default, but they are essential to maintain any movement of vehicles through the city streets. The calculation and administration of these are known as "traffic engineering."

Traffic engineers find themselves in the awkward position of responsibility for forcing the movement of the irresistible force of traffic through the impenetrable obstacle of congestion. Traffic engineers are repair persons rather than builders, devisers rather than planners, first-aid traffic "corpsman" rather than surgeons. Traffic engineering is necessary because the planning of the city circulation system has been neglected.

Traffic engineering embraces the host of devices with which the citydweller is familiar: stop-and-go signs at street intersections, slow-down warnings and speed limits, parking limits and prohibitions, the police whistle, the "safety islands" at points of boarding street cars and buses, the white and yellow lines painted upon the pavements to "channel" moving vehicles and the mechanical divisions sometimes employed for this purpose, and the one-way street. The list of these "solutions" is long, but none has singly, nor in combination,brought any genuine relief of the traffic problem.The devices are more appropriately described as stunts rather than solutions; they are expedient measures to cope with immediate traffic problems in the form of "first-aid" treatment and offer no real improvement in the capacity of the transportation system to move people.

The automobile travels at a reasonably rapid speed with relative ease, comfort, and convenience. Interruption of the flow of travel conflicts with the effectiveness of the machine as a means for the mass transportation of people, and this interruption also creates hazards to safety. The synchronization of "stop-lights" has improved the continuity of movement, but the effect of these interruptions remains. The average cycle for change of the traffic signal is one minute; cars travelling in one direction are stopped for 30 seconds and move for 30 seconds. The effect of this interruption is a reduction to 40 per cent of the number of cars which could pass a given point if the flow were uninterrupted. In other words, a street intersection controlled by traffic-lights can accommodate only two-fifths the number of cars a free flow of traffic will carry.

The conversion of streets from two-way to one-way travel is a familiar system that traffic engineers are frequently forced to employ. It is a method for channeling traffic that avoids the conflict of left-hand turns across lanes moving from the opposite direction, but the traffic signal is still necessary to permit the passage of pedestrians, and traffic flow continues to suffer periodic interruptions.

There is a reluctance to design streets for peak loads because of the alleged wasteful space during the periods of less intensive use. The alternative is conversion of six-lane trunk streets to four lanes in the direction of heavy flow and two lanes for the opposite direction during the morning rush and reversal of this process for the evening peak. While the painted channel lines are usually the only means for marking these lanes, some cities have mechanical barriers which may be raised and lowered from continuous slots along the channel separations.

Traffic engineers maintain data on the movement of people and vehicles, they measure the service of commercial centers by traffic counts of registered automobiles that park there, they measure the capacity of sidewalks by counts of pedestrians who traverse them; the probable effectiveness of street widening of new streets and freeways is estimated by counts of local and through traffic. The need for and effectiveness of traffic signals, prohibitions on left turns and curb parking, and special lanes for traffic flow are calculated by the traffic engineers from the variety of traffic counts and data compiled, and they aid the public transit companies in the routing of mass transportation vehicles.

The traffic engineers maintain a gallant struggle to cope with the imponderable traffic tangles they confront and, until the urban street system is designed for the vehicles which traverse it, their devices will remain essential ingredients of our city circulation. It is a choice between two traffic evils: no control and complete chaos or negative control to avoid paralysis.

THE RIGHT-OF-WAY

Since one-third of the land in the urban community is devoted to the road system, it is pertinent to observe how this land came into public ownership. In early times travel over the safest and most easily traversed routes created "public" roadways through usage. Since the basic ownership of all land was the sovereign right of the state, it was normal for the ruler to designate "post" roads and highways to assure protection for channels of communication between communities. When ownership was granted to individuals, the head of the state provided for a means of access to property, although some passageways remained toll roads until a very late date. In cities the subdivision of land into individual parcels was regulated by decree to maintain certain open spaces for travel and safety against fire. This practice is reflected in modern subdivision design whereby the state, in granting the right to individuals to subdivide land, requires that the roadways which give access to property be dedicated to public use. Streets thus dedicated to public use and accepted by the city for maintenance may either remain as public easements for such time as they are required as streets or they may be deeded to the city in "fee simple.' When streets are vacated by the city, the land occupied by them is usually divided, based on the original dedication or deed, and title to it returned to the abutting property owners.

STREET DESIGN

The gridiron street plan formed a pattern of rectangular blocks divided into rectangular lots which were usually very narrow to conserve on utility lines and very deep to conserve on streets. The curvilinear design was then devised to give some semblance of "character" to the subdivision, or subdue the deadly monotony of parallel streets stretching to infinity. The alterative soon developed into a curved grid, a series of parallel curved streets, with no more living amenities than the rectangular grid provided. The more exaggerated of the "designs" assumed the form of a violently swirling street system in which orientation was completely obscured.

It is customary to maintain the narrowest practicable width for local residential streets which serve only the abutting property. When parking is desired on each side of the street, the right-of-way is between 54 and 64 feet wide, with a pavement width of 36 feet. The paved surface may be as narrow as 30 feet, but this suggests parking on one side only since the traffic lanes should not be less than 10 feet wide. Although local streets of narrow width are more economical in their initial cost, the weaving of automobiles about parked cars is a hazard to the safety of children in the neighborhood.

Economy of street design has been more rationally approached through the effort to reduce the total length of streets rather than their width. Care in site planning brought about an abandoning of the artificial picturesqueness to the arbitrary street system and led to the use of the cul-de-sac and the loop street.

The cul-de-sac, or dead-end street, came into use to eliminate through traffic in a positive manner. Cul-de sacs terminate in a circular or hammer-head "turn-around," and, to retain their inherent advantages, they should be short—a maximum length of 450 feet is recommended. The advantages are dissipated in long cul-de-sacs, since they induce accelerated traffic speeds and render access for service and fire-protection facilities more complicated. Probably the most renowned example of the cul-de-sac street is the community of Radburn, New Jersey. In this development the system is fully exploited by the consolidation of open space and reduction of street crossings, the separation between vehicular and pedestrian circulation being enhanced by the use of pedestrian underpasses beneath the major streets. Although this separation of traffic is desirable, the narrow tunnel shape of the usual pedestrian underpass tends to accumulate refuse and dirt, and presents dangers which may be avoided by convenient pedestrian overpasses above slightly depressed streets.

The loop street is a variation of the cul-de-sac and is employed in substantially the same manner. However, it eliminates the necessity for the "turnaround" and provides continuous circulation required by some communities to assure no interference with accessibility for fire protection and other services. While it does not offer complete separation between vehicular and pedestrian traffic, it is as effective as the cul-de-sac in eliminating through traffic. The length of the loop street is not as important as that of the cul-de-sac, since the movement of traffic is continuous, but like the cul-de-sac, traffic is normally confined to vehicles of the residents or for service and delivery within the block.

There are some disadvantages in the cul-de-sac and the loop street, but careful planning can reduce these to a minimum. It is sometimes alleged that circulation about a community becomes confusing, although a simple plan can overcome much of this objection. House-numbering and street-naming require attention since they vary from the customary pattern for which the usual systems have been devised.

The collector street is, as the name suggests, the street into which the local residential streets feed. It may be designed to flow into the secondary or major traffic arteries, in which case the right-of-way is usually 60 feet wide with a pavement 36 feet in width. Frequently, however, the collector streets are comparable in traffic load to a secondary highway and must be so designed.

The traffic load from the local residential streets and their collector roadways is carried by the secondary and major highways and, although a difference in function is suggested by this terminology, there is often little real distinction between the traffic they carry. The secondary highway is intended to serve areas intermediate between the major traffic street and thence connect to the major highway. However, major highways have grown so congested that much traffic escapes along the secondary and collector streets, thus rendering each the equivalent of a major traffic artery.

Secondary highways are usually 80 or 86 feet in width of right-of-way with a pavement width of 64 feet having four lanes for traffic and two for parking. The major highways are customarily 110 feet in width with a pavement width of about 76 feet having six lanes for moving traffic and two for parking.

It is gradually becoming apparent that access from abutting property to major and secondary highways must be denied. The movement of traffic cannot be maintained when it is repeatedly interrupted by the ingress or egress of vehicles from side streets. Frontage along these main traffic routes must obtain their service access from either alleys or minor service roads parallel to the highway. A service road is generally 28 feet in width, allowing parking on one side only, and the usual width of alleys is 20 feet with parking prohibited. Service roads may be screened from the highways with a planting strip; the highway is thus enhanced while the abutting property is shielded from it, an asset to the development of residential neighborhoods contiguous to highways.

THE REGIONAL SYSTEM

Following old Indian trails, the winding. twisting, meandering routes between communities became the post roads, the plank roads, and the high roads. These were the trade routes between centers of population and between the rural areas where products were grown and the towns where they were marketed. Like the roads in the center of the early city, they followed the easy way irrespective of property boundaries. As property ownership was formalized the roads served as dividing lines. They represented access to property and a way to and from markets. Most of the important regional links follow, to some extent, these original lines. With the expansion of communities, many of these primitive roadways have been lost in the maze of internal growth. They left their mark, however, as the basis for orientation of other streets and highways, parallel and perpendicular to these original spinal lines.

With the expansion and congestion of cities, the intercommunity roads collapsed under the impact of traffic loads. They carried less and less traffic. Accidents were a by-product of too many intersections, ill-designed roadbeds and curves, lack of sufficient sight distances, and vertical curves. Widening the roads only intensified the situation by drawing more of the ever-increasing

Highway and Street Standards*

Type of Facility	Function and Design Features	Spacing	R.O.W. Width
Freeways	Provide regional and metropolitan continuity and unity. Limited access; no grade crossings; no traffic stops.	Variable; related to regional pattern of population and industrial centers	200–300 ft.
Expressways	Provide metropolitan and city continuity and unity. Limited access; some channelized grade crossings and signals at major intersections. Parking prohibited.	Variable; generally radial or circumferential	150–200 ft.
Major roads (major arterials)	Provide unity throughout contiguous urban area. Usually form boundaries for neighborhoods. Minor access control; channelized intersections; parking generally prohibited.	1 mile	120–150 ft.
Secondary roads (minor arterials)	Main feeder streets. Signals where needed; stop signs on side streets. Occasionally form boundaries for neighborhoods.	½ mile	80 ft.
Collector streets	Main interior streets. Stop signs on side streets.	¼–½ mile	60–70 ft.
Local streets	Local service streets. Non-conducive to through traffic.	at blocks	50–60 ft.
Cul-de-sac	Streets open at only one end, with provision for a turnaround at the other.	only wherever practical	50 ft. (90 ft. dia. turn-around)

* *Urban Land*, May 1961, by George Nez, Director, Inter-County Regional Planning Commission, Denver, Colorado. Standards revised 1979 by William A. Law, Linscott, Law, and Greenspan, Transportation Engineers, Los Angeles, Cal.

Pavement Width	Desirable Maximum Grades	Speed	Other Features
Varies; 12 ft. per lane; 10–14 ft. shoulders both sides of each roadway; 8–60 ft. median strip.	3%	55 mph 88.5 km/h	Depressed, at grade, or elevated. Preferably depressed through urban areas. Require intensive landscaping, service roads, or adequate rear lot building set-back lines (75 ft.) where service roads are not provided.
Varies; 12 ft. per lane; 8–10 ft. shoulders; 8–30 ft. median strip.	4%	50 mph 80.5 km/h	Generally at grade. Requires landscaping and service roads or adequate rear lot building set-back lines (75 ft.) where service roads are not provided.
84 ft. maximum for 4 lanes, parking, and median strip.	4%	35–40 mph 56–64 km/h	Require 5-ft.-wide detached sidewalks in urban areas, planting strips (5–10 ft. wide or more) and adequate building set-back lines (30 ft.) for buildings fronting on street; 60 ft. for buildings backing on street.
60 ft.	5%	35–40 mph 56–64 km/h	Require 5-ft.-wide detached sidewalks, planting strips between sidewalks and curb 5–10 ft. or more, and adequate building set-back lines (30 ft.)
44 ft. (2–12 ft. traffic lanes; 2–10 ft. parking lanes)	5%	30 mph 48 km/h	Require at least 4-ft.-wide detached sidewalks; vertical curbs; planting strips are desirable; building set-back lines 30 ft. from right of way.
36 ft. where street parking is permitted	6%	25 mph 40 km/h	Sidewalks at least 5 ft. in width for densities greater than 1 d.u./acre, and curbs and gutters.
30–36 ft. (75 ft. turn-around)	5%		Should not have a length greater than 500 ft.

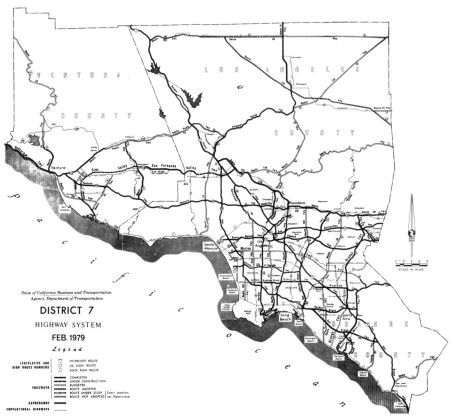

State of California Business and Transportation Agency, Department of Transportation

THE FREEWAY SYSTEM, Los Angeles

A portion of the California Freeway and Expressway system of 12,500 miles. The plan illustrates the 1,525-mile network in the Los Angeles region.

number of vehicles to them. Then the "free-way" introduced the first change in highway design.

The freeway provided a new approach; it released the roadway from old alignments, from abutting property, from intersections at grades, from outmoded design standards, from old right-of-way limitations. The traffic problem remains unsolved, and it is true that the freeway can, at peak hours, become the longest parking lot in the world. The freeway nonetheless has embraced the salient characteristics of the travel way for free and fast-moving vehicles. It has yet to find its appropriate relation to the future shape of the evolving modern city.

THE FREEWAY

A freeway is essentially a pair of parallel roadways, each of which carries one-way traffic moving in opposite directions, with complete separation from each other and free from all cross-traffic. Ingress and egress in either direction flow via accelerating and decelerating lanes. Traffic moves unimpeded by any interruptions from light signals or stop signs. All cross-traffic is carried over or under the freeway, and access from abutting property is closed from the freeway right-of-way.

The freeway appeared on the American scene during the early 1930's, with the construction of the Downtown Expressway parallel to the Hudson River in New York City, the Pulaski Skyway from Newark, New Jersey, to New York, and the commencement of the great Chicago Outer Drive. Later developments soon followed in New Jersey, Pennsylvania, New York, Connecticut, Delaware, California, and in the vicinity of Washington, D.C.

Many of these early routes were limited in scope, but they were designed for the unimpeded movement of vehicles by the shortest feasible route between points. The freeway may parallel existing streets or cut across their present pattern. It marks the beginning of a new form of artery which may aid in solution of the traffic problem and create the huge cells that will ultimately frame the groups of neighborhood units as the city grows and is rebuilt. With the freeway a new urban form emerges.

The right-of-way for a freeway is necessarily broad; it must provide adequate space to be depressed or raised without adversely affecting abutting property. Limitations on the width vary with circumstances. Land cost may be one obvious prospect for forcing economy in land area, but another may appear

Courtesy Department of Public Works, Division of Highways, State of California

FOUR-LEVEL INTERSECTION, Los Angeles

in state laws which restrict the acquisition of property for public improvements to that required for the principal function of the facility. Such restrictions would limit the right-of-way to the area required only for the traffic lanes and adjacent parkways, the acquisition for contiguous buffer spaces being considered excessive. To cope with such a situation in New York City, the routes were acquired by the Park Depatment as park strips and the traffic ways were built within them; the term "parkway" is consequently applied to them. Some states have enacted statutes to permit the acquisition of ample space for the freeway right-of-way; in California a space 150 feet on each side of the centerline of the roadway may be acquired, thus providing for purchase of marginal property to avoid the creation of small remnants of land otherwise unusable for development.

The freeway is usually designed for three lanes of traffic in each direction, and rarely more than four lanes. These are intended for the free movement of vehicles, and the greater the number of lanes, the greater is the interference from vehicles weaving between them seeking a satisfactory channel of speed or access to the decelerating lane from which to leave the freeway. The lanes for acceleration at the entrance and deceleration at the exit of the freeway, and for emergency parking for disabled cars, should be in addition to the number of channels of clear traffic movement.

Ingress and egress are at infrequent intervals, not less than one-half mile apart and preferably at one-mile distance; this frequency will permit adequate stops for bus connections if they are permitted on the freeway system. Lanes should be 15 feet in width rather than the usual highway standard of 12 feet, and loading and unloading zones must be separated from the clear channels of movement with transition lanes leading to the stopping places.

The dividing strip between the roads traversing in opposite directions will vary in width according to the nature of the right-of-way. Some separations are broad enough to permit service stations, emergency parking bays, and fully landscaped spaces, but the usual width is between 10 and 20 feet. Because the freeway presently intended for personal automotive vehicles may someday provide a channel for mass transportation vehicles, an ample dividing strip may one day demonstrate the economy of its original purchase; a minimum of 30 feet and a desirable width of 50 feet should be planned. Oversight, indifference, or lack of vision in planning freeways will cost the people much in money as well as time, confusion, and discouragement; it is demonstrated today in some cities where the freeway and mass transportation plans failed to be integrated.

Safety and efficient flow of traffic have been enhanced by improvements in lighting and directional signs. Lighting for night travel has made great progress, some highways having become ribbons of lighted pavement requiring no headlights on vehicles for adequate vision and safety. Although not yet fully developed and employed, color may be advantageously used to identify certain lanes for speeds and points of departure from the roadway. The scale of letters and placement of signs which indicate directions, places, and distances are important factors in the design of traffic-ways for smooth and safe circulation.

THE TRAFFIC LANE

Traffic hazards arise from excessive speed, but they may be due also to deficiencies in the design of roadways. Separations between traffic traveling in opposite directions and the elimination of intersections are essential. The provision of off-street parking so curb parking may be prohibited is necessary; only one disabled car can reduce a three-lane roadway to a two-lane street and add the hazard of rapid accumulation of vehicles at this bottleneck. Given the free flow of traffic which these improvements offer, the effectiveness of the motor car depends upon the shape of the roadway over which it travels.

Traffic lanes vary from 8 to 15 feet and this variation is not a fault until it occurs within the same line of travel. The local street may have a width of 10 feet and the through-traffic artery may be 12 feet, but the width should be constant for each. Local streets serving residential areas are customarily designed for a lane of 10 feet, being 4 feet wider than the standard automobile and none too great a separation between two moving vehicles passing at a rate of 35 miles per hour. On highways and freeways the width is generally 12 feet, increased to 13 or 14 feet on the curves.[5] When the freeway or highway is designed for the operation of trucks and buses, a lane 15 feet wide should be provided.

The width of the lane intended for parking vehicles is usually 8 feet; this assumes the wheels will be one foot from the curb and allow 3 feet between it and a vehicle passing along the centerline of the adjacent moving lane. If the parked vehicle is a truck, it will project into the adjacent lane, creating a hazard of side-swiping. It seems more sensible to make no distinction between the width of a lane for parking and one for moving vehicles; in peak hours when curb parking is prohibited, this lane adds a traffic way to the otherwise over-crowded street.

One-third of all trips by motor vehicles of all types are within the city limits, and 90 per cent of the rest are within a radius of 30 miles. The automobile is adapted to use for local travel and is readily maneuverable and quick-starting. However, it can achieve high, comfortable and relatively safe speed, depending upon the roadbed and the driver at the wheel.

The appropriate roadway is an uninterrupted straight run or sweeping curve. A car traveling at 10 miles per hour requires a turning radius of about 40 feet with a level roadbed and 30 feet if the road has a 10 per cent slope. When the speed reaches 30 miles per hour, the curve should be 400 feet on a level road and 230 feet with a 10 per cent slope. At 60 miles per hour the radius of the curve should be 1,400 feet if level, and 900 feet with a 10 per cent bank.[6] Since the average critical speed of automobiles has been between 30 and 35 miles per hour, it would appear that road curves of some 250 feet, well banked, would be adequate, but it is necessary to provide for the far more rapid travel which will

---

[5] Frank H. Malley, *Location and Function of Urban Freeways, Post-War Patterns of City Growth,* American Transit Association, New York.

[6] Based upon standards of the *American Association of State Highway Officials..*

continue to occur upon our freeways, a free flow needing a radius of at least 1,000 feet. Banking is commonly known as super-elevation.

The combined factors of human response and the mechanical action in bringing a car to a halt make clear visibility at street intersections mandatory. The driver of an automobile traveling at a speed of 10 miles per hour quickly perceives a necessity to stop the car, but by the time he has translated this perception into the action of applying the brakes the car has traveled a distance of 8 feet. Another 8 feet will be traveled before the brakes bring the vehicle to a stop. Traveling at 30 miles per hour a car will go 20 feet between the time the driver detects the need to stop and has translated this perception into action against the brakes. The car will travel another 60 feet before it is stopped. At 60 miles per hour the car will have moved 45 feet between perception and action on the brakes, the braking distance being another 230 feet.[7]

Previous reference has been made to the effect of weaving on the flow of traffic. This injects both a hazard and a deterrent to speed. The absence of left-hand turns reduces the problem to some degree, since cars entering a roadway have no necessity to move out of the traffic stream to the left. The weaving action is nevertheless present in a street of more than one lane in width since cars in the left lane will have to leave the traffic stream on the right. A car traveling in a traffic stream moving at a speed of 10 miles per hour will need only 170 feet to weave from left to right in a two-lane highway and 320 feet in a three-lane road. When the traffic stream is moving at 30 miles per hour, however, the weaving distance in a two-lane road increases to 750 feet and 1,230 feet in a three-lane road. At 50 miles per hour the weaving distance is 1,890 feet in two lanes and 2,900 feet in three lanes.[8]

Elimination of grade intersections removes stop-and-go signals and increases both the speed and the safety of vehicles. Despite the fact that higher speeds increase the time it takes to stop a car and can increase the damage done in an accident, good highways do tend to decrease the accident fatality rate. A study in 1970, for example, showed that on the portion of the Federal interstate system in operation at that time, the accident death rate was 2.8—significantly lower than the national figure of 4.9. Had the national average prevailed on the interstate system, 3,300 more deaths would have occurred that year.[9]

Not only is safety improved by the elimination of street intersections, but economy in time and money is effected. Estimates by the Automobile Club of Southern California indicate the freeway is seven times as safe as the normal street system, saves 50 per cent in driving time, and is 30 per cent cheaper in operating costs of the automobile.

The county of Los Angeles undertook a study of the relationship between street intersection design and accidents.[10] It embraced 86 residential tracts

[7] Herman Herrey, "Comprehensive Planning for the City: Market and Dwelling Place, Part 1: Traffic Design," *Pencil Points,* April 1944.

[8] *Ibid.*

[9] National Safety Council, *Accident Facts,* Chicago, 1971 edition.

[10] Harold Marks, Traffic Engineer, County of Los Angeles.

HIGHWAY INTERCHANGES

Simple Grade Separation between Two Highways

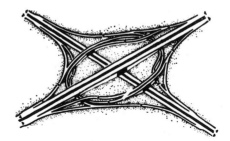

Universal Interchange

Braided or "T" Interchange

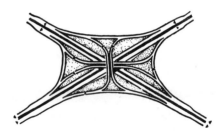

Four-Level Interchange

Simple Interchange of Freeway with Highway

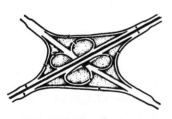

Cloverleaf Interchange

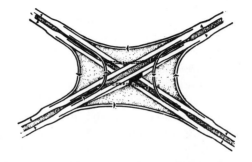

Bel Geddes Interchange

involving a total of 4,320 acres, 108 miles of residential streets, and 660 intersections. The study disclosed that the accident rate in "gridiron" street design
was almost eight times as great as in an internal system with limited access to
major traffic arteries. An internal cellular plan offers the opportunity for safer
living as well as economy, privacy, and attraction.

These statistics indicate the nature of the horizontal space dimensions the
auto has introduced to the urban traffic pattern and emphasize the basic fact
that streets intended for smooth and safe traffic flow cannot have frequent
intersections without destroying the effectiveness of the vehicle.

Adjustment to the new character of modern vehicular travel has been slow
and the change in approach to the design of roadways has probably been most
apparent at the points of intersection. Traffic circles were the first attempts to
merge traffic flow and avoid the conflicts of left turns. While traffic was light, the
circle was adequate, but the increase in number of vehicles re-created congestion
at these points.

The "cloverleaf" was the next step toward a solution of traffic interchange,
but it has a weakness. Drivers intending to turn left must cross beyond the
intersecting street for which they are destined and then make a right turn into
a curve which leads back to the cross street they seek. It is confusing for drivers
traveling at a fair rate of speed to find themselves beyond the intersection they
seek and then to turn right for a left-hand direction. Familiarity with a roadway
offsets this sort of confusion, but it is not assurance of the safest form of traffic
artery.

Other types of interchange structures have been designed for the purpose of
overcoming the weaknesses of the circle and cloverleaf, and most have incorporated the best features of each. However, all designs assume that slow vehicles
remain on the right-hand side of the roadway and, because left-hand turns on
level roads are a handicap to speed and safety, movement from the freeway is
channeled to the right regardless of the destination of the vehicle. In the General
Motors Exhibit at the New York World's Fair 1939, Norman Bel Geddes
presented a highway design in which a driver would turn left from the left-hand
lane, and this turn would have the same radius of curvature as the right-hand
turn. He observed that the term "slow lane" is a contradiction of the freeway
system and that the speed of vehicles would probably be similar in all lanes. Bel
Geddes proposed that the number of through-lanes continue undiminished
regardless of the left and right turns, and he provided a lane for transition into
the left-hand turn as was customary for the right-hand turn. Similarly the
transition lanes for entrance to the freeway would be from both left and right
sides of the roadway.

The adoption of this logic is rather slow since it suggests some changes in the
normal habits of drivers accustomed to the present formula for turning right out
of a freeway no matter what direction may be the ultimate destination. It also
necessitates some changes in the habits of the engineers who design the highway
system. Meanwhile, the knotty problem of the smooth and safe intersection of
traffic is met by some rather fantastic combinations of the circle, the universal,
and the cloverleaf.

THE INTERSTATE HIGHWAY

For many years names like "Sante Fe Trail" and "Lincoln Highway" have lent romance to the roads that cross our vast countryside. The Bureau of Public Roads has supervised the construction of highways and has received Federal aid since 1916, but until the late thirties highway planning was generally performed by the separate states. In 1956 the Congress authorized a vast interstate highway program. It was planned to build 36,000 miles of freeways outside urban areas by 1972 as part of the National System of Interstate and Defense Highways. These will connect with 6,700 miles of urban freeways to augment the 2,900 miles of urban freeways existing in 1961.

It had been estimated that passenger car registration will reach 120,000,000 in 1980, and require an additional 5,600 miles of urban interstate freeways.[11] However, since the projections of the 1960s were made, U.S. freeway constructions has been curtailed.

Great highways, such as the Pennsylvania Turnpike, have been designed for modern motor travel over long distances and at rapid and steady speeds. Uninterrupted by traffic crossings and modeled to the topography of the countryside, these sweeping freeways are unmarred by the stigma of commercial advertising. Roadside restaurants and service stations punctuate the route at convenient intervals. It is now possible to travel from New York City to Chicago and beyond on roadways with limited access rights and few, if any, crossings at grade.

MOVEMENT OF PEOPLE AND GOODS

In the movement of people and goods about the city every form of mass transportation, except railways and subways, is routed on a street system originally laid out for the easy subdivision of land and in the time when the horse and buggy was the common mode of conveyance. The result is a paradox: the automobile receives the most attention in plans for the improvement of urban traffic but is the least efficient form of urban transport, whereas the bus is replacing the electric train, although the latter is essentially the most efficient form of rapid transit for the mass movement of people. That the development of effective transit is the most economical, as well as the most efficient means for the mass transportation of the urban population may be apparent by comparison of the characteristics of vehicles and the roadways they use.

A typical traffic street with the usual intersecting streets will accommodate 700–800 private passenger automobiles per lane per hour passing a given point. It will carry about 180 buses and 150 streetcars per lane per hour. Since it is the movement of people rather than the movement of vehicles with which we are concerned, the capacity of the street must be translated into the number of

---

[11] A report by Wilbur Smith & Associates, Consulting Engineers, for the Automobile Manufacturers Association, 1961.

people these vehicles will transport, Studies have demonstrated that private autos carry an average of 1.5 perons per car. A bus will carry about 40 persons seated and a streetcar about 50 seated persons. The single lane of the typical trunk street will therefore accommodate about 1,200 passengers per hour in private autos whereas the bus carries 7,200 and the streetcar 9,000. The capacity of the bus and streetcar may be further increased with standing passengers raising the capacity of the bus to 9,000 and the streetcar to 13,500 per hour.[12]

These figures apply to the capacity of a single lane for each type of vehicle. A proportionate increase in the capacity would occur by the addition of lanes if they could be retained as clear channels. Painted white lines demarcating the lanes are of some aid in the typical street, but they do not prohibit the weaving of vehicles from one lane to another, and the effect of weaving measurably reduces the efficiency of the street. Surveys have shown that weaving reduces the capacity of the second lane of traffic to 75 per cent of the single lane, the capacity of the third lane is 56 per cent of the single lane, and a fourth lane is only 26 per cent of the single lane.[13] Three lanes in one direction with unrestricted weaving have a capacity of only 2⅓ lanes of clear channels with no weaving.

Studies by the American Transit Association demonstrate the increase in movement of people by the addition of mass transportation facilities on the city streets. A typical city street with a pavement width of 60 feet and no curb parking provides three lanes of traffic in each direction. This street will accommodate about 2,100 private autos in three lanes, assuming reasonable restrictions on weaving, and carry 3,700 passengers per hour. If one lane of autos is replaced by a bus, the number of autos is decreased to 1,200 and their passenger load to 2,100, but the bus line carries 7,200 seated passengers and 9,000 including standees, increasing the total capacity of the street to 9,300 seated and 11,100 including standing passengers. If the bus line is replaced by a streetcar, with a capacity of 9,000 seated passengers and 13,500 seated and standing, the total load of the street is 11,100 seated and 15,600 passengers seated and standing.[14] In each case the standing passenger load is assumed to be 25 per cent of the seated passengers in buses and 50 per cent of the seated passengers in streetcars.

This study shows that the substitution of a bus lane for a lane of cars on the ordinary trunk street will carry two and one-half times the number of people carried by three lanes of cars alone, and the substitution of a streetcar line for one lane of autos will carry three times the number of people. In both cases all passengers are seated. When standing passengers are included, the capacity of the street is increased to three times the number of people in buses and nearly four times the number in streetcars.

A limited access roadway with no crossing materially increases the capacity of private automobiles, but this capacity is not increased proportionately with the speed which cars can reach with uninterrupted flow. Studies show that the

[12] American Transit Association, *Moving People in the Modern City*, New York City, 1944.
[13] *Ibid.*
[14] *Ibid.*

theoretical maximum number of vehicles is accommodated at a speed of about 32 miles per hour, and that the theoretical maximum number of cars is about 2,060 per hour per lane. The practical maximum number of cars that can be carried at this speed, however, is only about 75 per cent of this number, or 1,500 cars per hour per lane, the capacity decreasing above and below this critical speed.

A freeway carrying 1,500 cars per hour will move 2,500 people in a single lane as compared with 1,200 passengers on the ordinary city street. The number of seated passengers carried by a bus increases from 7,200 to 10,000 per hour and 13,000 including standees. The capacity of the electric streetcar is likewise increased when interference of other traffic is removed; it increases from 9,000 seated passengers and 13,500 including standees on the ordinary street to 13,500 seated and 20,000 including standees per track per hour with uninterrupted movement. The free flow of uninterrupted rail lines further permits the effective use of multiple trains which carry 27,000 seated and 40,000 including standees per hour on a single track, while two tracks in the same direction, with one local and one express train, can increase the total capacity per hour to 70,000 seated and 100,000 or more including standing passengers.[15]

A six-lane freeway—three lanes in each direction—will reduce the capacity per lane for automobiles from 1,500 cars per hour for a single lane to about 2,700 cars for two lanes and 3,500 cars in three lanes. Three lanes will carry about 6,000 passengers per hour in private automobiles compared with one bus lane carrying 7,200 seated and 9,000 including standees.[16] Buses operating on a three-lane freeway would probably also be reduced in efficiency because of the inevitable conflict with automobiles. If the same decrease as automobiles were applied to the bus, the latter would still carry 8,000 seated persons and more than 11,000 including standees.

The freeway incorporating rapid transit lines (the expressway) or some form of overhead train system (the "elevated train" or monorail) both require a fairly commodious right-of-way for protection to abutting property. Because there is a firm reluctance to retire any of the land surface from present or potential use for commercial development in the urban centers, there is resistance to either of these surface forms of transportation into the heart of the city. Because of the overwhelming congestion on city streets and the inadequacy of rapid transit systems to move the people with convenience, comfort, or speed, the subway was constructed as the natural alternative.

Unfortunately the subway marks the final evidence that the city has succumbed to strangulation by urban congestion. An uninterrrupted flow of travel for multiple electric trains is accomplished, but at a cost that exceeds every other form of mass transportation. Only the private automobile exceeds the cost of subways and it is four or five times the cost per passenger mile.

---

[15] *Ibid.*
[16] *Ibid.*

MASS TRANSIT SYSTEMS

Every large city in the world has some type of mass transit system. One can imagine what travel would be like in cities such as New York, Paris and London if mass transit did not exist and automobiles carried no more than 1.25 passengers per unit. In New York City, for example, the streets and the space required for parking would eliminate all sites for buildings. Congestion would be absolute, movement would not be possible.

The subway is a mass transit means that does not impinge on vehicular street movement. There are subway systems in London, Paris, São Paulo, Peking, Hong Kong, San Francisco, New York, Chicago, Montreal, Washington D.C., and Moscow as well as in other cities. One may be critical of a system that at times packs people together as if they were inanimate objects, but a better method for moving large numbers of people has yet be found.

Recent mass transit systems such as the BART system in San Francisco, have been criticized because their highly sophisticated mechanisms break down easily. Another criticism has been that these systems do not fulfill their intended purpose—the reducing of automobile traffic into the central city. Further, critics claim these systems do not serve poor people, the people who need them the most, as service runs mainly through affluent areas where personal transportation is more readily available.

How to finance mass rapid transit has been a controversial public issue. Studies all over the world indicate that nearly all systems need heavy subsidy, even if fares are substantially raised.

The Hong Kong System. The Modified Initial System is 15.6 kilometres (9.7 miles) long with 15 stations and comprises part of the Kong Kow Line from Kwun Tong to Mong Kok in Kowloon and runs southwards along Nathan Road across the harbour terminating at Chater station in Central District on Hong Kong Island. It is scheduled for operation in March 1980.[17]

This system has 12 underground stations and three above ground. Apart from a short overhead section at the Kwun Tong end, construction has mainly been accomplished by bored tunnel with an immersed tube under the harbour.

In July 1977, approval was given to extend the Modified Initial System from Prince Edward station in north Nathan Road to Tsuen Wan in the New Territories. The extension is scheduled to commence operation in late 1982.

The underground stations are being constructed by the "cut-and-cover" method. They have been designed around the central island platform concept in order to segregate passenger movements in urban areas. Stations are spaced at about one kilometre intervals, while the maximum spacing is 2.4 kilometres (1.5 miles) across the harbor between Admiralty station and Tsim Sha Tsui.

---

[17] Hong Kong Government Information Service Publication, June 1978.

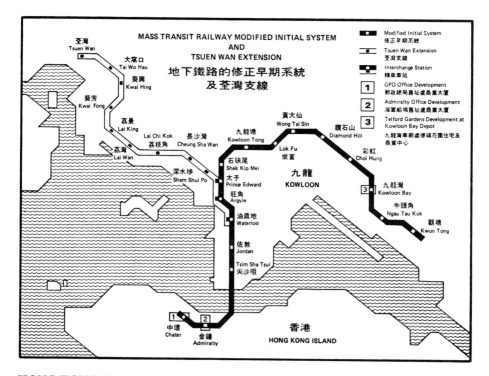

HONG KONG MASS TRANSIT SYSTEM

Hong Kong Government Information Services Publication, June 1978

OTHER ALTERNATIVES

Buses are another form of mass transit. Some routes are rapid, occupying specially designed lanes on a freeway. For the most part however, buses occupy street space and add to a city's congestion.

At one time cities in the United States had electric powered street car systems. For reasons not easily determined these carriers of large numbers of people disappeared from the streets of most American cities. The buses that replaced them spew fumes and smog into the air. The argument against the fixed rail system as compared with the flexibility of the busses with their passenger pick up at the curb creates questions of safety related to the weaving patterns that occur when the vehicle moves from a traffic lane to the curbside.

Monorails have captured the imagination of futurists. Examples, however, indicate that they are no more than a modernized elevated railway, with the same blighting effect on street architecture. The stations occupy large spaces at critical locations. The posts and columns in the street and the heavy structure of the monorail track interrupt the streets and reduce their carrying capacities.

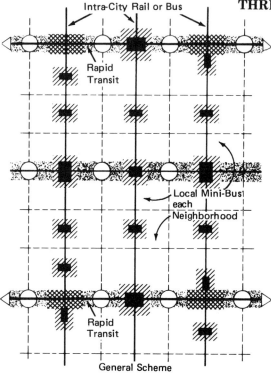

Intra-City Rail or Bus

Rapid Transit

Local Mini-Bus each Neighborhood

Rapid Transit

General Scheme

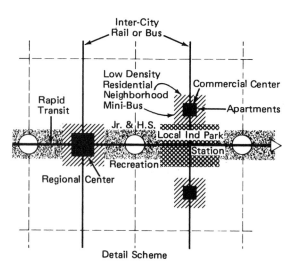

Inter-City Rail or Bus

Low Density Residential Neighborhood Mini-Bus

Commercial Center

Apartments

Rapid Transit

Jr. & H.S.

Local Ind Park Station

Recreation

Regional Center

Detail Scheme

THREE-PHASE MASS TRANSIT

The neighborhood unit is the common denominator in the urban structure. In this plan, a minibus system serves each neighborhood, circulating to and from the local commercial center, parks, playgrounds, and schools. An intracity or intercity rail or bus system links the commercial centers with major rapid transit service to central business districts, cultural facilities, airports, railroad lines, and concentrated industrial, or other, employment centers.

Although technically the system would be organized in a general "grid," this does not imply a "gridiron" street layout or pattern of land uses. Alignment would be adjusted to variations in natural terrain and, in existing cities, to established and desirable permanent land uses.

Weaning people from the automobile to mass transit will require both convenient and frequent local transit—the minibus—and restrictions on parking in concentrated business and cultural centers. Until most of the urban community recognizes the extravagance of the automobile, and until a convenient mass transportation system is available, massive automobile parking space will be required at rapid transit stations.

In the diagram, solid lines indicate the transit lines; solid spaces, the local and regional commercial centers; crosshatched areas, the local industrial parks; circles, community elementary or high schools; dotted areas, recreation facilities. Dash lines outline neighborhood areas.

The future of mass transit lies in the development of an integrated system that will serve the people who need the service most. The fares must be geared to the income level of its users. The aged and the lowest income groups should ride free. The system must be built to take people to places of employment and centers of activity. Most of all the system should be a part of the reconstruction of those portions of the city that have fallen into decay. In this way the system would be built into the development itself and people would use it, especially if there were no garages for the storage of automobiles and no off-street or on-street parking permitted other than for visitors or in cases of emergencey.

TERMINAL SPACE—OFF-STREET PARKING

Man's struggle to achieve speed has been successful, and we are confronted with a paradox: inadequate space to slow down and stop. Automobiles, buses, and trucks must have a storage place at both the origin and the destination of their travel routes. And they must have a place to come to temporary rest for the conduct of business or pleasure en route. This is the parking problem.

The requirements for parking space will vary according to the structure of the city and the habits of motor travel, but experience suggests some standards which may serve as guides.[18] These standards are generally related to the building floor space, and this underscores the issue of excess zoning and congestion. The issue may be restated by a question of whether it is our intention that cities become gargantuan parking lots occupied by buildings. The prospect that mass transportation may offer the solution seems remote; the private automobile is a phenomenon of our age, satisfying a basic instinct for freedom and choice of movement whatever the consequences. The form of cities must be adapted to man's nature and the vehicles he creates. To be effective, cars must have the room to move *and* to stop.

Motorists wish to park as near their destination as possible, and surveys have indicated that they will do this, in many instances, at the expense of illegal curb parking. Surveys have also indicated that motorists entering the downtown district for business or shopping do not wish to walk from their parking place a distance of more than 1,000 feet. In a midwestern city, Rockford, Illinois, the following desires were indicated by motorists: Of those who parked for one-half hour or less, 41% would walk one block, 36% would walk 2 blocks, and 14% would walk 3 blocks, 4% would walk 4 blocks; of those who parked for one hour, 15% would walk one block, 37% two blocks, 28% three blocks, and 12% four blocks, 4% five blocks; of those who parked up to two hours, 6% would walk one block, 28% two blocks, 29% three blocks, 23% four blocks, 6% five blocks, and 5% six; of those who parked for more than two hours, 20% would walk two blocks, 33% three blocks, 20% four blocks, 13% five blocks 8% six blocks, and 4% more than six blocks. If we assume the city block to be 600 feet long, it is apparent that those who wish to park for a short time—one-half hour or less—wish to be within 500

---

[18] See Chapter 21.

to 600 feet of their destination; those who park for about one hour wish to be no farther than about 1,000 feet from their destination, and those who intend to remain for a longer time would wish to be no farther than about 1,200 feet from their destination.[19]

It must be granted that these surveys deserve qualification. Consider the environment through which the urbanite must travel; it is little wonder the shopper dislikes to walk in the downtown district, or in many other sections of the contemporary metropolis. Ugliness is abhorrent and it repels a human being; it can hardly be expected that people will wish to walk about a business district fraught with every disagreeable feature and lacking convenient shopping and business facilities. When the cities acquire the self-respect which comes with pride in the physical beauty of an environment, the willingness of motorists to walk through these surroundings will probably reveal quite a different set of statistics.

About 80 per cent of the parkers in the central business district remain for one hour or less, the number ranging from 60 to 90 percent. When curb parking is permitted, the average time is about 30 minutes because of the preponderance of people who enter the business district for brief periods. Relating these several factors, the parking facilities for the downtown business district could be consolidated in areas ranging between 500 and 1,000 feet in radius from the center of a well-planned group of stores, and office buildings. Convenience would be enhanced by the elimination of congestion, discomfort, and hazard caused by the conflict between pedestrian and vehicular traffic, and it is possible that this new element of convenience might encourage pedestrians to walk more and further increase business.

Requirements for parking vary considerably, but experience has divulged some factors which assist in estimating the requirements. The average space per occupant in commercial buildings—office space—is approximately 150 square feet in floor area. If all regular occupants in these business structures were to use private automobiles for their transportation, an area of 150 square feet per person would be required in parking, the equivalent of one square foot of parking for each square foot of building floor space.

This space does not provide for people who patronize the business enterprise, and it may be estimated that an equal number enter the commercial district for this purpose as those who occupy the commercial buildings. In the average city, however, about 50 per cent of the people entering the downtown district use the available means for mass transportation—rail or bus. This results in a required space for parking equal to the building floor area, a figure generally confirmed by authorities. Retail shopping imposes a considerably heavier burden upon parking space, It is therefore necessary to adjust the required area for parking in central business districts according to the estimated uses to which

[19] Chicago Motor Club, "Parking in Downtown Rockford, Illinois," January 1942, from *Parking*, Wilbur S. Smith and Charles S. LeCraw, The Eno Foundation for Highway Control, Inc., December, 1946.

the land will be put. These estimates will likewise warrant adjustment as mass transportation is improved and becomes capable of adequately moving the largest possible number of people who enter and leave the business district.

RAILROADS

Builders of the railroads sought level terrain or followed the easy grades along water courses. As cities sprang up along these routes industry developed on the lines of transportation. The passenger station was the entrance to the town and the center of the city grew about it. Providing convenient commutation to the suburbs, the commercial district expanded about this hub.

With the passing of time and the neglect of orderly urban development, industry continued to creep along the railways and waterfronts. The city grew and new railroads entered to help build the metropolis. These lines of transportation were vital to the economic development of the city, and industries were accorded preferential sites along the rights-of-way as encourgement to locate in the city. Blocked by spur tracks and sidings, the street system was interrupted, and traffic problems and hazards were created.

Replacement of the various independent and scattered stations by the "union station" improved the reception, dispatch, and interchange of passengers and freight, but the city still suffers from the chaotic network of separate rail lines that stretch like tentacles in all directions. Consolidation of the various competing lines is slow because of complicated joint agreements, the abandonment of rights-of-way, the high cost of building new facilities for roads already equipped with terminals and the necessity for coordination which would tend to reduce possibilities for independent expansion. Reduction in the duplication of facilities which would result from such consolidation, however, would be of immeasurable profit to the city. Simplification of the street system, traffic routes, and grade crossings would alone vastly improve urban circulation and reduce the present hazards and disorderly pattern.

The shipping of freight comprises a far larger part of railroad business than passenger traffic and presents the more complicated planning problems. Except for some terminal locations, a large part of the freight business is "through shipping" that is, freight destined for points beyond the city. As the city grew up and spread away from the railroad, the "yards" remained a no-man's-land within the heart of the urban core. Occupying valuable land and disrupting the circulation system of the city, the "yards" are generally too cramped for the efficient handing of the tremendous operations involved in the classification, assortment, and redistribution of freight, as well as storage, switching, and make-up of trains.

Studies for the City of Detroit[20] suggest the appropriate rearrangement of

[20] *Proposed Generalized Land Use Plan,* City of Detroit Master Plan, City Plan Commission, May 1947.

the railroad lines for the metropolis of today. Designating many of the present rights-of-way as future routes for freeways, the railroads are consolidated upon an integrated system of trackage. A great belt line intercepts the incoming roads about the circumference of the city; along this belt line the "yards" and freight stations are located. From this circumferential belt line the freight is assorted and distributed to the industrial and commercial areas of the city or sent on its way to other points. A sub-belt system may be necessary to serve industrial areas in many cities, from which spurs would provide access to the individual plants.

Replanning of the railroad lines, consolidation of trackage, development of union stations where practicable, removal of "yards," and distribution along belt lines will facilitate the operation of this vital system of transportation and release the city from another of the bonds which now strangle circulation.

THE THIRD DIMENSION

People's ability to free themselves from the face of the earth created new problems. While the airplane was an experiment, terminal facilities were located as far as possible from people. With millions of people now flying each year, location of the airport in urban centers and rapid delivery of passengers to their destination are the joint concern of air line operators and the public. Connections from the airport to the destination in the city have become a greater problem than the flying time between cities.

Airport planning is a component part of the Comprehensive Plan for the city. It requires a complete analysis of the market comparable to the research conducted for other forms of transportation: an analysis of the present and potential passenger, cargo, and mail business which may be expected in the community: meteorological data; the present and planned land use within and about the city; extent of training program proposed by operators; the local traffic—intercity and state; transcontinental and international air routes; and prospects for development of private fields.

Air transportation is in a state of flux, developments in the type of equipment continuing to change and policies of airline operators being subject to modification with experience. The attitude of the urban population also varies, some desiring complete immunity from proximity to flying fields and lanes, others inclining to the development of residential communities designed about the airplane as a vehicle for commutation.

Planning for air transportation must be conceived at a regional scale, the distribution of airports being arranged for convenient and rapid connections to the strategic parts of the city and by a variety of means which have not yet been settled. Downtown feeder airports to which light ships may bring passengers into the heart of the city are being considered and helicopter flights from the major port to landing space in the city center for air mail service are already in operation. Air transport is an integral part of the transportation of the city, both passenger and cargo, and must be a component part of the city plan.

Airports   The location of airports and the relationship that these modern day transportation centers have to the development of urbanization is at a crisis state in many communities. Not only is the safety of the millions of passengers that use air travel at stake, but so are the lives of persons living in the areas surrounding airports.

Examples of the problem exists in all parts of the world. The crash of a plane adjacent to Kennedy airport some years ago and the 1978 accident in the vicinity of San Diego are two well known tragedies that should make us pay heed to the probability of future occurrences.

The dangers of collision may not be the major problem. Noise from the ever increasing size of the planes has been a major environmental problem. Overflights at low levels in the take-off and landing areas have caused people to petition for the closing of airports, or for the regulation of their hours of operation.

The future use of this "dead land" after acquisition and clearance still remains. In the Los Angeles area, some of the land has been turned into a parking lot. This use could be expanded and, if reasonably related to the air terminal by shuttle bus, would be a productive use. In other areas thought has been given to the use of the land for cemeteries or golf courses. High density housing or mobile home developments should be discouraged as a violation of NEPA and common sense.

SEA LANES AND HARBORS

In former times the harbors of the world were the centers of transportaion activity, the locale for romance, the heart of developing civilization. It was to ports that ships of many nations brought their goods and passengers. They were the ties to the trade centers, the distribution points for all exchange.

While in the developed nations the airlines now lead trains and ships in passenger travel, ships still perform the important function of handling bulk merchandise while also providing a means of travel for those seeking leisure and recreation. The harbors of the world and the rail lines leading from them must still be figured in any planning program. Harbors, unlike airports, cannot be moved from their natural locations. They may be deepened or extended or altered in function from industrial to recreational, but they are always at the water's edge.

THE PEDESTRIAN

People walked on all occasions during the urbanization in prehistoric times. With the use of the horse people moved a little more rapidly, but only few were able to utilize this means of rapid transit. After the wheel was used in conjunction with the horse, locomotion became still more rapid. During the mechanical age, steam, electrical energy and petrochemicals gave the wheel added power. For all practical purposes, motorized vehicles took people off their feet. Briefly stated, industry had produced mechanized mobility for the masses.

Today seldom does one go to the marketplace on foot. In cities where rapid transportation is inadequate, the individual automobile is practically indispensible. In others, like New York, it is generally more impractical due to limited and expensive parking facilities.

When the automobile is put to rest in a parking lot, people momentarily become pedestrians once again. They are on their feet as they travel the short distances from parking to place of employment or the shopping areas that have been designed to make pedestrians activities convenient and comfortable.

At these places, unless the automobile is separated from pedestrian travel lanes, people become targets for the automobile. Statistics indicate that more than 300,000 pedestrian accidents occur across America each year with more than 8,000 fatalities.[21] This latter statistic represents one sixth of the total national highway death toll.

Urban Sidewalks   As the accident and death tolls increase there have been efforts to provide for greater pedestrian safety through better street design and lighting of cross walks, the use of traffic lights and the slowing of traffic in areas where pedestrian movement is greatest.

Shopping areas too have been improved as central mall areas provide for pedestrian movement. Almost all of the newly developed major shopping centers are enclosed groupings of stores with a pedestrian safety area in the center. While this is not a new concept, most of the "planned" commercial centers now incorporate this feature. However, between the place where the automobile is parked and the safety pedestrian areas, it is still open season on pedestrians.

Pedestrian grade separations have been a part of the more sophisticated and costly arterial designs but are seldom placed in local areas where people are supposed do most of their walking. These separations can go over or under the arterial. They were given their best treatment by Clarence Stein and Henry Wright. Here the separation caused the roadway to rise slightly and the underpass to depress about an equal amount. The dangers associated with the overpass, such as vandals throwing objects at moving automobiles was eliminated, as was the dark, often dirty corridors of the underpass. The midway approach provided safety for the pedestrian as well as visibility in the corners. This type of underpass can be found in many of the new towns in Sweden.

The following recommendations were made in an article in the *Traffic Quarterly,* published by the Eno Foundation, July, 1978.[22]

---

[21] David I. Davis and Lawrence A. Pavlinski, *Traffic Quarterly,* July 1978.
[22] *Ibid.*

1. *Pedestrian Midblock Crossing Barriers.* At locations where significant numbers of pedestrian accidents result from midblock street crossings, physical barriers along the curb—line or in the median of a divided roadway are effective in channelizing these crossings to intersections, where vehicular movements can be controlled by traffic signals or stop signs.

2. *Midblock Crosswalks.* Although midblock crossing of streets by pedestrians is generally more hazardous than use of intersection crooswalks, under certain conditions a marked crosswalk at a midblock location between two widely spaced intersections will reduce pedestrian accidents.
An example would be a midblock location that has a large parking facility on one side of the street and a major pedestrian trip generator on the other side—such as the entrance to a large shopping center, a university campus, or a sports stadium. Rather than erect barriers to force people to walk relatively long distances from the parking area to their destination, a marked crosswalk may be preferable particularly if traffic signals are installed to control vehicular movements.

3. *Diagonal On-Street Parking.* On main streets with business frontages, and with only one or two lanes for traffic in each direction, diagonal on-street parking has been found to be hazardous in terms of collisions between motor vehicles. But in terms of pedestrian accidents, such diagonal parking has been found to be safer than parallel parking at the curb. This is because it reduces "dart out" accidents—the leading type of pedestrian accident—which occur when a person runs between parked cars onto the street.

So while diagonal on-street parking is not recommended on main streets unless they have ample width for vehicles to back out of parking spaces without disturbing the traffic flow, it can sometimes be applied with pedestrian safety benefits on wide residential streets.

INTEGRATION OR DISINTEGRATION

How may these various and diverse characteristics of contemporary vehicles be merged into an effective transportation system?

It is apparent that a change must be made in the present street system and this change may affect other aspects of land use. The freeway is hailed as an instrument with which to create a new framework for the community of tomorrow. The freeway can aid in relief of congestion in the central areas of the city, but the rebuilding of these areas to provide ample parking space and an environment as attractive as the outlying areas of the city must be created; otherwise, the freeways may become the arteries which carry the people past the outmoded central districts to the shopping districts which have their stakes in a well-planned, convenient, and pleasant environment of this day.

Adequate parking space and planned open space and commercial development may be substituted for the futile "strip" zoning along traffic arteries which themselves will be replaced by the freeways. Removed from traffic congestion, replanning will obtain ingress and egress to the business district for vehicles and pedestrians. Curb parking may become a thing of the past; with some exceptions the space along the curbs in central areas is less than one-fifth the amount of parking provided in lots and garages, and yet it is all hopelessly inadequate. Traffic flow is reduced about one-half by curb parking on the average street, making it a serious obstruction to traffic movement. The courts have held that streets are for the movement of traffic and not places for storage of vehicles. Being separate functions, terminal parking space for cars, the traffic arteries, and the space for circulation of pedestrians with their access to shopping and commercial enterprise, will be planned as separate elements.

There must be a plan for transportation and this plan must become a guide for each improvement in the city. During the long and arduous period in which the plan is being formulated, first-aid remedies will be necessary. Traffic bandages and tourniquets, splints and casts will be needed. It is necessary, however, that the distinction between the expedient nature of these first-aid measures and permanent solutions be continuously recognized. The breakdown represented by traffic congestion must be treated in the most infectious spots to keep the urban traffic stream flowing, but these devices of traffic engineering must not be confused with basic improvements in the street pattern and mass transportation. Too frequently they are interpreted as one and the same, with the result that the prospect of a solution to the urban traffic and transportation dilemma is given up as hopeless. Students of the problem realize that disintegration will eat deeper into the core of the urban environment and lead gradually, though eventually, to a complete loss of values, unless basic changes are made.

The evidence is already present in cities. We see the decay at its worst in the movement or, to put it more accurately, the retreat of sound business from the blight that has consumed one-time "high-class" districts. We also see the creation of entirely new business centers and we see them growing temporarily prosperous at the expense of the older established areas. Finally we see the first-aid methods being repeatedly used in the vain attempt to revive the dying areas.

ALTERNATE MEANS OF TRANSPORTATION

The bicycle, used as a health and pleasure vehicle for many years has become an important link in the transportation chain. The energy shortage in 1976 caused widespread purchases of bicycles. Perhaps their use in urban areas in America has not yet become as important as it has been in many of the European cities, such as in Amsterdam, Holland, but it is approaching this in certain localities, such as Davis, California, where the college students attending the University of California campus use the bicycle as their major means of transportation within the city.

In the People's Republic of China the bicycle is the major means of transportation in cities. While buses serve along major routes, the bicyclists are major occupants of public highways.

BICYCLE TRANSIT—A WAY OF LIFE IN CHINA

BICYCLE   AND   PEDESTRIAN   WALKS, Tapiola, Finland
The routes are carefully marked to separate the pedestrian from the cyclist.

The bicycle, like the pedestrian, poses many problems as it competes with the automobile for the use of the streets. The visibility of the bicycle rider, going in the same direction as the automobile traffic, creates a target with uncertain reactions on the part of both motorist and cyclist. Bike lanes, adjacent to the curbs often end at parked vehicles when the bicycle must veer out into the traffic flow. Where this danger is overcome by prohibiting parking, there are still the problems of enforcement and movement across intersecting streets. Night riding, when the bicycle may not be as visible, may also lead to accidents. The proper training of bike riders has become as essential as the proper training of automobile drivers. Bike riders should be licensed only after passing tests dealing with their safety and that of others.

However, the only truly safe approach for the bicyclist will be by constructing separate roadways paralleling sidewalks. The separation of the pedestrian from the motor vehicle has been a part of the Radburn plan since the 1940's. It is only reasonable to extend this idea to the bicyclist.

19

Conservation

We have become inured to early obsolescence. Goods are plastic-packaged for early discard. Fashions are outdated as soon as acquired; the trim on automobiles is still shiny when they are replaced by new models. Commercial prosperity has been geared to the principle of early obsolescence; quantity production substitutes for quality.

Wasteful consumption by an affluent society has become a malady; the passion to consume has been satisfied by the remarkable productivity of an aggressively expanding industrial system. Our appetites have become so gluttonous that the Environmental Protection Agency had to report in 1970: "The United States, with about 6% of the world's population, consumes 40% of the total non-replacable materials and 40% of the world's energy."The oil shortage, dubbed the "energy crisis," which surfaced in 1973, exposed only one aspect of the over-consumption which plagues the industrial nations of the world.

The urban environment directly reflects the excesses to which society has become habituated. Commercial enterprise has created gigantic symbols of economic power in urban centers. For more than three decades the 1,250 foot tower of the Empire State Building was the tallest emblem of commercial aggrandisement. But in the sixties, the two 110 story towers of the World Trade Center rose 1,350 feet into the air, while in Chicago the 100 story John Hancock Tower, looming 1,127 feet high, was soon topped by the 1,136 foot Standard Oil Tower, and in 1972, the Chicago Sears Tower triumphed over all competitors with a height of 1,450 feet. The famous architect Eliel Saarinen had pleaded, "Surely the city's form and coherence must not be left at the mercy of commercial speculation," [1] yet the architect of the World Trade Center, Minoru Yamasaki, claimed that venture was the "living representation of Man's belief in humanity."[2]

Lower Manhattan seen from the Statue of Liberty, the view of mammoth towers through the trees of Central Park, the silhouette of San Francisco from the Bay, the lakefront skyline of Chicago are among the dramatic spectacles of

[1] Eliel Saarinen, *The City—Its Growth, Its Decay, Its Future,* Reinhold, New York, 1943.
[2] Paul Heyer, *Architects On Architecture,* Walker, New York, 1966, page 195.

urban America. But these are not the views seen by most urban dwellers. Most of the people some of the time and some of the people all of the time experience streets denuded of trees, paved with oil-stained asphalt and concrete, over-burdened with buildings and vehicles, strung with wires and glaring advertising signs. Their intimate environment is a jungle of noise, tainted odors, incessant movement, and visual chaos. The refuse of the industrial system, spewed with abandon into rivers, lakes, and the atmosphere, pollutes the water and air nature has bountifully supplied. An economy of planned obsolescence scars the urbanscape.

Psychological and physiological damage is wrought upon the human mind and body. Those who can afford it find refuge in suburbia. Precious open space is devoured, hills are unmercifully bull-dozed, and valleys filled to accommodate the burgeoning population. When God created men and women, He admonished them to "replenish the earth and subdue it," but they neglected to distinguish between "subdue" and "destroy." We has impared the balance of nature and contaminated our environment.

This, then, is the challenge we confront as we prepare for the twenty-first century. A beginning has been made with our growing awareness of our impact on the environment; these lessons have slowly grown clear as the twentieth century progresses.

Previously unfamiliar words have entered the popular vocabulary. "Environmentalists" protest against the destructive exploitation of natural resources. A new awareness of "ecology" reveals the scope and intricacy of the interlocking relationships between land uses and services required in a man-made environment. Disposal of the waste created by over-consumption and planned obsolescence is a difficult, complex task and unforeseen scarcities give the term "recycling" a new significance.

CONSERVATION—THE ROUTE TO SURVIVAL

Many farsighted individuals and groups have fostered the conservation of our natural resources. Missionaries succeeded in obtaining presidential support for a National Park System and the conservation of some of the historical areas of America. For many years European nations have worked to preserve natural landmarks. In recent years, the importance of preserving our soil and forests has received much public attention.

Frequently, however, we think of conservation as being applicable only to wilderness areas. While conservation in this area is crucial, the protection of our urban environments is equally important. Cities and their hinterlands are an intertwined entity. If we are careless with either both will fail. We seldom realize the role that rural areas play in the lives of city dwellers. Without farms and forests the basic necessities of life—food, clothing, and shelter—could not (except for synthetics) be produced.

Securing food in the city usually means going to the supermarket or the restaurant. Our concept of the creation of clothing is going through racks in a department store. Our understanding of energy sources, until recently, was limited to the pump at the gas station. We are dependent upon the unknown producers of these items, and we would have a difficult time surviving if the real sources ceased to exist. Nevertheless, we encroach upon the best agricultural land, and foul the air giving little thought to our actions.

Conservation, therefore, implies both the protection of the open lands and the preservation of urban areas. Our propensity torward a discard economy and planned obsolescence must be changed. Many states require conservation guidelines in their comprehensive plans. The purpose of these guidelines is to promote the prudent use of our natural resources. Understanding the interconnection of these resources through the activities of man is important to achieving effective conservation.

Implementing land conservation policies through the zoning and subdivision ordinances will help forestall premature expansion of the city into the agricultural areas. The city zoning ordinance can provide for an agricultural district requiring large minimum lot sizes to protect the integrity of agricultural activity within and surrounding the cities in its area of influence.

CONSERVATION AND OPEN SPACE

During the latter days of World War II, people in Los Angles became aware that the air in their city had become unpleasantly murky. Tests showed the atmosphere was contaminated. The contaminants increased and it became a favorite laboratory exercise to measure the "parts per million." Sources were traced to oil refineries, industries, incinerators, and automobile exhausts. Their emissions, combined with the fog, were exaggerated by a natural phenomenon of temperature inversion in the southern California basin. The result was "smog."

As industrial garbage was discharged into the air, evidence of similar atmospheric contamination appeared in other cities. People died on one occasion in London. Tokyo experienced near-disasters. Some control measures were gradually and grudgingly adopted by industry. But smog persisted. The automobile was finally declared to be the principal source, and changes in the internal combustion engine and fuel were demanded. Although new models are produced each year, basic changes in automobile manufacturing are not easily achieved. Powerful lobbies have brought delay after delay.

Then pollution was discovered in water courses, streams, rivers, and lakes, a result of the discharge of industrial refuse. Insecticides disrupted agricultural crops. Fish in the rivers were poisoned. Fish in Lake Erie were dead. Oil spills threatened wildlife in the sea. Beaches were contaminated. Strip mining for coal laid waste the Appalachian landscape. Disastrous floods followed. Forests were decimated. The effects of a careless "throw-away" society is taking its toll on the natural resources in a rich land. Space in which to safely deposit waste is disappearing. Burial of nuclear waste and excess poison gas threatens areas beyond state and national boundaries.

Ecology suddenly became a *cause célèbre* in commercial and industrial public relations propaganda. Environmentalists, long concerned with ecology, took up the challenge to preserve natural resources. Legislation could not keep pace with the revelations of abuse to which society had become habituated. "Conservation"became a popular cause. In 1973, 1976, and 1979 the "energy crisis" shocked not only America but the entire western world. Realization gradually dawned that the continuous squandering of irreplaceable resources has become the western way of life.

The course of shifting social values is evident in the observations of the prominent Public Health Engineer, Frank Stead.[3] When he began his career in public health in 1931, public health occupied a privileged position: "When we said something was hazardous to health . . . that ended it. Everything else yielded—economics, property rights, everything." "Administration of more recent water and air regulations, however, is intended to "balance environmental quality against economic production," the unacceptable concept of "trade-offs" with public health. Stead defines the imperative of protecting the "total biospheric support system . . . that relatively thin zone at the surface of the earth that contains the land surface only a few hundred feet below the surface and ground waters, and the atmospheric envelope only a few thousand feet above the surface of the earth. Together with solar energy, these are the total resources on which all living things depend." "The real fact is," he emphasizes, "that we must give first place to the preservation of the biosphere, and within that mandate develop the ability to support an economically productive system to keep our civilization viable." To achieve that, he says, "We will have to make changes far more fundamental than getting rid of the internal combustion engine."

Conservation is not new. In ancient lands flood control was necessary for human survival. Blessed with apparently unlimited land and resources, the United States has been tardy and erratic in conserving its resources. When one resource is depleted, it has been taken for granted that some new technology will certainly replace it. That optimism cannot be applied to land. The land on this earth is fixed, and when the supply, for whatever purpose it may be used, is exhausted, there is no substitute. Land is not yet recognized as the precious natural resource it is, and the civilized concept of limiting speculative gains from land exploitation has not penetrated the American consciousness.

The nineteenth century was rife with disposition of public lands for the ostensible purpose of encouraging economic development. In the early twentieth century the public interest was asserted by creation of the National Park and Forest Services. A third (765 million acres) of the land area of the fifty states is still owned by the Federal government. Of this federal reserve, 312 million acres

---

[3] A graduate in Public Health Engineering from Harvard University, Frank Stead instituted the first industrial hygiene program by the Los Angeles County Health Department, and for twenty years was Chief of the Division of Environmental Sanitation, California Department of Public Health. In the early sixties he asserted that by 1980 "The gasoline-powered engine must be phased-out." Excerpts from *Healthnews*, August, 1974.

have been allocated to specific jurisdictions: The National Park Service, the Forest Service, the Department of Defense, the Bureau of Indian Affairs, the Bureau of Fisheries and Wildlife, the Bureau of Reclamation, the Department of State, the Atomic Energy Commission, the Tennessee Valley Authority, and the National Aeronautics and Space Administration. To administer the remaining 435 million acres, the Bureau of Land Management was created in 1946. Occupying nearly one-half of the western states, this precious resource is, in the words of Charles S. Watson Jr., "the lands nobody knows."[4]

With increased commercialism and urbanization, "conservation" has become a necessary element of the General Plan for cities. To preserve the theory of "local autonomy," most legislative authority is delegated by state governments to local communities. With public authority thus divided among various local governments, essential conservation measures are beyond the authority of competing local jurisdictions. Although some internal flood control, preservation of water sheds, protection of historic sites and extraction of minerals may be effectively administered at the local level, the broad conservation measures related to public health and welfare, domestic water supply, fish, plants and game, land and water reclamation, disposal of refuse and sewage, air quality, timber supply, and agriculture extend beyond city boundaries to regional, state, or interstate dimensions. Conservation at the local level has, consequently, been equated with provisions in the Comprehensive Plan and zoning ordinances for preservation of parks and recreation areas.

Each city determines the space and distribution of its playgrounds and parks. Rampant land subdivision practices have often failed to provide space for recreation. Planned developments have improved this situation, but cities must require *all* residential development to allocate land for recreation and schools in accordance with local space standards. In the event that scattered subdivisions are too small to provide a park, prorated payments should be substituted, and the funds maintained in a revolving fund for acquisition of parks, playgrounds, and school sites as the demand evolves.

The county tax assessor, more than the planning commission and city council, influences the disposition of open space. The office of property tax assessment is required by state law to assess taxes on the basis of "fair market value," and those appraisers determine the values. Regardless of the zoning designation, land which is in the path of development usually acquires a "value" consistent with that potential development. Land thus taxed cannot be long held off the market for development, nor can the pressure for zoning changes to accommodate "higher economic" use be long resisted by local authorities. Urban sprawl eats into agricultural zones, speculators are rewarded, non-committal plans are ignored, and open space disappears.

One tentative remedy is the contract between the state and land owner to maintain an agricultural use for a specified period (ten years) in return for tax

----

⁴ *Sierra Club Bulletin,* September, 1973.

assessments based upon agricultural value.[5] This tax shelter only postpones the inevitable change to urban development, unless the Comprehensive Plan and zoning ordinance become the recognized reference for land value and tax assessment or, as recommended by the American Institute of Architects,[6] unless public policy provides for the public to recover that increase in land value which is created not through the productive enterprise of the owner but as the result of public investment and community prosperity.

This policy deserves thorough exploration by civic leaders and authorities on urban law and economics of development. Comprehensive planning of the urban environment is seriously impeded by ineffective land use controls which, according to Professor Robert H. Freilich, "stems from a supposed constitutional inability to adequately govern the decisions of the private land owner. It is stated to be a constitutional problem limiting the extent of regulatory powers over land use regardless of the political unit which is exercising decision-making authority. The United States has a deep-seated tradition which believes in 'absolute' owership of land. The view that land ownership is 'absolute' is, of course, erroneous under American law. All property is held subject to police power, regulations of the State being necessary to preserve the public health, safety and welfare of the Community, a power which is the least limitable and most expansive of all governmental power."[7]

It should be within the power of government to recover that increment of land value which is created by community action through zoning decisions and investment of public funds for capital improvements. Value created by the action of a City Council (or other governing body) to change a permissible land use from residential to commercial, for example, or the installation of public facilities which enhance the use of property, is unearned by a landowner; it is an increment of value created by public action and should be recovered by the public. Conversely, changes in land use which are necessary to achieve an improvement of the environment, such as "roll-back" zoning from high to low density of land use, and which result in a reduction of the vested land value, should be accompanied by compensation to the owner by the public for that increment of lower value. Professor Donald Hagman has referred to the policy as "trading windfalls for wipeouts."[8]

This policy is comparable to the British program of compensation and betterment and, benefiting from the experience in England, both the success and the equity of the policy will depend in large measure on the simplicity of the administrative procedures designed for its implementation. It should be insti-

[5] Hawaii State Zoning ; Williamson Act in California; Land Conservation and Development Act, 1973, in Oregon.

[6] American Institute of Architects, *A Strategy for Building a Better America,* 1972.

[7] Robert H. Freilich and John W. Ragsdale Jr., *Development Framework Data Report,* Metropolitan Council ot Twin City Area, January, 1974. Refer also to the *Minnesota Law Review* (58 Minn. L. Rev. 1,009) (1974).

[8] Donald Hagman, "A New Deal: Trading Windfalls for Wipeouts," *Planning,* Association of Planning Officials, September, 1974.

tuted neither as a punitive measure nor as a means to produce revenue and, in order to avoid a possible disruption of the land market, it should be implemented in stages.

Open space for parks, playgrounds, and other amenities for built-up-districts in accordance with local standards must be acquired with public funds, or special assessment districts. Efforts to preserve open space to enhance the general amenity and enrich the esthetic quality of a city confront the eternal conflict between the public good and private property rights.

Cities blessed with hilly terrain within of around them can turn this natural asset into a beautiful urban form, or allow it to be chewed up for homes of status seekers. We seem to have great difficulty in accepting the fact that the modern city is not the natural habitat of hill-dwellers. The site for a medieval castle was not selected for its view, although views of a beautiful countryside were magnificent. The noble's real concern was for observation of approaching enemies, and the compact hill towns that huddled about the castles were built for protection of the inhabitants. Modern city builders generally seek plains and broad valleys for industry, business, transportation and housing. Lovely hills should be looked at, not cut to ribbons for "flat-land" lots. The undulating ridges and slopes should be preserved. Development should not climb above a 20 per cent slope.

If we intend to halt further destruction of the natural character of our environment, the public and the government must act. Philanthropy rarely extends to gifts of land to enhance the amenities of a city, and political action to restrict development of land for either utility or beauty meets with the claim of "inverse condemnation."

Cherishing the beautiful site of their city along the foothills of the Rocky Mountains, the people of Boulder, Colorado, took action to protect their birthright. Adding to an original Federal grant of 3,000 acres of foothills (1899), donations by enlightened citizens increased their Mountain Parks System. The people of Boulder took the initiative in financing the preservation of open space when potential development threatened Boulder, as it does other cities. A "Greenbelt" program was approved by referendum in 1967; the people assessed themselves an additional 1 per cent sales and use tax for land acquisition, lease, or retirement of bonds. A cooperative City-County Comprehensive Plan encompassed a "Greenbelt" system of parks, recreation, wildlife sanctuaries, and scenic trails. By means of "density transfer"[9] (compensatory density), open space in "planned developments" became integral links with the "greenbelt." The people of Boulder demonstrated that when the people are determined to maintain their environmental assets, they can. Aspen, Colorado, followed suit; other cities should.

The resolute determination of the people of St. George, Vermont, to maintain the quality of their environment is also instructive. With their

---

[9] The basic density for residential development is 4 dwelling units per acre. It may increase to 6 d.u./acre with open space thus consolidated to link with the "Greenbelt."

population more than tripled in a decade, from 108 in 1960 to 477 in 1970, the people of St. George acted. Recognizing that they must deal with the right to *develop* land rather than land ownership, St. George arranged for and required the transfer of development rights from the open space of its lovely environment to the new village center it planned for the future.[10]

Fearful that "development" would destroy the foothills of the city, Palo Alto, California, undertook a comparative study of open space versus urbanization. The study revealed that the cost of public services for residential development would exceed acquisition cost for preservation as open space.[11] Failing to support a $4,000,000 bond issue for land purchase, the city rezoned the land to minimum lot sizes of 10 acres.

The California Office of the Bureau of Land Management has, in cooperation with the City of Palm Springs, prepared plans to preserve a band of Desert Big Horn Sheep. By this action, a large open space in mountainous terrain will become a permanent open area to provide a refuge for the endangered species and breathing space for people. Another of the Bureau's recent projects is preservation of the great California desert, which was abused by uncontrolled off-road vehicles, ranging from motorcycles to dune buggies. The plan has provided for areas where these recreational uses could be continued, while declaring the more fragile section off limits to all but persons on foot or horseback.

---

[10] Leonared U. Wilson, "Precedent-Setting Swap in Vermont," *Journal of American Institute of Architects,* March, 1974.

[11] The professional study was conducted by Livingston and Blayney, Planners, San Francisco, California.

PART 5

This is not inflaming or exaggerating matters, but trying them by those feelings and affections which nature justifies, and without which we should be incapable of discharging the social duties of life, or enjoying the felicities of it.
—*Thomas Paine, Common Sense*

Implement-ation

20

The Implementation Process

RECENT DEVELOPMENTS

The step from the general to the specific, from plan to action, in the Comprehensive Planning process has become more difficult, complicated, and time consuming as cities impose more controls over their environment. With the major emphasis on land use planning resulting in little or no improvement in the quality of cities, the socio-economic specialists relegated this process to oblivion as an archaic and valueless exercise. Social planning, economic planning, policy planning, and program planning became the substitute for the existing limited land use practice without recognition of the importance that the physical structure of the land has on the realization of those goals.

Into this vacuum came the environmentalists, concerned with the damage being done to nature. Environmentalist groups merged and organizations such as the Sierra Club were born. They demanded that legislators be given more information so that the law makers could make more prudent land use decisions. They pressed for review of the impact that a development might have on the natural and human resources in a given area. The Federal government passed a major new law dealing with the environment: the National Environmental Policies Act. In addition, laws designed to protect the environment tend to form a "sieve" that a proposal has to filter through before permits can be issued to begin construction. Environmental Impact Studies became a requirement in many communities.

PROBLEMS IN PLAN IMPLEMENTATION

The implementation of a land-use plan requires that government and the private sector have a reasonably similar view of the future. This presupposes that the

Comprehensive Plan has been prepared on a rational basis and decisions have been made without collusion with special interest groups. If the Comprehensive Plan is followed up with sound growth management (the timely meeting of people and the facilities that they require) then development can be readily implemented.

However, in many areas of the country long range planning is still considered only a guide for future growth, to be respected if the politicians see fit and to be disregarded if short range personal gain is considered paramount. In the latter case development will be uncontrolled, the decisions on the uses of land being made based on momentary advantages to the land owner with little concern for the consequences in long term cost of services and inconveniences to residents at large.

Perhaps the most important obstacle to appropriate plan implementation exists in the political process that permits the plan to be amended without sound reason or ignores the plan as though it did not have a definitive role in producing compatible development. A major problem with many plans is that there is no schedule for their development. The past lack of growth management techniques has created plans that are not time- and sequentially-phased. There was no sound basis for the extension and installation of the infrastructure, and thus there was no indication of where, how, or when the community could implement the plan.

PUBLIC OPPOSITION

Objections by citizen groups often will delay or halt the implementation of portions of a plan. For example changes in a zone to permit a shopping facility in a location indentified on an adopted Comprehensive plan can bring out area residents to oppose the facility on the basis that it will be incompatible with the concept that they have had of their area. Proposals for including such facilities in the hillside areas in Montecito, California, brought strong objections from the residents. The people said they did not mind travelling on narrow streets to obtain convenience items, preferring the travel problems to the danger, as they saw it, of the intrusion of commercial uses and the possibility that these uses might spread to further depreciate their rather pristine properties.

In Arcadia, California, tremendous local opposition was registered to the development of a regional shopping center by local residents. Local opposition was overcome when a city-wide referendum on the matter indicated that the residents in areas away from the site supported the proposal. The matter was decided on political grounds even though the site was admirably suited for the project insofar as strategic location was concerned. However the shopping center did present the problem of heavy traffic in the area, and so special traffic and aesthetic design features were initiated to protect the area.

21 | The Zoning Plan

THE PRECISE PLANS

The Comprehensive Plan sets the basic policies for development of the city, the general relation between the various land uses—residential, commercial, and industrial—and forms the framework of the urban structure. From time to time this general framework is translated into *precise* plans which specify the zoning for land use, streets and highways, mass transit, recreation and conservation, subdivision expansion, utilities, railways and airports, civic centers, schools, and urban redevelopment. The precise plans interpret the basic policies for urban development reflected in the Comprehensive Plan and serve to adjust the Plan to new situations and conditions as they arise.

The precise plans serve a dual function. On one hand, they define the standards for development of the city, the standards of population density, the design of the circulation system, and the amount and location of open space and physical facilities for business and residence. On the other hand, the precise plans provide a *program* for development, a basis for timing proposed improvements in the city, the location, design, and installation of utilities, schools, parks, the extension of subdivision development, and the redevelopment of blighted areas. Thus, the need for public improvements may be geared with the ability to finance such improvements and maintain a coordinated pace with expansion of private development.

These functions presume continuous attention to the process of urban planning. A Comprehensive Plan which collects dust in the archives of the city hall is a monument on the grave of lost opportunities in urban improvement. Planning is a *process* which anticipates the needs of a community, proposes ways and means for the satisfaction of these needs, and relates these proposals to the orderly development of the city and realization of the Comprehensive Plan. The precise plans are the instruments with which these functions are performed.

299

ZONING DEFINED

Zoning is the legal regulation of the use of land. It is an application of the police power for the protection of the public health, welfare, and safety. The regulations include provisions for the use of property and limitations upon the shape and bulk of buildings that occupy the land. The law comprises two parts: the ordinance in which the regulations are defined, and the zoning map which delineates the districts within which the provisions of the ordinance apply.

Zoning is not a substitute nor an alternative for the Comprehensive Plan. The plan expresses the basic policies which shape the community character, the general land use, circulation, and relationships among the variety of urban facilities. The zoning plan establishes the specific limitations which apply to the use of land as an instrument for achieving the goals set forth in the Comprehensive Plan. Serving as a comprehensive guide for urban development, the Comprehensive Plan is usually adopted as a *resolution* by the legislative body. The zoning plan is adopted and rendered effective as a legal ordinance.

Validity of the zoning ordinance has been subjected to several tests by the courts, whose decisions have generally supported the following criteria:

1.   The plan shall be comprehensive.

2.   The same regulations shall apply to all districts having similar zone classifications.

3.   The plan shall demonstrate protection of health, welfare, and safety.

4.   There shall be neither discrimination nor capricious intent in the plan.

5.   Administration of the ordinance shall be reasonable and free from arbitrary decisions.

IS ZONING NECESSARY?

Many people believe that zoning or any public regulation of the use of land is not only unnecessary but unconstitutional. In their opinion zoning has a detrimental effect upon the development process. The process that they would subsitute would be the free market where economic forces at any time determine what is best use for a given parcel of land.

Often quoted as an example of a city without zoning is Houston, Texas. Not mentioned in these discussions is the fact that there are many land use regulations that affect the free use of land in that city, such as deed restrictions and regulations enforced by resident associations. The difference may be only in whether the regulations are applied on a citywide basis by official governmental institutions or by a private local body.

Over the years zoning has been an accepted manner of regulating the use of land, not only in the United States but in almost every nation of the world. In some nations the democratic processes involved in the United States are not observed, the government making land-use decisions and applying them as they see fit. Planning in these countries is in many cases arbitrary, expressing only the will of a few in the administration.

ZONING PROCEDURES

Complications inevitably arise in the administration of zoning, and procedures must be provided to cope with them. These situations may involve natural or man-made conditions of the land, unusual demands not evident when the ordinance was adopted, or developments in which the exacting limitations of zoning do not accommodate reasonable latitude for the adaptation of new ideas.

The Zone Change or Amendment. The most frequent alterations occur when property owners request a change for the classification of their properties from one zoning district to another, usually for the purpose of enjoying greater economic values from the use of their land. Changes on the Zoning Map should be made only when such changes conform to the Comprehensive Plan. Otherwise they may, while being beneficial to an individual, be detrimental and costly to the community in terms of the effects on utilities and public facilities.

Amendments to the text of the ordinance are also made quite often. These amendments include changes in terminology; inclusion or deletion of certain uses; changes in standards, either raising or lowering them; and changes in procedures.

Regardless of whether the map or the text is modified, the procedure requires public hearings and discussions prior to any changes becoming effective. The procedure is generally identical with that required for the adoption of the original ordinance.

The Zoning Variance. A variance is a permission granted as relief from some specific and unusual hardship imposed by the strict interpretation of the ordinance. It is a means to adjust the property development standards of the ordinance which, by reason of specific location, topography, shape, or size, are impossible to comply with. The variance permits a property owner to use his land at the same intensity allowed others in the same zone; it should not allow *uses* not permitted in the zone. Being readily subject to discriminatory administration and unsound planning, the variance is perhaps the most abused of all zoning procedures. It is not intended to be an alternative to "spot" zoning or a device to circumvent the intent of the ordinance by a grant of special privilege, nor is it proposed as a means to solve personal problems. The following advice by a high state court, in its review of a case involving rezoning, brings the issue into clear focus:

> We feel impelled to express briefly our view of the proper theory of zoning as relates to the making of changes in an original comprehensive ordinance. We think the theory is that after the enactment of the original ordinance there should be a continuous or periodic study of the development of property uses, the nature of population trends, and the commercial and industrial growth, both actual and

ZONE CHANGE PROCEDURE AS IT RELATES TO THE GENERAL PLAN

Initiation of zone change

By petition of owner

By council

By commission

To commission

Check against general plan for conformity

If conforming	If not conforming

Criteria for conformity

Advise owner or council

Owner may request change in general plan

Or Council may authorize restudy and hearings on amendment to general plan

Commission restudies general plan

Commission holds one public hearing

Commission makes findings and recommendations to council

Council holds one public hearing

Council approves or disapproves change in general plan

If favorable   If unfavorable

No zone change at this time

Set date for public hearing

Publish notice of public hearing

Hold at least one public hearing

Make findings and recommendations to council

Council sets date for public hearing

Publishes notice of public hearing

Holds at least one public hearing

Approves or disapproves zone change

302

prospective. On the basis of such study changes may be made intelligently, systematically, and according to a coordinated plan designed to promote zoning objectives. An examination of the multitude of zoning cases that have reached this court leads us to the conclusion that the common practice of zoning agencies, after the adoption of an orginal ordinance, is simply to wait until some property owner finds an opportunity to acquire a financial advantage by devoting his property to a use other than that for which it is zoned, and then struggle with the question of whether some excuse can be found for complying with his request for a rezoning. The result has been that in most of the rezoning cases reaching the courts there has actually been spot zoning and the courts have upheld or invalidated the change according to how flagrant the violation of the true zoning principles has been. It is to be hoped that in the future zoning authorities will give recognition to the fact that an essential feature of zoning is *planning*.[1]

Conditional Use Permit. There are occasions when a special "use" is necessary for the welfare of a community, but not permitted within the applicable zone. Permission for such uses may be granted by the Conditional Use Permit. Unlike the variance, evidence of unusual hardship in the development of a property is not required. The Conditional Use is for the purpose of meeting a special need of the community based upon evidence that the proposed location will serve this special purpose. Protection from adverse effects on abutting property must be assured and measures for this must be included in the Permit. As with the Variance, the Conditional Use is not a substitute for rezoning. It is designed to meet a special situation in the public interest; it is not a device by which a new use may be indiscriminately introduced within an established zoning district. The zoning ordinance does not usually provide for a variety of sharply defined uses within a district, and the Conditional Use offers a degree of flexibility in adjusting to new demands within the framework of the ordinance.

There remains a difference of opinion on the manner in which a Conditional Use Permit should be granted. Some authorities hold it to be essentially an administrative decision at the discretion of the Planning Commission. Others contend that it should be subject to approval by the legislative body. It is generally agreed that the ordinance should clearly stipulate the circumstances and indicate the areas under which Conditional Use Permits may be granted as a protection to investors in property.

Administrative Committees. Zoning ordinances contain a variety of provisions, compliance with which may require some form of review and approval. Among these may be the location and size of signs, or engineering and architectural design and arrangement. The ordinance may therefore provide for Administrative Committees vested with the responsibility and authority to pass upon plans subject to these provisions. Such committees are particularly effective when both public officials and lay persons comprise their membership.

---

[1] *Fritts v. City of Ashland,* Court of Appeals of Kentucky [highest court], 348 S.W. 2d 712, (June 16, 1961), quoted in *Zoning Digest,* October 1961, American Society of Planning Officials.

ZONING DISTRICTS

In the zoning plan the community is divided into districts in which the land is restricted to certain classified uses. The size, shape, and location of these districts reflect the major uses indicated by the Comprehensive Plan and should be formed to invite the natural development of neighborhoods. The Comprehensive Plan may indicate an area to be appropriate for single-family dwellings, whereas the zoning plan may permit a commercial use within specified limits to be developed as a shopping center and contribute to the neighborhood quality of the area. A site for a school and a park may also be provided within such an area. Such developments of the precise plans are refinements of the General Plan, their purpose being the creation of balanced community design.

Most zoning ordinances provide for different densities of population in different districts. One residential district may permit only single-family houses with a density of five families per acre, whereas another district may permit "unlimited multiple residential" use in which the density can reach hundreds of people per acre. These variations in population density must be reflected in other precise plans for the city since they affect the provisions of all community facilities and services. The size and location of schools, commercial land use and transportation, police and fire protection, and the size of utility services vary considerably with the number of people to be served.

The following description of land uses indicates the variety of districts which may appear in the zoning ordinance. The classification of these districts will differ in various communities, and local customs and requirements will determine the definition of each classification.

Open Land Districts.   This classification of land use, though not included in most ordinances, applies to areas in which the public interest requires the prohibition or restriction of urbanization to protect or enhance reasonable growth and development of the community. Open land districts may include areas of particular scenic or historic importance, areas too steep to be built upon, areas subject to flooding, and areas where water and sanitary facilities or police and fire protection cannot be provided without excessive cost to the community.

Agricultural Districts permit the use of land consistent with economically feasible agricultural enterprise, the subdivision of land being governed by the type of agriculture normal to the area. Agricultural districts about some urban areas may establish minimum lot areas of 40, 20, 10, 5, and 2 acres, while some include one-acre lots in this classification. Uses considered generally permissible in this type of district include farming, poultry-raising, dairying, and cattle and horse grazing. Restricted residential uses may also be permitted provided the agricultural uses are not adversely affected. Hog raising may be prohibited in some agricultural zones because it is generally interpreted as an obnoxious use. There are usually provisions in the zoning ordinance for exceptions by special permit if an investigation of the particular situation demonstrates no prospect of endangering the general welfare.

Estate Districts are sometimes created to provide property owners the opportunity to establish a character of residential development measured primarily in terms of large-size lots. In some suburban areas it is desired to develop a rural quality, and the estate zone is for such a purpose. This is generally the most restricted residential zone, the minimum lot sizes ranging from 20,000 to 40,000 square feet or more in area. Some "agrricultural" uses are frequently permitted in this zone, like poultry for domestic consumption or saddle horses. Estate zones are usually established at the behest of the property owners or developers who desire to attract clientele wishing reasonably large tracts protected from the infiltration of small-lot subdivision. Other factors sometimes warrant the establishment of estate zones; when facilities for sewage disposal are absent or limited, or where police and fire protection are not readily available, or community facilities such as schools or commercial districts are remotely situated, it may be advisable to limit the population an area is permitted to accommodate.

Single-Family Districts are zones in which the land use is restricted to a single dwelling unit per lot. The zoning ordinance establishes a minimum lot area permitted in these zones and frequently specifies the minimum lot width. The standards vary considerably, some cities still permitting lot widths of 25 feet street frontage, but a width of 60 feet or more is being accepted in most communities as the minimum, with a minimum lot area of 6,000 square feet. Such restrictions are not retroactive, and property owners are not obliged to comply with area and lot size regulations enacted subsequent to the recording of subdivisions with lesser restrictions.

Multiple-Family Districts. This classification applies to any residential district in which more than a one-family dwelling is permitted to occupy a single lot. A gradation of dwelling densities is usually provided within this classification.

Two-Family Districts This classification has been rather generously used in the past to permit the "duplex" type of dwelling, i.e., two dwelling units within a single structure. With the increasing use of density control rather than classification of building type, a provision which specifies the density, such as a minimum lot area per dwelling unit, is more equitable than a limitation of two dwellings per lot. Application of a uniform density provision offers a desirable flexibility for lots of varying size, rather than freezing the limitation regardless of the lot area.

Medium-Density Districts. The density permitted in this classification will be quite different in a great city than in a small town. In large cities a medium density ranges from 20 to 40 dwellings per net acre. It may be prescribed as four times the density of the single-family district. If the minimum single-family lot area is 6,000 square feet, the medium density would then require 1,500 square feet of lot area per dwelling. Some communities permit a lot area as low as 1,000 square feet per dwelling in this district.

High-Density Districts. Densities ranging from 50 to 150 families per net acre are not uncommon in large cities, and 200 to 300 families per acre are permitted in some laws. With the increasing congestion of traffic and intensity of the parking problem, zoning ordinances are due for a critical review of these high densities. The classification may be defined as a multiple of the minimum single-family lot size. Assuming a density standard of some 50 dwellings per acre and a minimum lot size for the single-family district of 6,000 square feet, the high-density district would permit about eight times the single-family density, or about 750 square feet of lot area per dwelling unit. Some ordinances further grade these requirements according to the size of the dwelling apartment. Thus 300 square feet of lot area may be permitted for "bachelor" units, 400 square feet for one-bedroom units, 600 square feet for two-bedroom units, and 800 square feet for three-bedroom units.

Mobile-Home Districts. The mobility of the population in this country is demonstrated by the expanding use of the "trailer" as a relatively permanent dwelling type. It possesses unique characteristics and plays an important role in the housing supply in moderate climates. The essential amenities for this mode of living should be regulated in zoning ordinances. Well designed mobile-home "parks" accommodate a density of between 6 and 8 trailer units per acre, or approximately 4,000 square feet of ground space for each unit. The Federal Housing Administration standards and the recommendations of the Mobile Homes Association support the lesser density as the desirable space requirement.

Hotel Districts. The density and lot area requirements for hotels are the least restrictive of the residential zones, except in areas where the particular character of the environment warrants special attention to density. Hotels may also be included in the provisions for Commercial Districts. With the exception of limitations upon setbacks for side, rear, and front yards, there has been little control of density in these districts, but reconsideration of hotel densities is as urgent as high-density apartment and commercial zones.

Commercial Districts. The complex structure of the modern urban community has introduced changes affecting the arrangement of commercial facilities as it has in other land uses. The "mamma and papa" grocery store has blossomed into the neighborhood convenience center, the expanding suburbs have forced the decentralization of retail enterprise and the development of the regional shopping center. The destiny of "downtown" hangs in the balance. Special service facilities, ranging from professional offices to light manufacturing establishments where commodities are also sold across the counter, must be accommodated within the fabric of commercial zoning regulations. Consideration of the relation between these several commercial functions and other land uses must be reflected in the Comprehensive Plan as a foundation for the zoning plan. Excessive land area and permissible floor space, typical of present zoning, is related to traffic congestion and the parking problem. Transition from the burden of "strip" zoning for business uses along the major streets to the consolidation of commercial centers will be an arduous task and require a long period of time. The shopping center has confirmed the necessity and provided the impetus for this conversion in the pattern of commercial land use.

Historical Preservation Districts.   A national carelessness about our rich natural and cultural heritage has been another by-product of building for commerical enterprise. The unique grandeur of many natural wonders has been protected through the National Park Service, but efforts to preserve structures and sites of historical or artistic importance have been severely hampered by economic infeasibility and cultural indifference. In some regions significant historic buildings are protected by special government action, and a few have been saved by private philanthropy. The continued maintenance of existing structures, however, is a serious problem. A proposal by Professor John J. Costonis, of the University of Illinois, is therefore pertinent. Historically important buildings are often not economically practical especially since zoning regulations usually permit buildings of greater height and bulk in those areas. Professor Costonis proposes to allow owners of such landmark buildings to sell the "development rights" to additional stories or bulk which zoning would permit to the developer of a building on another acceptable site, with the provision for the protection of the Vieux Carré (French Quarter), a famous and Historic buildings or places may thus be protected without the sacrifice of the property rights which usually preclude preservation.[2]

Several cities followed the lead of New Orleans, which adopted a zoning provision for the protection of the Vieux Carré (French Quarter), a famous and popular area of the city. The principle involved in this zoning system is the protection of the unity of an area. This is intended to preserve not only a historical structure, a natural feature, or a site, but the entire surroundings.

The important feature of the historical area is that it must have a distinct and desirable character worthy of preservation. The standards for its preservation should assure a continuity of scale and design even if demolition, alteration, renovation, removal, or relocation takes place. A certificate of appropriateness is often required for any change in occupancy, construction, demolition, removal or relocation or any modification of the site that would alter its original form or structure.

Historical preservation commissions are created by the legislative body.

---

[2] The first application of this proposal is the Heurich House, a Victorian mansion in Washington, D.C. owned and occupied by the Columbia Historical Society. A building ninety feet high could legally occupy the site. The City Zoning Commission permitted a developer of a "high-rise" structure on a nearby site to erect a building forty feet higher than the zoning code usually allowed, from which the additional income is to be used for the maintenance of the old building. A similar application is considered for the Chicago "Loop," where many significant buildings of the Ninteenth Century "Chicago School" remain. Report in the *AIA Journal,* American Institute of Architects, March. 1974.

The members of the commission must be residents of the special zone. All of the members of the commission must demonstrate knowledge of and interest in the preservation of the area. Santa Barbara, California, always deeply concerned about its early history, has adopted a Historical Preservation Zone to protect the old "presidio" area where remains of the early days of the city are found. San Diego, California, has also adopted such an ordinance to protect an area containing remnants of its historical heritage.

In Warsaw, Poland, after World War II damaged areas were considered of great historical importance and rather than rebuilding new structures the existing buildings were reconstructed to keep contact with the past. The cost of this technique is often far greater than clearance and rebuilding with "modern" structures. However the value of retaining of a taste of the past sometimes appears more important than the cost involved. There can be no doubt about the need to preserve architecturally and historically important buildings, especially if they can be made functionally suitable.

Industrial Districts.   This classification ranges from the most restricted uses for "light" industry, in which electric power only may be employed or in which smoke, odors, and sound are rigidly controlled, to the unrestricted "heavy" industrial areas in which any type of manufacturing enterprise or process is permitted. Certain industrial uses which may endanger the public are frequently restricted to specific areas whereas still others may require special permits by legislative action in order to conduct business. The manufacture of fireworks or fertilizer, or the dumping of refuse and garbage, may be confined to areas at least 500 feet from other unrestricted uses , if permitted at all.

The manner in which operations are conducted, rather than the type of the industry, is the basis for classifying industrial districts in recent ordinances. The adoption of "performance standards" may obviate the need for arbitrary distinctions between "light" and "heavy" industry and provide a more rational utilization of industrial land. It could also become a means for closer integration between places of employment and places of residence.

In some regions and states the emission of chemical contaminants from the internal combustion engine has necessitated an independent Air Pollution Control Agency to enforce regulations of atmospheric contamination, not only from manufacturing processes, but from the product (the automobile) as well.

Performance standards prescribe regulations for control of smoke, odor, glare, vibration, dust, sound, radiation, water or sewer pollution, and moisture. They are enforced through the measurement of the effects of plant operation at prescribed points.

The "industrial district" has acquired an unsavory association with run-down hovels in the shadow of the factory. The successful development of the Planned Industrial District, or Industrial Park, has therefore been a singular advance in planning. The intensity of land use identified with the crowded workshops of the past is relieved in the Industrial Park. A density of some 30 to 50 workers per acre is not uncommon in industrial areas, but the density in

Industrial Parks ranges between 15 and 20 per acre, with areas of heavy industry having less than 10 workers per acre. Regulations prescribe restrictions on building height, space between buildings, setbacks from property lines, signs, off-street parking and loading, and landscaping.

The reservation of Industrial Parks for the exclusive use of industry encourages the planned integration of residential communities with mutually beneficial results: efficiency in industrial operation and convenience to employment in a desirable residential environment.

PERFORMANCE STANDARDS FOR INDUSTRY[3]

A. Fire and Explosion Hazards

All activites involving, and all storage of inflammable and explosive materials shall be provided with adequate safety devices against the hazard of fire and explosion and adequate fire-fighting and fire-suppression equipment and devices standard in industry. All incineration is prohibited.

B. Radioactivity or Electrical Disturbance

Devices which radiate radio-frequency energy shall be so operated as not to cause interference with any activity carried on beyond the boundary line of the property upon which the device is located. Radio-frequency energy is electromagnetic energy at any frequency in the radio spectrum between 10 kilocycles and 3 million megacycles.

C. Noise

The maximum sound pressure level radiated by any use or facility when measured at the boundary line of the property on which sound is generated shall not exceed the values shown in the following table:

Octave-Band Range in Cycles per Second	Sound Pressure Level in Decibels, 0.0002 dyne/cm²
Below 75	72
75–150	67
151–300	59
301–600	52
601–1200	46
1201–2400	40
2401–4800	34
Above 4800	32

If the noise is not smooth and continuous or is not present between the hours of 10 p.m. and 7 a.m., one or more of the following corrections shall be applied to the above octave-band levels:

[3] This material is derived from the zoning ordinances of the cities of New York, Chicago, Denver, and others, and critical analyses of this type of regulation by the Urban Land Institute and the American Society of Planning Officials.

	Correction in Decibels
Daytime operation only	+ 5
Noise source operates less than 20% of any one-hour period	+ 5
Noise source operates less than 5% of any one-hour period	+ 10
Noise of impulsive character, such as hammering	–5
Noise of periodic character, such as humming or screeching	–5

The sound pressure level shall be measured with a sound level meter and associcate octave band analyzer conforming to standards prescibed by the American Standards Association as set forth in a pamphlet published by the Association, entitled: "American Standard Sound Level Meters for Measurement of Noise and Other Sounds No. Z24.3," published in 1944, and in another pamphlet published by the same Association, entitled: "American Standard Specification for an Octave-Band Filter Set for the Analysis of Noise and Other Sounds No. Z24.10," published in 1953.

D. Vibration

Every use shall be so operated that the ground vibration inherently and recurrently generated is not perceptible, without instruments, at any point on any boundary line of the lot on which the use is located.

E. Smoke

No emission shall be permitted at any point, from any chimney or otherwise, of visible grey smoke of a shade equal to or darker than No. 1 on the Power's Micro-Ringlemann Chart, published by McGraw-Hill Publishing Company, Inc., and copyright 1954 (being a direct facsimile reduction of the standard Ringlemann Chart as issued by the United States Bureau of Mines), except that visible grey smoke of a shade equal to No. 1 on said Chart may be emited for four (4) minutes in any thirty (30) minutes. These provisions applicable to visible grey smoke shall also apply to visible smoke of a different color but with an apparently equivalent capacity.

F. Emission of Dust, Heat and Glare

Every use shall be so operated that it does not emit dust, heat or glare in such quantities or degree as to be readily detectable on any boundary line of the lot on which the use is located.

G. Emission of Odors

No emission shall be permitted of odorous gases or other odorous matter in quantities which exceed those proportions shown in Table III, "Odor Thresholds," in Chapter 5 of the "Air Pollution Abatement Manual," copyright 1951 by Manufacturing Chemists' Association, Inc., Washington, D.C.

H. Outdoor Storage and Waste Disposal

All outdoor storage facilities for fuel, raw materials, and products shall be enclosed by a fence or wall adequate to conceal such facilities from adjacent property. No materials or wastes shall be deposited upon a subject lot in such form or manner that they may be transferred off the lot by natural causes or forces. All materials or wastes which might cause fumes or dust or which constitute a fire hazard or which may be edible by or otherwise be attractive to rodents or insects shall be stored outdoors only in closed containers.

Special Uses.   In some communities there may be special uses to which land may be subject, such as drilling for oil and mining for rock or minerals. It is customary to control uses of such a special nature by requiring individual action by the planning commission and issuance of permits by official action of the city council. The establishment of cemeteries may also come within this category and be subject to a similar control.

The development of nuclear energy has introduced a new element of regional concern. The location of nuclear power plants, as well as performance standards, becomes a matter of state concern. Citizens, as well as wildlife and coastal waters, must be protected from the pollution which can result from the disposal of the plants' waste, and must also be protected from possible ill effects of radioactive material.

HEIGHT AND BULK

One of the most critical problems in zoning is the relationship between buildings and the space about them. The issue of space about buildings was once predicated upon the necessity to preserve adequate light and air for interior space. Examples of adequate setback requirements to serve this purpose are rare, but the remarkable progress in the technical design of the interior environment has altered the demand for such provisions. Preservation of space for light, air, sound control, and privacy continue to be criteria in measuring adequate space between buildings, but their relative importance has been modified by advances in artificial illumination, sound insulation, and air conditioning. It is possible that the necessity for space in the future will derive far more from the *exterior* requirements than the interior demands. The amount of building floor space in relation to exterior circulation—streets, sidewalks, parks—may become the critical factor. The space for vehicular and pedestrian traffic circulation now presents an almost insurmountable problem, and it is compounding annually. The dissipation of exterior space in which the environment may be enriched with landscaping, and in which the human scale may be restored, is a mounting challenge. This thesis will, however, apply best in the new areas where open land is to be developed or in the renewal areas where land is assembled into large plots. The current concern for space to protect light, air, etc., will still be an important consideration in dealing with old areas, divided into small, narrow, individual lots.

Over the years there has been a constant effort to increase the distances between buildings and property lines, and to devise methods by which setbacks might compensate for increasing building heights. The ground space reserved by these provisions has never been sufficient for its purpose; the setback distances and lot coverage restrictions have been rather token grants of space sacrificed after the land had acquired great value. The initial method of front, side and rear yard requirements was later augmented by "envelope" provisions to cope with excessive building heights. The modest side yard of 5 to 6 feet in residential zones has increased to 10 feet for multiple family districts in some ordinances, with provisions for setbacks above the first or second floors. The space between buildings reserved by these provisions is not adequate for reasonable privacy, but opposition to increasing the space has been adamant. Awareness of the deficiency, however, has induced the subdivision of land into larger lot sizes and consolidation of small properites. This trend has increased the efficiency of land use and site planning, but successful large-scale developments demonstrate that the conventional regulations have no actual bearing on good planning.

There is an inflexibilty in current methods for preserving open space; the minimum standards permitted by law become the maximum standards in practice. The primary issue in the future seems to be the need for regulations directed to a balance between building bulk and exterior space required for circulation, vehicular storage, and the evolution of an urbanscape which satisfies more of the basic material needs of humanity.

The principle of the "Floor Area Ratio" offers some encouragement in this direction. This is a regulation of the ratio between the area of building floorspace and the area of the lot it occupies. A Floor Area Ratio of 2, for example, would permit 100 per cent of the lot to be covered by a two-story building, or 50 per cent of the lot to be covered by a four-story building. Recent applications of the Floor Area Ratio introduce the features of "bonus," or premium, space. Chicago adopted such inducements in its revised ordinance of 1957, and they have been proposed in Philadephia. The first major overhaul of the New York City ordinance since the history-making zoning law of 1916 occurred with the revisions of 1960. The conventional "setback" requirements that produced the familiar shapes variously referred to as "cakemold" or "ziggurat" were modified by adoption of the "Sky Exposure Plane" for commercial zones and the "Open Space Ratio" for multifamily residential districts. The effect of these provisions, in combination with the inducements of increased permissible floor space in proportion to the open space reserved at the ground level, is comparable to the Floor Area Ratio method of regulation.

This approach affords a flexibility in the shape of buildings to serve their particular functions and removes the arbitrary limitations upon building heights unless such limitations may be desirable for particular purposes. As with other regulations to control the bulk of buildings on the land, the Floor Area Ratio will be effective to the extent that it produces the required balance between enclosed floor space occupied by people and adequate ground space for vehicles and living things, be they human, animal, or plants.

FLEXIBLE ZONING

Exploration of methods by which flexibility may be incorporated within the framework of zoning has produced the technique of "density control." The monotony of subdivision design which has resulted from the single-family land use classification combined with lot-size regulations is relieved by this method. The zoning classification and prescribed lot size that prevails for a given tract establishes the overall density and maximum number of lots permissible in the subdivison. The density control provision permits the developer to reduce the minumum lot size providing the maximum number of lots is not exceeded and the balance of the land area is developed for recreation or park space.

The technique identified as "planned development" or "community unit" is another advance in the achievement of flexibility in zoning. This permits the planned integration of land uses and, although its application is directed primarily to large developments of raw land in suburban areas, it may be applied to built-up sections of the city. It offers the opportunity to plan for the full range of uses required by a well-balanced community—shopping, parks, schools, and a variety of housing types—uses not generally provided for within the framework of conventional zoning.

OFF-STREET PARKING

Substantially 85 per cent of all surface travel in urban areas, except in a few large cities, is by means of the private automobile. The road system upon which these vehicles circulate is a major element in the Comprehensive Plan of the city. A component of this element is the accommodation of these vehicles at their destination. The moment when a driver is transformed to a pedestrian plagues the planner. The zoning plan must provide for this.

The horseless carriage inherited the narrow street as a traffic route and the hitching post as a parking place. When the automobile attained its own identity the number of vehicles burgeoned. They filled the streets, the rate of movement declined, slot machines were put on the hitching posts, and curb parking absorbed two street lanes urgently needed for moving vehicles. Although the parking meter produces some revenue for the city, the movement in and out of curb parking seriously interrupts the free flow of traffic along the free lanes. Off-street parking is the urgent need, and methods for both voluntary and mandatory parking have been varied. Parking districts and merchants' associations have been created, but relief from the parking jam in commercial districts remains inadequate.

With decentralization of commercial facilities, ample parking was a primary prerequisite of the shopping center. This obvious competition forced a recognition of the necessity for off-street parking in built-up commercial districts. Provisions for off-street parking have been accepted in many zoning ordinances applicable to both residential and commercial areas during recent

Off-Street Parking

Use	Minimum Standard

Residential
Single family dwellings .... 2 spaces per dwelling
Multifamily dwellings .... 2 spaces per unit, except for low income dwellings and university dormitories.
Apartment hotels .... 1 space per unit
Hotels and clubs .... 1 space per room up to 40 rooms, and 1 space per 2 rooms over 40 rooms
Tourist motels .... 1 space per sleeping room or living unit
Trailer parks ....1¼ spaces per trailer

Shopping Centers
Neighborhood .... 6 spaces per 1,000 sq. ft. gross floor area
Community and regional .... 8 spaces per 1,000 sq. ft. gross floor area

Food Markets .... 10 spaces per 1,000 sq. ft. gross floor area

Retail Stores
Less than 5,000 sq. ft. gross
   floor area .... 1 space per 200 sq. ft.
5,000-20,000 sq. ft. gross
   floor area .... 25 spaces plus 1 space per 150 sq. ft. over 5,000 sq. ft.
More than 20,000 sq. ft. gross
   floor area .... 25 spaces plus 1 space per 150 sq. ft. over 5,000 sq. ft. plus 1 space per 100 sq. ft. in excess of 20,000 sq. ft.
Restaurants and Bars .... 1 space per 150 sq. ft. gross floor area
Central Business .... 1 space per 300 sq. ft. gross floor area when mass transit is available, 2 spaces per 300 sq. ft. gross floor area if not available

Office Buildings
General business .... 1 space per 400 sq. ft. gross floor area

Banks, Professional Offices, and Service Shops .... 1 space per 250 sq. ft. gross floor area

Medical-Dental Offices .... 1 space per doctor and each employee plus 1 space per examining room or 1 space per each 100 sq. ft. gross floor area

Public Assembly
Theaters, auditoriums, and
   stadiums .... 1 space per 5 fixed seats or 35 sq. ft. of seating area
Churches .... 1 space per 3 fixed seats

Schools
Elementary schools .... 1 space per classroom
High schools and trade schools .. 1 space per 5 seats
Colleges .... 1 space per 3 students

Hospitals .... 1 space per 1,000 sq. ft. gross floor area or 1 space for 2 beds

Recreation
Bowling alleys .... 5 spaces per alley

Amusement centers	25 spaces per 1,000 sq. ft. gross floor area
Dance halls	1 space per 5 seats or 35 sq. ft. seating area, plus 1 space per 35 sq. ft. of dance floor area
Beaches	1 space per 250 sq. ft. beach area
Golf courses	10 spaces per hole, 1 space per 35 sq. ft. floor area of public assembly, and 250 sq. ft. floor area for other uses
Industries	1 space per 300 sq. ft. gross floor area
Warehouses and wholesale houses	1 space per 800 sq. ft. gross floor area plus 1 truck space per 5,000 sq. ft. gross floor area

years. The requirements vary, but none have coped with the situation in central business districts.

The necessity of freeing the streets of standing vehicles is hardly more pressing in the business districts than in the high-density multiple-family apartment districts. Off-street parking is but one important feature for improvement of the total environment, and it would aid in achieving a balance between bulk and the capacity of the street system to accommodate the traffic flow.

The requirements for off-street parking will vary according to the conditions of each community, but the table on page 314 indicates standards which may serve as a guide. The local circumstances—general density of commercial and apartment districts, and driving habits—should be weighed in their application.

SOME CONVENTIONAL DEFICIENCIES

Zoning is the instrument which permits regulation of the use of land to be administered in the public interest by protecting the interests of each individual who invests in the urban community. These regulations are predicated upon good *principles* of land control, but they fail to establish *standards* of urban development that produce good cities. Harland Batholomew has said:

> Zoning has come about partly through the desire of certain better residential districts to obtain a protection which is difficult, if not impossible, to secure by private initiative, and partly through municipal authorities seeking to curtail the enormous losses brought about by uncontrolled growth. Zoning as now practiced, however, has scarcely succeeded in attaining either of these objectives. Owing to inaccurate and, more particularly, insufficient information, our zoning ordinances have been quite out of scale with actual needs. The same forces of speculation that have warped city growth in the past continue to do so through distortion of zoning ordinances.[4]

[4] Harland Bartholemew, *Urban Land Uses,* Harvard City Planning Series, Harvard University Press, Cambridge, Mass., 1932.

Because it is a vital instrument, these deficiencies deserve attention. The design of commercial zoning persists in retaining "horse and buggy" features. It is an established community attitude in most areas that all land on highways should be zoned for business. In the early days of the village the road led to the door of the shop. The horse was tied to the hitching post in front and "parked at an angle." This form of curb parking has lingered on while the automobile replaced the horse and buggy, while the number of motor vehicles leaped from 8,000 at the turn of the century to more that 120,000,000 in 1970, and while the electric streetcar and motorbus made the horsecar extinct.

The shopping promenade of yesterday has become the traffic artery of today, but the design of business zoning remains unchanged. Mile after mile of highways are "stripped" with excessive zoning for commercial use. Strip zoning with its curb parking has become a curse. Through-traffic does not mix with the ready ingress and egress for parking and service needed on shopping streets. Submarginal business enterprises, blighted houses, and acres of weed patches on unimproved lots stretch along streets zoned for business, creating a state of built-in blight. The result is a plan which is impractical for traffic and undesirable for shopping.

The property protection expected of zoning has been largely confined to excess single-family dwellings. It is a peculiarity of current zoning that each lesser economic classification is permitted in zones of greater economic intensity. Single-family dwellings are permitted in multiple-dwelling districts and both uses are permitted in commercial districts. Some ordinances still permit all uses in industrial zones. As a result, the only zone restricted to the use for which it is designed is the single-family zone; in this zone *only* single-family dwellings are permitted. The "industrial park" is a step forward, because it is restricted to industry, but this feature has thus far been infrequently incorporated into zoning ordinances. Mixed land uses are not economically sound. Land occupied by dwellings in an industrial zone reduces the efficiency of service facilities for industrial operations, and the safety and convenience of a residential community are denied to the residents scattered through an industrial district. Zoning and planning will achieve compatibility only when the zoning ordinance restricts uses in each zone to those for which the zone is designated.

The areas of land zoned for their respective uses are usually far in excess of the requirements of the city. The amount of land zoned for commercial use has been estimated at three to ten times the area that will ever be needed in the locations zoned. This not only compels the mixture of incompatible uses but induces the spread of uneconomic commercial enterprise. Submarginal business degenerates into blight and, in turn, creates an unhealthy environment for its more prosperous neighbors. Were land uses restricted to the classifications for which they are zoned, the temptation to retain or seek zoning for uses which cannot be sustained economically would undoubtedly fade.

The tremendous burden of building bulk occupying urban land has contributed to the congestion of people and traffic, the disappearance of space, and ugliness. Zoning regulates the type of use permitted on the land; it also regulates the amount of permissible floor space. The regulations are expressed in terms of setbacks from property lines—front, side, and rear yards—volume envelope, sloping planes from street lines, maximum heights, lot coverage. The building volume resulting from these regulations is the measure of the floor space and population density set by the zoning ordinance. The maximum density permitted by prevailing ordinances is so excessive that open space has disappeared, the streets cannot handle the traffic generated, and there is no room to store vehicles. A final consequence, more elusive to measure but nonetheless vital to the economic health of the community, is the imbalance between the demand for space and the amount of excess space permitted by zoning laws. Neither the total amount of land nor the total amount of permissible floor space can be absorbed for the designated land use. As land development reaches a saturation point, new improvements, exploiting the permissible zoning volume, drain away the opportunities of less fortunate neighbors to sustain economic business operations. Physical deterioration follows economic blight, and the adverse effects injure both the overbuilt and the underbuilt properties. The potential intensity permitted by the ordinance defeats its purpose as a regulatory measure. Land values are subject to extremes of speculative irresponsibility, and decent standards of open space and site planning occur, if at all, despite the law. Zoning must allow adequate space for dynamic growth, but it must also avoid the excesses which nourish economic and physical blight.

An indiscriminate mixture of different land uses can be detrimental to the quality of the physical environment. This is observed in the careless practice of "spot-zoning"—the intrusion of service stations in residential neighborhoods, for example. The convenience of a modest shopping center, however, may enhance a residential neighborhood, if it does not lead to undesirable noise, night-lighting, and an increase of traffic on residential streets, and if adequate on-site parking and landscaping are components of the plan. With appropriate density control, apartments may not only harmonize with single-family districts, but enrich the appearance of a neighborhood with a variety of form and open space. Compatibility, rather than similarity of uses, is the key to a harmonious relation between land uses.

The dull uniformity of mass-produced houses in suburban "cookie-cutter" sub divisions has prompted the effort to achieve visual interest, and some degree of individual identification; a variety of setbacks and decorative exterior designs are used to camouflage the similarity in floor plans. These superficial efforts are unpleasant reminders that few custom-built homes have been erected in recent decades. Most homes are produced by a new profession of speculative, large-scale home-builders. The home, once every man's castle, has been reduced to a piece of merchandise, a commodity for trade.

22

Subdivision Practices

THE USE OF LAND

The earth is our primary resource. It took tens of thousands of years to create the few inches of soil that support humanity. The greed and neglect of man have often destroyed what took nature eons to develop. The story of man's improvidence with the land is suggested by Walter Havighurst:

> In 1823 a little Norwegian wanderer, named Cleng Peerson, walked overland from New York to the western territories. At Chicago he turned north. For six days he printed his steps in the blank sands of Lake Michigan. At evening he boiled his kettle at the lake's edge. He slept under the soothing drones of water. At the site of Milwaukee (three log huts, one of them empty) he found a tall man, naked to the waist, beside a cabin hung with traps and snowshoes.
>   "What will I find if I continue north from here?" Cleng Peerson asked.
>   Solomon Juneau was a fur trader. He know the great twilight of the forests.
>   "Woods to the world's end," he replied.
>   It was literally true. Woods for 600 miles. In that day six-sevenths of Wisconsin was forest. Two-thirds of Minnesota was forest. The upper peninsula of Michigan was all forest. And the forest began beyond Lake Superior, stretching away toward Hudson Bay. A country as big as France and every mile of it mysterious with forest twilight and haunted with the sound of running water. . . . Cedar, hemlock, tamarack and pine. A forest rich and vast enough for the needs of a nation forever.
>   Try to find that forest now. . . .
>   The timber cruisers came, walked through the country. . . . Behind them came the lumber kings and the great corporations. They logged off the forest in a furious assault. "Come and get it" was the cry of the lumber camp. . . . "Come and get it" was the slogan of the corporations. . . .

How did the big corporations get hold of all the timber? There was the Stone and Timber Act of Congress, designed to safeguard national resources. But the corporations found the loopholes, and they got the timber. . . .

Following the mining of timber came the fires that swept not only the fallen timber but the seeds as well ... so there was no second growth. Conservation of this forest preserve came 50 years too late.[1]

This is so with all of our resources. In our desire to provide a maximum of opportunity and a minimum of regulation, we are prone to pass on a heritage of poverty in natural resources. So often our willingness to protect our resources emerges only after irreparable damage has been done. The control of land subdivision has been similar to that of soil conservation. It is accepted only after most of the urban land has already been butchered into pieces that render our city the unhappy affair we now experience. Carol Aronovicci said: "Wisdom is knowing what to do. Virtue is the doing it. . . . " In the subdivision of land as in many other affairs our virtue precedes our wisdom and, it might be observed, the "doing" of many subdivisions is without much virtue.

PRIVATE OWNERSHIP OF LAND

The history of land ownership commenced when people formed tribes. Living on wild food and game, primitive tribes appropriated the territory they occupied. Like the American Indian or the pastoral people of the Asiatic steppes, the primitives guarded their territory from intrusion by other tribes, but equality of use was open to all the members of their own community. Remnants of these ancient customs survive; in territorial waters all have the right to fish, and in our national forests the birds and beasts are stalked during hunting seasons.

The land belonged to the tribe and not to the individual; in this we detect a precedent for the sovereign state as the true owner of all land. As the tribes grew in size and acquired territory by conquest or peaceful consolidation, they subdivided into villages. A degree of local autonomy was tolerated, but the land remained as community holding.

This ancient tradition that the land is vested primarily in the community, with rights to its use being granted to individuals, has persisted despite the forms which these rights have assumed from time to time. This concept of land ownership, derived from tribal possession of the land, was later reflected in the feudal system when land was vested in the king as the head of the state.

In the feudal system land was "granted" by the king to his lords for their pledge of military support. The lords in turn allocated rights to the use of land to their serfs and villeins, these rights becoming an integral part of the social and political caste system. As the feudal system dissolved, the privileges of the lords were transformed into a form of ownership, and the landlord was born. In

---

[1] Walter Havighurst, "The Land and the People," *Land Policy Review,* June 1941.

England the system of leasing land estates to tenants reached a stage in which the tenants were assured rights to the land even more firm than those of the landlord-owner; the tenants' intimate association with the land and its use warranted secure protection against unfair eviction and assurance of full compensation for improvements they might effect in the land.

The character of land tenure is complicated and has varied in different countries at different periods of history. While the landlord-tenant system prevails in some countries, the peasant proprietorship is predominant in others. The concept of land-ownership has gradually moved from that of possession—the act of presence on the land as a place to live and to cultivate or capture food for survival—to that of land as property; in this latter concept the land becomes a commodity and we associate it with private land-ownership.

Because of this identification it is necessary to recognize the relation between private ownership and the interest retained by the community in the land. The legal rule has been expressed that there is no absolute private right to land in our system, the state alone being vested with that right which it concedes to the individual possessor only as a strictly defined subordinate right, subject to conditions enacted by the community from time to time. Quoting from the *Encyclopaedia Britannica:*

> Land tenure, throughout the world, shows that it has pursued one unvarying course; commencing in the community of tribal possession, land has everywhere by degrees been appropriated to the village, to the families and to the individuals. But in every stage the condition of its enjoyment and use have been absolutely regulated by the community in reference to the general welfare. . . . Those who refuse to admit the right of the state to impose such conditions on private property as it deems for the general benefit, may be dismissed with brevity. Not only do they show entire ignorance of the history of land tenure at all times, but they belie the daily action of the British legislature. Parliament seldom lets a session pass without making some laws which assert the right of the state to take possession of property for private or public benefit, to tax it, and to restrain or regulate the rights of its owners over it. Nor is there any theory of the basis of property which does not tacitly admit that it is subject to the authority of the community.[2]

Land in the United States was originally vested in the Crown of the country which colonized the area. The British king made grants of land to the trading companies, and they in turn transferred the grants to individuals or groups of settlers. It was customary for these settlers to establish compact villages in the New England country with each family receiving a holding of 20 acres. Outside the area of these individual holdings, the land remained in custody of the community for use by all members of the group. In the South, however, large tracts were granted for agricultural development.

The King of Spain held absolute title to the land in the Spanish colonies. His

---

    [2] *The Encyclopaedia Britannica,* The Werner Company, Chicago, 1893, Vol. 14, p. 259 (American Revision).

subjects were dispatched to those areas the Crown desired to be populated, and the land was leased for cultivation. The crops were specified, and, if for any reason settlers neglected to cultivate the land, they were deported from the colony. Provisional grants of huge estates were made to favorites of the Crown in the western country which later became California. The first of these was in 1784, and *ranchos* like those of José Verdugo in the San Fernando Valley and Manuel Nietos between the Santa Ana and San Gabriel Rivers occupied areas of 68 leagues or 390,000 acres stretching from the mountains to the sea. These great holdings were roughly measured; the *vara*, the measurement of distance, was calculated on horseback, and the later problems of untangling disputed claims may well have originated with the relative spryness of some caballero's horse.

Like the Roman *praesidium*, the German *marktplatz*, and the New England common, the plaza occupied the center of the Spanish colonial pueblos. House lots were grouped about the plaza, with the planting fields and public pasture land lying beyond them. Although this form was originally adopted for protection from attack by hostile tribes, the social advantages were later realized, and the Spaniards used this pueblo form in all the cities they founded in North and South America.

Founded in 1781, the town of Los Angeles illustrates the typical village plan. Eleven families traveled overland to settle this new town, and history records what was probable the first of the "super-colossal premiers" for which Hollywood later was to become famous. The Indians and the garrison joined with the settlers in a gay fiesta marking the establishment of the town.

Each of the settlers was permitted to cultivate 14 acres of land outside the residential area, and an equal allowance of stock and equipment was given to each family. All had free range for their stock on the pueblo lands lying outside the land designated for cultivation.

> The first subdivision of the City of Los Angeles was quite simple. It covered an area of 4 square leagues or about 36 square miles centered about the plaza which measured 275 by 180 feet. In accordance with de Neve's instructions, the old plaza lay with its corners to the cardinal points of the compass, the streets extending at right angles so that "no street would be swept by the wind." Upon three sides of the plaza were the house lots, 55 feet in width. One-half of the remaining side was reserved for public buildings, the other half was for open space.[3]

After the American Revolution, land formerly held by the Crown of England went to the respective states and, in order to resolve the conflicting interests of the states in this land, much of it was made a public domain under the Federal government. The United States thereby became proprietor of the great frontier areas. Because the government of the new nation needed revenue

---

[3] *El Pueblo,* Security Trust and Savings Bank, Equitable Branch, Los Angeles, California, 1948.

for its operation and the expansion of the vast country, settlement was encouraged by the sale of land at nominal prices, and grants were offered in return for development. The Homestead Act was one such method, entitling the citizen to 160 acres of land on the condition that he bring it under cultivation within a period of 5 years. Huge grants were made to the railroads as encouragement to extend their rails across the western territories, about 10 per cent of the public domain in 1867 being turned over to the several railroad companies.

These policies overlooked the possible dissipation of natural resources in forests and minerals that later took place, and it has been subsequently necessary to devote much legislation to the restoration and protection of these domains. In urban communities the abuse of land through speculative excesses has paralleled the dissipation of the natural resources in rural areas.

LAND SUBDIVISION AND SPECULATION

As our nation grew in size and the urban centers became large metropolitan areas, there was increased competition for land for all purposes. Great estates were broken up and sold in parcels of varying size. Land was still considered, for the most part, as a base for some economic or social use. Not until recent years did it become a speculative commodity, to be bought and sold, like stocks and bonds, for a profit and, not infrequently, a loss.

Some of the wildest exploits in land sales occurred in Florida and California during the early 1920's. Florida land was sold at fantastic prices to people in New York and the New England states, and much of the land was under water. When the boom broke, thousands of people found themselves with worthless property and their life savings lost.

Real estate speculation in California was somewhat reminiscent of the exploits of the *Americanos* following the Spanish occupation, when tales of fantasy colored the accretion of large land holdings. One such tale cites a case in which all land was to be registered in the land office at the specified time or be declared free for claim by anyone desiring it. Various tricks were employed to deceive the Spanish *rancheros*: some notices were never published, or they were "lost"; some were phrased in language not understood by the Spanish landowners; or, as a last resort, owners were terrorized to keep them from the registry office until the deadline had expired.

In later days of speculation, land was subdivided and sold in flood areas and on precipitous hillsides; in one area the gridiron plotting of streets rendered the lots so useless that 90 per cent of the land has since reverted to the state for failure to pay taxes. A multitude of 25 by 100 foot lots were laid out and sold for "a dollar down and a dollar a week." There were no sewers and no paved streets, and heavy rains washed out roads and water pipes. These subdivisions were not only poor investments for the purchasers, but they were wanton wastes of the urban land resources.

As lots in these scattered "wildcat" subdivisions were sold off, there followed the demand for urban services and facilities and for transportation which could not be supported. When the boom died in California, as in Florida, thousands of lots, some improved and some devoid of pavements or utilities, remained as evidence of premature and irresponsible subdivision. Assessment districts, which had been formed to pay for the improvements promised by the subdivider, defaulted on their bonds and the scene was one of economic desperation.

The depths to which abuse of urban land subdivision sank is best illustrated by the contrast of fine residential suburbs which were begun during the same period. Such developments as the Palos Verdes Estates near Los Angeles, St. Francis Woods in San Francisco, Roland Park in Baltimore, Forest Hills on Long Island, River Oaks in Houston, and the Country Club District in Kansas City are among a number in which the best techniques in land division and development were employed.

ESCAPE!

The wanton neglect of the congested centers of our cities has been equaled only by the wastefulness of its sprawling expansion. People are fleeing from the city in search of relief from the ugly evils of congestion in their living and working environment. This does not raise the question of decentralization versus rebuilding. Cities are being continuously rebuilt, after a fashion, and decentralization is not only coming, it is here. The central problem is to turn the current exodus from a rout into an orderly expansion by way of planning and effective legislation to implement the execution of the plans.

Thus far, expansion has amounted to a scattering of homes over the available outlying countryside. This has provided a means to escape from the outmoded living environment within cities rather than a means to accommodate gracefully the growing urban population. It has not been guided by the foresight of planners, enlightened civic leadership in business and government, nor wisdom in urban economics and finance. Credit for meeting the demand for better living must go to that aggressive group of patent medicine men of real estate we have identified as "lot hawkers." Only they were prepared for the call and they made a contribution to improved urban living. Of those who could afford to escape, there are few not living in some subdivision promoted by the early hawkers of real estate or their more recent offspring. The process was chaotic, unplanned, and it created more problems for the future than it solved. But the people were served.

Henry Ford said, "Plainly, so it seems to some of us, that the ultimate solution will be the abolition of the City, its abandonment as a blunder. . . . We shall solve the City problem by leaving the City."[4] This thesis reflects the underlying discontent with cities, but can it be a milepost on the way to reaching a decent environment?

People have congregated in cities for their mutual welfare. They are now retreating from the congestion. Commercial and industrial expansion is moving

[4] From "Mr. Ford's Page" in the *Dearborn Independent,* Dearborn, Michigan, 1922.

LONDON

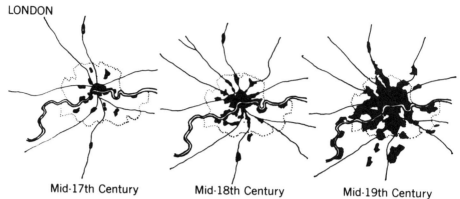

Mid-17th Century   Mid-18th Century   Mid-19th Century

THE EXPLODING METROPOLIS

Cities everywhere are growing with disorder along the same pattern, each becoming a metropolis sprawling unplanned over the countryside. These diagrams illustrate the urban explosion since the industrial revolution of the nineteenth century. Rare among such cities, London has planned a "green-belt" to restrict its expansion.

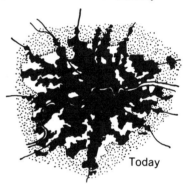

Today

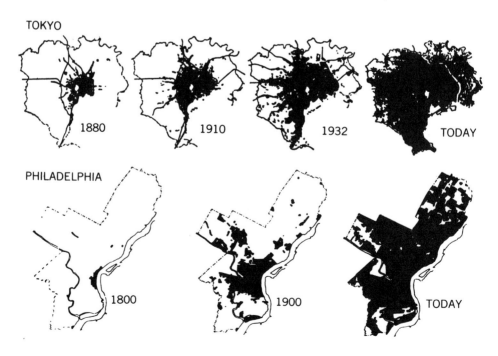

TOKYO

1880   1910   1932   TODAY

PHILADELPHIA

1800   1900   TODAY

324

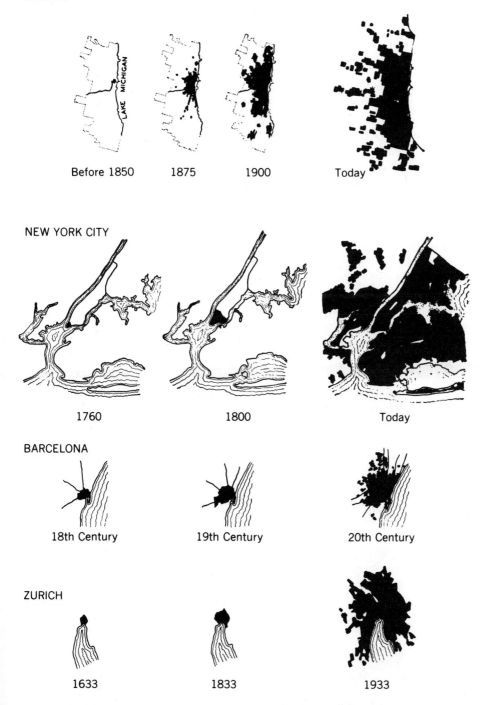

CHICAGO

Before 1850   1875   1900   Today

NEW YORK CITY

1760   1800   Today

BARCELONA

18th Century   19th Century   20th Century

ZURICH

1633   1833   1933

325

to the outskirts to dodge the incredible land prices in the older areas. Decentralization is on the march, but this is an industrial age and the urban framework forms the basic pattern of our economic and social system. It is in the cities where people find their work. The surge of population to the cities has occurred at a remarkably accelerated rate, but it is not a phenomenon of recent origin. During the thirties three-quarters of all industrial jobs were within the major industrial centers, and these centers were confined to only seven per cent of all the counties in the United States. More than one-third of all jobs were in large cities and one-fifth in the peripheral areas and satellite communities contiguous to them.[5]

The urban population of the country was only 3 per cent of the total in 1790, and it is almost 70 per cent of the total today, having increased nearly 30 per cent during the 1950—1960 decade. But the great central cities are *losing* population. This trend has also been evident since the thirties when the suburban districts of metropolitan areas under 1,000,000 population gained twice as fast as the central cities themselves, with a similar trend in areas over 1,000,000. The suburban and satellite areas of Detroit and San Francisco-Oakland increased twice as fast as the central urban districts; the suburban and satellite communities around Chicago, New York, and Pittsburgh gained three times as fast as the central cities; around Philadelphia they gained six times as fast; St. Louis more than ten times; and around Cleveland nearly eleven times.[6] The trend has advanced to the point where the population in 10 of the 12 largest cities, with populations in excess of 700,000 and including the above-named cities, *decreased* during the 1950—1960 decade; only Los Angeles and Houston showed gains. The people are moving to the suburbs and satellite communities about them, but they seek to retain the advantages of the urban environment. More than three-quarters of the urban population live in the 212 metropolitan areas, and 40 per cent of this urban population occupies the sixteen metropolitan areas of more than 1,000,000 people.

The population trend indicated in these statistics from the U.S. Census of 1960 shows prospects for continuing. The trend is evident in metropolitan growth between 1960 and 1968: Houston gained 31.7%; Phoenix, 31.4%; Atlanta, 30.8%; Dallas, 30.4%; Fort Lauderdale, 57.5%; San Jose, Calif., 53.4%; Anaheim-Santa Ana-Garden Grove in Orange County, California, 79.1%.[7] Congestion in the cities will probably continue to drive middle and upper income people to the suburbs.

Spreading at random about the metropolitan countryside, the subdivisions exact a heavy toll upon the city. Extension of public services—utilities, streets, schools, transportation, police and fire protection—over sparsely occupied sections has heaped a burden upon the city treasury. Financing the urban com-

[5] Daniel B. Creamer, *Is Industry Decentralizing?* University of Pennsylvania Press, Philadelphia, 1935.

[6] Ladislas Segoe, *Population and Industrial Trends,* American Society of Planning Officials, 1935.

[7] George Prytula, *Community Mobility Systems,* Urban Land Institute, Special Report, 1970.

munity has become a lingering illness. Debt hovers over property and improvements until a day when it is either paid up in full or foreclosed. It hangs over the City Hall and drains the taxpayer. Investments are unplanned; lending institutions compete for loans in the expanding suburbs, mushrooming over the countryside and sapping the strength of the central districts. "Lenders thus find themselves in the unpleasant situation of financing their own funeral."[8] The city invites chaos and awaits the day when the Federal government must be summoned to bolster the crumbling local economy. Encouraged by the prospects for cheaper development, uninspired builders surge to the outskirts, create the blight of tomorrow, and retreat to other equally fruitful fields.

Within every city is much land which is either vacant or inefficiently used. The speculative prospect for a future increase in the selling price is a strong inducement to withhold this land from development. The penalty of high real property taxation on improvements is a further deterrent to development. Henry George, in 1879, evolved his theory of the "single tax" on land as a remedy for the situation,[9] and the graded real property tax in Pittsburgh assesses land at twice the value of improvements. Various methods have been proposed to emphasize taxation on land as a means to remove the speculative advantage of withholding land from development and conserve the public facilities and services of a community. Applied to all land, this principle could also discourage speculation in unproductive vacant land in the suburbs.

The role of cities is vital. They provide the range and diversification of employment essential to free existence. Our task is not to destroy the city, but to build a better one.

SUBDIVISION REGULATIONS

The questionable practices of the 1920's placed the subdivider of land in an extremely poor light, and the able practitioner was unavoidably identified with the unscrupulous. Reforms were overdue, and the necessity for regulations over the subdivision of urban land was urgent. These controls are based upon the principle that the use and development of land constitute a right bestowed by the community upon the individual, and this right may be withdrawn or withheld when and if the individual, violates the conditions upon which it is vested in him. The power of eminent domain, the police power, the power to tax real estate, and the power to regulate the use of land are expressions of this principle, and it provides the structure upon which the development of urban land is built.

A subdivision may be defined as follows: "Any land, or portion thereof, shown on the last preceding tax rolls as a unit or as contiguous units which is

---

[8] Miles Colean before Mortgage Bankers Association, New York City, 1943.

[9] Henry George, *Progress and Poverty,* 1879.

divided for purposes of sale, either immediate or future, by any subdivider, into five or more parcels within any one year shall be considered to be a subdivision and requires the filing of a map for the approval of the planning commission and legislative body."[10] Such a definition, or one of similar form, is usually contained in state laws which vest in cities and counties the right of police power for the regulation of land subdivision, or in planning acts which outline the procedure for preparation of the Comprehensive Plan.

The definition of a subdivision like the foregoing does not preclude the sale of a portion of an individual lot; this right is retained by the individual property owner. A parcel of land may be sold in whole or in part at the discretion of the owner without the necessity to follow the subdivision procedures. It is only necessary to inform the county recorder and the tax assessor of the sale so that the official records may be adjusted and the taxes reassigned. The regulations applying to the development of individual parcels of land are the zoning laws, the housing laws, health and building codes, and sanitation laws. The divison of property falls within the classification of subdivision regulations when (according to a definition like the preceding description) a piece of land is divided into at least five separate parcels each of which is to be separately sold within a period of one year. Many communities regulate the division of property into less than five lots through local ordinances.

There are many interests involved in the subdivision of land including those of the original owner, the developer, the prospective buyer, and the city as a whole. Ladislas Segoe stated:

> To the land developer the subdividing of land is primarily a matter of profit. He is chiefly interested in realizing as much money as he can from the sale of his land in the shortest possible time. To the community the subdivision of land is a matter of serious public concern. The activities of the developers shape the future of the community and condition in a considerable measure the quality of the living and working conditions of its inhabitants. Where such activities are uncontrolled or inadequately controlled, they also may place an undue burden on the public treasury by reason of excessive cost of public improvements and maintenance, unnecessarily high operating costs of public services, and through the participation of the community in the financing of improvements in premature subdivisions.[11]

One of the first steps taken in some states for the control of subdivisions was the licensing of the subdivider. To obtain a license some education was necessary in the principles and practices of land sales as well as a knowledge of state and local laws pertaining to the subdivision of land. In both state and local laws it was generally necessary for the owner to employ a licensed engineer to prepare the subdivision map for recording. This was an effort to ensure the accuracy of the

---

[10] This should not be confused with the more popular definition of a subdivision as "an area of land where they tear out all the big trees and plant little ones for a suburb."

[11] Ladislas Segoe, *Local Planning Administration,* International City Managers' Association, Chicago, 1941, p. 495.

subdivision maps and avoid alteration in the development after it was recorded. In more recent years it has been frequently mandatory to record on the subdivision maps any unusual or hazardous conditions such as the danger of floods in low areas. Such land has not been necessarily precluded from sale, but the purchasers was warned of what they were purchasing. If life was endangered, however, the public body could deny the right to subdivide and sell the land.

Subdivision of land is the method of transforming a city plan into a reality. Many elements in the overall plan are realized at the time the land is developed. Highways are dedicated, streets and alleys are paved, sewer and water lines and electric power are installed, new schools are constructed, transportation lines are extended, and police and fire protection is expanded. The city plan is either realized or it is lost in the subdivision of land. The control a community retains over land subdivision is the means by which the elements of the Comprehensive Plan are enforced.

Having sovereign rights over the land within their boundaries, state laws govern the ownership, transfer, and use of private property, and they vest in cities and counties the right of police power to regulate the subdivision of land. Some states establish the procedures for subdividing land and have real estate commissions which ensure compliance with these procedures. The real estate commission operates in a manner similar to that of a corporation commission that regulates the sale of stocks and bonds. They check the legitimacy of sales organizations, the quality of the lots offered for sale, and ascertain that the required improvements are either installed or assured by a bond posted by the subdivider prior to approval of the subdivision and sale of land.

The design of subdivisions is the responsibility of the local government of the community in which the land is situated. Under the provisions of the Comprehensive Plan, the local planning agency is generally charged with the responsibility for administration of the standards for "community design" of subdivisions, the shape and size of lots, the size and length of streets, the spaces to be reserved for community facilities, schools, and recreation.

In effect, the community reserves an equity in the land and vests in the individual the right to own and use land subject to the requirements for the general welfare of the community. Thus the city may require the subdivider to dedicate certain streets for access to property and it may demand that sewer lines be installed. If this facility is not available, the city may require larger lots to avoid the possibility of water and soil contamination by effluents from cesspools or septic tanks. The city may require service roads where land abuts a principal traffic way to control the ingress and egress to property, and it may require the installation of specific utilities and roads, walks and curbs, street lighting, electric distribution, or require the subdivider to post a bond to cover the cost of such improvements before the final map of the subdivision is approved. The subdivider may be required to conform with a major highway plan for the community and the grades and proposed alignment of city streets.

The local planning agency aids the subdivider in planning his land, suggests improved methods of site planning, and recommends to the legislative body exceptions to established regulations which may be warranted by peculiar characteristics of the various sites. Material assistance has been rendered by the Federal Housing Administration in the improvement of subdivision design; this Federal agency has performed a service in raising the quality of subdivision design in communities where local laws are ineffectual or no trained planning officials are active.

One of the principal deficiencies in subdivision practice is the difference in improvement standards which prevail in adjoining communities. These differences are apparent in the strange street alignments, blocked roadways, alternately wide and narrow streets, and differences in type of pavements we frequently observe as we move from one community to another. Less discernible, perhaps, but more disastrous to the general community welfare and regional development are the differences in standards for the design and construction of real estate subdivisions, some communities willfully lowering their standards below those of their neighboring areas to invite the subdivision and development of land within their boundaries only to suffer the pain of a degenerated community at some later date. Many cities have made agreements to cooperate in matters of subdivision where the developments are within a certain distance of their respective boundaries. Where regional planning agencies are active, they have coordinated the subdivisions of the various cities within their jurisdiction and here is a field ripe for significant service and progress.

A method for the exercise of quantitative control over land subdivision is yet unresolved, but it is urgently needed as a means to restrain excessive and premature expansion of subdivisions. Repetition of the economically disastrous practices of the 1920's, many of which are recurring today, need to be forestalled, but the method of legally accomplishing this purpose has not been developed. There were suggestions for issuing "certificates of necessity" during the 1930 decade when the effects of "wildcat" operations became painfully obvious. These certificates were to allow subdivision of land only when the developer could demonstrate the need for developing his property and produce some evidence of bona fida purchasers for it.

The most effective means to cope with excessive subdivision thus far has been the requirement that a subdivider install all utilities and improvements, including streets and walks, in conformance with the standards established by the community. The subdivider must thus install, at his expense and prior to sale, all the required improvements. This transforms the subdivider from the usual position of a land speculator to that of a land developer. When required to meet the full capital costs of a complete improvement, it is likely that the developer will consider more thoroughly the financial soundness of his development in terms of its timeliness before he ventures willfully upon a highly speculative enterprise.

SUBDIVISION PROCEDURE

Our conception of land has changed from that of the soil we cultivate for food and the earth from which we extract the minerals and materials to sustain our civilization. The change has come about almost imperceptibly, but nonetheless surely. Land is still used for the same primary purposes. However, it is not only used for the goods it produces; it itself is treated as a good to be bartered for trade. As such a commodity, trading in urban land is frequently conducted independently of its productive usefulness in the traditional sense. Ostensibly the value of land is linked with the manner in which it may be used, but possession is quite generally acquired for the purpose of exchanging it as a commodity rather than for its natural productive use.

As a result of this gradual shift in emphasis upon land, we have grown unaware of the vital impact which the process of transforming raw acreage into improved urban lots exerts upon the community welfare. It is to assure the protection of the general welfare that subdivision regulations have been devised, with the knowledge that, in the final analysis, it is the general welfare that protects sound investment in urban development.

Although procedures vary in different localities, the following steps may serve as a description of the general sequence from an unimproved site to the development of parcels available for sale:

1.   The land is surveyed to ascertain the precise description of its boundaries, the abutting streets, local drainage conditions, contours of the land, and the special features or structures that may occupy the site.

2.   Official records are consulted to define the location of special easements or rights-of-way that must be retained in developing the land. There may be a proposed highway passing across the site or easements for sewers or power lines to serve the site or adjoining land. All restrictions on the use of the property must be determined: deed restrictions and zoning, the location of existing sewers or other requirements for sanitation, the height of the water table, the type of soil. The data on orientation and wind directions may affect the layout of streets and building sites. The surrounding land uses, both existing and permitted, require investigation.

3.   Schools, parks, playgrounds, and other cultural and social facilities are located, and availability of transportation and shopping facilities is evaluated in reference to the services they may provide to the residents in the proposed development.

4.   The subdivision ordinances are consulted for restrictions which may apply to the size and shape of lots, the width and grade of streets, the set-back lines to be observed, and the methods for presentation of the maps required by the local government agency: the planning department, real estate commission, or city engineer.

5.   The developer should employ a planner or engineer to prepare the tentative or preliminary plan for the development of the property. This map should show, with reasonable accuracy, the manner in which the land is to be subdivided: the approximate size, shape, and the number of lots, the location of streets, their radii of curvature and grades, the method for providing drainage in all areas, and the utilities to be installed. The zoning and proposed land uses —open space to be reserved or developed for recreation, shopping, or other community facilities—should also be indicated.

SUBDIVISION MAP CHART

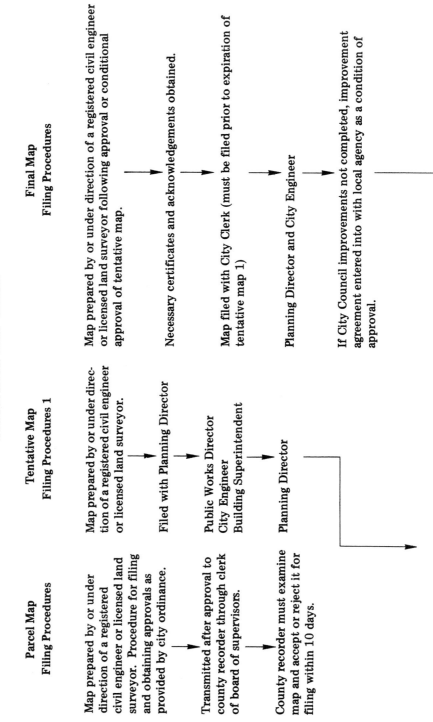

Parcel Map Filing Procedures	Tentative Map Filing Procedures 1	Final Map Filing Procedures
Map prepared by or under direction of a registered civil engineer or licensed land surveyor. Procedure for filing and obtaining approvals as provided by city ordinance.	Map prepared by or under direction of a registered civil engineer or licensed land surveyor.	Map prepared by or under direction of a registered civil engineer or licensed land surveyor following approval or conditional approval of tentative map.
	Filed with Planning Director	Necessary certificates and acknowledgements obtained.
Transmitted after approval to county recorder through clerk of board of supervisors.	Public Works Director / City Engineer / Building Superintendent	Map filed with City Clerk (must be filed prior to expiration of tentative map 1)
County recorder must examine map and accept or reject it for filing within 10 days.	Planning Director	Planning Director and City Engineer
		If City Council improvements not completed, improvement agreement entered into with local agency as a condition of approval.

332

Planning Commission

Approves, conditionally approves, or disapproves within 50 days after filing with clerk. (Deemed approved if no action taken within 50 days, but only insofar as map complies with act and city ordinances.)

If dissatisfied, subdivider may appeal within 15 days to the City Council

City Council

At next regular meeting sets date (within 30 days thereafter) to consider map.

Approves, conditionally approves, conditionally approves or disapproves within the 30 day period. (Deemed approved if no action taken within the 30 day period, but only insofar as map complies with act and local ordinances.)

Decision of City Council within 10 days. (Deemed approved if no action taken within time limits, but only insofar as map complies with act and city ordinances.)

Appeal to City Council by either subdivider or any person adversely affected.

Map approved by City Council within 10 days or at its next regular meeting, if in substantial compliance with previously approved tentative map and conditions, if any, imposed on the tentative map have been met. (Deemed approved if no action taken within 10 day period.)

Map transmitted after approval to county records through clerk of board of supervisors.

County recorder must examine map and accept or reject for filing within 10 days.

6. An estimate is then prepared to show the probable total cost for development of the site and indicate the minimum selling price for the lots to defray the cost of the land, the improvements, and the overhead for subdivision commissions and profits.

7. Before filing the tentative map with the local agency, planning department, or city engineer, it is generally considered good practice to consult with the Federal Housing Administration land planning officials and lending agencies. This is particularly important if approval for mortgage insurance by FHA is expected to be ultimately sought by purchasers of the lots.

8. The tentative map is then filed with the local agency, planning commission, or engineer, and this agency submits it to the various city departments for advice on engineering, health, schools, fire and police protection, and recreation. The suggestions and requirements of each department are co-ordinated by the planning commission, and the specific conditions for approval of the proposed subdivision are then issued, these conditions being based upon the public health, safety, or the general welfare of the community. On many occasions the planning staff will prepare a revised plan to suggest improvements in the design of the site or indicate the manner in which the plan may better conform to local conditions and the Comprehensive Plan for the city.

9. After approval by the planning department and the legislative body, the developer proceeds with the preparation of the final or "precise" engineering map for the land. The street improvements and utilities are shown, the lots are staked on the ground, and minor changes which may be dictated by peculiarities in the site, such as hilly areas, are recorded. The final map is then filed with the city authorities who check it for conformity with the approved tentative map. If compliance is apparent, the final map is submitted to the local legislative body and the mayor for final approval. It is then officially recorded.

10. Before sale of the land may be undertaken the final recorded map must usually be filed with the state real estate commission and approval of sale obtained from that government agency.

CURRENT SUBDIVISION TRENDS

The subdivision of land is responding to the techniques of large-scale planning, and the magic words of mass production and prefabrication are having their effect. Jerry-building persists, to be sure, and the city faces a struggle to combat the insidious effect of the cheap product of unprincipled, speculative developers. Pressure to retreat from decent standards of land development is strong, and resistance is difficult in periods when a housing shortage and high costs create social as well as economic problems for city dwellers. Subdivision standards for minimum lot area and width, street rights-of-way, design and construction of pavements, sidewalks and curbs, water and sewer lines, have become accepted controls administered by city authorities. In the interest of economy or greater profit margin, the pressure to reduce standards is ever present, but the necessity for and desirability of such standards is generally recognized. It is in the broader implications of urban expansion that regulations of land subdivision need serious attention.

Conservation of the land is vital, not only to avoid reckless waste of this precious resource, but for the economic and social stability of the community. The sprawl of suburbia is a symptom of the revolt against congestion and exploitation in the central city. The crying need for re-examination of the nature of urbanism in our society is urgent, but the extension of urban facilities *ad infinitum* to serve the symptom postpones treatment of the malady. A common, perhaps national, fervor comparable to that which brought the London Plan and New Towns to England after World War II may be necessary to force the search for a pattern of urbanism appropriate to our time. Meanwhile, and without relaxing this search, the uneconomic expansion of suburbia will require some measure of curtailment. The unpleasant reality of deterioration throughout great areas of the central city demands attention, but prudent conservation of land is companion to economy in the cost of government.

The requirement that the land developer assume the cost of street and utility improvements in new subdivisions is accepted practice. Expansion creates the demand for a variety of facilities—schools, parks, playgrounds, health, fire and police protection, highway and utility extensions. It is a public responsibility to assure the provision of these facilities. When the services are required to accommodate an increase in population, the added tax revenue to the community may maintain an economic balance with the cost of the facilities. Imbalance occurs, however, when the municipal facilities are necessarily duplicated to serve the population escaping from the central city, or where expansion is into an area that has no economic support.

The power to withhold permission to subdivide land is one control with which balance may be maintained. Denial of the right to subdivide land, however, is strong medicine, and other means may serve with greater equity and equal effectiveness. Independent of the market value of land, the public improvements and services necessary to the development of raw land enhance the basic land value. Since this increment of increased value is created by public expenditure, it seems reasonable to assess a pro rata share of the cost against the subdivision.

A policy adopted in a growing number of cities is the requirement that the developer shall provide the new subdivision with a neighborhood park and playground. The policy is based upon the premise that recreation space to serve a residential subdivision is in a similar category to public rights-of-way and improvements for streets, sidewalks, service roads, and parkways. Since the size of subdivisions varies, some being too small to require a local recreation area, a charge is assessed the subdivider as a deposit with the city to assure the development of this facility when the demand arises.

PLANNED DEVELOPMENT— THE COMMUNITY UNIT

The growing acceptance of the principles of *community* planning is one of the encouraging signs of an improvement in standards. Land in the heart of cities is already subdivided. Improvement in city planning within these huge areas of the city must necessarily emerge with techniques of urban renewal and redevelopment. The major activity has been consequently taking place on the outskirts of the cities and will undoubtedly continue until renewal becomes an effective instrument for rebuilding the central areas.

Attention to the amenities of good community planning is apparent in the standards espoused by such organizations as the Urban Land Institute. The members of this organization include some of the pioneers in the development of subdivisions and the planning and building of residential communities. That good planning may also be good business is attested to by the appeal of such men and organizations for an improvement in subdivision development. The mediocre product of speculative ventures has succeeded in the past and will continue to succeed so long as it remains a profitable enterprise. As the initiative of creative enterprise in community building produces better standards in the living environment, the ventures in speculative practices will be reduced to a diminishing level of investment; by this form of competition and the maintenance of decent standards of land subdivision—land planning—our cities may gradually improve as an environment for the people.

In the Comprehensive Plan, the location of future neighborhood centers—shopping centers, parks, and schools—are only approximately defined within the undeveloped areas of the city. The land use is usually shown as low density or classified as single-family residential zoning. The principles of community planning applied to large-scale subdivisions imply a balanced range of dwelling accommodations as well as a full range of community facilities. A provision for *planned development*, or the "Community Unit," has been incorporated in zoning ordinances to encourage and facilitate this integration of land uses. Under this provision an owner or group of owners, may produce a complete development plan which, upon approval by the Planning Commission, may be adopted by the legislative body as the zoning plan for the entire area in lieu of prevailing zoning. This feature affords a flexibility in planning subdivisions not heretofore available. It implements planning for a diversification of dwelling types, characteristically lacking in conventional zoning, and assures harmonious density within the plan.

The "neighborhood association" is a familiar instrument for property owners to secure and maintain common amenities. Membership is usually stipulated in property deeds. The Planned Unit Development embraces this legal instrument as a new level of self-government through cooperative or condominium ownership. The owner of a dwelling (apartment or house) in a cooperative owns shares of stock in the entire development with the right of occupancy in a specific dwelling. The owner of a condominium has title to the dwelling itself and a proportionate interest in the land and exterior facilities. The governing organization in both cases is an association of all owners with responsibility and authority for levying assessments for management and exterior maintenance. The condominium is generally preferred since owners are financially responsible only for their own dwellings and for a portion of the related common areas, and are not liable for obligations incurred by other owners.

The prospects for an improved environment offered by this enlightened approach to planning of subdivision expansion warrants encouragement. The cumbersome procedures involved in the modification of conventional zoning fortify entrenched resistance to the flexibility demanded for community planning. Planned development may be a means by which the current complications are overcome and accomplish a variety in urban expansion not previously feasible. It could release the future subdivision of land from the strait jacket in which the built-up city and current subdivision practices are bound, and provide the amenities and character of an urban environment we associate with the central city without its concomitant faults. It may lead to a broader concept of planned decentralization for the metropolitan regions in which the great majority of the population is destined to find itself in the future industrial and scientific age.

DENSITY CONTROL

Conventional residential zoning classifies land uses according to building types—single-family or multiple-family. This method has its roots in the historical beginning of zoning when "fine" residential sections were protected from intrusion by undesirable uses. The precedent has lingered on while the form of protection has become a myth. Vast changes in the social and economic structure have completely altered the physical character of the city. The multifamily dwelling is no longer reserved to "tenement house" class, nor is the single-family dwelling district the sole domain of the privileged class. The apartment and the detached house are not now distinguished by the difference in *type* of dwelling but rather by the quality of each, the geographic location, and particularly the family composition and preference. Incompatibility revolves about the differences in the density of each type—the relative adequacy of interior and exterior space for comfort, convenience and safety.

Planned development implements a desirable "mix" of dwelling accommodations to serve the needs of a balanced range of family sizes and preferences. The quality of the improvements which are placed upon the land and the level at which they are maintained contribute to the character of a community, but density is the key factor in planning. It establishes the texture of the physical form. It reflects the distinction, for instance, between a community of single family homes and a community of multistory apartments. It is a unit of measure for establishing a balance among all community facilities and circulation.

The term *density* is commonly employed as a measure of the number of dwellings which occupy, or may occupy, an area of land. "Net density" is identified with the number of dwellings in relation to the land area exclusive of public rights-of-way—the streets and sidewalks, parks and playgrounds, schools and commercial areas—whereas "gross density" usually pertains to the number of dwellings in relation to an area of land including all public rights-of-way and other related land uses. A distinction between these definitions may serve a useful purpose for certain technical measurements and comparisons, but the significant measure for the general texture of the physical form is expressed by *gross* density.

The pressure of urbanization has intensified the demand for land to accommodate the expanding urban population. Efforts to maintain the traditional single-family dwelling on its individual lot has forced the subdivision of land into increments of inadequate size and the typical "cookie-cutter" subdivision pattern has been inevitable. This, in combination with the economic pressure to reduce building and site development costs, has resulted in vast areas

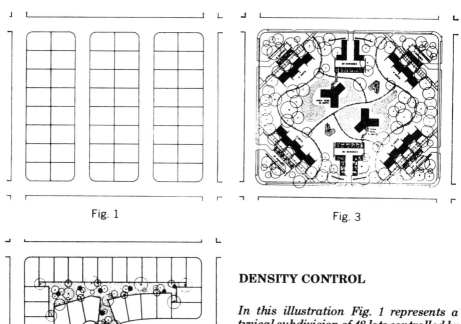

Fig. 1

Fig. 3

Fig. 2

DENSITY CONTROL

In this illustration Fig. 1 represents a typical subdivision of 48 lots controlled by the minimum lot size. In Fig. 2 relaxation of the minimum lot size as the basic control results in the same number of lots but reduces the area of internal streets, eliminates through-traffic, and provides a common open space for all dwellings. Fig. 3 retains the same number of dwellings but introduces a diversification in streets and increase of recreation space.

Fig. 1
Conventional
Subdivision

DENSITY CONTROL

With the minimum prevailing lot area as the unit of measurement for the overall "gross density" in the illustration, the site would accommodate as many as 200 dwellings. Adjusting the internal street system to the topography in a typical subdivision plan, with the usual odd lot sizes which result, would produce only 137 individual lots in conformance with the standard regulations (Fig. 1). With the principle of density control applied, permitting 200 dwellings, an arrangement of clusters of row (alias "town," "group," "garden," or "patio") houses about cul-de-sac roads results in the allocation of about one-fifth of the site for park development (Fig. 2).

This is the primary community interest served by density control. Other advantages may accrue in the planning of individual dwellings, cul-de-sac roads, attractive planting along the main circulation roads, and economy in site improvement costs. These costs may be reduced to as much as one-half those of the conventional subdivision because of economy in grading, paving, drainage and utilities. The degree to which the consumer of housing shares in these economies will extend the broad social advantages which may also accrue. (Plans by courtesy of Richard Leitch, Architect.)

Fig. 2
Density Control
with Clusters

339

of mediocre residential "tracts" about our cities. Every city will have its districts of single-family detached homes; this traditional form of family dwelling has amenities of particular value. These districts in the very large metropolis may be removed to the distant outskirts, but they should be planned upon standards of adequate lot size and shape which actually produce the amenities of the detached house upon its separate piece of land. In seeking to preserve the single-family detached dwelling, however, the minimum lot size has been reduced to dimensions which actually nullify the real advantages of this form. The narrow width of sideyards which separates dwellings denies privacy and renders the space wasteful, and the conventional street "setbacks" have lost almost all semblance of usefulness since the automobile converted the street from a promenade to a service roadway. Insistence upon a distinction in zoning between subdivisions of *high*-density single-family lots and *low*-density apartment destricts has consequently contributed in large measure to the extension of urban sprawl.

The genuine unit for measurement of adequate standards of planning is the individual human being. Family composition and characteristics vary, as do personal desires. Families need space in proportion to their sizes: children need space for active recreation, adults for sports, and the elderly for relaxation. Variations in these requirements may be more than absorbed in the "psychological elbow room" people need and now find wanting in their living environment. A diversification of dwelling types is necessary to the satisfaction of the wide range of desires and family needs in a city. Insistence upon the distinction between a single-family classification of land use and the apartment district has tended to obscure the wide gap which exists between the amount of land area per family in these two categories of residential zoning. If the amenity of space on the earth were related to the common denominator of the human being, the importance of *density* rather than the type of dwelling structure or the size of a lot could be employed as the desirable control for residential planning. It is within the space of this wide gap that conventional subdivision practice and apartment zoning require overhauling. Were a relatively common standard of population density to be adopted as the measure of control for residential development, varied patterns could be woven within the overall texture of the physical form of the city. The apartment and the single house, the tall building and the low building would then approach equal acceptability as neighbors and as places in which to live.

The application of density control may be extended by the interpretation that the conventional minimum lot size represents an acceptable unit of measurement for the gross density in a community. The number of dwellings which may be placed upon an area of land is thereby controlled by this density rather than the minimum lot size *per dwelling*. This method of control offers flexibility in planning the internal street system and the arrangement of the dwelling units. Efficient planning may also produce economy in development cost. As compensation for these advantages a predetermined proportion of the property would be reserved as open space for community recreation.

This approach to density control may open further opportunities in land planning and tract development. The "row" house has acquired an unpleasant connotation for various reasons, ranging from the dull aspect of the conventional row buildings in some older cities to the "barracks" with which public housing was identified in the early years of the program. When we recognize that the disagreeable impressions have not been produced by the *type* of dwelling but rather by the manner in which it has been planned and designed, a block to improvement in planning and economy will have been removed, and the inherent advantages of density control in stemming the course of urban sprawl may be exploited. A step in this direction has been taken through the curious attraction which the term "town house" has aroused.

Old districts of the city which are in a state of limbo, described as "transition" zones in Chapter 21, lend themselves to a form of progression zoning from a "single-family" classification (one dwelling per lot) to a graduated density increase as compensation (or incentive) for the assembly and consolidation of individual lots. Applying the principle of "planned development," transition areas may thus be rehabilitated without the damage to environmental quality which the careless intrusion of conventional apartment zoning imposes.

A feature of density control is the consolidation of open space for community use, and the effective maintenance of this common space is essential. The subdivision of large land areas may warrant a consolidated reservation of sufficient size to be accepted as a public park and playground in the recreation program of the public authorities. For open space in subdivisions of less magnitude the "neighborhood association" may serve as an acceptable alternative. "Special Assessment Districts" have been employed in many communities to provide for street lighting, sanitation, recreation and other special facilities or services not supported by the general tax. In some states the counties may contract with cities or with "special districts" to provide specific services. These districts may be created at the time the land is subdivided and purchasers of homes informed of the special tax to be levied for the services rendered. This form of assessment for the maintenance of community facilities such as open space is thus collected with the "ad valorem" tax and renders assurance of an equitable distribution of the costs.

It is in the public interest to develop planning techniques which may avoid the wasteful and uneconomic extension of urban services. Density control suggests a method by which the current disparity between the single-family classification of land use and the alternative of apartment zoning may be resolved. It also suggests an approach in planning which may recover a desirable physical texture which can be identified as *urban.*

23

Urban Design

URBAN DESIGN

Critics of the concept of urban design say that in fact it does not exist. "Towns are not designed," said one, "they are pasted together, piece by piece." If that is true, it is the result of too many persons being involved in the developmental process and insufficient cooperation among them.

In recent years several interesting concepts have been put forward to bind individual efforts into a compatible whole. The Comprehensive Plan, with its emphasis on a coordinated, unified system of land use and circulation, is at the heart of this effort. The creation of new techniques and acceptance of greater responsibility by the land developer in subdividing property is another important gain. The emphasis on building developments in a subdivision has tended to reduce the speculation in vacant land; thus the city has become a place for living rather than a "hop-scotched" checkerboard of partly used real estate. A concern for the environment—especially in the areas of fire prevention and land erosion—has also made urban design more acceptable to many people.

The most effective impact of urban design comes about when the architect or planner develops a "planned unit" subdivision. It is here that all of the theories of serving the residents with open space and amenities come into play. In the planning stage, sound judgment must be applied to the relationships between the permitted number of dwellings and the spaces between them. The economics of building types, provision for access and parking, the responsibility for the maintenance of the open areas are issues that must be resolved before construction can start.

SYMMETRY OR FREEDOM?

Democracy in city building is a framework in which the manifold functions of contemporary urban life may be accommodated with freedom of expression. Such freedom in organized society, as we are gradually coming to realize, implies self-dicipline and respect for the dignity of others.

342

Building laws not only permit but have actually forced an enormous bulk to be loaded on the land. Consequently, the city has been reduced to a network of street pavements lined with façades of unrelated buildings. Architectural banality and chaos are inevitable. The "right" to build as one wishes has approached a degree of license, and the ugliness has frequently provoked the panacea of architectural control.

In the name of democracy the proponents of architectural control suggest it will not interfere with free expression. Actually there is little else it can do. By its nature architectural control sets a form, usually in terms of some particular "style of architecture" or its equivalent, and the designer is henceforth bound by the capricious taste of a select few.

There are designers who produce a higher order of creative work than men of lesser talent, but should their genius deny the right of self-expression to those of lesser competence? Rare is the genius in the welter of men that can capture the sublime in steel, stone, and space. This is clear when we observe all the buildings of past ages rather than the isolated monuments alone. If talent to produce appropriate and beautiful buildings is limited, it is the task of society to raise the level of competence and widen the cultural horizon, not remove freedom of expression.

The city takes shape over the years through the enterprise of all the people. Moved by their desires, their opportunities, and the evolution of changing conditions, the city is in a continuous state of flux and its plan must accommodate a variety of forms. Eclecticism cultivated the impression that harmony of form is synonymous with symmetry, and planning assumed a rigid formality. Symmetry about an axis was assumed to produce a grand unity among the forms of the city. City building did not follow those plans, however, and the result was most discouraging if not a little puzzling; it seemed that planning was futile enterprise and indeed the form it had acquired was futile.

There was reason for the failure of "grand" planning: boldly reminiscent of imperial domination over the lives of people, its forms were inimical to the tenets of democracy. Not only is the urge for free expression an integral characteristic of democratic society, it is a distinct right. There can be no "centerline" about which the city of democracy is built; it is a fluid, changing form. The rigid symmetry of formal planning is alien to democracy. An autocrat may decree a great plan and he has the power to draft the labor of people to execute it accordingly, but when that power transfers to the people a new concept of urban conduct emerges. It is then the people seek a set of standards we call laws adopted according to the will of the people as guides in the conduct of their mutual and independent affairs. A new concept of planning also emerges, not less compelling but more plastic and sensitive to the will and expression of individuals in society. The "grand" plan was conceived by a single mind to be imposed upon the future. Thenceforth skill in its execution was not the creative power of the individual to solve a problem, but the ingenuity with which the requirements of a later time could be warped into a precast mold. It was suggestive of a solution before the problem was stated.

That democracy imposes great responsibility upon the individual is self-evident; with the privilege of freedom goes responsibility. Harmony in the city of democracy calls for the exercise of individual responsibility and the mutual self-respect of people. Since it was by means counter to democratic processes that a monarch carried out a vast venture like Versailles, so it is contrary to democratic behavior that individuals should ignore the works of others to memorialize their own vanity or expand the contents of their purses. Rivalry for "bigger and better" cities can do no more to open the way to creative civic design than can the stamp of classic planning.

The harmonious integregation of various forms is the art of planning space, and the Piazza of St. Mark's in Venice is a dramatic illustration. Building the Piazza of St. Mark's spanned five centuries. In it we find no sterile symmetry. It was an open space in which throngs of people could congregate. The ornate church of St. Mark's was erected in the eleventh century in the flourishing Byzantine style. The Palace of the Doges, built in the fourteenth and fifteenth centries, was designed in the Gothic style of that period. It was a colorful building, but the façades were simple rectangles facing the sea and forming one side of the Piazzetta. The façade leading from the waterfront was set back to frame a view of the church from the canal. Detached from the church, the Campanile was a powerful accent in the group arrangement. When the Procuriatie buildings were built—late fifteenth and early sixteenth centuries—the Renaissance style was in flower. They were arranged about a long Piazza placed at right angles to the Piazzetta. Located at the intersection of these two plazas, the Campanile was visually linked with the long façades of the Procuriatie Vecchie and Library; the tower was not isolated in space like a centerpiece.

There was variety among the forms, each successive addition to the plaza built in the "style" of its period. The spaces were planned to harmonize these variations; no part was tacked on to complete an "original." The differences in architectural styles enhance the effect of this great plaza, the absence of axial symmetry impresses the observer. The flat façades of the Doges' Palace was not imitated elsewhere to conform to a preconceived "scheme"; the façades of the Procuriatie buildings were stretched into an oblong plan at an angle to the Piazzetta, and the contrasts in the forms and spaces were emphasized by slanting the buildings in plan. The plastic quality of this great plaza is eloquent refutation of the sterile process of symmetrical planning which has been frequently substituted for monumentality in our period of eclecticism. Forms may be harmoniously integrated by appropriate contrasts—contrasts in plan forms adjusted to accommodate the contrasts in contemporary expression as it evolves in successive periods of culture.

NEW DIMENSIONS

With the abundant labor of slaves ancient cities were built of blocks of stone and wood, their heavy forms refined by sculpturing the structural members. Laying stone upon stone, medieval builders formed soaring arches, flying buttresses, and intricate tracery. During all these centuries all construction was wallbearing; all structural stresses were in compression.

The industrial revolution brought a violent change. The massive construction of ancient cities was transformed to the lightness of steel in tension. Processed in the crucibles of smelting plants and testing laboratories, materials were refined, their basic qualities extracted and synthesized. A wide range of synthetic materials were assembled mechanically upon light structural frames. The dynamism of forces in tension replaced the static forms of compression, and the machine released a new freedom in the organization of space.

With the positive thrusts of railway, highway, and airway, new dimensions penetrated the twentieth-century city. Vehicles of transportation no longer mingled informally in the fashion of the Middle Ages. Seeking channels of uninterrupted directness, moving with uncompromising direction, straight ribbons stretch across level spaces and merge with irregular terrain in graceful sweeping curves. The highway is shaped to the contours of the land. Continuity is uninterrupted by natural obstacles; with almost defiant sureness bridges span chasms and tunnels pierce mountains. Unimpeded continuity is essential and insistent. Almost unnoticed, this new dimension has forced a new scale in city building.

The new scale appears in the Mount Vernon highway, the Westchester County Parkways, the New York City freeways, the Outer Drive in Chicago, and the freeways of Los Angeles. More rural than urban, the parkway combined with clear channel rapid transit for mass transportation is the salvation of the traffic dilemma in the heart of the city.

Matching the expanse of the parkway is the horizontal span of enclosed floor space. The city of today is a series of horizontal planes, one above the other, and the relatively constant floor heights retain the impression of human scale. Utility and economy are inconsistent with the inflated scale of eclecticism; excesses in scale that characterized the Baroque city are restrained. Scale is not absent in the volume of floor space enclosed in tall buildings; it has been lost in the congestion of these buildings upon the land—the absence of open space as a foil for their size. The skyscraper readily expresses the mulitiplicity of its floors, but the sense of scale has been destroyed by the depressive bulk of buildings in proportion to the open space about them. It is toward the restoration of adequate space that the new dimensions of the city are forcing urban development.

THE PENETRATION OF SPACE

The parkway brooks no interference; freedom of movement is continuous. The futility of the usual network of streets is exposed. Like an irresistible force meeting an immovable object, the freeway meets the gridiron. The static form of the right angle meets the dynamic thrust of free form.

A rectilinear street arrangement has been generally interpreted as evidence of conscious planning. The assumption must be qualified by an appraisal of the purpose and functions for which the form was devised. The Roman city was patterned after the military camp, and agricultural and urban land has been subdivided into rectilinear plots, but it does not necessarily follow that the organization of a military camp or a convenient form for legal description and recording of deeds are keys to the conscious design of cities for the residence and commerce of people. On the other hand, Hippodamus adopted the checkboard street arrangement for the purpose of allocating lots which would provide proper orientation of all the dwelling units erected upon them. Vehicular traffic was light, towns were small, and direct communication about them was of no particular import.

Today the city is the battleground between the right angle and the curve; the tight gridiron of the surveyor versus the swirling twists of our "planned" suburbia. The battle is being waged in a vacuum; chaos prevails in both, the monotony of one, the variety of disorder in the other. The process is one of dividing the land rather than forming spaces, laying out roads and lots rather than planning appropriate and related uses, and allocating parcels as merchandise tagged with a price rather than arranging space for living or business.

Planning circulation about the city implies a twofold purpose: the direct and natural connection between two or more points, and clear direction for those traversing the roadways. The gridiron provides the latter, but it is essentially a devious zigzag route between two points. Complete loss of orientation is the curse of curving roadways, and no amount of picturesqueness can compensate for the confusion it creates.

A test of planning is the order it produces, and the freeway is a new instrument for orderly space arrangement. Its horizontal expanse clearly defines it as an artery with positive direction in contrast to minor roadways. Reliance upon signs of nature or the rigid orientation of the gridiron in the old city is supplanted by the positive identification and direct action of the sweeping freeway. A dominant feature of the modern city, it brings time and space into harmony. The parkway is destined to force an orderly development not yet apparent in the cluttered urban environment, or it will sweep the city clean.

Just as the freeway has rendered obsolete the corridor and gridiron street, a new relation between buildings and open space was introduced in the great housing developments during the 1920–30 decade. Park-like open space was incorporated in the eighteenth-century "terrace" dwellings of the Royal Crescent and Lansdowne Crescent in Bath and Regent's Park in London, and the "squares" of Bloomsbury introduced the garden to residential streets. However these developments were generally confined to the aristocratic classes, and the amenitites were absent from the living environment of the majority of the urban population. Berlage in Holland and Otto Wagner in Vienna, during the early twentieth century, strove to treat the dwellings of the people as integral parts of civic design, but they retained the corridor street and uniform façades reminiscent of Baroque planning.

When the international housing crisis after World War I forced a widespread program of dwelling constuction, the new dimensions pierced the archaic armor of the city. Large-scale planning, freed from the restrictions of single lots, completely altered the relation between dwelling and open space. The corridor street was abandoned, space between building façades was no longer devoted exclusively to vehicular circulation, and building units were arranged in orderly groups within free open space.

Space was designed for use, traffic arteries by-passed residential groups, and internal circulation was by way of service roadways and pedestrian walks. Recreation space was accessible from all dwellings, and buildings were planned so each dwelling unit enjoyed the same orientation as every other dwelling. For the first time since the building of Hellenic cities a common standard of amenities was applied uniformly to all dwellings in the community plan. There was an affinity between the continuity and breadth of space along the parkway and the flow of space through the developments of large-scale housing.

The infiltration of space in the center of the city is insistent although it expresses the anachronism of urban growth. While automobile parking lots expand and slums are cleared, adjacent lots are improved with a greater density than before and congestion persists round about; one ugly improvement is substituted for another. Nevertheless, space is forcing its way into the heart of the city.

Much land still lies vacant within the city and more lies fallow on the periphery. No pattern, no plan, and little thought have been directed to the future destiny of this land save for outmoded zoning and ineffective building laws. Should we not profit by experience? The tragic results of chaotic expansion lie all about us, the heavy hand of public debt gropes frantically to support the crumbling environment, and all because we waited too long!

To pursue this course is to invite the same ills that now plague the central urban areas—and incur the same debt for blight and redevelopment again and again. It is a challenge to invest in the future.

Laws to prevent the abusive use of land is one step. Common sense suggests another: the reservation of space for public use—plan today our program for tomorrow. We will not save by waiting; now is the time for decision. Now is the time, not later, to decide upon the orderly expansion of the urban pattern or abandon it to the termites of civic decay. If we intend to restore decency to the environment, now is the time to prepare.

The failure of inaction is written in the spectacle of present cities. The success of action is demonstrated in those rare instances when vision triumphed. What would Manhattan do without Central Park, Chicago without Lincoln Park, San Francisco without Golden Gate Park? In contrast, what a price the people have paid to "make" the land for Chicago's lake front, and the Moses parkways in New York! If ample space for public facilities is not reserved now, speculation will grip only more firmly—sink its roots deeper into the nourishment of urban expansion. To delay the day of reckoning will cost the future much too much.

Reservation of open space—"greenbelts" for recreation, broad thoroughfares, public services—is the least our urban program should include. It would make sense to plan regional park systems as permanent lungs and circulation to protect future expansion. It would make more sense for cities to acquire sections of outlying land as an antidote to the insidious effect of future speculative inflation.

There is need for civic enterprise to provide leadership for urban growth and development rather than remain forever a step behind. Our society requires such leadership— it represents the dominant will of the people. Civic enterprise is the joint participation of private and public initiative; it is neither one nor the other alone. The ultimate goal in our democracy—the general welfare—is approached when both act in unison. And it is then that profit becomes a healthy motive in our economic, social, and political system. This purpose can be well served by preventing urban ills from infecting new development while the cancer is being carved from the old city. Prevention will come by reservation of ample space before the cost renders adequate room too expensive.

THE HABIT OF CONGESTION

Congestion has a strong grip upon the megalopolitan city. Excess upon excess of people and buildings are heaped upon the land. Size is an accretion of ever-increasing population; people are piled in a pyramid expanding at the base in proportion to the accumulation at the center. The heavy burden of building bulk has created a Frankenstein of land values, and the result is a paradox.

The value of land is a product of its use. Presumably the use is designed as a service to people, and the value of the land is measured by the income derived from performing that service. When by increasing the intensity of land use, the income from it can be increased, the value of the land is likewise increased.

Following this logic with enthusiasm, city building proceeded according to the "highest and best use" to which urban land could be put. Absorbed with pursuit of this theory, attention to the basic concept that land value is derived from service to people shifted to the concept of land as a speculative commodity, and this is the status of urban land "economics" today.

It is not a new situation since exploitation of land has been common throughout history and its effect upon the development of cities has been one of degree, the extent to which urban growth in any period has been deominated by speculative excess or implemented by tempered investment. The novel character of this process today is the self-consuming nature of land economics. The upward spiral of value has created congestion and, seeking to maintain an economic balance, more congestion is the usual antidote. As a result, value is not measured in terms of service to people; on the contrary, the people are now obliged to adjust themselves to congestion in order to maintain land values.

This paradox is at the root of the urban problem, but it is being resolved. Decentralization is gnawing at the values in congested areas, even though the unplanned and disorderly process has the effect of shifting the disease about the urban anatomy rather than curing the malady.

Congestion is a habit hard to break and we see it illustrated in some of the most courageous efforts to release the city from its shackles. The remarkable program of highways directed by Robert Moses in New York City may be fairly compared with achievements of the Roman Empire or Baron Haussmann in Paris. Yet the administrative prowess and engineering skill it represents are unconsciously tangled in the web of congestion.

Struggling to escape from congestion, the smooth freeways loosen themselves from one complicated intersection only to find themselves caught in another. High land cost is a challenge to engineering ingenuity and the results are triumphs of technical skill but the capacity to build these structures is sometimes a delusion. The ready escape from congestion offered by the freeways is part of the formula for dissipation of excessive land values, but the highway design is threatened with early obsolescence when it is warped into complicated and extravagant intersections to avoid high land cost. Avoidance of high land cost is inadequate compensation if the civic improvement is a crippled rather than a permanent asset to the community. A full statement of the problem cannot omit the necessity for the most direct system of circulation integrated with redevelopment of congested areas.

24

Development Issues

Before any development can take place the developer must follow a number of steps. These include observing the provisions of the Comprehensive Plan as it affects the land being proposed for urbanization, the Zoning Ordinance and its many regulations, the subdivision laws of both the local community and the state, the Environmental Review Agency which will determine if the project impacts unfavorably on use of energy or endangered species, the building code and all of its many components and, if the site is near the coast, the critical eye of the Coastal Commissions, both local and state. Finally, citizens' committees, the environmental protection associations and others may be opposed to development on personal or philosophic grounds.

Having cleared all of the prerequisites to development, the developer is then faced with the costs that are related to the procedures and the improvements that are required. It is important to recognize that many of the costs now part of the developmental process are due to the past excesses in poor land development and the problems directly related to the former lack of regulation.

THE INFRASTRUCTURE

Before any property can be offered for sale, there must be a major investment in the infrastructure. The infrastructure includes all essential facilities such as water, sewers, streets and highways, public utilities, schools, libraries, parks, police and fire services and many other facilities related to the protection of the health, safety and general welfare. The installation of the various elements of the infrastructure involves both the public and private sectors identified with a proposed development.

350

The infrastructure must be in conformity with the Comprehensive Plan and all other regulations dealing with services to people. All must be related to the density of population proposed or the intensity of the commercial or industrial uses intended for the land.

Many of the elements of the infrastructure are installed prior to the occupancy of the sites. Others can follow when the need arises. Schools must be in place at the time the people and children are on the land. Water, sewers and other utilities must be available at the time the land is to be occupied. The utilities must be in the streets before paving is done. The timing and sequence of installing improvements must be carefully planned. They must be tied into existing lines with the capacity to accept the additional loading. Offsite connections may become a critical financial problem for the developer.

Funding Improvements. Improvements, as defined in most land subdivision programs, consists of the infrastructure required to serve the occupants of the land. All of these are usually required to be installed and paid for by the developer but like all other costs, they are passed on to the consumer. If the proposed development is detached from the already urbanized area, the "off-site" costs are also born by the developer, but as the in-between spaces are filled, the funds collected are returned to the initial activist. In many ways the return of the funds are clear profit since the total cost of the development has already been passed on to the occupants of the home, industrial, or commercial uses.

Beyond the base line items mentioned above, there are several other costs that enter into the development picture. Schools and parks are often assessed against the developer either in the form of demands for land or for in-lieu fees. This cost is, of course, related only to those facilities that serve the people who directly benefit from them. In California, after lengthy court actions where early efforts to secure neighborhood parks were declared illegal on the grounds that the State Subivision Law did not list them as improvements, the state law was thereafter amended to include parks. A formula was devised to require the subdivider of land to allocate either land or in-lieu fees. In addition, in 1977, the State recognized the overcrowded conditions in the local schools and adopted legislation to require the allocation of land or in-lieu fees to assist communities to secure temporary buildings and sites for school purposes.

Some of the fees assessed the subdivider are indicated in the fee chart. These are determined at each local level and relate to the costs of both material and manpower at a given time. The data are only illustrative of the impact that local government has in adopting requirements to assure the ultimate land user that he is not walking into an untenable situation insofar as future expenses are concerned. Often, later installations involve lengthy individual negotiations with a multitude of land occupants and a variety of economic situations. In many instances the "after occupancy" efforts to bring a development up to acceptable levels of urbanization result in failure and frustration. It is far better to have the improvements included in the original costs where the installations can be done on a mass basis and at much lower cost.

Typical Fees Related to Land Subdivisions

A. The following fee shall be paid to the Community and deposited into
    the general fund.

    1.   Tract No. — $3.00

B. The following fees shall be paid to the Planning Director and
    deposited into the general fund:

    1.   Tentative land division map, preliminary filing — $25.00

    2.   Tentative subdivision map, filing — $100.00 plus

    3.   Tentative statutory condominium subdivision map, filing — $100.00 plus
         $10.00 per gross acre.

    4.   Revised tentative subdivision map, filing — $50.00 plus
         $2.50 for any additional lot.

    5.   Revised statutory condominium subdivision map, filing — $50.00 plus
         $10.00 per additional gross acre.

    6.   Tentative parcel map, filing — $50.00 plus

    7.   Revised tentative parcel map, filing — $50.00 plus
         $2.50 for any additional parcel.

    8.   Tentative commercial or industrial parcel map, filing — $100.00 plus
         $2.50 per parcel.

    9.   Revised tentative commercial or industrial parcel map,
         filing — $50.00 plus
         $2.50 for any additional parcel.

    10. Land projects — $50.00
         in addition to the regular fee.

    11. Land division unit map, filing — $50.00

    12. Reversion to Acreage, filing — $100.00

    13. Certificate of Compliance, filing — $100.00

C. The following fee shall be paid to the Planning Director and depo-
    sited into the appropriate flood control fund or agency fund
    providing flood hazard reports.

    1.   Tentative land divisions map, filing — $100.00 plus
         $1.50 per lot or parcel.

    2.   Tentative statutory condominium subdivision map, filing — $100.00 plus
         $10.00 per gross acre.

3. Revised tentative land division map filing within one year of the
    date of approval —   No Fee

4. Revised tentative land division map filing after one year — $100.00 plus
    $1.50 per lot or parcel, except that for statutory condominium,
    the fee shall be $100.00 per gross acre.

D. The following fee shall be paid to the Planning Director and depo-
    sited into the appropriate road fund or gas tax fund.

    1.   Tentative land division map, filing — $30.00

E. The following fees shall be paid to the City and deposited into the
    appropriate road fund or gas tax fund:
    1.   Final subdivision map, filing — $100.00 plus
         $6.00 per lot.

    2.   Final parcel map, filing — $60.00 plus
         $7.50 per parcel.

    3.   Final statutory condominium subdivision map, filing — $100.00 plus
         $40.00 per gross acre.

    4. Plan checking and field inspection including survey monuments
        fee shall be 3 per cent of the total cost of improvements as
        estimated by the City Engineer and shall be paid as follows:

        a.   Filing of map for checking — $5.00 per lot

        b.   Planned residential development including statutory
             condominium — $ .25 per
                                                                   linear foot.

        c.   The remaining portion of the 3 per cent shall be paid prior to
             recording of the final map.

    5. Lot revision after checking — $6.00 per lot

    6. Reversion to acreage — $100.00

    7. Recordation of the final map — $5.00
        for the first sheet plus $2.00 for each sheet thereafter.

DEVELOPMENT COSTS

Aside from the costs related to the processing and installation of certain
improvements required by local law the developers are confronted with a
mulititude of direct costs. These include:

> The cost of the land
> The cost of the money with which to buy the land
> The cost the following additional improvements:
> > Planning and engineering
> > Grading of lots and the streets
> The cost of advertising and sales promotion.

In many cases the developers do not have funds to pay the cost of all of the improvements. They obtain bonds and pay the interest on these guarantees for the period between the requirement of the posting and the installation of the improvements. Where the project is large there may be several years between obtaining plan approval and obtaining the final occupancy permits for potential buyers. Some cities, where intensive building is encouraged, have eliminated the usual tax on property entirely. They have substituted a development tax on all new structures and through these funds have been able to provide the minimal services new development requires.

CAPITAL IMPROVEMENTS

The investment of public funds in the construction of community improvements is done through capital improvement programs. Each community anticipates its income over a period of years and prepares a budget for the accomplishment of certain essentials to the growth and prosperity of the area over which it has jurisdiction. The types of improvements may include expansion of a sewerage treatment plant, extension of trunk sewer or water lines, the development of new parks and recreational areas and many other projects of this type.

With the new growth management plans it is becoming easier to project future needs since they are under the control of the agencies responsible for implementing the capital improvements.

The location and nature of public improvements such as streets, public buildings, etc. are a major factor in determining environmental quality. Expenditures for these public improvements should be allocated in accordance with a planned program that balances needs and priorities against available resources and in accordance with the provisions of the Comprehensive Plan.

Capital Improvement Planning should not be limited only to those things that require funds from the city budget, since significant programs carried out by other levels of government can have a great effect on the timing, financing, and location of city projects.

PART 6

Slowly but surely humanity achieves what its wise men have dreamed.

—Anatole France

New Horizons

25

Regional Concepts

URBAN ECOLOGY

In the final decades of the twentieth century, complicated social, economic, and technological phenomena have extended the dimensions of urbanization beyond the concentration of traditional cities. It should be the objective of a civilized society to achieve a harmonious, attractive, convenient, and healthy living environment. The extent to which we meet this challenge will be the test of contemporary society. Thus far, the prospects are not encouraging. Creeping urbanization is engulfing entire regions, reducing the significance of political boundaries betweeen cities and counties to a shamble of legal technicalities.

The growing regional agglomerations along the north Atlantic and southern Pacific coasts are well known, and no viable mechanism of government has been devised to deal with these massive groupings of people and conflicting, overlapping public and private institutions. New public policies are required, fashioned at national and state levels of government, to direct the distribution of population, industry, transportation, and the conservation of resources essential to sustain the structure of the national economy. An ecology of natural and human resources is linked inextricably with the ecology of urban resources in the industrial age.

REGIONALISM IN PLANNING

In the latter days of the National Resources Planning Board a study of regional planning was prepared and a voluminous report was submitted to the President and Congress. The report listed a great number of different regions, each defined for the special purposes that it served. The Army divided the nation into its own form of regions, the Federal Reserve created others and so on.

The one great regional planning effort supported by the President and Congress was the TVA. This project achieved the goals that had been set for it including flood control and the development of electric power in an area badly needing it. At about the same time the Port of New York Authority was created.

REGIONAL PLANNING IN ANCIENT TIMES

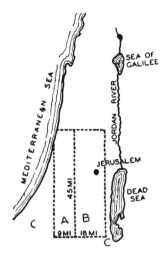

A Lands for City People

B Lands for Priests

C Lands for Princes

While in captivity in the sixth century B.C., *the Israelites planned their return to Jerusalem and Ezekiel described in his book (Ezekiel 25:45) the plans desired by God for the allocation and use of the land upon their return. Within their land, from Dan to Beersheba, an area of 10,000 by 25,000 reeds (18 by 45 miles) was to be set aside for the priesthood and within it was to be the sanctuary of worship. An area of 5,000 by 25,000 reeds (9 by 45 miles) was to be set aside for the people of the city. The land on both sides of these areas was reserved as princely lands.*

There was no indication of the precise location of the boundaries and it is probable that Ezekiel understood God's wishes were directed more to the area of land needed for the production and distribution of abundant goods than the exact location surrounding the city of Jerusalem. Perhaps the amount of land allocated to production for the people of the city was less than that for the priests since Jerusalem was a crossroads for trade routes and the people derived considerable wealth from the resulting commercial enterprise in which they were engaged. The princely lands supported the kings who maintained residences on the Mediterranean and the Dead Sea as well as Jerusalem.

Like TVA, its activity has affected several states. Its function has been to promote commerce and transportation in the New York Metropolitan area.

A more limited example of regional planning is the Los Angeles County Regional Planning Commission. Created in 1923, it was initially charged with drawing up a master plan for Los Angeles County. The commission's main objective was to develop a network of major and secondary highways.

Regional planning offers a marked advantage for contiguous areas sharing common interests. Such matters as air pollution, unified circulation systems, water distribution, sewerage and solid waste disposal cannot be regulated by an individual community. An overriding authority with the power to enforce decrees is needed to deal with these problems.

WHY SO LITTLE REGIONAL PLANNING?

The main reason why so little regional planning has been done is that local political entities fear a loss of their power. Another reason is that a regional agency, if it is to have real authority, must have the power to tax. This alone is enough to frighten local communities into opposition. One more taxing body, one more layer of government seems to add up to additional expenses for a superflous governmental body.

In the early 1970's the state of California, tried to establish regional planning districts. Meetings were held in various areas of the state to determine the districts that had common economic, social, and cultural interests. The result was that the local communities resented the initiative that had been taken by the state; as a result the project ended in a fiasco.

Professor John Friedman, in his treatise "The Concept of a Planning Region" States:

> Regional Planning in the United States has at various times had reference to different types of activity as well as to different types of area. There was a time, roughly 1933 until the end of World War II, when regional planning meant primarily the development of water resources and the adjacent land resources within a given river basin. The basic planning unit was the watershed and the objective, the fullest possible use of all physical resources for the improvement of living levels within the area. The Tennessee Valley Authority has been the outstanding example of this type of planning, but a number of other river basins have followed suit; the Columbia; the Central Valley of California; the Missouri; the Arkansas, and the Red River. The TVA however, remains the only authority in full charge of a comprehensive development program.[1]

During the past few years there has been created, in almost every state, one or more coordinating agencies concerned with aspects of regional planning. These Councils of Governments are usually voluntary associations with little or no power other than to make an effort at coordination of the individual planning going on in the various member communities. They perform A95 reviews for projects seeking Federal assistance.

THE CITY AND THE REGION

Cities are the focal points of intensive economic development within most regions. They are intimately related to the hinterland from which the raw materials are imported. They are also, to a large extent, the purchasers of the finished products. No effective planning can be done without a deep concern for the interrelationships that must be protected and conserved. There can be no waste of resources, either land, water or energy in this partnership without the community structure becoming unbalanced and uneconomic. The social consequences result in both areas losing their viability. Sound planning must take into consideration the total environment that makes the city function as the core for the total economic structure.

Recent efforts at metropolitan area planning takes into account the importance of concern for both the urbanized core and the surrounding areas which in some instances are called the "areas of influence." However, it is important to

---

[1] *Regional Development and Planning,* ed. John Friedman and William Alonzo, M.I.T. Press, 1964.

realize that in most cases the power to control the development of areas surrounding a city lies with the county government.

STATE PLANNING

Despite the inability of independent city jurisdictions to cope with air contamination, transportation, sanitation and water supply, the theory of "local control" is retained with fanatical fervor. The rule of "divide and conquer" breeds intense rivalry between cities and counties for economic advantage. Competition to capture the maximum tax-productive enterprise justifies irrational land uses, induces the relaxation of development standards to attract business and industry, and favors local politicians bent on perverting the public interest to the benefit of special interests. National planning is needed for the conservation of natural resources, the designation of areas in which new urbanization would be compatible with related land uses, new industrial and energy development, and transportation by land and air.

With the possibility for a population increase of 60,000,000 in the United States by 2000 A.D., urban centers will have to accommodate nearly 40,000,000 more people than now occupy the nation's cities, or the equivalent of 40 new cities of 1,000,000. New forms of urban development will be needed.

Land use planning at state and national levels of government is either faltering or non-existent. A galaxy of "regulating agencies" struggle within limited and often competing jurisdictions. The annual cost (1972) of preparing Environmental Impact Statements by only three of the Federal agencies was $16,000,000 and countless man hours, with few, if any, national policies by which to measure the validity of these studies.[2]

Planning is a costly undertaking, but consolidation of the fragmented budgets for administration of public resources would provide a tidy sum with which to launch a comprehensive national planning program. It will call for a national commitment to the public interest unprecedented in the nation's history. Some measure of the gap between necessity and realization has been illustrated by the fate of Federal Land Use Planning legislation[3] in the Congress. After strong support by environmentalists, state governors, and the House Committee on the Interior, as late as 1974 the legislation was sidetracked by adverse political manipulation, in what the *New York Times* referred to as "a perversion of the democratic process" on a "question of immense national importance."

National planning will require implementation by the individual states, and state plans are slow to emerge. Hawaii is the first state with such a plan.

---

[2] Estimated cost for Environmental Impact Statements by the Atomic Energy Commission was $6,000,000; Department of Agriculture, $2,000,000; Department of the Interior, $8,000,000. *Traffic Quarterly*, Eno Foundation, January, 1974.
    [3] H.R. 10294.

Planning was initiated in Hawaii with creation of a Planning Commission for Honolulu in 1915, and a zoning law was initiated in 1922. A Territorial Planning Agency, established in the late thirties, became the State Planning Office when Hawaii became a state in 1957. The State Land Use Law of 1961 defined three basic land use zones for all land in the state: urban, agricultural, and conservation. Regulation of land uses within designated urban zones is administered by the county governments, which also maintain a measure of control within agricultural districts. The conservation zone is administered by the state. Zonal boundaries are defined by a State Land Use Commission.

Both planning and land use zoning are aided by several unique advantages. Overlapping governmental jurisdictions are absent. Each island, with a small number of exceptions, is a county, and each county is surrounded by the permanent "Blue Belt" of the Pacific Ocean. Each has a city-type government and there are no independently incorporated cities. Authority for property assessment and taxation is vested in the state govenment, and taxes are assessed in accordance with land use zoning. The Director of the State Planning and Economic Development is a member of the governor's cabinet.

In this idyllic setting, however, the people of the island paradise display characteristics similar to those of citizens elsewhere in the nation. Shortly after adoption of the zoning districts, a fourth zone, rural, was incorporated by the legislature. Within this zone the provision for one-half acre lots allows for land exploitation, which the legislation was intended to curb. The rural district was omitted from Oahu, where the declining role of agriculture in the economy leads to the pressure for urbanization of agricultural land, a trend progressing at such a rate that urbanization of the entire island seems imminent.

There is little contemporary evidence that urbanization in Hawaii will be more humane than elsewhere. There have been urban slums in Honolulu for generations, although a benign climate somewhat tempers the harshness of typical ghettos. It is apparent that the tradition of plantation "villages" has been foresaken for suburban sprawl, as in other American cities, and the same brutalism is present in the proliferation of ever-taller commercial and residential structures.

The natural beauty of Hawaii has been impaired in the course of accommodating tourists, attracted by climate, tropical character, traditions, and racial blend of the islands. It is not, however, the welcome to brief visitors which presents the major threat. It is the insidious trend toward exploitation of a lovely land for an unlimited increase in permanent population which will inevitably compound the burden of economic support from sources beyond the island shores. How this strong temptation will be controlled is the pressing issue for state and county leadership. In the words of Robert Wenkam, stalwart conservationist; "Tread gently. These are the only Hawaiian Islands we have."[4]

Issues which prompted state planning in Hawaii are even more critical in states on the mainland. The tangled political boundaries between counties and

[4] Robert Wenkam, *Hawaii,* Rand McNally & Company, Chicago, 1972.

cities, the desperate competition for tax-productive enterprise, and the rivalry between cities to outstrip their neighbors in population statistics, present formidable obstacles to the prospects for rational and essential planning at state and Federal levels of government. Yet these same obstacles render the need for planning even more urgent. State planning and broad classifications of land use zoning are as essential to administration of the public business as the General Plan and detailed zoning ordinances are at the city and county levels of government.

The annual flood of 300,000 new residents and the 57,000 acres of land converted to urbanization in Florida demands not only measures like the Environmental Land and Water Act, the Water Management Act, and the Land Conservation and Comprehensive Planning Act that the State adopted in 1972; there must be a comprehensive State Land Use and Zoning Plan as the basic reference for administration of the state agencies and county or regional authorities. Without such a definition of land use zoning, the ambitious program to evaluate "Developments of Regional Impact" can only drift ineffectually.[5]

Thwarted by political ineptitude, and a State Planning Department *with no plan*,[6] a group of enlightened California citizens[7] determined to construct a framework for comprehensive planning for the state. Taking into account all aspects of the state's economy, its social structure, and its physical characteristics, the "California Tomorrow Plan"[8] is a guide to state planning. Adopting land use categories similar to Hawaii's, the Plan divides the state into four zones: urban, agriculture, conservation, and regional reserves, administered by regional government authorities.

In states where urbanization and industrial concentration infringe heavily upon land resources, state zoning and national policies (planning) for industrial allocation and population distribution are imperative. Yet conservation of agriculture, timber, water, and mineral resources is equally vital in the states which thus far have been saved from excess urbanization. The "energy crisis" of the early seventies emphasizes the urgency of this problem.

The necessity for both Federal and state financial assistance to support urban functions amply demonstrates that cities and counties cannot "go it alone," however attractive the concept of local autonomy may be. Thus far, most states rely on reviews by state agencies or on the preparation of Environmental Impact Statements for approval of various types of development in designated "critical areas." The inevitable increase in population can only

---

[5] "Developments of Regional Impact" are equivalent to "environmental Impact Statements" and are administered under the Comprehensive Planning Act.

[6] Alfred Heller observed that after ten years and an expenditure of $4,000,000, the State Development Plan Program simply recommended further studies. (Speech at National Forum on Growth With Environmental Quality, Tulsa, Okla., September 25, 1973.)

[7] Alfred Heller of San Francisco was President of "California Tomorrow" until September, 1974.

[8] *The California Tomorrow Plan,* published by William Kaufman, Los Altos, California, 1972.

compound both the number and extent of so-called "critical areas." It would demonstrate appropriate public responsibility to establish land use zoning regulations both to preserve state resources and to set parameters for economic and urban development. Meanwhile, city and county governments struggle at the administrative level and in the courts to maintain some semblance of environmental equilibrium.

Acknowledging the limitations of independent cities in attempting to cope with the full range of urban ills, some forms of regional authorities have already been created. The San Francisco Bay Conservation and Development Commission was created by the State of California in 1965. The Miami Valley Regional Planning Commission has jurisdiction within the metropolitan area around Dayton, Ohio, and the Twin Cities Metropolitan Council encompasses

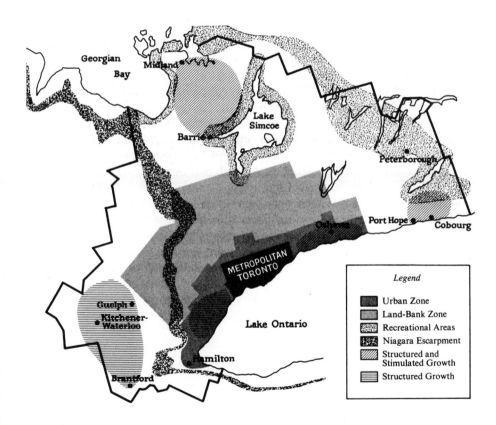

Legend

- Urban Zone
- Land-Bank Zone
- Recreational Areas
- Niagara Escarpment
- Structured and Stimulated Growth
- Structured Growth

A DEVELOPMENT CONCEPT FOR THE TORONTO-CENTERED REGION

In 1965 the provincial government of Ontario initiated a program for regional planning and development, centered about the city of Toronto. The program was under the direction of Dr. Richard S. Thoman between 1967 and 1971. (Map from Richard Thoman, "A Checklist for California," Cry California, Fall 1974, California Tomorrow.)

Minneapolis and St. Paul, Minnesota. The Hackensack Meadowlands Development Commission includes fourteen cities and two counties in New Jersey. Dade County, in Florida, which has jurisdiction over all local communities, is considered a highly effective Regional Government. Councils of Government (C.O.G.) with limited powers have been created in some areas to conform with Federal requirements for a regional clearing house for programs involving Federal grants.

Acquisition of land within and around cities has been a policy and practice in a number of European countries since the turn of the century. The policy has been implemented in Sweden since 1904; some 200 square miles are now owned by the City of Stockholm, a program which made possible the new towns of Farsta and Vallingby. The development of "land banks" in the United States has been confined to New York, Louisiana and Puerto Rico. The appropriate responsibility for stewardship of the land has been generally abdicated in favor of private interests in land ownership and development. Partially filling the vacuum, nonprofit "trusts" are acquiring or leasing land to remain as open space. The Nature Conservancy preserved some 377,000 acres in various parts of the country, holding the land until public agencies are financially able to acquire it. The Trust for Public Land (TPL) is directly concerned with preservation of a 672 acre ranch for the City of Los Angeles.

It is a gross irony that state legislatures require cities and counties to make plans and enact zoning ordinances in conformance with them, yet reject their own responsibility to create plans and land use zoning for the states. The situation is further aggravated in states which require local communities to plan for open space and conservation and, in the absence of funds for the necessary land acquisition, communities are confronted with threats of "inverse condemnation" suits as a result of conforming with state laws.

26

The New Towns

Problems of the urban community multiply with the increasing complexity of our age. The physical expansion of cities is running out of control, and the economic and social consequences command the attention of civic leadership in government, business, and industry. The practical limitation of the pyramidal form of the city has forced decentralization. As people, buildings, and traffic pile higher the upper crust slides down the sides and outward to the suburbs.

When the weight of congestion at the core becomes unbearable, the inner layers slip out from under. This process has not been accompanied by rational planning to forestall the inevitable economic and social disorder.

An appropriate form for the future city has not yet emerged, but serious attention has been directed to the nature of the modern city in two major areas: the internal urban structure—redevelopment—and planned decentralization—the New Towns. The results have not been conclusive in either of these areas, but our present consideration of the New Towns may serve as important experience in shaping our vision of the city of tomorrow.

TWENTIETH-CENTURY CITIES—PRELUDE TO TWENTY-ONE

The cities of the twentieth century inherited the buildings, streets and ownerships of past centuries. The cities' leaders made little effort to have the new or expanded areas of the older cities respond to the life style of the new age or the needs of the tremendous increases in urban population. Overcrowding has occurred everywhere in the world as people leave the rural areas for the imagined more affluent and interesting life of the big cities.

Current Trends in Urbanization. Two diverse trends can be observed in the current urbanization process. On the one hand, the urban areas are growing into gigantic hedropolises—many-headed metropolitan elements welded physically but not politically into one great expanse. On the other hand, people are becoming more disunited, uniting usually only as the result of a common problem. This can be exemplified by megapolitan cities on the coasts of America and by the fragmentation of people into tiny defensive cells until an issue such as the bussing of school children causes them to get together for momentary unity in protest.

NEW TOWNS—U.S.A.

Creating facilities to accommodate 40,000,000 more urban inhabitants in the United States by the turn of the century cannot be left to chance. Cities will require massive rehabilitation, regrouping of densities, allocation of open space, and effective mass transportation. Left to speculation and exploitation by free enterprise, suburbanization outside corporate city limits seriously impairs the economic viability of the cities. Decentralization in Europe, notably around London and Stockholm has been planned by the government authorities to distribute the population, industry, and commerce in satellite towns. As socially responsible attitudes develop in the United States, large American cities will collaborate with county or regional authorities for an orderly decentralization of population and industrial and commercial enterprises to satellite communities withing their sphere of influence.

Big cities are swollen and decaying. They can only accommodate substantially more people through planned decentralization. It is the responsibility of the separate states to establish policies for growth and urbanization. Some states can accept more population only to their own detriment, economically, socially, physically. Florida is already suffering. Oregon chooses not to grow in population. Each state has to consider its particular attributes in its plans and land use regulations. Responsibility devolves upon the Federal government to harmonize state policies with the national imperative. There is much land, and though it is perhaps underdeveloped, it is precious.

A "New Cities" program, comparable to the British New Towns or Swedish satellites, may be implemented in the United States, though no such program has yet been initiated. The equivalent of British public development corporations will conflct with the ingrained assumption in America that the public role shall be subordinate to the role of free enterprise, which is necessarily contingent upon the degree to which financial profit is assured. Free enterprise has thus far been primarily engaged in existing cities and in urban expansion where a full range of public facilities and services are available.

In his review of the New Communities Act of 1968, the veteran British New Town proponent Sir Frederic J. Osborn anticipated the administrative problems "of a Federal department without town-funding experience confronting developers necessarily concerned for profitability but themselves not having staffs adapted to building complete towns, and local municipalities accustomed only to providing public services for adventitious growth rather than cooperating in town design. Some think that good new-town creation is only possible if a public body comparable with our development corporation is entrusted with the landownership and groundwork, leaving the provision of building mainly to commercial developers. They are probably right."[1]

The record of large land development companies across the nation does not bode well for their effectiveness in town building. From Cape Coral and Palm Coast in Florida to Adirondack Park in Pennsylvania, Treasure Lake in Georgia to Colonias de Santa Fe in New Mexico, Lake Winnebago near Kansas City to Lake Tahoe in California, the consuming objective has been the rapid sale of land, not the building of cities. "Decisions about where millions of Americans should be encouraged to migrate are left to land speculators while the National, State and Local Goverments give up by default the right of the public to say what land use or growth policy should be."[2]

Time is growing short. As the population grows, vigorous redevelopment of existing cities can upgrade the environment and accommodate more people. Based upon the assumption that "most of America's expected growth from now until the end of the century will occur within existing metropolitan areas,"[3] National Task Force of the American Institute of Architects[4] recommended that future urban growth should proceed in neighborhood increments identified as "Growth Units." The estimated increase in national urban population during that period, however, can hardly be absorbed in existing metropolitan areas without a massive multiplicity of such "Growth Units."

Exploitation of desirable open space proceeds in the guise of "new towns," although most serve as expansion of suburbs for discontented refugees who can afford to escape from the city or own a second home. The growth of suburbia is not confined to ticky-tack subdivisions for the middle class. Wealthier citizens are in the market for fine, well-planned and expensive communities with a full complement of commercial and recreational enterprise.[5] These are not independent new towns, however, and the economic and social stratification increases pressures upon low income families, ethnic minorities, and the elderly.

The Urban Land Institute defines a "new town" as a "land development project having acreage sufficiently large to encompass land use elements of residence, business, and industry which, when built, provide opportunities for (a)

[1] "Planning Commentary—USA On the Way to New Town" *Town and Country Planning,* October-November, 1968.

[2] Robert Cahn, "Land in Jeopardy," seven articles in *The Christian Science Monitor,* January 17 through January 24, 1973. Reprinted by permission from *The Christian Science Monitor.* ©1972 The Christian Science Publishing Society. All rights reserved.

[3] American Institute of Architects, *A Plan for Urban Growth: Report of the National Policy Task Force,* January, 1972, Page 3. Item G.

[4] American Institute of Architects, National Task Force: *Strategy for Building a Better America,* December 1971; *Report of Constraints Conference,* May 1972; *Structure for a National Policy,* October 1973.

[5] Florida is "blessed" with such high class developments, like North Palm Beach, and California has its share; Rancho San Bernardo and Laguna California in San Diego County, Laguna Niguel in Orange County, Conejo Village in Ventura County, Valencia and Westlake Village in Los Angeles County are examples.

living and working within the community; (b) a full spectrum of housing types and price ranges; (c) permanent open space in passive and active recreation areas with sufficient land on the periphery to protect the indentity; (d) strong esthetic controls.[6]

Planning new towns is certainly not a novel activity for Americans. Williamsburg was a new town in 1633, New Amsterdam (New York) in 1660, Philadelphia in 1682, Savannah in 1733, Washington in 1791 and Chicago as late as 1833. The "company town" of the nineteenth century was notorious, such as the town of Pullman, built near Chicago in 1881 for the Pullman Car Company. Many large and fine residential communities were developed near large cities early in the twentieth century and independent new towns were promoted to serve major industrial enterprises—Gary, Indiana (1906), Kingsport, Tennessee (1910), Kohler, Wisconsin (1913), Tyrone, New Mexico (1915) and Longview, Washington (1923), among them. Radburn, New Jersey begun in 1928 as the "New Town of the Motor Age," will be remembered for the greenbelts circulating through the community. The Resettlement Administration Communities of Greenbelt, Maryland; Greendale, Wisconsin; and Greenhills, Ohio in the thirties were planned after the Radburn prototype.

An ambitious program for the new "city" of Irvine was incorporated in 1972 on a huge singly owned ranch in southern California. With a new campus for the University of California, an airport, and large industrial park, the new city emerges as a series of planned real estate developments in a street system for automobiles. Although elaborately planned for a population of nearly 500,000, the community depends upon neighboring cities for most urban facilities and services.

Begun in the early sixties, the new towns of Reston, Virginia (planned for an ultimate population of 75,000) near Washington, D.C. and Columbia, Maryland (planned for an ultimate population of 100,000) between Baltimore and Washington, are well planned privately financed communities. Although some industrial-research development is anticipated in both, the principal economic base is the nearby Federal government. Robert Simon, developer of Reston, proposes a new town to be called Riverton, near Rochester, New York, while Philip Klutznick, developer of Park Forest, Illinois, near Chicago, proposes a new town of 50,000 near Aurora, some 34 miles from Chicago.

In Europe new towns are public ventures of a high order. A city is a political entity of citizens; it is not a private domain, a corporate "company" town. Although the city in the United States is, for many, a "fat calf" to be exploited for private gain, accommodation of the growing population will require aggressive public initiative, implemented by the equivalent of the British development corporation, to administer public funds for initial investment in land and public facilities. New York set a precedent with the creation of the State Urban Development Corporation in 1968. With some tax support from the state, the Corporation is empowered to issue tax-exempt bonds as its major source of

---

[6] The *Community Builders Handbook,* The Urban Land Institute, Washington, D.C., 1968.

Lake Anne Village Center　　　　　　Courtesy Gulf Reston, Inc.

Aerial view of Reston's first village center, Lake Anne—designed by architects Conklin & Rossant—showing 15-story Heron House apartments; J-shaped Washington Plaza shopping area; 30-acre Lake Anne, with townhouse clusters, single-family detached and patio homes, rental and condominium garden apartments around the lake.

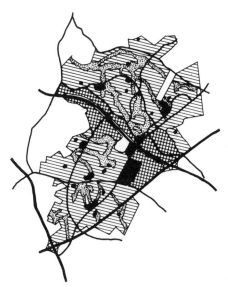

RESTON, VIRGINIA

Master Plan

Hatch areas indicate residential, which includes low, medium, and high density mixtures; crosshatch includes industrial and "advanced educational" uses; solid areas denote commercial centers. Round dots are elementary schools; square dots, high schools. The dotted areas indicate internal recreational space, lakes, and ponds; no permanent surrounding open space is planned.

funds. Its function is to initiate needed public facilities with emphasis upon housing for low income families. With power of eminent domain and deviation from local codes and zoning ordinances where necessary, the corporation uses private capital in its developments. A major project is Roosevelt Island, with Federal assistance under the Communities Development Act.

Alert to the need for new urban communities as the population increases in the United States, competent and experienced developers recognize the necessity for public participation in new town building to achieve the full range of housing and urban facilities. "There is absolutely no means whatsoever by which the home-building industry, as it is now constituted in America, can develop the sensibly organized new communities that America needs to accommodate its future growth," said James Rouse, developer of Columbia. "The country needs to enlarge the application of the process by which Columbia was built. It cannot afford to rely on the capacity or the whim of the private developer alone."[7] Philip Klutznick observed the need for public assistance to meet the housing needs for all income groups, as well as basic facilities, and Emmanuel Cartsonis, Director of Planning and Design of Litchfield Park near Phoenix Arizona,[8] asserted the need for Federal assistance in site acquisition and low-interest financing.[9]

NEW TOWNS INTOWN

Dr. Harvey S. Perloff, Dean of the School of Architecture and Urban Planning at the University of California at Los Angeles, developed the concept of the New Town Intown and presented his vision in an article published in the AIP Journal, May 1966. The following excerpt indicated the premises upon which his ideas are based:

> The heart of the new town idea is the creation of an urban community conceived as an integrated and harmonious whole. Starting from scratch in an open area, the new town can provide the most modern of facilities, whether schools, shopping or parking. The ability to develop through an overall plan makes possible community amenities and aesthetic qualities normally not realized. Because people today have both rising income and expanding leisure time, recreation receives an important role in the new town plan. (Reston, Virginia, for example, has made a golf course, an artifical lake, riding stables and bridle paths, and other recreational facilities the very backbone of the community.) The more advanced new town makes an effort to provide a balance between workplaces and homes. It has a distinctive center with important functional and visual purposes. High-rise

---

[7] James Rouse, *Taming Metropolis: How to Manage an Urbanized World,* Doubleday & Company, Inc., Anchor Books, New York, 1967.

[8] For Goodyear Tire and Rubber Company.

[9] Shirley Weiss, *New Town Development in the U.S.,* New Towns Reseach, Center for Urban and Regional Studies, University of North Carolina Press, Chapel Hill, March, 1973.

apartments as well as low-lying buildings and individual homes help to provide variety as well as a superior design for living.

With adequate imagination and purpose, the essence of all this can be applied to the older parts of the metropolis. Since replanning is much more difficult than starting from scratch, it will require particularly good planning — aimed at the same goals of harmony and balance. It will normally require some strategic rebuilding as well as rehabilitation for continuous improvement according to a plan. An essential element would be a working partnership in planned urban development between the people of the area, a variety of public agencies, and private enterprise. The aim should not be to create communities that are all alike; each should have its own special character, its own focal points, it own attractions.

The New Town Intown concept can greatly help in transforming the physical environment of the city in keeping with social objectives and human resources needs. It cannot *solve* the human *problems* of the city, nor even all the physical problems. It can provide a valuable lever for both. If we hope to achieve the objectives of the antipoverty and other social programs, it will be necessary, among other things, to transform the total environment of poverty — the physical aspects as well as the social, economic, and political. It is important to create an environment in which the community as well as the individual family are important.

The concept of the "New Town Intown" involves large-scale rehabilitation, modernization, and redevelopment of the core of the city. It is proposed that the functions of the area be changed to make for a viable living environment that will be attractive and safe for persons of all ages who like to be in the heart of a city where activities are both interesting and exciting. The concept involves recognition that the central city areas are too important to discard. The changes called for will take time and monumental efforts on the part of both government and the private sector to complete. To reconstitute the central core as a total living environment is a challenging idea. To make it an economically sound as well as socially desirable part of the total city is imperative. In this approach, the old format for the area must be abandoned. Vehicular traffic must be reduced or confined to special locations, the concentration of pollutants must be eliminated, the streets must be lighted and protected against vandalism and crime.

Presently, plans are being developed for the rehabilitation of buildings that have been vacated by their former occupants. These buildings, like the warehouses in the "SoHo" artist district of New York City, can be converted to special uses bringing people with like interests together. The effect of this rehabilitation is to bring economic stability into areas on the verge of collapse.

As a means of coping with the tremendous urban dilemma, the Urban Growth and Community Development Act of 1970 provided Federal financial aid for the "New Towns Intown" program. Intended to recover a human scale through comprehensive redevelopment of large cities, it provides more flexibility than was embodied in previous redevelopment "projects." The Housing and Urban Development Agency requires that a site be a minimum of 100 acres and wholesale condemnation is not necessary to assemble an acceptable site. A full range of urban facilities and social amenities may be incorporated to achieve an

New York State Urban Development Corporation

NEW TOWN INTOWN, Roosevelt Island,
New York City
New York State Urban Development Corporation

A 150 acre site development for 25 percent housing, 16 percent commercial/industrial, 44 percent open space and public use, 15 percent circulation. Of 5,000 dwellings units, 30 percent are planned for low income 25 percent for moderate income, 45 percent unsubsidized.

effective *community*. Cedar-Riverside in Minneapolis is the first development to be undertaken; Roosevelt Island in New York is the second.

Plans for sweeping redevelopment should open avenues to the essential restructuring of the urban form, to phase out strip commercial zoning and substitute genuine commercial *centers*, and to readjust land uses to a system of mass transportation without which large cities will continue to strangle themselves in an endless network of streets, highways, and parking facilities. It will take time, in some cities a desperately long time, to achieve the transformation. But it has taken a long and dreary time for cities to reach the current stalemate and it should be worth the time to recover from the *malaise*. It is the public's responsibility to replan cities for the integration of renewal through redevelopment programs, and a combined public and private responsibility to assure that each new development will serve that purpose.

BRITISH PLANNING POLICY

Throughout the nineteenth century the British were stirred by the woeful impact of the industrial revolution on the living environment. Improvement in housing conditions was the center of concern and action. In 1909 there began a series of legislative steps up the ladder of urban planning. It was a cogent, complete experience in the search for a physical structure to accommodate the people and the functions of urbanization. The Housing and Town Planning Act of 1909 granted powers to local authorities to prepare plans for their respective jurisdictions. To encourge building after World War I the Housing and Town Planning Acts of 1919 for both England and Scotland introduced the policy of joint planning action among several local authorities and in 1923 the Act empowered the local authorities to plan for built-up as well as undeveloped areas. In 1925, for the first time the planning functions were separated from the field of housing alone. The Town and Country Planning Acts of 1932 for England, Wales, and Scotland extended the responsibility of local authorities to both urban and rural land, and included the preservation of historic buildings and the natural landscape. The powers under this Act were only permissive, and they were conferred on all local authorities. As a consequence, the local authorities were subject to excessive compensation for any claims which might result from the exercise of their powers. These Acts, however, provided the basic framework in Great Britain for the following 15 years, with the addition of the Ribbon Development Act of 1935 that regulated the space along the highways.

In 1937 a Royal Commission was established under the chairmanship of Sir Montague Barlow to inquire into the distribution of industrial population and the social, economic, and strategic disadvantages arising from the concentration of industry and working people in large built-up communities. The Commission report, published in 1940, contained recommendations for redevelopment of congested areas, the dispersal of population from such areas, the creation of balanced industrial employment throughout Great Britain, and the establishment of a national authority to deal with these matters.

In 1941 two new committees were created to study the recommendations of the Barlow report—the Scott Committe on Land Utilization in Rural Areas and the Uthwatt Committee on Compensation and Betterment. From these committees came recommendations for the creation of a central planning authority, measures to insure state control of development, increased powers of local planning authorities for compulsory purchase (eminent domain), and major revisions in the laws on compensation and betterment.

The Scott and Uthwatt Committee reports led to the adoption of a new series of Town Planning Acts. The first, in 1943, created a new office of Minister of Town and Country Planning for England, Wales and Scotland, and strengthened the powers of local authorities to control development. The Town and Country Planning Act of 1944 for England and the 1945 Act for Scotland gave local authorities power to enforce comprehensive redevelopment of obsolete and war-damaged areas, and implemented the acquisition of land for both open space and a balanced arrangement of land uses. These Acts culminated in the Town and Country Planning Act of 1947 for England and Wales and a counterpart for Scotland. The principal features of this Act were (a) to establish a framework of land use throughout the country based upon development plans by local authorities, approved by the Minister of Town and Country Planning (now the Minister of Housing and Local Government) or the Secretary of State for Scotland; (b) to control all development by making it subject to permission from the local planning authorities; (c) to extend to local authorities all necessary powers to acquire land for planning or development and provide for grants from the central government for these purposes; and (d) to assure the preservation of buildings of historic interest and the natural character of the landscape. In contrast to prior legislation, this Act conferred these powers upon only 188 local authorities in the large cities and county boroughs and rendered their exercise mandatory rather than permisssive.

COMPENSATION AND BETTERMENT

During the past hundred years the policy of "compensation and betterment" became an accepted procedure in the regulation of land use in Great Britain. The principle that the use of private property is subject to regulation for the community welfare was implemented by the dual provision that just compensation is due to private owners for restrictions by public authorities which impair the value of land, whereas the enhancement of property values which accrue through public planning decisions may be assessed by the local authorities. In the administration of this policy it was assumed that the public funds expended for compensation to property owners would be balanced by the assessments for the betterments which resulted from land use regulations. The administration of this policy, however, became unduly complicated. Assessments for betterments for improved values were awkward to determine and almost impossible to collect. As a consequence, local authorities had inadequate resources upon which to draw to fulfill their obligations for payment of compensation.

A major task of the Uthwatt Committe was the investigation of this entire policy and recommendations for improvement in its administration. Based upon the report of the Committee, the 1947 Act introduced a comprehensive modification in land policy with the provision that the state shall reserve all rights to the *development* of land.[10] This sweeping revision followed the principle of compensation and betterment but was intended to remove the involved processes in the collection of betterments and the determination of appropriate compensation. The government was empowered to expropriate all "development rights" in the land. Owners of property approved for development at the time the legislation was enacted were entitled to compensation for the loss

---

[10] Beverley J. Pooley, *The Evolution of British Planning Legislation,* University of Michigan Law School, Ann Arbor, Mich., 1960.

of these rights at land values prevailing in 1947. A Central Land Board was appointed to administer these negotiations and a fund of 300 million pounds was set aside by the national government for this purpose. As permission was subsequently granted by local planning authorities to develop property, the land owners were required to pay a "development charge" to the government. This charge was in the amount of the difference between the value of the land for the existing use and the land value for the new development approved by the planning authority. Since, under the Act, owners who had suffered loss through expropriation of "development rights" were to have been compensated for this loss, all land owners were subsequently liable for the "development charge." A permitted use which resulted in a lesser land value entitled the owner to compensation for the difference, whereas a permitted use which would support a land value greater than the existing use entitled the government to "charge" the owner for this difference.

Perhaps this remarkable land policy could have been developed only through a coalition government such as that under Winston Churchill as prime minister. The Committee which recommended it included conservative members with a sound knowledge of British tradition and the problems of land development. The chairman, Honorable Augustus Uthwatt, was a Lord Judge of Appeal, a high rank in the public affairs of England. But opposition to the entire procedure formed soon after passage of the Act. The growing resistance generated misunderstanding about the purpose of the Act and its administration became increasingly cumbersome. In 1951 a Conservative government came into power and, in the Act of 1953, abolished this feature. Permission to develop land was still required, but land owners were thereafter free to realize the values on the open market. The long tradition embraced in the principle of compensation and betterment as a basic policy for the equitable regulation of land in the implementation of the planning process was ended.

The administration of planning in England has been vested in the public authorities of large localities, the county and borough councils. Contrary to the practice in the United States, zoning as a means to regulate land use has not prevailed. Local planning authorities are required to prepare a 20-year development plan, approval of which is required by the government. This plan is reviewed every five years and has the statutory effect of establishing the land use policy by which the authorities are guided in granting permission for development. The power to grant permission is the vehicle for the control of development within the policy set forth in the plan, and this procedure has been retained for the purpose of maintaining flexibility to meet changing conditions. Although the enlightened land ownership policy embraced in the Act of 1947 is absent and the British experience demonstrated the difficulties in its administration, the tradition of responsibility by public authorities in Great Britain may yet offer the prospect for favorable land development in that country. There are planning authorities who believe these difficulties might have been materially altered if the land owners had shared in the increment of increased property value by a "development charge" fixed at a lower level, such as 75 per cent of the difference in value.

This issue will undoubtedly remain alive. It revolves about the relation between the necessary public control of land use and the element of monopoly which such control vests in land values. Any form of public control over land use, whether it may be permission for development from planning authorities as in England, or by zoning regulations as in the United States, conveys to some owners and withholds from other owners privileges which accrue because of the relative location of land. The maintenance of a balance between the open channels of competition and the effect of monopoly values which sound planning may confer upon land is an unresolved issue in the United States as in Britain. An equitable distribution of all the benefits of planning was the basic purpose of "compensation and betterment," and the operation of this principle may yet restore an appropriate measure of equity in the conduct of urban affairs.

THE LONDON REGION

To the people of Britain, London is their great and noble city, the capital of the Commonwealth, and as colorful as any city in history. It is also synonymous with overcrowding. Mercilessly damaged by bombs in World War II, London was ready for major change, and the scope of the planning program was significant—the replanning of a great city integrated with related communities—the New Towns.

England suffered heavy damage to its cities during the war. One third of its 13,000,000 dwellings were damaged, and there was practically no new building. With devastation all about them, the people found it necessary to consider plans for reconstruction. The 1944 Town and County Planning Act had extended financial aid to local authorities for the purchase of land when rebuilding was possible. The destruction of large urban areas, however, impressed many throughtful people with the possibility of recapturing some open space within their congested urban centers.

Athough agriculture in England can support only about half the population, and a large proportion of the people live in urban communities, there are only seven large industrial centers, which are agglomerations of urban areas ranging from two to eight million people. Congestion in these cities is acute, but it remains the British ideal to live in "cottages." A density of 12 families per acre was suggested by Ebenezer Howard; it became the standard density for the Garden Cities, and Sir Raymond Unwin dwelt upon it at length as a desirable standard. It remains today the standard toward which enlightened planners strive.

After World War II, the British realized that, in the large-scale rebuilding that was necessary, they should try to cope with the problem of congestion in their cities. Over the years, the British have cultivated a remarkable political common sense. With astutensess they somehow realize their aims and ambitions. Launching the postwar planning program, they began where they were with what they had and sought the way to a new concept of the urban structure.

The elements of the Garden City held strong appeal for the British; the characteristics of the village, in contrast with the metropolis, attracted them. Proximity to the beautiful countryside was a natural desire. They prefer the bicycle to the subway. They probably enjoy walking more than motoring. The two successful garden cities, Letchworth and Welwyn, were before them for comparison with the huge and congested cities. The English people have seen the advantages of the small community as a better way of life. They have been justly proud of their delightful rural country, and preservation of the countryside has occupied the aggressive attention of the most influential peers of England.

The County of London has an area of 117 square miles. In 1944 it had a population of 4,000,000. At the core of this area is the city of London, one mile square, with 5,000 people. This is the financial and political heart of the British Commonwealth. Fanning out from this center, Greater London had a population of 8,000,000 in an area of 700 square miles. The planning program of 1944, under the direction of Professor Patrick Abercrombie and F. J. Forshaw, was directed toward a dual objective: rebuilding the war-torn city and relieving the intolerable overcrowding and congestion.

The essential concept of the Abercrombie plan for Greater London was reduction of the population within the congested center, creation of a greenbelt ring to contain Greater London, and movement of industry to an Outer Ring. This theme was consistent with the enlightened tradition of planning in England, but it demanded courageous conviction and bold decision. A major issue at the outset was the standard of population density which should be sought within the overcrowded center. Although some authorities held to a density of about 70 to 75 persons (20 dwellings) per acre as a desirable maximum in the center, the London planners proposed a density of 100 to 150 persons per acre, and the inner districts of the County are being redeveloped in this latter range. The density within the Inner Ring ranges from 70 to 100 persons per acre and in the Suburban Ring it is maintained at about 50 persons per acre. About this complex a broad Greenbelt Ring ranging from 5 to 15 miles wide was reserved. Within this greenbelt the existing towns were permitted to increase within the platted areas of their jurisdictions, but the balance was reserved for recreation. Beyond the greenbelt and within the Greater London region was the Outer Ring of villages and small towns separated by open countryside.

The plan encompassed a total area of some 2,600 square miles. The population densities adopted for the several areas involved a population reduction of about 40 percent, or more than 600,000, in the County, and more than 400,000 persons in the Inner Urban Ring of the metropolis. Some increase was proposed for the Suburban Ring, but the population of Greater London was reduced by a total of over 1,000,000 people. This program for decentralization of vast population resulted in the New Towns Act of 1946.

As in the United States, the structure of urban government in Great Britain was designed for an era when the administration was relatively simple. With the growth of the metropolis and its accretions of urban entities, the governmental organization bears no relation to the real character of a metropolitan area.

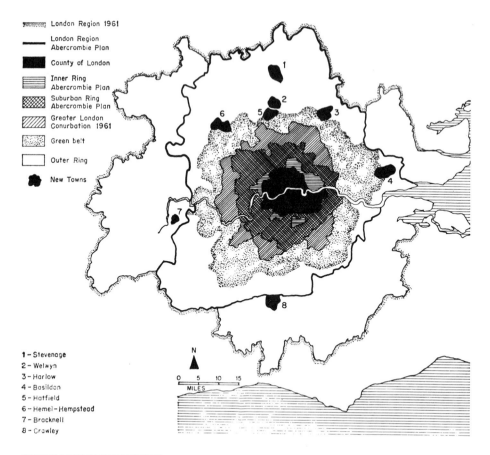

THE LONDON REGION

The Greater London Plan of 1944, by Patrick J. Abercombie and F. J. Forshaw, embraced a region of 2,600 square miles. A series of four rings surrounded the County of London. The population within the heavily urbanized areas of the County and the Inner Ring was to be reduced by some 1,000,000 people by dispersal within the Suburban and Outer Rings. The urban conurbation (concentration) of the region has extended the boundaries of the Suburban Ring beyond the limits of the plan and has forced attention to the preservation and expansion of the greenbelt. The regional sphere is also extended to some 4,600 square miles since the plan was conceived, and the total population has grown from 8,000,000 to 10,000,000.

The planned decentralization of London, by a reduction of population denstity within the inner core of the metropolitan area and a dispersal of people and industry from the center, was implemented by the New Towns program. Of the 33 New Towns in England, Scotland and Wales, eight are located within the London region. These have invited industrial development and will accommodate more than one-half million people.

Legislation has been introduced to establish a single authority, the Greater London Council, for the 800 square miles and 8,000,000 people of metropolitan London. Within this structure of the Council there are 34 boroughs, each with a population of about 200,000, which will be responsible for all local administration except the functions of metropolitan scope, including planning.

LONDON REGION NEW TOWNS

The adoption of the policy that more than a million people must be removed
from the central districts of London was of major consequence. It represented a
conviction that the overcrowding within the city must be relieved, that the
expansion of the city must be controlled, and that the amenities of urban life
could be accomplished only by decentralization of employment and residential
communities. The new towns were conceived, in the tradition of the garden
cities, as self-contained communities with all facilities that make an independent environment. They were not intended to be satellite dormitories connected
to the central city. Some were related to the larger orbit of London, however, to
make available to the people of the new towns the special facilities of the central
city, and being thus attractively near, to encourage movement from London to
release the city for a program of redevelopment.

The New Towns Act provided for the creation of *development corporations*
to plan, build, and manage the new towns. The corporation obtained sixty year
loans from the Ministry of Housing and Local Government (now the Department of the Environment) to finance the acquisition of land, prepare the plans,
and improve the land with all utilities and road systems. The corporation could
construct buildings to rent to business and industry, or could lease sites for
private development. Lease arrangements were generally for a period of ninety-nine years. Housing could also be built by the corporation; to insure adequate
housing for employees of industry, most of the housing was built by the
corporations. Increasing participation by private enterprise has been encouraged. The Minister of Housing and Local Government has general jurisdiction
over the program and all plans for development are subject to approval by the
Ministry. The New Towns Act of 1959 determined to dissolve each corporation
when the town was completed and transfer management to a Commission for
New Towns, made up of members appointed by the Minister of Housing and
Local Government.

The earliest towns, beginning with Stevenage in 1946, were located in the
London region. Eight were so designated, including Welwyn, which was begun
in 1920, but taken under the jurisdiction of the New Towns Act. These towns,
from 18 to 30 miles from London, were intended to accommodate the overspill
of people and industry to implement the London Plan for decentralization and
redevelopment. Nearly 500,000 people lived in these towns in 1973.

Overspill from large cities has not been the principle reason for building
more new towns. The purpose has shifted to economic support and development
on a regional scale. As reported by the Town and Country Planning Association:
"The regional aim of new towns is both to assist the restructuring and growth of
our major urban regions and to bring the advantages of strong growth points to
relatively depressed regions."[11]

---

[11] Report by the Association to the House of Commons Sub-Committee of the Expenditure
Committee, November, 1973.

Thirty-three new towns had been authorized by the end of 1973. The original plan for each called for a population of between 60,000 and 80,000 people. However, population redistribution and the development of regional resources in existing cities have led to plans for much larger new towns. Those within the London Ring are expected to remain within the specified limits, but a number elsewhere are planned for between 250,000 and 450,000 people, becoming major urban population centers in their regions.

This planning for the distribution of population and industry at a national level, in support of regional development, is an important first step toward the redevelopment of congested urban centers and the general improvement of the living and working environment, as well a rational approach to accommodating a growing national population.[12]

Planned as clusters of neighborhoods around a business and civic center, the new towns are predominantly made up of row cottages, ranging in density from 12 to 15 per acre. The neighborhoods have populations of 4,000 to 8,000, each neighborhood has its own schools, recreation facilities, churches and a small shopping center. The industrial area has convenient access and is efficiently arranged. In an effort to overcome the monotony of the standard two story cottage, some high apartment buildings (high points) have been introduced. Commenting on this trend, Dame Evelyn Sharp, Permanent Secretary of the Ministry of Housing and Local Government, said, "The architect likes the occasional high block; whether the new town tenant really does is one of the great debates."[13] The apartment is considered objectionable for the large numbers of families with children; 5 to 15 per cent of the dwellings are planned as apartment buildings for single people and childless couples.

Industrial enterprise, though initially slow to move to the new towns, became attracted by the efficient operating conditions, the availability of good sites, and the stable employment conditions. The expanding range of industries settling in the new towns offers a desirable diversification of employment, although skilled and professional workers predominate.

Retail services in the new towns are arranged in the conventional manner of shopping centers in the United States, with a variety of facilities arranged around a pedestrian mall or plaza. Automobile ownership increased in the new towns beyond that anticipated in the early plans, and it has been necessary in some towns to build garages to augment shopping center parking. Automobile ownership in the original eight towns within the London Ring ranged between 50 per cent and 60 per cent and has reached 70 per cent in Stevenage, as compared with 42 per cent in greater London and 46 per cent in Wales and England.[14]

An experimental "superbus" system in Stevenage doubled bus travel (from 20 per cent to 39 per cent) between 1971 and 1972, but the new towns in Great Britain were not planned for internal mass transit. The London region towns are

[12] See Chapter 21 for a discussion of national and state planning in the United States.

[13] *Town and Country Planning,* January, 1961.

[14] *Report of United Nations Seminar, London, June, 1973,* the Office of International Affairs, U.S. Department of Housing and Urban Development, Washington.

connected by rail to London. Only in Runcorn is there provision for an exclusive bus lane along the road system, but Cumbernauld near Glasgow was designed for complete separation of pedestrians and motor traffic. Cumbernauld is also unusual in the design of its commercial center. Geoffrey Copcutt, principal designer for the town, consolidated all facilities within an elongated, multi-level, concrete megastructure situated along a topographical spine through the town site and adjacent to the Glasgow Railroad. Vehicular circulation and parking occupy the lower levels; entertainment, shopping, offices, and civic facilities are distributed on upper levels, with so-called penthouse dwellings on the roof deck.

The new towns, in the words of Dame Evelyn Sharp, "have been a great experiment and are on their way to being a great success. Mistakes have been made and there are many problems still to resolve. But for thousands of families they are providing living conditions among the best in Britain; and for industry they are providing the conditions for efficiency. They will prove a first-class investment, in money as well as health and productivity."[15]

In conclusion, an American assessment states:

> The crowning achievement of British planning is not the new towns themselves, but rather the protection of the bulk of the beautiful landscape around London and other major cities. Along with control of development in new towns and expanded areas designated for growth, all are coordinated with a sensible rapid transit system. The British have found the formula for coordinated regional and national planning and curbing of urban sprawl, which may be 10 years away in the United States. There is no *direct* cost for this 610,000 acre greenbelt. It would have been impossible to purchase in full fee at market prices, which is the only permanently successful way to protect the landscape on a significant scale.
>
> The success with the greenbelt is not immediately transferrable to the United States. It is based upon several factors which makes it successful, but which are difficult to transfer ... [including]:
>
> A concept of government ownership of the incremental value of property derived from public improvements and zoning, where property owners need not be compensated for permanent freezing of land use in open space or existing uses. This would be impossible under current court rulings under the 14th Amendment in the U.S., where freezing of large areas, not subject to natural hazards, in non-development could be challenged as a taking without just compensation.[16]

VARIATIONS OF THE THEME

The British New Towns are an expression of the national disposition. Whereas most of the people live in the great industrial centers, the English village and the

---

[15] *Town and Country Planning,* January, 1961.

[16] A report by the Office of International affairs of the Department of Housing and Urban Development on the United Nations Seminar on New Towns in London, June, 1973. The report was written by Jack A. Underhill of the Office of New Communities Development, HUD, and clearly stipulates that "the material presented does not necessarily represent the views of the Department."

NEW TOWNS IN
GREAT BRITAIN AND
NORTHERN IRELAND

Town and Country Planning Association

THE NEW TOWNS

*Locations of the 33 New Towns in the current program are shown on the map of England,
Wales and Scotland. The towns are experiments in the design of an environment in
which the human scale predominates. They are self-contained communities seeking a
balance between sources of employment, business enterprise, shopping, education and
recreation for those who live in them. They are, however, significant for another
important reason: they are essentially an organic element in a broad program of
decentralization of the congested urban centers, the London region having received the
principal attention.*

  *Two of the towns related to the London region are shown in diagrammatic plans.
Stevenage, begun in 1949, was the first of these towns. The site comprises 6,100 acres, and
the original population of 60,000 for which the town was planned has expanded to 80,000.
Harlow, begun in 1949, was also planned for 60,000 and that population has increased
to 80,000. Located on a 6,400-acre site on the River Stort, Harlow has 13 neighborhoods.*

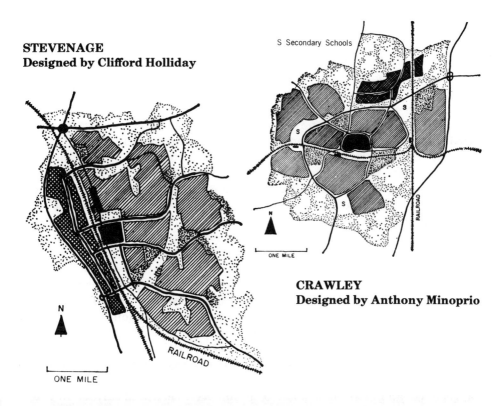

STEVENAGE
Designed by Clifford Holliday

S Secondary Schools

CRAWLEY
Designed by Anthony Minoprio

N

ONE MILE

RAILROAD

N

ONE MILE

RAILROAD

The neighborhood units have populations ranging from 3,500 to 6,000. Three suburban shopping centers serve clusters of these units. Two industrial districts are located on sites of 300 acres in the eastern section and 265 acres in the western section to avoid undue concentration. A total of 14,000 workers is anticipated. The town of Crawley, originally planned for a population of 50,000 on a site of 6,000 acres, will have a population of 70,000. Two existing villages—Three Bridges and Crawley—have been absorbed, and the town center occupies the latter. An industrial area of 264 acres is planned for 8,500 workers. Nine neighborhoods have populations of 4,000 to 7,000, and the density is about 29 persons per acre.

    Each neighborhood in the New Towns has a small subcenter for shopping, a primary school, playfields, and social facilities. The secondary schools serve several neighborhoods; in Crawley they are combined in three separate campuses (S).

    The residential neighborhoods are indicated by crosshatched areas, industrial areas by heavy crosshatching, and the town centers by black. Open space and farm land, forming a greenbelt about the towns, are indicated by dotted areas.

    A desirable attribute of the New Towns is their relatively small size, designed to encourage pedestrian circulation and maintain close proximity to surrounding open space. The plans indicate an abundance of space flowing throughout the community as separations between the neighborhoods. The preservation of natural wooded areas or unusual topographical characteristics within this space is advantageous, but the proportionate quantity of land reserved for permanent open space may be excessive in view of the surrounding greenbelt, low density, and internal recreation fields. This abundant open space may over-extend walking distances, exaggerate the separation between neighborhood cells, and thus tend to nullify the advantages of the modest size of the towns.

383

open countryside represent the cherished qualities of an ideal environment. This ideal was given tangible expression by Ebenezer Howard and established the garden city as a traditional British objective. Urban desires have not followed this firm direction in other places, however. The self-sufficient community as a module for decentralization of the urban metropolis does not present the same attraction in other countries as it has in Great Britain. The strong affirmative approach to decentralization represented by the New Town program has exerted positive influence elsewhere, but the traditional bond with the older cities in most countries is strong. As a consequence, the movement of planned decentralization is marked by variations of this theme.

The theory of new towns has been adopted by the Soviet Union in their extensive plans for decentralization. Industries are discouraged from settling in cities which have reached a population of 500,000 or more, but new communities are to become satellites of large cities, to assure proximity to the cultural activities in existing cities. Eighteen such towns have been proposed for the region around Moscow, the first of which is Kryukov. The future size of this great urban complex will be limited to 5,000,000 people. Three population sizes are favored for new towns: 30,000–50,000; 80,000–100,000; and 100,000–300,000. In 1974 plans were made for five new towns of 100,000 for the region around Odessa.

The places of greatest historic interest in Paris, most of the important commercial, financial, educational, and political activity, and the entertainment center are confined to an area of less than ten square miles in the heart of the city. The city, however, covers an area of 40 square miles with a population of 3,000,000, and more than 4,000,000 people have settled in surrounding districts. This region of between 7,000,000 and 8,000,000 people occupies 300 square miles. Since an urban population increase of 20,000,000 is anticipated by the turn of the century, a multiplication of housing "colonies" is inadequate. Implementation of an urban policy of planned decentralization in France has been slow. But the pressure of population and industrial growth has required positive action, and with the passage of the Boscher law in 1970 financial assistance for new towns has become available. Five new towns with populations between 330,000 and 500,000 are planned within a ten to twelve mile radius of Paris. New towns are also planned near Marseilles (for 750,000) Lyon (for 200,000), Lille (for 150,000), and Rouen (for 140,000). Existing villages will be integrated within the new town developments.

In Spain, where the same concentration of population in large urban centers exists, a 1970 legislative decree created the "Urban Urgent Action" (ACTUR), a plan for eight new satellite towns, ranging in population from 60,000 to 120,000. Three of these are near Barcelona, the principal industrial city of Spain, and the others serve Madrid, Zaragosa, Seville, Valencia, and Cadiz.[17]

Although Sweden was the first country in Europe to enact legislation for

---

[17] The data on new towns in France and Spain are from "New Communities in Selected European Countries," U.S. Department of Housing and Urban Development, Wash., D.C., April, 1974.

planning, with the Urban Building Act of 1874, the social and economic circumstances there have not compelled attention to planning on a regional scale, such as that which prevailed in England. The first Town Planning Act of 1907 and the 1931 Act were similar to the 1909 and 1932 Town and Country Planning Acts in England, but emphasis was placed on site planning, street and building arrangements, rather than regional relationships.

The consumer cooperative movement reflected the direct and pragmatic approach to the solution of economic and social conditions for which the Swedish people have demonstrated capability. The self-help small cottage, or "Magic-House," program initiated in 1927 is another example. One-tenth acre plots on city-owned land were made available for 60-year lease and a ground rent of 5 per cent of the land value. Pre-fabricated houses were also made available for erection by the owner, his labor amounting to 10 per cent of the cost. The balance of 90 per cent of the dwelling cost was to be repaid to the city in thirty annual installments. This program presented a practical means for families of low income to acquire decent homes as a substitute for substandard tenements in the congested city.

The plan for decentralization of Stockholm has resulted in two noteworthy developments in urban planning—Vallingby and Farsta. Some 50,000 people, whose sources of employment are in the central city, have had to seek dwellings within the suburban districts. This is equivalent to about one-third of the housing in the new suburban developments. These two new communities are therefore related to the general plan of the city and are served by a subway to the center. It was intended that the usual development of small suburban increments, unable to support an adequate community center, be avoided. The Vallingby group was therefore planned for a population of 60,000 which, including the immediate existing suburbs about it, could support a complete shopping and commercial center. The Farsta district, with a surrounding population of 35,000, was planned for an equal number of 35,000 people. Industrial sites were reserved within the vicinity of these new communities as part of the decentralization program.

These towns, built on publicly owned land, attest to the wisdom of the policy adopted by the city many years ago to acquire large tracts of land about the periphery of the city. Planning for the greater city of Stockholm was thus implemented and the complete development of these new communities was made possible. Whereas the city built some of the housing, land was leased to the cooperatives and other private organizations for housing and commercial and industrial development. Open space for recreation was reserved between these towns and Stockholm, but the relatively convenient proximity (Vallingby seven miles and Farsta six miles) to the central city offers a diversification of employment and the advantages of cultural facilities in the city.

Since these successful towns were founded, Skarholmen-Varherg and Soderby-Salem have been built around Stockholm, and a dozen relatively small communities are distributed through the southern part of the country. This policy of planned decentralization is also illustrated in the new town of Tapiola in Finland. Situated on a superb wooded site, six miles from Helsinki, the new satellite town is exemplary. Although it is relatively modest in size—a population of 17,000 on 670 acres—Arne Ervi's town plan, chosen by a competition in 1952, reflects the sensitivity and skill of the several architects who participated in its design.[18] Residential groups are situated among the forest areas in three neighborhoods of about 6,000 people. Each is provided with convenient shopping centers with indoor and outdoor recreational facilities. Bicycle and pedestrian ways are carefully separated from motor roads. Housing ranges from one and two story dwellings, three and four story "walk-up" apartments, to eleven story apartment towers. Dwellings are puchased with the aid of loans at low interest from the State Housing Board.

A light industrial area provides employment for about half the residents, and a short bus trip to Helsinki extends employment and cultural opportunities. Completed in 1965, Tapiola was carried out by the Housing Foundation, an association of consumer, civil servant, and trade union organizations created in 1951. The town site was purchased by the Family Welfare League before the establishment of the Housing Foundation. With aggressive private initiative, this new town achieved an environment of unique distinction under the direction of Heiki von Hertzen, Chief of the Planning Department for the Foundation.

Around the middle of the twentieth century century Copacabana, near Rio de Janeiro, was a seaside paradise. A quarter of a century later, 250,000 people occupy tall buildings in three square miles by the sea. A new city is now planned 10 miles away. Barra de Tijuca, occupying 75 square miles of open space and mountains stretching along 14 miles of beach, was planned in 1969 by Lucio Costa, the planner of Brasilia. Planned as a series of urban communities of 12,000 separated by greenbelts and two large centers for 80,000 to 100,000 people each, the new city is expected to accommodate a population of 2,000,000. Designed with the flair of architect Oscar Niemeyer, the first center is dominated by seventy 34-story apartment towers, six office buildings, and elaborate amenities.

The grandiose concept of Barra de Tijuca is in the Latin American tradition of dramatic scale. Aratu, an extension of Salvador in the province of Bahia, was also planned by Lucio Costa. Planned for a population of 1,500,000, Aratu is a neighboring port city rather than a satellite community; Salvador itself has a population of less than one million. The land for Aratu, the first completely planned industrial city in Brazil, was purchased by the State and sold at low cost to developers of industry and housing. Tax incentives are also granted for development. The National Housing Bank (NHB), founded in 1964, is the primary source of financing for urban development, and several thousand low income dwellings have been built in Aratu with NHB loans.

Funds with which the NHB operates are obtained by an 8 per cent tax on payrolls of all private enterprise in the country. The NHB borrows from this

---

[18] Besides Ervi, Jorma Jarvi, Keija and Heiki Siren, Viljo Rewell, Aluis Blomstedt are among the prominent architects who designed portions of the town.

special fund (Fundo de Garantia do Tempo de Servico) at a rate 5 per cent interest to provide the capital to finance its urban housing programs which are directed primarily to housing for families in slum areas of the *favelas*. These families pay from 1 per cent to 10 per cent interest on the loans, according to their income.

This unique program has elicited the interest of other countries, but it is not without problems. New outlying housing communities are far from sources of employment. The degree of authoritatian direction concerning the movement of families from the *favelas* to the new and unfamiliar living conditions, some of which include the proverbial "high-rise" apartments, has aroused resentment. The Bank has also been confronted with the not uncommon predicament of many low income families unable to meet the continuing financial obligations of home-ownership.

A series of urban concentrations in a linear alignment, know as the "Finger Plan," was adopted in 1949 for the extension of urbanization about the city of Copenhagen. It is estimated that the urban population of this region will increase 70 per cent, about 1,000,000 people, by 1980, and applicaton of the "Finger Plan" was expanded in 1958 with the recommendation for two large urban centers southwest of Copenhagen. Each of these new centers will accommodate 250,000 people, a population considered by the planners to be an optimum size to support all necessary major urban services, provide a desirable diversification of industrial employment, and yet facilitate the convenient circulation of motor vehicles without the congestion which afflicts the larger cities. The concept of this plan is the development of an integrated decentralization of the entire metropolitan region of Copenhagen. Although the new communities are intended to have a self-sufficient economic base, and their size and facilities would exclude them from the category of satellite towns, a key purpose of the "Finger Plan" is convenience of communication between the new centers as well as to the central city of Copenhagen. The aim is integration with, rather than isolation from, the metropolitan complex, and this linear structure is therefore dependent upon a rapid and efficient system of rail transportation.[10] Numerous and extensive land subdivision has occurred on the periphery of the cities of America. Many of these developments have incorporated parks, schools, and shopping centers, but usually they have been random residential tracts without benefit of a plan for decentralization of the cities to which they are attached. The planning and development of complete self-comtained towns in North America are rare. Kitimat, a company town in British Columbia for the Aluminium Company of Canada, planned by Clarence Stein, is an exception. Another is Don Mills, near Toronto in Canada.

This community was begun in 1953 by the Don Mills Development Corporation, a private land investment company. Being part of North York, one of the 13 municipalities in the Toronto metropolitan area, it is not politically

---

[19] Eric Reade, *Journal of the Land Planning Institute,* London, December 1961–January 1962.

independent but represents an approach similar to the New Towns of England. Occupying a site of 2,058 acres, it was planned as a new industrial community for a population of 25,000. Located one-half mile from a limited access highway and 25 minutes from the Toronto airport, it is served also by two railways that traverse the site. The entire town has been developed by private companies, and the sponsoring development company has encouraged a wide diversification of industrial enterprise. The town is distinguished for the high level of architectural quality that prevails.

Perhaps the most significant aspect of this new town is the policy of the development company to seek an economic balance between residential and

Courtesy Hugo Priivits   FARSTA—Town center   *Courtesy Hugo Priivits*

Courtesy Hugo Priivits   *Courtesy Hugo Priivits*

VALLINGBY—Town center

VALLINGBY—Town center
and apartments

VALLINGBY AND FARSTA

Neither Vallingby nor Farsta are, nor were they intended to be, self-contained "New Towns." They are integral developments of the general plan for the decentralization of the city of Stockholm. They were planned however, to support a complete marketplace and business center, provide industrial employment to complement the employment opportunities in the central city, and accommodate a diversification of dwelling types to meet the wide range in family composition in a balanced community. When completed, Vallingby will have nearly 500,000 square feet of shops and more than 1,000,000 square feet in office space, social and welfare facilities, and entertainment. Some 40 per cent of the employment has been within the nearby new industrial district.

industrial or commercial development. It is the objective to maintain a ratio of 60 per cent in the assessed values of residential development and 40 per cent in industrial and commercial development. This policy of a balanced economy in the administration of urban affairs suggests an approach to the regulation of urban growth and development.

The importance of economic balance was also illustrated in the community of Yorktown, in Westchester County, New York. This community, with a 1960 population of 16,500, was originally developed as a subdivision of single-family homes. Concern for the increasing tax rate and an annual tax deficit of some $100 for each dwelling led to a study to ascertain the proportion of land uses which might produce a balanced tax structure. The results indicated the need for the community to have 8 per cent of the area in industrial and laboratory facilities and 4 per cent of the area in business and commercial uses.[20] With the rapid and continuing increase of urbanization in the United States, other communities may profit from attention to the economic balance in tax revenue and expenditure as a guide to planning control.

CHANDIGARH AND BRASILIA

The planning of government capitals is outside the context of towns as they relate to the mammoth problems of metropolitan urban expansion, but two recent examples warrant attention. Capital cities have offered the opportunity for expression of dramatic form, and Chandigarh in India and Brasilia in Brazil are no exceptions. Razing of the city walls about Vienna created the Ringstrasse, for which that city is famous. Moved by the splendor of Paris, Pierre L'Enfant delineated the plan for Washington, D.C. The classic influence was impressed upon the governmental section of New Delhi. An international competition was held in 1911 for Canberra, the new capital of 35,000 for Australia, and won by Walter Burley Griffin, an American. But the occasion to undertake the building of new cities to serve as government capitals is rare, and those in progress in Brazil and India are unusual both in this respect and in the boldness of their expression of urban form.

The Constitution of the Republic of Brazil in 1889 included a provision for a new capital for that country. The location was not determined until 1955, when a site at the confluence of two rivers some 600 miles from Rio de Janeiro was selected. A development corporation, appointed by the President, assumed charge of the building of the new city, and a competition for the plan was held in 1957. It was won by the Brazilian architect Lucio Costa.

The concept is bold—two huge axes in the sign of the Cross. The principal

---

[20] *American City*, December 1961. This study was sponsored by the original developer, David Bogdarff, with the planning services of Frederick P. Clark & Associates, and Mickle and Marcon. It indicated that for each increment of 500 homes, occupying 312 acres, 25 acres should be devoted to laboratory and industrial uses and 12 acres to business and commerical uses.

multi-level traffic arteries traverse these axes. Separate centers for government, commerce, and entertainment are located along one axis and the residential districts are distributed about the other. Building of the city has progressed as rapidly as funds were available, and the creative talents of Oscar Niemeyer are among those employed for the virile architectural forms throughout the city. Great blocks of tall apartment buildings dominate the residential sections, and the entire theme of the city is a monumented expression of concrete and glass.

The positive conviction, uncompromising courage, and daring forms represented in this new city are inspiring. Perhaps a faint question can be heard through the powerful thrusts of this dynamic place: is it really for people?

The ancient capital city of the state of Punjab in India was Lahore. When India and Pakistan were partitioned, the city of Lahore was contained within Pakistan. The site of Chandigarh, on the rolling plains near the foothills of the Himalayas, was selected for the new capital of the Punjab. Prime Minister Nehru appointed Le Corbusier to serve as advisor to the government for the plan of the new city. In collaboraton with Maxwell Fry and Jane Drew of England and P. L. Varma, chief engineer for the state, a master plan was developed in 1951.

A future population of 500,000 is anticipated, but the initial stage of the plan provides for a population of 150,000 on a 9,000-acre site. The plan is a huge gridiron of major roads intersecting at distances of one-half mile in one direction and three-quarters of a mile in the other. These roads define neighborhood "sectors," each 240 acres in size and housing about 15,000 people. The commercial and civic center occupies the heart of this great square.

The Capitol complex is set apart along one boundary of the city on a site of 220 acres. Comprising the Palace of Ministers or Secretariat, the Palace of the Assembly, the Palace of the High Court, and the Palace of the Governor, this complex and the buildings within it were designed by Le Corbusier, who added a symbolic sculptural feature—the "Open Hand" —to the group.

The plan is no more bold than might be expected from the creative mind of Le Corbusier. Situated on a vast plain in a hot and arid region, it nevertheless evokes positive response from those who view it. The highly disciplined order and the sweeping scale of the entire concept is at once impressive. In this respect it shares an affinity with the tradition of the Mogul empire when, during the period of Islamic domination in India, unsurpassed strokes of bold planning and city building were executed. Yet a basic difference distinguishes the monumental group of this new Capitol from the earlier Mogul tradition. It is a distinction in quality expressed by the scale of space and the shape of the forms which enclose it. Even in a dead city like Fatepur-sikri a human scale seems to pervade the paved courts and the varied structures within and about them. This city lived for only 50 years but, stark and empty though it now is, the relation between buildings and space, the light and shade of arcades and sheltered areas, convey a vivid impression that the place was meant for people. Somehow this quality is not present at Chandigarh.

The Palace of Ministers, a tremendous concrete structure 800 feet long and

BRASILIA—Central Mall, 1973

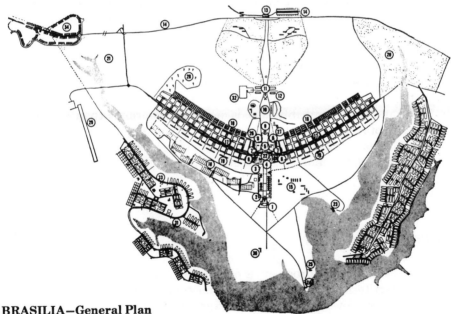

BRASILIA—General Plan

1. Plaza of the Three Powers
2. Esplanade of the Ministries
3. Cathedral
4. Cultural Area
5. Amusement Section
6. Books and Offices
7. Commercial Area 8. Hotels
9. Radio and Television Towers
10. Sports Area
11. Municipal Plaza
12. Sentry Outpost

13. Railroad Station
14. Warehouses, Small Industries
15. The University
16. Embassies and Legations
17. Residential Zone
18. Twin Houses
19. Twin Super-Blocks
20. Botanical Gardens
21. The Zoo
22. Highway Terminal
23. Yacht Club

24. Residential Palace
25. Tourists' Hotel
26. Exhibition Grounds
27. Horse Club
28. The Cemetery
29. Airport
30. Golf Club
31. Individual Residences (So.)
32. Printing Facilities
33. Individual Residences (No.)
34. Suburban Residences (Pky.)

nine stories high, is one-quarter of a mile distant from the High Court Palace. Perhaps trees may one day provide a welcome canopy of shade within this vast space, but a rich landscape to cover the dimensions of the open space in this complex is hardly indigenous to the region nor reminiscent of the delightful gardens which once graced this country. The great structures are powerful expressions of abstract form and pattern, and the space between them is of mighty proportions. Yet they seem to withhold an invitation for people to share in the experience, and tender no protection from the burning sun. Thus one may ponder the *art* of planning and await the emergence of Chandigarh as a complete reality to evaluate the grand concept it represents

When the new nation of Pakistan was created, the capital was shifted from the ancient City of Lahore to Rawalpindi along the foothills of the Himalayas in West Pakistan, and a Capital Development Authority was appointed in 1959 to develop a new capital, Islamabad, nearby. The rigid geometrical plan, by the Greek architect Doxiadis Associates, is divided into residential sectors (neighborhood units) of some 800 acres. Each sector is served by civic facilities, schools, health services, recreation facilities, and mosques. The Administration Center at the crossing of two main avenues contains the President's house, the Secretariat, the Assembly, the Supreme Court, and cultural buildings, with a large enclave for foreign missions. With a great National Park and extravagently monumental public buildings in the Muslim tradition, the City of Islamabad should reflect the ambitions of the new nation.

As one meditates upon the qualities which charge a city with the human spirit, the images of many places loom in contrast to these remarkable new towns in Brazil and India. Probably none is more heart-warming than that of Paris. The charm of its monumental spaces, the saucy animation of its avenues, the delight in its varied perspectives, seem less to have been "planned" than to have blossomed. Perhaps, more than an efficient arrangement of its streets or the abstract shape of its buildings, it takes "the music of men's lives" to give a city character.

HONG KONG (Kowloon)

As land is scarce in the urban areas of Kowloon, most new building must be in the New Territories.[21] To provide good living conditions for the inhabitants who move there, the government is building three new towns—largely on reclaimed land—which have been carefully planned to provide balanced communities.

These new towns have all the essentials of modern life—schools, clinics, parks, playgrounds, shopping centers, markets, police, fire, and ambulance services, as well as community buildings. There are also sites for private, industrial and commercial development, as well as for private housing. When fully developed each of the towns will be self-sufficient, with employment and

[21] Hong Kong Government information service, 1978.

entertainment and all social amenities. Additionally, good transport links to urban Kowloon will be provided by the extended underground railway system to Tsuen Wan, the second Lion Rock Tunnel to Sha Tin, and a new expressway to Tuen Mun.

The first of the new towns is Tsen Wan Kwai Chung, based on the existing community of Tsuen Wan, which already has a population exceeding 485,000. An area to the north of the existing development will provide housing for 114,000 people together with 47 acres (19 hectares) for industrial development and a site for a town center incorporating administrative, commercial, and cultural facilities.

Also to be developed is Tsing Yi Island, which is now connected to the mainland by a bridge and highway. Here it is planned that 158,000 people will live in new homes, and good progress has already been made on the early phase of Cheung Ching Estate, with the first twin-town blocks already occupied. Tsing Yi, although an integral part of Tsuen Wan New Town, will have all the facilities required to make it a self contained community. It will also provide a number of sites suitable for heavy industry requiring sea access. When the new town is completed by the mid-1980's Tsuen Wan will have a total population approaching one million.

The second new town is Sha Tin just north of the Lion Rock Road tunnel from Kowloon. Its first new public housing estate, Lek Yuen, was completed during 1975 and has a population of 22,000 most of whom enjoy panoramic views of the nearby sea and rolling countryside beyond, and all of whom are served by a major shopping complex.

Another estate, Wo Che, is now under construction next to Lek Yuen and when completed in early 1979 will provide 40,000 people with homes. Phase One of Wo Che was completed in mid-1977 and tenants have been moving in since. An industrial area of 13.5 acres (5 + hectares) is also being developed to provide job opportunities for new town residents. The town, expected to reach rapidly a population of 475,000, will have both public and private housing.

The third new town is Tuen Mun—previously know as Castle Peak—which already has a population of 70,000. It is being built on the west coast of New Territories where some 350 acres (138 hectares) of land have been reclaimed from Castle Peak Bay and a major new highway is under construction to link Tuen Mun to Tsuen Wan and Kowloon. This new highway is expected to open in the first half of 1978. The populaton of Tuen Mun is expected to grow to 460,000 within eight years, and as in other new towns most residents will live in public housing estates. Industrial sites are part of the development of Tuen Mun so that job opportunities will be provided for the population.

ISRAEL

Israel has built many new towns in addition to the reconstruction and expansion of Jerusalem, Haifa, and Tel Aviv. Along the coast of the Medeterrranean two important centers were constructed in the late 1960's and early 1970's, Ashdot and Askelon. At the northern end of the Gulf of 'Aqaba, the new town of Eilath was constructed. New communities were developed, some as defense outposts, others as permanent homesites, for immigrants arriving from many parts of the world.

The government of Israel utilized the British town planning standards and techniques. Most structures are two or three stories in height. They are built of masonry materials. The site planning is, for the most part, very good, with adequate open spaces for recreation and outdoor living in the temperate climate.

27

Art in the City

COMMUNITY APPEARANCE

Not since the City Beautiful movement at the turn of the century has the planning of cities been accepted as an *art*. Planning shifted from the province of the landscape architect to engineers and techniques of zoning. Industrial genius created the productive capacity of the world, but it was commercial genius that produced the wealth. The city became a vast commercial enterprise; everything was for sale. Planning was dominated by technicians. The city as an art form disappeared. The attention of planners was diverted to zoning administration and urban management.

The "billboard syndrome" defaces strip commercial streets in every city, freeway rights-of -way, and most rural highways. Power poles and wires, competing traffic signals, a convulsive mass of distracting color, form and motion, obscure the identity of individual signs. Every street looks every other street; in the words of Gertrude Stein, "When one gets there, there is no there there."

It has now become customary to include community appearance as part of the Comprehensive Plan for a city. It is perhaps the most nebulous element in the planning process. The refinement of urban form and space, respect for natural topographic features, scenic approaches, views of sea and sky, open space, relationships and identity of structures, have been skillfully advocated by competent designers.[1]

But, caught up in the technicalities of urban housekeeping, and confronted with apathy among the urban populace, administrative planners, public officials, and citizens have become inured to the ugliness around them and incompetent to make judgements on urban esthetics.

Public authority has absolute jurisdiction over some 40 per cent of the city area: streets, parks, and public facilities. Yet a street will be widened to accommodate more automobiles, even though doing so destroys trees and ruins the visual quality of adjacent property; a school or other public building will be crowded onto an inadequate lot, and acquisition of enough space is alleged to be

[1] Kevin Lynch, *The Image of the City*, The Technology Press and Harvard University Press, Cambridge, Mass., 1960.

CIVIC ART—
IMAGE OF A CULTURE?

ART INSTITUTE—Chicago, 1897

PICASSO'S "WOMAN," CIVIC CENTER—Chicago, 1967

"uneconomic" because it would cost more. An old city hall will be abandoned and a modern facility built elsewhere without concern for the historical value of the old building or disruption of the city's sense of identity.

Despite official insensitivity to urban aesthetics, the city may improve, or preserve, attractive features within the area of its authority, if an alert citizenry and a competent planning staff are vigilant. But the balance of 60 per cent of the city area is within the province of private enterprise, and regulation of esthetic quality by legislative processes is largely ineffectual. Strategic locations may be controlled by regulations of height and bulk, and billboards may be eliminated in time by imposition of amortization zoning. The 1954 Supreme Court decision offers some encouragement, but the courts are generally reluctant to impose judgement on aesthetic issues alone. Subdivision ordinances can require underground power utilities, building setbacks, and open space. The Planned Unit Development introduces the advantages of large scale planning. But a city can exercise its major influence on aesthetic quality by the degree to which an orderly structure of land uses is planned, the relationship of streets to abutting property and their effectiveness for traffic movement, the elimination of strip commercial zoning (also by amortization zoning) and the consolidation of commercial facilities in shopping center, the maintenance of street trees, the preservation of open space and historic land marks, the location and intensity of street lighting, and the design of street furniture.

In the wake of Le Corbusier's polemics some recent New Utopians have become increasingly esoteric. Abstract terminology is drawn upon to support imaginative concepts of urban form. Words acquire their own subtle and occult significance: a "continuum of constant change," "ever-fluid movement," "transciency of life-cycles," "mobility," a "new objectivity." The rhetoric is eloquent; words in the lexicon are employed with enviable conviction. Yet, when the terms are converted to delineations of tangible form, they reflect a strong basic similarity to the conventional city. Alternatives seem even less appealing than existing cities. At one time, a platform is proposed to cover Paris; at another an urban bridge leaps across the English Channel.[2] Buckminster Fuller proposes a series of "floating neighborhoods" moored in the East River.[3]

In their plan of 1958 for the Hauptstadt in Berlin, Peter and Alison Smithson were intent upon the theme of "mobility." Pedestrian and vehicular traffic were separated by a network of pedestrian decks and bridges elevated above the road system. Sinuous "walls of office slabs" to contain the inner city would become as rigidly fixed as any conventional urban structure. In that proposal, like their plan for Mehring Platz, in 1963,[4] the Smithsons featured the

---

[2] Illustrated in Udo Kuterman, *New Architecture in the World*, Universe Books, New York, 1965. The Paris Platform is by Yona Friedman; the Channel Bridge is by Schulze-Fiedlitz and Friedman.

[3] The "floating city" was developed under a grant by the Triton Foundation, Cambridge, Massachusetts, 1968.

[4] The Haupstadt Plan of 1958 by the Smithsons and Sigmonde-Wonke. The Mehring Platz Plan of 1963 by the Smithsons and Gunter Nitschke. See David Lewis (ed.), *Pedestrian in the City*, D. Van Nostrand, New York, 1966.

"Motor Way," rather than a dynamic concept for mass transit which might have been expected to shape the modern city. Bearing strong resemblance to freeways in American cities, the new planning vision appears remarkably conventional and rather *old*. There is little evidence that the new aesthetic of urban form would be any more adaptable to "fluid change" than existing cities.

Kenzo Tange and the "Metabolists" of Japan envision dramatic vertical and horizontal forms linked by automobile highways projecting into Tokyo Bay. The forms are ¡exhilarating, but the fundamental difference between their proposal and the cities we have and know to be outmoded is not readily discernible.[5]

Where among the broad roadways in these theatrical visions is the mass of motor vehicles to be lodged? Where in the incessant movement of traffic can the automobiles *stop*? That function was featured in the visions of Louis Kahn for Philadelphia in 1956. He glorified the multi-level garage; among images of tall shafts, pyramids and tinker-toy cages, a collection of great cylindrical garages, or "ports," dominated the scene.

The popular credence accorded the mechanistic beehives designed for a million or more by the desert mystic Paolo Soleri,[6] as recently as the seventies and George Favre's reference [7] to the "cellular agglomerates, clip-on or plug-in cities, grid structures, containers, submarine cities, cities in outer space, megastructures and all the gidgety-gadgety et ceteras," reflect the desperate malaise of a technologically-oriented society. The incredible impact of the electronic computer on every aspect of contemporary human existence is evident in a widespread reliance upon that ingenious instrument for solutions to problems of the urban environment. It has value as a mechanical tool, but it is gifted with neither a conscience nor ultimate wisdom; it cannot make the *decisions* related to social and economic welfare or the physical form of the city.

Encompassing the full range of human activity, the city is the living image of the culture that spawns it. It reflects the social values, aspirations and aesthetic sensibilities of the people who create and occupy it. These character-istics will be represented in the Comprehensive Plan and zoning ordinances, the allocation of land uses and regulations which accommodate individual and collective *participation* in city building. A city which functions adequately may not be aesthetically satisfying but, conversely, it will not become an art form unless the functional parts work effectively.

In the final analysis, the aesthetic quality of the city is the measure of the cultural values of a community, values identified with the elevation of mind, morals and taste of a society. Beautiful cities in the world are not only charming because of a colorful history or the patina of age. Cathedrals of Europe were beautiful when the stone was white. Paris and Venice were built to be beautiful, and they show that beautiful cities can grow old gracefully.

[5] Illustrated and described in *The Pedestrian in the City.*

[6] Paolo Soleri, *Arcology: Cities in the Image of Man,* PIT Press, Cambridge, Mass., 1969.

[7] George Favre, "Cities Are For People . . . or Are They?" *Christian Science Monitor,* June 14, 1972.

The city needs space for the free flow of transportation and movement of people, space in which to create a desirable environment for living and for work, space in which the functions of the city and the aesthetics of our time may be welded into an inseparable unity. Space in the city will encourage the inventive genius of mankind to fulfill the wants of people and free them from the wanton congestion that renders the city a detestable place in which to live and work.

The urban environment shrieks with the production of science and industry and the commodities of commercial enterprise. The city is like a cave in which a multitude of weird and raucous echoes create a psychological din. Self-discipline in organizing the advantages of our industrial age is lagging, and the city dweller is suffering distraction.

Reams of statistics show the habits of the urbanite. They reveal, for example, the short distance people will walk from their parking place to their shopping destination. This reluctance to walk is interpreted as a significant characteristic of the present-day shopper, but the fact that these statistics also measure the repellent character of the urban environment is overlooked. There is ample evidence of the response of the people to studied civic design and their hunger for open space. The diminutive plaza in Radio City evokes spontaneous response, and the success of planned residential communities and neighborhood shopping centers attests to the good business of adequate space. Statistics may show the characteristics of the urban population, but they may also reveal the deficiencies of the environment that induce those traits; they may tell the story of how rank congestion violates human sensibilities and how abhorrent are slums to the human spirit.

THE CULTURAL VACUUM

City building is neglectful of human feeling; it is a cold harsh enterprise devoid of the amenities for living. It explains the desire for escape which eclecticism provided, a refuge from reality in which the people could draw the walls of romanticism about themselves. It was not a real existence the people lived, but it showed that they could still dream, and it is dreams that will lead civilization out of the darkness—dreams of the future rather than the past.

The significance of freedom is not yet fully grasped; society is not yet adjusted to the democracy of our industrial age. Political rights have been won, and mechanical tools of phenomenal number and variety are at our disposal, but the significance of man's achievement is blurred in its whirling presence. It was entertaining and amusing fiction that Jules Verne wrote in the nineteenth century. Today reality so far surpasses his visionary anecdotes that society is bewildered. There is a strangeness about the powers science has thrust into the hands of man; his capacity to manipulate these powers and the responsibility it bestows cast a spell upon society. When we contemplate their effect upon our social and economic life, the stupendous possibilities are appalling. Imagination pulsates with the vibrating tempo of the modern world.

Evidence of technical progress is all about us. The material benefits of our age are delivered ready-made; gadgets are a part of our daily existence and we take for granted the marvelous developments of science. But the assimilation of these accomplishments into our cultural environment is coming hard. Forging a culture from the technology of our time is a complicated process. Ultimately adjustment of civilization to the reality of our age will generate the cultural climate in which the creative work of artists flourishes.

Meanwhile we are moving in a cultural vacuum, into which has been drawn the technological progress we misinterpret for culture itself. Mediocrity is the standard bred of materialism. Inured to this standard, we are hardly conscious of its reality and unaware of the cultural potentials present but undeveloped. Their development offers a whole new frontier in our world of progress—the cultural expression of democratic freedom in which the vitality of contemporary art will shape our physical environment. There is resistance to a new aesthetic, but it is more passive than active. The pursuit of material welfare distracts attention from cultural achievement as we bow low before the great god Mammon, but the result is indifference more than wilful denial. Economic distortions exert more convincing pressures for improvement of the urban environment than does the creative urge for a fine city. The loss of land values due to congestion and the economic burden of blight and social maladjustments are more impressive than the aesthetic and spiritual baseness to which the city has degenerated.

UNITY OF PURPOSE

The search for form in the urban environment would stagnate without the imagination of fertile minds. It is the more regrettable that official planning agencies are so timid in their leadership. The aspirations of city people are suffocating. Some cities may have illusions of grandeur, others have ambitions for greatness, but false pride obscures their decadence. We can hardly conclude that the ugliness of our environment is due to a complete absence of civic pride, that nerve-racking congestion and unhealthful overcrowding answer the natural desire for activity and vitality, and that people have become so inured to their surroundings they prefer mediocrity to an environment of decency and culture regardless of their social or economic station in life.

What is there to stir the city-dweller in the prospect of nothing better than more of the same? The people need to see new plans. Civic leadership needs to emerge with standards of urban development that will convince the people it will be worth the cost to restore decency to their cities. Planning implies a goal to be reached. This, in turn, suggests some unity of purpose. Sorely needed progress is frustrated by disunity and unimaginative leadership. Unity of purpose—a conviction about the form and character we desire for our cities—has been absent. Consequently, planning has wandered aimlessly, frequently promising much but delivering little.

Cities have not yet reached the stage of crowding and congestion that present laws permit, and yet they are already pitifully overcrowded and congested. These legal limits have induced a state of anarchy in city building. Feeble innovations for improvement are not enough. Face-lifting will not do the job; it will take a major operation. Our conception of unlimited exploitation in urban property and people will need modification; the relation between the amount of space occcupied by buildings and the amount of land about them must be altered. An inspiring projection of the City of Tomorrow by Le Corbusier, a studied group like Radio City, a well-planned subdivision like River Oaks, and the Parkways of New York and Chicago have pointed the way. If we expect our cities to be shaped in their images, however, we must look to the laws that set the standards for that accomplishment.

Cities are breaking down. As they are rebuilt they must conform to standards which ensure they will not break down again. This will require major decisions, and we must be prepared to make them. Unless these decisions are made wisely, it would be far better and more economical to beat a hasty retreat from the congested urban centers and build new communities elsewhere.

We can build better cities when we quit gnawing at the fringe of the urban garment and accept some of the bitter with the sweet. We will replan our cities to provide a rational density of population, and from these plans we will lay a foundation of law that prohibits crowding and congestion of people and buildings. We will plan for such expansion and decentralization as the regions about our cities require, and we will plan for such rebuilding as obsolescence and decay demand. We will go about this as civilized human beings with due consideration for each other, rather than barbarians bent upon destruction or as creatures of greed and deception bent on personal power and profit. We will seek the values in cities Thomas Guthrie described in the early nineteenth century:

> They have been as lamps of life along the pathway of humanity and religion. Within them science has given birth to her noblest discoveries. Behind their walls, freedom has fought her noblest battles. They have stood on the surface of the earth like great breakwaters, rolling back or turning aside the swelling tide of oppression. Cities indeed, have been the cradles of human liberty.

The tragic impact of the great city upon human welfare aroused the search by the new utopians, and their vision may light the way toward a metamorphosis of the city. Statistics, economic analyses, graphs, and charts urge a popular plea that planning must adopt scientific methods for the direction of future urban growth. The facts are essential; there can be no question about the necessity for full and complete information about our cities. But cities are the creatures of people, built by people for people, and their form is subject to the will of the people. Scientific analysis may indicate trends, but it does not direct action.

Science is an invention—an instrument with which man reaches his objectives, the goals he may set for himself. The force that moves mankind in the selection of these goals is Morality, not science; it is a Morality rooted deep in his culture and sharpened by his intuitive capacity. Man has the power to control his environment; he can mold it to his purpose. He can observe trends, determine their direction, then reverse or shift them to suit his purpose. The course of human events is not some inevitable fate to which the people are destined; it is subject to their will. They can examine the facts and from them they can select their course. This is the power of man and it is the purpose of planning. Guided by a high moral sence, and acting with freedom, the people can plan their cities of tomorrow. And, in the words of John Ruskin, "Let it be as such work that our descendants will thank us for, . . . and that men will say, as they look upon the labor and the wrought substance of them, 'See this our fathers did for us.' "

28

Environmental Practices and Growth Management

CONCERN FOR THE ENVIRONMENT

The changes that we have allowed to occur to the earth's ecological system clearly demonstrate that the welfare of other people is not upper most in our minds. We profess to love our children and grandchildren but we are little concerned with the world we are leaving them. Our negligence would not be so deplorable were the damage that we do to our environment less manifest.

Halting efforts are being made in all parts of the world to check the undisciplined exploitation of nature. Sometimes, the freedom to abuse continues in the guise of the costs involved in making the changes needed to ameliorate the problems. This is particularly true in the areas of pollution and wasted energy. The long term effects of our negligence have not been clearly determined.

IMPACT STUDIES

The environment has little to do with the political boundaries established by the individual communities or nations that we find all over the world. To develop a meaningful environmental impact assessment there is a need for a broad range including all of the elements that would be found in the study of at least a region or metropolitan area. Unfortunately the political entity needed to finance and develop the environmental basis for judgment is almost uniformly absent.

At present each community assesses its own area and the overlapping areas that fall into other jurisdictions. The cost of the individual studies can become monumental.

HOW SHALL WE GROW?

It has been traditionally assumed that continuous growth is essential to economic prosperity. But, an unpleasant fact of life has now become apparent: as urban population swells, public welfare and protection absorb increasing segments of city budgets. In the absence of a national or state policy to direct population distribution, individual cities are obliged to make their own decisions about growth and development. Within the Comprehensive Plan, land uses are designated and population densities distributed; thus the *"carrying capacity"* of the land in a city is measured. It is useful to know the *rate* of estimated population increase by immigration and birth-death rates in anticipating programs to improve and maintain city services. But it is the Comprehensive Plan which establishes how many people a city may accommodate and the quality of environment to be provided for those people. The zoning ordinance translates the land use provisions of the Comprehensive Plan into specific terms. These instruments of planning policy represent the ultimate "growth" policy of a city. Where they are not so designed and not so implemented, the entire planning process is invalid.

These processes for guiding urban development are invalidated to a large extent by the common assumption that a city must find ways and means to accommodate all the people who may choose to live and work within it and that regulations of land use which place limits upon density of use are infringements upon the "property rights" of land owners. Such allegations nullify the planning process and reflect a serious cultural and economic malady: the conflict between the recognition of land as the precious and rare natural resource it is and the concept of land as a *commodity* to be traded as merchandise. The "vested rights" of an owner to use his land as he chooses must be limited to uses that serve the public interest, which are determined by the Comprehensive Plan and the zoning ordinances derived from it.

The small city of Petaluma in northern California, with a population of some 30,000, illustrates the dilemma. Confronted with inadequate public services, sewers, water supply, and schools to accommodate an unprecedented population growth, the city undertook the unusual measure of restricting further development to 500 dwellings a year. The well-financed Construction Industry Association protested the City Ordinance and, in 1974 a Federal Courty Judge ruled "No city can control its population growth numerically."[1]

---

[1] Decision by Judge Lloyd H. Burke, Federal District Court, San Francisco, January 14, 1974.

ENVIRONMENTAL ASSESSMENT PROCESS FLOW CHART

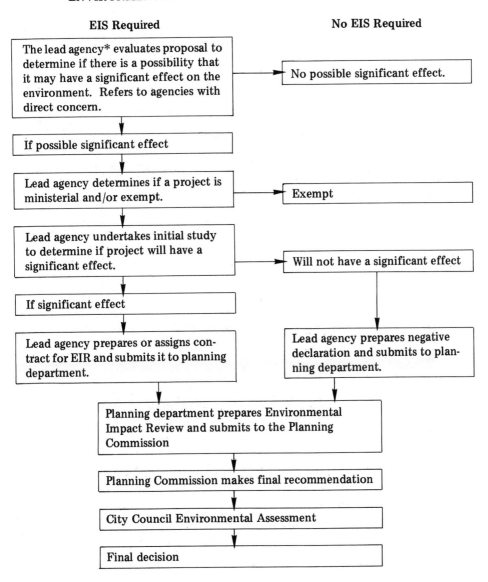

EIS Required

No EIS Required

The lead agency* evaluates proposal to determine if there is a possibility that it may have a significant effect on the environment. Refers to agencies with direct concern.

→ No possible significant effect.

If possible significant effect

Lead agency determines if a project is ministerial and/or exempt.

→ Exempt

Lead agency undertakes initial study to determine if project will have a significant effect.

→ Will not have a significant effect

If significant effect

Lead agency prepares or assigns contract for EIR and submits it to planning department.

Lead agency prepares negative declaration and submits to planning department.

Planning department prepares Environmental Impact Review and submits to the Planning Commission

Planning Commission makes final recommendation

City Council Environmental Assessment

Final decision

*In the majority of cases the planning department is likely to be the lead agency. In some cases, however, the lead agency might be a federal government agency.

The issue was drawn between the right of a city to determine its own character and the obligation to accept all the people who may choose to reside there. The Comprehensive Plan of 1962 (when the population was 17,000) provided for growth to an estimated 77,000 by 1985. The Plan provided a guide for capital improvements of facilities and services in conjunction with expected city revenues.

The Supreme Court however, reversed the lower court decision, holding that the city had developed a careful time table for the expansion of city services. It ruled, more over, that the city's carefully worked out plan was predicated on expected tax revenues and so could not be altered.

The legal strife in Petaluma represents the struggle of cities across the land to control their own destiny. A Zoning Ordinance in 1972 through which the timing and sequence of development in Ramapo, New York could be made consistent with necessary capital improvements for public services, was upheld by the Supreme Court.[2] The issue of "exclusionary" zoning, however, is not fully resolved, and the equitable distribution of housing for all income levels is a complex issue. An ordinance in Fairfax County, Virginia, required 15 per cent of all units in multi-family housing be available to low income families. It was declared unacceptable by the courts, who alleged the provision an illegal "taking" of private property for "public" purposes.

Growing at an alarming rate—from 7,000 in 1960 to 28,000 in 1970—Boca Raton, in Florida, placed a ceiling on its ultimate growth with a limit of 40,000 dwelling units. The impact of growth affects every city, town and village. Sanbornton, New Hampshire, population of 1,000, rezoned to a minimum of six acre sites to forestall compact development.

The issue of property rights versus public interest is subject to a variety of legal interpretations. When development of Great Salt Meadow in Stratford, Connecticut, was denied by the Environmental Protection Commission, already zoned for industrial use, the Rykbar Industrial Corporation contended that the action constituted a "taking" and claimed $77,700,000 in damages. On the same grounds, disapproval of development of a 17-acre site at Fleur de Lac at Lake Tahoe, California, by the Tahoe Regional Planning Agency resulted in a claim for $4,500,000 compensation.

The dilemma is not confined to development of open land. The great concourse of Grand Central Station in New York City, was declared a "landmark" by the New York City Landmarks Protection Commission in 1967. Owned by the Penn Central Railroad, U.G.P. Properties, Inc. leased the *air rights* above this historical monument. Denied the right to build a 59 story office

---

[2] In *Golden v. Planning Board of the Town Ramapo* (1972), the Court stated: "There is then something inherently suspect in a scheme which apart from its professional purposes, effects a restriction upon the free mobility of a people until sometime in the future when projected facilities are available to meet increased demands . . . What we will not countenance, then under any guise, is community efforts at immunization or exclusion. But, far from being exclusionary, the present amendments merely seek, by the implementation of sequential development and timed growth, to provide a balanced cohesive community dedicated to the efficient utilization of land."

building above it, the lessee claimed a "taking" and asked $8,000,000 a year in damages. After "high rise" apartments near the bay front in San Francisco had obliterated dramatic views for inland dwellers, the city created a 40-foot height limit in 1972. It did not apply to the downtown area where the increasing height of skyscraper office buildings was destroying the scale of the picturesque urban silhouette. Also threatened by high rise apartments, San Diego set height limitations along its waterfront and the people of Santa Barbara, by referendum, have limited the height of buildings in their charter, simply because they do not want high rise structures.

How we shall grow to accommodate the new urban population and achieve the civilized quality of the environment toward which we aspire remains a crucial issue confronting cities as we approach the twenty-first century. Violation of the "constitutional right to freedom of movement," alleged in the Petaluma case against the city's restrictive ordinance, is a transparently superficial argument on behalf of those whose interests are exploitation of land. It reinforces the necessity for distribution of population, but should not abrogate the city's obligation, as well as "right," to determine the number of people it shall accommodate and the environment it intends to provide for them.

Premature, scattered, or non-contiguous subdivision of land has perennially plagued city administration. Agricultural zoning is a common protection, but it is usually a device for postponement rather than planning. It has become common practice for cities to finance extensions of public services—water, sewers, roads, etc.—to encourage urban expansion. These costs are then recovered by the city, in whole or in part, through taxes on development over ensuing years.

A multitude of other services, however, must immediately be assured to the new residents—schools, fire and police protection among them. Uncontrolled exploitation of land for development about the periphery of large and small cities exceeds the capacity to provide services and maintain desirable open space. People's desire to escape from the oppressive environment of congestion in cities accelerates the trend toward suburban growth. A balanced use of land and services within the economic capacity of a city to achieve and maintain the quality of environment must be the goal of local administrations.

An enlightened attitude toward the "right" to develop property may emerge as civilized values mature. Meanwhile, this right must be coupled with responsibility to assume the burden of cost it imposes upon the public. This would require that land owners and developers accept the obligation for *all* costs which may be entailed, including extension of facilities and services. Such a policy does not deny the right to use property in accordance with the local land use regulations. It is simply a "carry your own weight" policy. Such regulations would act as one means of "growth control," and take the decision-making power away from the local bureaucracy, which is often arbitrary in its decisions or subject to political pressure.

There is flexibility in the planning process to amend plans and zoning ordinances, but that flexibility cannot be subverted by incompetent, capricious, or corrupt public administrators. Among the most damaging "changing conditions" to which a city is subjected is the subordination of the public interest to commercial exploitation, the easy zoning changes, casual conditional permits, and a variety of special concessions for private advantage.

A City Plan which is a vague diagram or is hardly more than a record of existing land uses transcribed on a map offers nothing but more of the same; for *that* there is no need for a plan. In contrast, a plan which embraces innovative and imaginative measures to correct social problems[3] and misuses of land can be a public commitment to progressive change.

GROWTH MANAGEMENT PLANNING

A central concern in plans for accommodating future population growth is determining where new residential development should take place, given the necessity of providing essential public service. While the costs of additional roads, sewer collector lines, and water lines will be borne eventually by new home buyers, there are other continuing services that must be provided by local governmental units. These latter services include police and fire protection, school bussing, street maintenance, water and sewer systems maintenance, waste collection and disposal, and other maintenance activities. The services in out-lying areas, moreover, are more costly than the same services close to the city's center.

For example, current expenditures for such services as police and fire protection, water and wastewater systems operation and maintenance, street maintenance, and solid waste collection amount to a substantial portion of General Fund expenditures. The costs of police protection, waste collection, and street maintenance alone amount to about 37% of El Centro, Cal. General Fund expenditures. The per capita costs of these services are particularly sensitive to the density of the residential developments so that a widely dispersed pattern of developments can have a substantial impact on municipal finances and local tax rates.

IMPLEMENTING THE COMPREHENSIVE PLAN THROUGH GROWTH MANAGEMENT

The management of community growth and development is not a new technique. Every step taken since the adoption of the first zoning ordinances has been an effort to direct the structural pattern of a city in a way that would bring about

---

[3] The Sketch Plan prepared by "California Tomorrow," published in 1971, lists greater political participation, reduction in unemployment, improved educational opportunities, improved access to health service, combating of hunger and the reduction of crime as social problems that strongly affect the poor of all ethnic groups.

the best, most efficient and desireable living environment for its people. Zoning, however, has not always taken into account the timing and sequence of development and, thus, has not been effective in indicating where or when services can be provided at levels essential to sound community living.

With the requirement that each community prepare a Comprehensive Plan for its future growth and development, there was still the lack of an instrument to provide, other than in a general way, for the phasing and direction of growth. Expansions into new areas are often piecemeal, without the essential studies to determine what the costs of scattered development might be.

In many instances the zoning of the land reflects the decisions before there was a Comprehensive Plan and in most instances, before the decision by the state legislature that zoning must be consistent with the Comprehensive Plan. In the past, community leaders felt that the Plan was s simple guide and therefore had no real meaning in law. In California, this has changed with the adoption of new state laws governing planning. The Plan is now considered critical in all land use decisions because it is the only real indication of how a community wants to grow and how it will attain its goals. Until the law was changed there had been a gap in the process. No ties between the Comprehensive Plan and timing of development existed. Now, however, growth management is to be the vehicle for implementing the Plan proposals by creating timing and directional guidelines based on the ability of the community to absorb growth.

The growth management program is, therefore, an outgrowth of the efforts by community leaders, not to stop growth and change, as much as to direct it and limit it to prescribed boundaries based on community capabilities.

The growth management plan is the bridge between planning and development. It is the evaluation system used to determine if the proposals submitted to the community can be accommodated within the fiscal abilities of the community without causing existing residents and commercial and indus-trial occupants to assume an unreasonable tax burden.

The growth management plan is the best means designed to date to bring about logical implementation of the long range proposals of the Comprehensive Plan. Zoning thereafter becomes the legal vehicle that permits development to proceed in those areas where growth management finds it appropriate and timely.

FACTORS IN GROWTH MANAGEMENT

There must be a well designed Comprehensive Plan which establishes the densities and intensities of land uses and gives an indicaton of the facilities that are required to meet the needs of the residents. Where facilities and services exist, they would be evaluated in terms of the potentials for expanded demands.

If there is a service short fall there should be a determination of the ability of the individual services to expand to meet new demands and when this expansion will be possible, physically and financially. Only after the deter-mination of the "when and how" should the zoning of the land be approved allowing for the development to take place at the densities and purposes set forth in the Comprehensive Plan.

A number of approaches and techniques have been developed to ensure that future growth occurs in a manner consistent with the community's ability to accommodate new growth. Below is a partial list and description of these techniques:

Zoning: The pace and distribution of growth can be affected by the following types of rezoning:

"Downzoning" is intended to reduce the ultimate holding capacity of an area, either in terms of the number of residences or the land available for business expansion. The objective is to reduce the pace of population or economic growth to a level consistent with the community's ability to absorb new people and businesses.

"Upzoning" is intended to increase the ultimate holding capacity of an area and can serve to attract development that might have occured elsewhere. For example, the upzoning of central areas can help reduce growth pressures on undeveloped lands.

Moratoriums: A moratorium is intended to prevent further development for a relatively brief time in order to allow for the completion of studies, plans and the implementation of controls directed toward managing and accommodating growth.

Quotas: These limit the number of housing units that can be built during a period of time and are intended to reduce population growth and to ease the burden of such growth on public facilities and services.

Total population densities: A variety of techniques such as downzoning, moratoriums, and building quotas are used to insure a city's total population does not exceed some stipulated maximum. The maximum is set on the basis of the city's ability to provide services affecting the safety, and general welfare of its residents.

Land banking: In this approach, land is actually bought by local government and then made available for private development under carefully specified conditions (such as consistency with the Comprehensive Plan and the provision for some low-income housing) according to a timed-sequenced capital improvements program. This insures that future growth occurs at a pace compatible with the city's financial resources.

Development rights transfer: All landowners would receive development rights in proportion to the amount of undeveloped land owned within an area, with no single landowner initially owning enough rights to develop all of the land. Unexecuted rights are bought and sold on the free market (independent of land ownership) and tend to be transferred from rural areas to growth areas.

To develop a specific piece of property to the intensity of use designated on the Comprehensive Plan, a developer must accumulate sufficient rights.

Timing and sequencing controls: These controls are intended to affect the distribution, as well as the pace of growth. A well-known application of such controls is Ramapo, New York. The controls were used in conjunction with a master plan and a capital improvements plan, to constrain growth around existing developed areas, to prevent hop-scotch devlopment into agricultural areas, and to forestall development until necessary public services could be made available at reasonable costs.

Each of these approaches must be evaluated on a number of legal, economic, and social criteria. The legality of a particular approach is complicated but tends to revolve around a number of basic questions: Is a regulation related to a "protectable goal" (such as health, safety, or general welfare)? Are equally situated landowners treated equally?

Is the regulation "reasonable" in application as well as intent, and not discriminatory in its application? Is the regulation exclusionary or does it restrict free movement? Answers to each of the above are currently being evaluated by the judicial process.

Economic criteria include the costs of applicaton and administration. For example, land banking can involve substantial public money. Also to be considered are the indirect effects of controls. Quotas, downzoning, and population ceilings can increase the costs of housing, and may accelerate the rate of growth as developers rush to beat impending deadlines (often at higher cost). Social criteria include issues of equity and exclusion and the political impact of governmental intervention.

GROWTH MANAGEMENT—A STUDY OF SMALL CITIES

The cities of El Centro and Holtville lie within 10 miles of each other in a highly productive agricultural area in southeastern California. The problem of growth confronts both of these communities but in different ways. Both are confronted with the potentials of growth, especially as it may be affected by the development of geothermal resources located in the nearby areas. But each has special problems associated with the anticipated growth and each has its own philosophic approach to dealing with growth. El Centro wants to encourage growth. Holtville would discourage it in order to maintain its present rural, low pressure way of living.

In both cities, most of the land within the city limits has been occupied and growth must come by either intensifying the uses within the current city or expanding into the agricultural hinterland. El Centro sees no philosophic problem in the expansion and annexation program, since the major support for the city comes from government and services (the city is the county seat). On the other hand, Holtville is governed largely by persons sympathetic to the preservation of its agricultural resources. Holtville sees any invasion into the agricultural area as a reduction of its economic base.

Both communities have utility problems. El Centro's sewerage disposal system is operating at capacity. The plant could handle the products of growth if the sewer lines were replaced to prevent seepage of ground waters into the lines. Holtville, on the other hand, is not troubled by line capacity, but the treatment plant is underdesigned and there should be a complete moratorium on building until the plant capacity has been improved to prevent the further pollution of local streams and the Salton Sea, a nearby recreational resource.

Water is a problem for Holtville, but does not pose any difficulty for El Centro. Other utilities are private or in special districts that can meet even explosive rates of growth that may come into the valley. The potentials of the geothermal resources may actually mitigate the energy problem for many years to come.

Thus, in the management of growth the entire planning depended on the abilities of the cities to meet the requirements of health and safety for both the current residents and for those who constitute the element of growth.

Two other cities base their growth management plans on entirely different criteria. Both San Juan Capistrano and Rancho Mirage, like many other communities in the world, are deeply concerned about the maintenance of the quality of their environment. They both fear that too rapid growth may allow some development to slip by without adequate project review. Local pressures against increasing the staff that deals with review projects suggests there will be reduction in the number of applications acceptable at any one time.

29

Metamorphosis

SYMBOLS OF PURPOSE

Freedom is a native characteristic of mankind. It has been sought and fought for from time immemorial. Transcending creature instinct for self-preservation, the human mind makes of man a social entity. The creature is conditioned by its environment, whereas man, through his intellect, has the capacity to mold his environment to his purpose. Purpose, then, lies at the vital core of human conduct.

Material progress marks peaks of civilization, but the culture of a people is measured by relative social values and the purpose that directs human progress. The cultivation of human sensibilities, the shaping of intuitive power, and the spiritual content of social institutions elevate a people to the cultural plane. These processes are nurtured in the soil of freedom wherein people share responsibility for society and each man is an active collaborator with his fellowman in directing their mutual affairs.

The city is a laboratory in which the search for freedom is carried on and experiences are tested. The design of the city is the warp and woof of people's lives; the pattern is woven with the toil of mind and hand guided by a purpose. We cannot dissociate purpose from achievement in evaluating the affairs of men or charting a course toward human welfare. We detect symbols of that purpose in city building; symbols of the dominant will of a tyrant or the common weal of free men, the rigid formality of ruling authority or the plastic form of liberty, the sumptuous pretension of aristocracy or the humble simplicity of democracy.

The Pharaohs of Egypt created their symbol of unity—the pyramid. Forged with the toil of countless slaves, the pyramid is a symbol of the unity of uncontested power wielded by autocratic rulers over the lives of people. The Emperors of Rome build great fora, a series of huge projects dedicated to the glory of mighty rulers. Each forum was designed about an axis, the arrangement of structures and spaces dictated by symmetry. Like a symbol of undaunted might, the centerline dominated the cities built by emperors, and when their power waned there were no strong citizens to sustain the social order.

The monarchs of France built avenues and plazas about the symbolic axis of autocratic power. The liberated space of the baroque city was appropriated by rulers rather than the ruled. Louis XIV built his palace and gardens at Versailles. Aloof from the motley crowd of the city, he transferred his court to these magnificent spaces and ordered the streets to focus upon them. *L'état, c'est moi.* ... Louis XV built the Place de la Concorde, and in the center of the formal square he placed a statue of himself. The city was a formless mass of slums on which the bloated forms of palaces and gardens, boulevards and plazas were grafted. The urban population lost its identity as people and became the crowd. Uniform façades lined the avenues as a frame for royalty. The people receded to the borders of the boulevards and took their places as spectators of the stately display rather than participants.

The city of Hellenic democracy was planned for the people. The houses were designed for the amenities of living—each dwelling arranged as every other dwelling for appropriate orientation and privacy. The agora was the meeting place for people and the market place and center of urban activity designed as an outdoor room for the mingling of citizens. The axis was incidental, it was not a dominant feature. Hellenic builders composed rectilinear forms with subtle refinement, shifted the scene from major to minor squares, and surrounded them with the continuous rhythm of colonnades. Streets did not bisect and obstruct the open space reserved for public assembly, and sculpture adorned the public square about the periphery of the open space. Size itself was not the aim of Greek city builders. The agora was large enough to accommodate the citizen population; its space was commodious, but the urban population was small. A monumental quality in public spaces was obtained through a juxtaposition of small and large spaces, contrast between the shape of forms, and the rhythm of voids and solids. The distinction between space for the movement across and circulation within the simple rectangular forms produced an order of quiet dignity.

Human scale was the measure of design in the Hellenic city, and it likewise guided the builders of the medieval town. Emerging from the Dark Ages and unprotected by the broad reaches of empire, the feudal town huddled within the confines of its encircling walls. The church provided the new common bond for humanity and, in response to the spiritual need of the people, the cathedral dominated the town but was not set apart from its surroundings. Built against other buildings, it formed an integral part of the enclosing walls of the plaza. Town life centered upon this plaza and it was designed for the mingling of people intent upon exchanging the products of their labor and learning the news of their fellowman. The urban facilities were designed for use and they were arranged accordingly. Roadways traversed the plaza but left open space free for the movement of people. Fountains served the vital function of water supply and they, like buildings and sculpture, were not isolated within the open space of the public squares.

City design is inextricably woven in the social order of people. The design reveals symbols of the dominant economic, social, political, and spiritual patterns of civilization. The city is a melting pot of cultural forces and its design is the expression.

ECLECTICISM

In the latter part of the eighteenth and early nineteenth centuries social upheaval burst the bonds of monarchical tyranny; the violent tensions of the industrial revolution broke the chain of cultural development. A new freedom was unleashed, but uncertainty of our cultural direction aroused emotional conflicts. An air of overconfidence concealed the indecision of society. The fancy of personal taste was the new right of every individual and it confused critical judgment. Taste sank to mediocre levels, and ugliness settled upon the city.

Recoiling from the dread monotony of the industrial city, people sought escape from the ugly reality. They cloaked public edifices with an artificial pomposity and found retreat in dwellings that simulated sumptuous surrondings of a glorified ancestry. As though to insulate themselves from aesthetic degradation, the arts donned the mantle of classic pedigree. A cultural veneer obscured the ugly environment of the "brown decades" and eclecticism engulfed society. Artificial taste flavored parlor conversation on the arts. Art became a commodity to be bought, sold, and collected; it moved from the streets of the people into the salon.

The muralist who once adorned the walls of buildings stepped down from his scaffold, retired to his studio, and painted pictures to be framed and hung in galleries. Works of art were no longer integral with the environment of people. The stained-glass legends of the cathedral were replaced by book printing. Sculptured figures draped in Roman togas were fitted into the classic pediments of banks and courthouses. Fountains no longer supplied water for the population, they dripped or spouted in memory of some event or person.

Civic design reflected the confusion and uncertainty about aesthetics. Scholars studied the cities of old; they observed the assurance and strong centerline of imperialism and the picturesqueness of the Middle Ages. The past was a vast storehouse of historic forms available for reproduction. New buildings, each with its historic prototype, were assembled about a whole complex of axes shooting off in all directions. Plazas were laced with major and minor axes, streets bisected open spaces at diagonals and at right angles, avenues focused upon pompous structures, and a galaxy of artificial features, statues, fountains, and formal landscape effects were arbitrarily distributed about these spaces. The variety of symmetrical effects interrupted the flow of traffic; both the utility and the scale of open spaces were lost to the people who traversed them.

The grandiose formality of open spaces was awe-inspiring, and the people were impressed. The grand planning of the World's Fairs "took." Like the great Mall in Washington, D.C., generous open space was admired but did not invite relaxation and rarely served as gathering places for the people. Their formal character was more like a picture to be observed rather than partaken of. The delightful quality of our capital city lies in the fine old elm trees that grace the

residential streets and the quaint Georgian houses of the eighteenth century.
Frederick Law Olmsted, the great landscape architect, strove to design open
spaces for the people rather than an abstract feature in a grand plan, and Central
Park in New York City is a case in point. While the people might be better served
if this hugh space had been more adequately distributed, it is nevertheless
designed as a natural park for the people to use.

Eclecticism was a masquerade, and a veritable bazaar of planning forms
appeared. The face of the city concealed the misshapen bulk behind the masque.
Once functional features occupying a graceful place in the environment of
people were now used as decorations on the false face of the city. The shopping
street became the main variety show, but there were also special features. Forms
of ancient Rome were frozen into civic centers, and plazas were carved out of
slums to reveal a railroad station or open a traffic artery. New obstructions were
then substituted: interrupting "squares" or "circles" as spots in which to isolate
diminutive statues. The entire range of architectual and planning styles from
the past were applied to the new city. Tastes were torn asunder in the process of
selecting the appropriate garment or applying the right cosmetic. Inspired by the
Gothic cathedral, the impressiveness of St. Peter's, the charm of the colonial
meeting house, and the dignity of the Georgian mansion, the choice was not an
easy one.

CITIES ARE DATED

Eclecticism with its parade of "styles" beclouded the tradition of city building,
concealing the fact that urban forms in all great periods of culture were the
contemporary expression of creative workers in their day. Neither order in our
cities nor culture in our society can be expected without the creative expression
of the contemporary character of our time.

There were undoubtedly accidental effects among the attractive features in
cities of old, but we may be reasonably confident that the harmony is not due
alone to the patina of age. There is an integrity of character in fine buildings and
spaces that commands respect through the years. It is the integrity of creative
effort, the quality of being *genuine*. It is the quality that gives harmony and
continuity to creative works of all cultures. The process of reproducing the works
from another period leaves a cultural void, and eclecticism is the expression of
that void in our present stage of civilization.

When we observe the cities of old, we find little evidence of the eclecticism
we suffer today. Cultures developed their own characteristics and it is by these
characteristics that we identify them. When we detect signs of imitation we
suspect a decline in civilization or a culture that is not yet mature. Cultures grew,
expanded, evolved; just so did the forms of their cities. Changes in the style of
buildings were reflected in the forms. A cathedral begun during the Romanesque
period was built with heavy walls and small windows, round arches and vaults.
Additions during the Gothic period were designed with pointed arches, refined
tracery, and flying buttresses. The parts of a building were *dated*; we identify the

time when they were built by the style in which they were built. The quality of thus speaking from the past is one we respect; it tells us of the character of the people; it has meaning for us.

Is it not significant that builders of today assume an opposite view of building design? How often we have observed objection to a design which would "date" a building? This contradiction marks a singular contrast with building of past ages and it is, in truth, the base following of fancy, the fashion of substituting artificial pedigree for creative expression. If we were to follow the tradition of great cultures of the past, we today would engage in the most powerful period of creative contemporary city building the world has ever seen. We have the people, the tools, the science, the industry, and the ingenuity to make the finest cities of all time.

CHANGING ATTITUDES

Persons familiar with the current trends and attitudes toward planning will recognize the changes of attitude toward planning when compared with that which existed thirty years ago. The changes and sophistications that have taken place in both the governmental and private levels reflect the concern felt for the public welfare and the understanding that planning is saleable commodity. There is a widespread demand for it. This should not imply that there is no longer a conflict between the regulators and the regulated. The battlegrounds usually pertain to the time delays and the costs involved in meeting regulations such as the new environmental and growth management procedures.

The restudy of the Comprehensive Plan lies ahead as some professionals advance the idea that the plan should be a series of broad policies rather a detailed map. The generality of this approach may please some, especially legislators, for it seems to provide them with a free hand to determine the consistency of their zoning plans and the prerogatives to make decisions that may be more flexible. We are not sure how the indivdual land owner will feel when his property is affected by some unpredicatable use. Some past "General Plans" were so general that the new idea seems but an extension of the approach of having a "no-plan plan."

As the world continues to be more urbanized there will have to be new approaches to solving the many problems associated with employment, housing, health, transportation, education, recreation and the many other needs of people. Each new step that is taken will require understanding of the impact that it will have on people. Each step will add to the responsibilities of the planning profession and will establish the need for the broadening of the scope of its involvement in community affairs. Real problems must be discerned; by working directly with the affected people, we must find ways to solve them. Democracy in the planning process has little place for an elitist, who "knows what is best" for the people.

In order to meet these challenges new tools are already being devised. They include the development of area—wide or regional environmental studies to relieve the pressure on the multiplicity of public agencies that are currently preparing and reviewing individual environmental studies. Data will not only be more extensive, it will be more readily retrievable for use in the decision making process.

All that will still be necessary is the wise decisions, based upon factual data, on the part of the legislators. There will still be the need to differentiate between short term political or economic gains for the few and the preservation of long term values and benefits for the general public.

"GENTRIFICATION"

The renaissance of the central core of cities appears to be under way in some of the most unlikely communities, such as New York City with its troubled economic conditions, Detroit, with decay appearing to etch at the core. In San Francisco, with the reconstruction and beautification of Market Street, the central area has assumed a new appearance and new life.

The trend of middle-class emigration appears to have come to a slowdown if not an end. Competition for close-in accommodations where the life of the city can be experienced is becoming an incentive to the redevelopment of older buildings and the rents on formerly abandoned structures are skyrocketing.

The "SoHo" section of New York City is a prime example of what is happening in many places.[1]

> The experience of SoHo (an abbreviation of Southern Houston) in New York, where an art colony was encouraged, is instructive. When the rehabilitated space was offered for rent or lease, the immediate attraction of the project for renters caused rents to skyrocket. Rents originally ranging from 60¢ to $1.60 per square foot escalated up to $3.00 or more a square foot. In addition, there are reports that persons desiring apartments have paid several thousands of dollars as "key money," in order to secure a lease. The people now occupying the facilities are only those who can afford to pay rents at the inflated prices or were able to buy accommodations before the area became glamorous.

An article in the *New York Times Magazine* cites many of the factors that are leading to the revitalization of the central core areas.[2] The decay that is setting in at suburban locations, the boredom and uniformity of the setting, the lack of cultural opportunities, the time spent getting to work each day, the rising crime rates, the increased cost of land and housing, the added burden of the rising cost of transportation, the threat of gasoline shortages and many other factors make the return to the central city attractive.

---

[1] Based on information provided by Ms. Adriana R. Kleiman AIP, Principal Planner on the staff of the Planning Department of New York City.

[2] "The New Elite and Urban Renaissance," Blake Fleetwood, *New York Times Magazine* January 14, 1979.

As these events take place, the poor and minorities now living in the central areas are driven out by the rising cost of living space. There may be a flight to the suburbs as the cost of housing in these outlying areas decreases. The need for places of employment for blue and white collar workers will become monumental in these outlying areas. New social and economic problems may surface outside of the areas where they have tended to concentrate in the past.

As the central areas become the haven for the new "gentry," as the *Times* article calls the new residents, the suburbs may have problems that will need much planning attention: economic planning, social planning and physical efforts to turn the changes in occupancy into advantages for the people who will live there.

BIBLIOGRAPHY

PART 1

Adams, Thomas. *Outline of Town and City Planning.* Russell Sage Foundation, New York, 1935.

Aristotle. *Politics.*

Bannister, Turpin. *Early Town Planning in New York State.* American Society of Architectural Historians.

Benson, Edwin. *Life in a Medieval City.* London, 1920.

Bonavia, David, and Editors of Time-Life Books. *Peking.* Time-Life International, Amsterdam, 1978.

Bosanquet, R. C. "Greek and Roman Towns." *Town Planning Review.* January–October 1915.

Breasted, James Henry. *Ancient Times: A History of the Early World.* Ginn & Co., Boston, 1914.

Bridgeport Brass Company. *History of Sanitation.* Bridgeport, 1930.

Brion, Marcel. *Pompeii and Herculaneum.* Crown Publishers, New York, 1960.

Churchill, Henry. *The City Is the People.* Reynal & Hitchcock, New York, 1945.

Davis, K. "The Origin and Growth of Urbanization in the World." *American Journal of Sociology,* 60 (5): 429–437, March 1955.

Gardner, Percy. *The Planning of Hellenistic Cities.*

Giedion, Sigfried. *Space, Time and Architecture.* Harvard U. Press, Cambridge, Mass., 1943; rev. ed., 1954.

Glotz, Gustave. *The Greek City and Its Institutions.* Kegan Paul, Trench, Trubner, 1929.

―――――. *The Aegean Civilization.* Alfred A. Knopf, New York, 1925.

Green, Alice Stopford. *Town Life in the 15th Century.* 2 vols., London, 1894.

Green, Constance M. *American Cities in the Growth of the Nation.* John de Graff, New York, 1957.

Hamlin, Talbot. *Architecture Through the Ages.* G. P. Putnam's Sons, 1940.

Hammarstrand, Nils. "Cities Old and New." *Journal of the American Institute of Architects, New York, 1926.*

Hatt, P. K. and Reiss, A. J., Jr. *Cities and Society:The Revised Reader in Urban Sociology.* Free Press, Glencoe, Ill., 1957.

Haverfield, Francis J. *Ancient Town Planning.* Clarendon Press, Oxford, 1913.

―――――. *Town Planning in the Roman World.* Town Planning Conference, Transactions, R.I.B.A., London, 1910.

Hilberseimer, Ludwig. *The New City.* Paul Theobald, Chicago, 1944.

Hiorns, Frederick Robert. *Town Building in History.* Harrap, London, 1956.

Korn, Arthur. *History Builds the Town.* Lund Humphries, London, 1953.

Lavedan, Pierre. *Antiquité, Moyen Age: Histoire de l'Urbanisme,* Vol. I, Paris, 1926.

Lee, R. H. *The City: Urbanism and Urbanization in Major World Regions.* J. B. Lippincott, Philadelphia, 1955.

"Lost Worlds," by the Editors of *Horizon* magazine. American Heritage, 1962.

Macaulay, Rose and Roloff, Beny. *Pleasure of Ruins.* Norwich Eng., Thames and Hudson, 1964.

Marinatos, Spyridon. *Crete and Mycenae.* Harry N. Abrams, New York, 1961.

Marshall, Sir John. *Mohenjo-daro and the Indus Civilization.* Arthur Probsthain, London, 1931.

Mayer, Harold H., and Kohn, Clyde F. *Readings in Urban Geography.* U. of Chicago Press, 1959.

McDonald, William A. *The Political Meeting Places of the Greeks.* Johns Hopkins Press, Baltimore, 1943.

Moses, Robert. "What Happened to Haussmann." *Architectural Forum,* July 1942.

Mumford, Lewis. *The Culture of Cities.* Harcourt, Brace, New York, 1938.

————. *The Condition of Man.* Harcourt, Brace, New York, 1944.

————. *City Development.* Harcourt, Brace, New York, 1945.

————. *The Natural History of Urbanization in International Symposium on Man's Role in Changing the Face of the Earth.* U. of Chicago Press, 1956.

————. *The City in History: Its Origins, Its Transformations, and Its Prospects.* Harcourt, Brace, New York, 1961.

Murphy, Raymond E. *The American City: An Urban Georgraphy.* McGraw-Hill, New York, 1966.

Our Continent: A Natural History of North America. National Geographic Society, Washington, D.C., 1976.

Our World from the Air: A Survey of Man and His Environment. Doubleday and Company, 1952

Peets, Elbert. "The Genealogy of L'Enfant's Washington." *Journal of the American Institute of Architects*, April, May, June 1927.

Pirenne, Henri. *Medieval Cities.* Trans. Frank Halsey. Princeton U. Press, 1925.

Plato. *The Republic.*

Poète, Marcel. *Introduction à l'Urbanisme: L'Evolution des Villes, La Leçon de l'Antiquité.* Paris, 1929.

Renard, Georges François. *Guilds in the Middle Ages.* London, 1919.

Robinson, David M. *Domestic and Public Architecture: Excavations at Olynthus, Part XII.* Johns Hopkins Press, Baltimore, 1946.

Robson, W. A., Ed. *Great Cities of the World: Their Government, Politics and Planning.* Macmillan, New York, 1955.

Roseman, Rose. *The Ideal City.* Boston Book & Art Shop, Boston, 1959.

Rostovtzeff, M. *The Orient and Greece: A History of the Ancient World, Vol 1.* Oxford U. Press.

Sandstrom, Gosta E. *Man the Builder.* McGraw-Hill, New York, 1970.

Seminar Research Bureau. *City in Crisis.* Boston College, Chestnut Hill, Mass., 1959.

Sitte, Camille. *The Art of Building Cities.* Reinhold Publishing, New York, 1945.

Smithsonian Institution. *Bureau of Ethnology, 8th Annual Report.* Government Printing Offce, 1891.

Stewart, C. A. *Prospect of Cities: Being Studies Towards a History of Town Planning.* Longmans, Green & Co., London, 1952.

Straus and Wegg. *Housing Comes of Age.* Oxford U. Press, New York, 1938.

Thomas, William L., ed., with the collaboration of Carl O. Sauer, Marston Bates, and Lewis Mumford. *Man's Role in Changing the Face of the Earth.* U. of Chicago Press, 1956.

Town Planning Review. *Haussmann.* June, 1927.

Triggs, H. I. *Town Planning.* London, 1890.

Tunnard, C. *The City of Man.* Scribner, New York, 1953.

Vitruvius. *The Ten Books on Architecture.* Harvard U. Press, 1914.

Wallbank, T. Walter and Taylor, Alastair M. *Civilization Past and Present.* Scott Foresman & Co., Chicago, 1942.

Williams, Henry Smith. *The Historian's History of the World.* The Outlook Co., 1904.

Wirth, Louis. "Urbanism as a Way of Life." *American Journal of Sociology* 44 (July 1938).

Wolfe, M. R. *Locational Factors—Suburban Land Development.* Prepared for the Weyerhaeuser Co. in the College of Architecture and Urban Planning, University of Washington, Seattle, July 1961.

World of Ancient Rome. Ed. Giannelli Giulio. Putnam, New York, 1967.

Wycherley, R. E. *How the Greeks Built Cities.* The Macmillan Co., New York, 1949.

Yugoslav Cities. Ed. *The Yugoslav Review Magazine.* Stampa, 1965.

Yutang, Lin. *Imperial Peking.* Crown Publishers, New York, 1961.

Zucker, Paul. *Town and Square.* University Press, New York, 1959.

PART 2

Abercrombie, Patrick. *Greater London Plan, 1944.* His Majesty's Stationery Office, London, 1945.

Abrams, Charles. *The Future of Housing.* Harper, New York, 1946.

Alm, Ulla. *Cooperative Housing in Sweden.* The Royal Swedish Commission, Stockholm, 1939.

American Institute of Architects. *Reports of Committee on Community Planning.* New York 1924, 1925, 1926, 1927.

Architectural Forum. "Limited Dividend Roll Call." January, 1935.

Aronovici, Carol. *Housing the Masses.* John Wiley & Sons, New York 1939.

Augur, Tracy. "Planning Principles Applied in Wartime." *Architectural Record,* January, 1943.

Bartholomew, Harland. *Urban Land Uses.* Harvard City Planning Series. Harvard U. Press, 1932.

Bauer, Catherine. *Modern Housing.* Houghton Mifflin Co., Boston, 1934.

Boardman, Philip. *Patrick Geddes: Maker of the Future.* U. of North Carolina Press, Chapel Hill, N.C., 1944.

Boyd, John Taylor, Jr. "Toward the Reconstruction of New York's Lower East Side." *Architectural Forum,* January, August 1932.

Buckingham, James Silk. *National Evils and Practical Remedies.* London, 1849.

Burnham, Daniel H., and Bennett, Edward H. *Plan of Chicago.* Ed. Charles Moore. Commercial Club, Chicago, 1909.

Childs, Marquis. *The Middle Way.* Yale U. Press, 1936.

Churchill, Henry. *The City Is the People.* Reynal & Hitchcock, New York, 1945.

Dean, John P. *Home Ownership: Is It Sound?* Harper & Brothers, New York, 1945.

DeForest and Veiller. *The Tenement House Problem, Vols. I and II.* Macmillan, New York, 1903.

Denby, Elizabeth. *Europe Rehoused.* W. W. Norton & Co., New York, 1938.

Dickens, Charles. *Hard Times.* London, 1854.

Encyclopaedia Britannica, "Land," vol. 14, R. S. Peale Edition, The Werner Co., Chicago, 1893.

Engels, Friedrich. *The Condition of the Working-Class in England in 1844.* Leipzig, 1845; London, 1887.

Federal Emergency Administration of Public Works. *Homes for Workers.* Housing Division Bulletin No. 3, Washington, D.C., 1937.

Filene, Edward A. *The Way Out.* New York, 1924.

Ford, James. *Slums and Housing.* Harvard U. Press, Cambridge, Mass., 1936.

Forshaw, J. H., and Abercrombie, Patrick. *County of London Plan.* Macmillan & Co., London, 1943.

Fortune Editors. *Housing America.* Harcourt, Brace & Co., New York, 1935.

Geddes, Patrick. *Cities in Evolution.* London, 1915; revised, Williams and Northgate, London, 1949.

_____. *City Deterioration and the Need of City Survey.* The Annals of the American Academy of Political and Social Sciences, July 1909.

_____. "Talks from My Outlook Tower." *Survey Graphic,* February, April 1925.

George, Henry. *Progress and Poverty.* New York, 1879.

Gerckens, Laurence C. "American City Planning Since 1900 A.D." 1976–77 Edition. School of Architecture, Ohio State University, 1976.

Gray, George. *Housing and Citizenship.* Reinhold Publishing Corp., New York, 1946.

Graham, John. *Housing in Scandinavia.* U. of North Carolina Press, Chapel Hill, N.C., 1940.

Hardy, Charles O., assisted by Kucznzki, Robert R. *The Housing Program of the City of Vienna.* The Brookings Institution, Washington, D.C., 1934.

Hegemann, Werner. *City Planning: Housing,* Vol. I, Historical and Sociological. Architectural Book Publishing Co., New York, 1936.

_____. *City Planning: Housing,* Vol. II, Political Economy and Civic Art. Architectural Book Publishing Co., New York, 1938.

_____. *City Planning: Housing,* Vol. III, A Graphic Review of Civic Art. Architectural Book Publishing Co., New York, 1938.

Hoagland, Henry. *Real Estate Principles.* McGraw-Hill, New York, 1940.

Home Loan Bank Board. *The Federal Home Loan Bank System.* Washington, D.C., August 1947.

Housing and Public Health Committee. *London Housing.* London County Council, 1937.

Howard, Ebenezer. *Garden Cities of Tomorrow.* London, 1902; First Edition—*Tomorrow*—London, 1898.

Hoyt, Homer, *100 Years of Land Values in Chicago.* U. of Chicago Press, 1933.

Johansson, Alf and Svenson, Waldemar. *Swedish Housing Policy.* The Royal Swedish Commission. In *Annals of the American Academy of Political and Social Sciences,* May 1938.

Johnson-Marshall, Percey. *Rebuilding Cities.* Aldine Publishing Co., Chicago, 1966.

Justement, Louis. *New Cities for Old.* McGraw-Hill, New York, 1946.

Le Corbusier. *The City of Tomorrow.* The Architectural Press, London, 1929.

_____. *La Ville Radieuse.* Boulogne, 1934.

_____. *When the Cathedrals Were White.* Reynal & Hitchcock, New York, 1947.

_____. *Concerning Town Planning.* Trans. Clive Entwistle. Yale U. Press, New Haven, 1948.

_____. *New World of Space.* Reynal & Hitchcock, New York, 1948.

_____. and Pierre Jeanneret. *Oeuvre Complet, 1910–1929,* Verlag Dr. H. Girsberger & Cie., Zurich, 1930. *1929–34,* Willy Boesiger, Zurich, Les Editions d'Architecture, Erlenbach, Zurich. *1934–38,* Max Bill, Editions Dr. H. Girsberger, Zurich, 1945. *1938–46.* Willy Boesiger, Les Editions d'Architecture, Zurich. *1946–52,* Editions Girsberger, Zurich, 1953. *1952–57,* Editions Girsberger, Zurich, 1957.

Leven, Maurice, Moulton, Harold G, and Warburton, Clark. *America's Capacity to Consume.* The Brookings Institution, Washington, D.C., 1934.

Lohmann, Karl B. *Principles of City Planning.* McGraw-Hill, New York, 1931.

Mayer, Albert. "Greenbelt Towns Revisited." Journal of Housing, 1967.

McAllister, Gilbert and Glen, Elizabeth. *Town and County Planning.* Faber & Faber, London, 1941.

McRae, John, "Elderly in the Environment: Northern Europe." U. of Florida, Gainesville, Fla., 1975.

McQuade, Walter. *Cities Fit to Live in and How We Can Make Them Happen.* Macmillan, New York, 1971.

Moore, Charles. *Daniel Burnham: Architect, Planner of Cities.* 2 vols., Boston, 1921.

Mumford, Lewis. *The Story of the Utopias.* New York, 1922.

Nolen, John. *City Planning.* New York, 1929.

Olmsted, Frederick Law. *Public Works and the Enlargement of Towns.* Cambridge, Mass.,1870.

Owen, Robert. *A New View of Society.* London, 1813.

Osman, John. *Architectural Forum,* August 1957.

Purdom, Charles B. *Building of Satellite Towns.* London, 1926.

_____. *Town Theory and Practice.* London, 1921.

_____. *The Garden City.* London, 1923.

Reps, John W. *The Making of Urban America.* Princeton U. Press, 1965.

Riis, Jacob. *How the Other Half Lives.* Charles Scribner's Sons, New York, 1934. Original edition, 1890.

Robinson, Charles Mulford. *City Planning.* New York, 1916.

Robinson, Joan. "Economic Management in China." Modern China Series. Anglo-Chinese Educational Institute, London, Nov. 1976.

Scott, Mel. *Cities Are for People.* Pacific Southwest Academy, Los Angeles, 1942.

Sennett, Alfred R. *Garden Cities in Theory and Practice.* 2 vols., London, 1905.

Sert, José. *Can Our Cities Survive?* Harvard U. Press, Cambridge, 1942.

Simon, Sir E. D. *Rebuilding Britain: A Twenty Year Plan.* Victor Gollanez, Ltd., 1945.

_____. *The Rebuilding of Manchester.* Longmans, Green & Co., New York, 1935.

Smith, Adam. *An Inquiry into the Nature and Causes of the Wealth of Nations.* 2 vols., London, 1776.

Steffens, Lincoln. *The Shame of Cities.* Collection from *McClure's Magazine.*

Stein, Clarence. "The Price of Slum Clearance." *Architectural Forum,* February 1934.

Stern, Sylvia, "Housing for the Elderly." Unpub. paper, U.C.L.A., 1978.

Straus, Nathan. *The Seven Myths of Housing.* Alfred A. Knopf, New York, 1944.

Survey Graphic. "Homes," a special number, February 1940.

_____. "The Case Against Home Ownership," by Stuart Chase, May 1938.

Thoreau, Henry David. *Walden*. Boston, 1854.

Unwin, Raymond. *Town Planning in Practice*. London, 1909.

_____. *Nothing Gained in Overcrowding*. Garden Cities and Town Planning Association, London, 1912.

Urban Renewal Division, Sears, Roebuck & Co., ABC's of Urban Renewal 1957.

Weimar, Arthur and Hoyt, Homer. *Principles of Real Estate*. The Ronald Press Co., New York, 1954.

Wendt, Paul F. *Housing Policy: The Search for Solutions*. U. of California Press, Berkley, 1962.

Winnick, Louis. *American Housing and Its Use: The Demand for Shelter Space*. John Wiley & Sons, New York 1957.

Wright, Henry. *Rehousing Urban America*. Columbia U. Press, New York, 1935.

PART 3

Abrams, Charles. *Revolution in Land*. Harper & Brothers, New York, 1939.

Action for Cities. American Municipal Association, Public Administration Service, Chicago, 1943.

Adams, Thomas. *Outline of Town and City Planning*. Russell Sage Foundation, New York, 1935.

American Bar Association. *Municipal Law Service Letter,* Vol. 10, No. 1, January, 1960.

Bauer, C. *The Pattern of Urban and Economic Development*. American Academy—Political Science Annual, May 1956.

Bettman, Alfred. "The Decisions of the Supreme Court of the U.S. in the Euclid Village Zoning Case." *University of Cincinnati Law Review, March, 1927.*

_____. *City and Regional Papers*. Ed. Arthur C. Comey. Harvard U. Press, Cambridge, Mass., 1946.

Bogardus, E.S. *Fundamentals of Social Psychology*. D. Appleton-Century Co., New York, 1942.

Bogue, D. J., ed. *Applications of Demography: The Situation in the United States in 1975.* Scripps Foundation Studies in Population, Oxford, Ohio, 1957.

Citizens' Housing and Planning Council of New York. *A Citizen's Guide to Rezoning.* 1959.

Friedmann, John. "The Good Society." U.C.L.A., June, 1976.

Hagman, Donald G. *Urban Planning and Land Development Control Laws*. West Publishing Co., St. Paul, Minn., Rpt., 1975.

Hallman, Howard W. "The Organization of Neighborhood Councils." Center for Government Studies, 1977.

Kingsley, S. C. *Methods of Winning Public Support for a City Planning Program.* Proceedings, 14th National Conference on City Planning, 1922.

Meyers, William; Dorwart, Robert; Kline, David. "Social Ecology and Citizen Boards: A Problem for Planners." *A.I.P. Journal,* April, 1977.

McClenahan, Bessie Averne. *The Sociology of Planning: Sociology and Social Research.* University of Southern California.

Moody, W. D. *Wacker's Manual of the Plan of Chicago.* Chicago Plan Commission, Calumet Publishing Co., Chicago, 1916.

National Municipal League. *The Citizen Association: How to Organize and Run It.* New York, 1958.

————. *The Citizen Association: How to Win Civic Campaigns.* 2nd ed., New York, 1959.

National Urban Policy. Report of The President's Urban and Regional Policy Group, H.U.D. Washington, D.C., March, 1978.

Scott, Mel. *Cities Are for People.* Pacific Southwest Academy, Los Angeles, 1942.

Siegel, Shirley Adelson. *The Law of Open Space: Legal Aspects of Acquiring or Othwise Preserving Open Space in the Tri-State New York Metropolitan Region.* Regional Plan Association, New York, 1960.

Walker, Robert Averill. *The Planning Function in Urban Government.* U. of Chicago Press, 1950.

Webster, Donald H. *Urban Planning and Municipal Public Policy.* Harper and Row, New York, 1958.

————. *Urban Planning and Municipal Policy.* Harper and Row, New York, 1958.

Wood, Robert C. *1400 Governments.* Harvard U. Press, Cambridge, Mass., 1961.

PART 4

Abrahamson, Julia. *A Neighborhood Finds Itself.* Harper and Row, New York, 1959.

Adams, Thomas. *Design of Residential Areas.* Harvard U. Press, Cambridge, Mass., 1934.

————. "What Proportion of Public Land and of Private Land Should be Reserved for Open Space." *American City,* June, 1928.

Alterman, Rachelle and Hill, Morris. "Implementation of Urban Land Use Plans." *A.I.P. Journal,* July, 1978.

American Association of State Highway Officials. *A Policy on Arterial Highways in Urban Areas.* Washington, D.C., 1957.

American Automobile Association. *Parking and Terminal Facilities.* Washington, D.C., 1940.

————. *Parking Manual: How to Solve Community Parking Problems.* Washington, D.C., 1946.

————. *Roadside Protection.* Washington, D.C., 1951.

American Institute of Planners. *Land Use and Traffic Models. May, 1959.*

American Public Health Association. *Planning the Neighborhood.* Committee on the Hygiene of Housing, Public Adminstration Service, Chicago, 1960.

————. *Planning the Home for Occupancy.* Committee on the Hygiene of Housing, Public Administration Service, Chicago, 1950.

American Public Works Association. *Airports: Location, Design, Financing, Zoning, and Control.* Chicago, 1945.

American Society of Planning Officials. *Preliminary Report of Committee on Park and Recreation Standards.* Herbert Hare, Chairman, S. R. DeBoer, Russell H. Riley; Proceedings, Annual Meeting, Chicago, 1943.

————. *A Program for Tax Abandoned Lands.* Chicago, 1942.

————. *A Model State Subdivision Control Acts.* Chicago, 1947.

American Transit Association. *Moving People in Modern Cities.* New York, 1944.

Anderson, Nels, and Lindeman, E. C. *Urban Sociology.* Alfred A. Knopf, 1928.

Architectural Forum, "By 1976 What City Pattern?" September, 1956.

Automobile Club of Southern California. *California Statutes Relating to Public Acquisition of Off-Street Parking Facilities.* Los Angeles, 1958.

Baker, Geoffrey, and Funaro, Bruno. *Parking,* Reinhold Publishing Corp., New York, 1958.

Barnett, Joseph. "Express Highway Planning in Metropolitan Areas." *Transactions of the American Society of Civil Engineers,* Vol. 112, 1947.

Bartley, Ernest A. and Bair, Frederick H. Jr. *Mobile Home Parks and Comprehensive Community Planning.* Studies in Public Administration, #19. Public Administration Clearing Service, U. of Florida, Miami, 1960.

Bartholomew, Harland and Wood, J. *Land Uses American Cities.* Harvard U. Press, Cambridge, Mass., 1955.

Bartholomew, Harland. *The Place of the Railroad in the City Plan.* Proceedings, National Conference on City Planning, 1926.

Bassett, Edward M. *Model Laws for the Planning of Cities, Counties and States.* Harvard U. Press, Cambridge, Mass., 1935.

————. *The Master Plan.* Russell Sage Foundation, New York, 1938.

————. *Zoning.* Russell Sage Foundation, New York, 1940.

Bibbin, J. R. *Planning for City Traffic.* American Academy of Political and Social Sciences, 1927.

Black, H. "Detroit: A Case Study in Industrial Problems of a Central City." *Land Economics,* August, 1958.

Black, Russell Van Nest. *Planning the Small American City.* Public Administration-Service, Chicago, 1944.

————. *Building Lines.* Harvard U. Press, Cambridge, Mass., 1935.

Blanchard-Nichols Associates. "The True Look of the Super Market Industry, 1958." *Super Market Merchandising,* Los Angeles, 1959.

Blucher, Walter H., Executive Director, American Society of Planning Officials. In *Planning,* 1945, Part 1, Chicago, May 16–17, 1945.

Blumenfeld, H. *Are Land Use Patterns Predictable? A.I.P. Journal,* May, 1959.

Breese, G. W. *Industrial Site Selection, Burlington County, N.J.: A Case Study of Existing and Potential Industrial Location.* Princeton U. Press, Princeton, N.J., 1954.

Brewster Publishing Co. *Patterns on the Land: Geographical, Historical, and Politcal Maps of California.* Los Angeles, 1957.

Brown, Thomas H. "Long Range Aviation Planning in the Northeast," *Traffic Quarterly,* Eno Foundation for Transportation, January, 1979.

Buckley, James C. "Comprehensive Transportation and Terminal Planning for Large Urban Centers." *A.I.P. Journal,* Winter, 1947.

Building the Future City. Annals of the American Academy of Political and Social Sciences, Philadelphia, 1945.

Bureau of Public Roads. *Toll Roads and Free Roads.* Department of Agriculture, Washington, D.C., 1939.

Butler, George. *Introduction to Community Recreation.* McGraw-Hill, New York, 1940.
_____. *Recreation Areas.* Ronald Press, New York, 1958.
California Committee on Planning for Recreation, Park Areas and Facilities. *Guide for Planning Recreation Parks in California. A Basis for Determining Local Recreation Space Standards.* Scramento, 1956.
California Divison of Highways. *Los Angeles Regional Transportation Study.* Los Angeles, 1960.
California State Reconstruction and Reemployment Commission. *Forecasting a City's Future.* Sacramento, 1946.
Caudill, Harry M. *My Land is Dying.* E. P. Dutton, New York, 1971.
Central Association of Seattle. *Planning the Future of Seattle's Central Area.* Planning Commission, Seattle, 1959.
Chamber of Commerce of the U.S. *Urban Transportation.* Washington, D.C., May 1945.
_____. *Making Better Use of Today's Street.* Washington, D.C., 1947.
Chamber of Commerce Parking Clinic. *Shopper Bottleneck.* U.S. Chamber of Commerce, Washington, D.C., March 1953.
Chapin, F. Stuart, Jr. *Urban Land Use Planning.* Harper & Row, New York, 1957.
_____. *Shopping Centers Design and Operation.* Reinhold Publishing, New York, 1951.
Churchill, Henry, and Ittleson, Roslyn. *Neighborhood Design and Control. An Analysis of the Problem of Planned Subdivisions.* National Committee on Housing, New York 1944.
City of Detroit, City Plan Commission. *Proposed Generalized Land Use Plan.* Detroit, 1947.
Civil Aeronautics Administration. *Small Airports.* Washington, D.C., September 1945.
_____. *Airport Planning for Urban Areas.* Washington. D.C., 1945.
Claire, William H. *Study of a Truck Terminal Under A Freeway.* Community Redevelopment Agency, Los Angeles, 1952.
Clawson, Marion. *The Dynamics of Park Demand.* Regional Plan Association, New York,1960.
_____. *Methods of Measuring the Demand For and Value of Outdoor Recreation.* Resources for the Future. Inc., Washington, D.C., 1959.
Clawson, Marion; Held, R. Burnell; and Stoddard, Charles H. *Land for the Future,* Johns Hopkins Press, Baltimore, 1960.
Cleveland City Planning Commission. *Downtown Cleveland—1975.* Cleveland, 1959.
Collison. Peter. "British Town Planning and the Neighborhood Idea," Oxford U. *Housing Centre Review* (British), Vol. 5, No. 6, December, 1956.
Contini, Edgardo. *The Renewal of Downtown U.S.A.* Victor Gruen & Associates, 1956.
County of Los Angeles Regional Planning Commission. Master Plan of Airports. Los Angeles, 1940.
Dahir, James. *The Neighborhood Unit Plan.* Russell Sage Foundation, New York, 1947.
Davis, Harmer E. *How May the Planning, Financing and Construction of Vehicular and Mass Transit Systems in the Modern Metroplitan Area Be Integrated? Part I: A Statement of the General Problem.* U. of California, Berkeley, 1955.
De Leuw, Cather & Co. *Report on Parking Facilities for the City of Chicago.* Chicago, 1956.
Denby, Elizabeth. *Europe Rehoused.* W. W. Norton, New York, 1938.
Denver Planning Office. *Lower Downtown Denver.* Denver, 1958.
Denver University. *A "Before and After" Study of Effects of a Limited Access Highway*

Upon the Business Activity of By-Passed Communities and Upon Land Value and Land Use. Bureau of Business and Social Research, 1958.

Detroit City Plan Commission. *Neighborhood Conservation.* Committee for Neighborhood Conservation and Improved Housing, Detroit, March, 1956.

Dobriner, William M. *The Suburban Community.* G. P. Putnam's Sons, New York, 1958.

Dowling, Robert. "Neighborhood Shopping Centers." *Architectural Forum,* October, 1943.

Duke University School of Law. "Land Planning in a Democracy." *Law and Contemporary Problems,* Spring, 1955.

Engelhardt, N. L., and Engelhardt, F. *Planning School Building Programs,* Columbia University Press, New York, 1930.

Eno Foundation for Highway Traffic Control. Saugatuck, Conn.:

"Layout and Design of Parking Lots: Aesthetic Consideration." *Traffic Quarterly,* January 1952.

The Legal Responsibilities of Traffic Agencies. 1948.

Parking. 1957.

Poissen & Traffic. 1955.

Shopping Centers. 1956.

Some Traffic Factors in Urban Planning.

Statistics with Applications to Highway Traffic Analyses. 1952.

Traffic Design of Parking Garages. 1957.

Traffic Performance at Urban Street Intersections. Elroy L. Erickson, 1947.

Turn Controls in Urban Traffic. 1951.

Zoning and Traffic. 1952.

Parking: Legal, Financial, Administrative. Joint Committe on Urban Traffic Congestion and Parking, 1956.

Highway Traffic Estimation. Robert E. Schmitt and M. Earl Campbell, 1956.

A Modified O. and D. Survey. Robert D. Dier, 1953.

Fawcett, C. B. *A Residential Unit for Town and Country Planning.* U. of London Press, London, 1943.

Federal Housing Administration. *Planning Profitable Neighborhoods. Washington, D.C., 1938.*

_____. *Neighborhood Standards.* Land Planning Bulletin No. 3, Los Angeles, 1953.

Federal Works Agency. *State Laws Related to "Freeways."* Public Roads Administration Washington, D.C., 1940.

Foley, Donald L. "The Daily Movement of Population Into Central Business Districts." *American Sociological Review,* 17, October, 1952.

Ford, G. B. *Building Height, Bulk, and Form.* Harvard U. Press, Cambridge, Mass., 1931.

Ford, Henry. *Ford Ideals: A Selection from "Mr. Ford's Page" in the Dearborn Independent.* The Dearborn Publishing Company, Dearborn, Mich., 1922.

Fordham, Jefferson B. "Local Government's Power to Provide and Finance Parking Facilities." *Traffic Quarterly,* Eno Foundation for Highway Traffic Control, Saugatuck, Conn., 1951.

Fowlkes, John Guy. *Planning Schools for Tomorrow,* Committee on Planning for Education, U.S. Office of Education, Washington, D.C., 1942.

Freilich, Robert H. and John W. Ragsdale Jr. *Development Framework Data Report.* Metropolitan Council of Twin City Area, January, 1974.

Freeways for the Region. County of Los Angeles Regional Planning Commission, Los Angeles, 1943.

Garrison, William L., and Marts, Marion E. *Influence of Highway Improvements on*

Urban Land: A Graphic Summary. Highway Economic Studies, University of Washington, Seattle, 1958.

Geddes, Norman Bel. *Magic Motorways.* Random House, New York, 1940.

Gruen, Victor, and Smith, Larry. *Shopping Towns U.S.A.* Reinhold Publishing Corp.

Haar, Charles M. *Land Use Planning.* Little, Brown, Boston, 1959.

Hagman, Donald. "A New Deal: Trading Windfalls for Wipeouts." *Planning, September, 1974.*

Harvard Graduate School of Design. *The Traffic Problem.* Department of Regional Planning, Cambridge, Mass., 1952.

The Heart Of Our Cities. Simon and Schuster, New York, 1964.

Heliport Design Guide. Federal Aviation Agency, Washington, D.C., 1959.

Heyer, Paul. *Architects On Architecture.* Walker, New York, 1966.

"Historic Preservation Plan, Savannah, Ga." HUD, Washington, D.C., 1973.

Hjelte, George. *The Administration of Public Recreation.* The Macmillan Co., New York, 1939.

Horack, F. E., Jr., and Nolan, V. Jr. *Land Use Controls.* West Publishing Co., St. Paul, Minn., 1955.

Horwood, Edgar M., and Boyce, Ronald R. *Studies of the Central Business District and Urban Freeway Development.* U. of Washington Press, Seattle, 1959.

Hoyt, Homer. *Urban Land.* September, 1961.

Hubbard, H. V. *Parks and Playgrounds.* Proceedings of the 14th National Conference on City Planning, 1922.

Hubbard, Henry V., Williams, Frank B., McClintock, Miller. *Airports.* Harvard U. Press, Cambridge, Mass., 1930.

Hurd, Fred W. *These Traffic Factors Are Involved in Intersection Design.* Eno Foundation for Highway Traffic Control, Saugatuck, Conn., 1953.

Hyde, D. C. "Fringe Parking." *Traffic Quarterly,* Eno Foundation for Highway Traffic, Saugatuck, Conn., July, 1953.

Ingraham, J. *Modern Traffic Control.* Funk & Wagnalls, New York, 1954.

Isaacs, Reginald R. "Are Neighborhoods Possible?" *Journal of Housing, July, 1948.*

————. *"The 'Neighborhood Unit' Is an Instrument for Segregation."* Journal of Housing, August, 1948.

Jurkat, E. H. "Land Use Analysis and Forecasting in Traffic Planning." *Traffic Quarterly,* April, 1957.

Kaptur, Marcia C. "Neighborhoods and Urban Policy: A View from the White House." *Practicing Planner,* AIP, September 1978.

Kelley, Eugene J. *Shopping Centers: Location Controlled Regional Centers.* The Eno Foundation for Highway Traffic Control, Saugatuck, Conn., 1956.

Kennedy, G. Donald. *Modern Highways.* Conference Committee on Urban Problems, U.S. Chamber of Commerce, Washington, D.C., 1944.

Kostka, Vladimir Joseph. *Neighborhood Planning.* U. of Manitoba School of Architecture, Winnipeg, Manitoba, Canada, 1957.

————. *Planning Residential Subdivisions.* University of Manitoba School of Architecture, Winnipeg, Manitoba, Canada, 1954.

Lavanburg Foundation. *The Village in the City.*

Lederman, Alfred, and Trachsel, Alfred. *Creative Playgrounds and Recreation Center.* Frederick A. Praeger, New York, 1959.

Lewis, David. *The Pedestrian in the City.* D. Van Nostrand Co., Princeton, New Jersey, 1966.

Lohmann, Karl. *Principles of City Planning.* McGraw-Hill, New York, 1931.

MacElwee, Roy S. *Ports and Terminal Facilities.* McGraw-Hill, New York, 1926.

Malley, Frank H. *Location and Function of Urban Freeways: Post-War Patterns of City Growth.* American Transit Association, New York.

Mandelker, Daniel R. *Green Belts and Urban Growth.* U. of Wisconsin Press, Madison, Wisc., 1962.

Marketers Research Services, Inc. *Baltimore Central Business District Projections.* Planning Council of the Greater Baltimore Committee, 1958.

Marks, Harold. "Subdividing for Traffic Safety." *Traffic Survey Engineer,* Los Angeles County Road Department, Ninth Annual California Street and Highway Conference, U. of California, Berkeley, Calif., 1957.

Master Plan of Airports. County of Los Angeles Regional Planning Commission, Los Angeles, 1940.

Master Plan of Highways. County of Los Angeles Regional Planning Commisssion, Los Angeles, 1941.

McClintock, Miller. *Short Count Traffic Surveys and Their Application to Highway Design.* Portland Cement Association, Chicago, 1935.

McKaye, Benton, and Mumford, Lewis. "Townless Highways for the Motorist." *Harper's,* August, 1931.

Minneapolis Planning Commission. *Goals for Central Minneapolis—Its Function and Design.* No. 0.103, Series 2, Minneapolis, 1959.

Mitchell, R. B., and Rapkin, C. *Urban Traffic: A Function of Land Use.* Columbia U. Institute, Urban Land Use and Housing Studies, New York, 1954.

Mott, Seward H., and Hayden, Buford. *Providing for Automotive Services in Urban Land Development.* Eno Foundation for Highway Traffic Control, Inc., Saugatuck, Conn., 1953.

Mott, Seward, and Wehrly, Max S. *Shopping Center: An Analysis.* Technical Bulletin No. 11, Urban Land Institute, Washington, D.C., 1949.

Moulton, Harold G. *The American Transportation Problem.* The Brookings Institution, Washington, D.C., 1933.

Muncy, D. A. "land for Industry." *Harvard Business Review,* March, 1954.

Murphy, Raymond E.; Vance, J. E. Jr.; and Epstein, Bart J. *Central Business District Studies.* Clark U., Worcester, Mass., 1955.

Nader, Ralph. *Politics of Land: Report on Land Use in California.* Ralph Nader's Study Group, Robert Z. Fellmuth, Project Director, Grossman, New York, 1973.

National Advisory Council on Recreation. *A User-Resource Recreation Planning Method. Loomis, Calif., 1959.*

National Association of Home Builders. *Home Builders Manual for Land Development. Washington, D.C., 1950.*

National Association of Real Estate Boards. *Blueprint for Neighborhood Conservation.* The Build America Better Council, Washington, D.C.

National Resources Planning Board. *Human Conservation.* Washington, D.C., 1938.

_____. *Transportation and National Policy.* Washington, D.C., 1943.

National Resources Board. *A Report on National Planning and Public Works in Relation to Natural Resources and Including Land Use and Water Resources with Findings and Recommendations.* Washington, D.C., December 1, 1934.

_____. *State Planning: A Review of Activities and Progress.* Washington, D.C., June, 1935.

National Resources Committee. *Urban Planning and Land Policies,* Vol. 2. Supplementary Report of the Urbanism Committee, Washington, D.C., 1939.

_____. *Better Cities.* By Charles Ascher, Washington, D.C., 1942.

National Committee on Urban Transportation. *Better Transportation for Your City: A Guide to the Factual Development of Urban Transportation Plans.* Public Administration Service, Chicago, 1958.

National Conservation Bureau. *Manual of Traffic Engineering Studies.* New York, 1945.

National Federation of Settlements and Neighborhood Centers. Neighborhood Goals in a Rapidly Changing World. Action Research Workshop held at Arden House, Harriman, N.Y., 1958.

National Recreation Association. *Play Space in New Neighborhoods.* A Committee Report on Standards of Outdoor Recreation Areas in Housing Developments, New York, 1939.

National Resources Board. *Recreation Use of Land in the United States, vol. IX,* Report of Land Planning Committee, Washington, 1938.

National Resources Planning Board. *Transportation and National Policy.* Washington, D.C., 1943.

Neff, Edgar R. *Planned Shopping Centers vs. Neighborhood Shopping Areas.* Marketing Series No. 3, Business Research Center, College of Business Administration, Syracuse U., Syracuse, N.Y., 1955.

Neighborhoods, Schools, Recreation, and Parks. The Metropolitan Planning Committee and the Winnipeg Town Planning Commission, Manitoba, Canada, 1947.

Nelson, Richard Lawrence. *The Selection of Retail Location.* F. W. Dodge, New York, 1958.

Nolting, Orin F., and Opperman, Paul. *The Parking Problem in Central Business Districts.* Public Administration Service, Chicago, 1938.

Owen, Wilfred. *The Accessible City.* The Brookings Institution, Washington, D.C., 1972.

————. *Cities in the Motor Age.* Viking Press, New York, 1959.

Pennsylvania State U. College of Agriculture. *The Economic and Social Impact of Highways: A Progress Summary of the Monroeville Case Study.* Agricultural Experiment Station, University Park, Penn., Progess Report 219, 1960.

Perry, Clarence. *The Neighborhood Unit,* vol. 7: Neighborhood and Community Planning. Regional Survey of New York and Its Environs, New York, 1929.

Pfouts, Ralph W. *The Techniques of Urban Economic Analysis.* Chandler-Davis Publishing Co., West Trenton, N.J., 1960.

Peterson, John Eric. *Airports for Jets.* American Society of Planning Officials, Chicago, 1959.

Philadelphia City Planning Commission. *Philadelphia Central District Study.* Philadelphia, 1951.

"Plan of Bikeways," Los Angeles County Regional Planning Commission, 1975.

Planning Facilities for Health, Physical Education, and Recreation. Athletic Institute, Inc., Chicago, 1956.

President's Airport Commission. *The Airport and Its Neighbors.* Washington, D.C., 1952.

Rannels, John. *The Core of the City: A Pilot Study of Changing Land Uses in Central Business Districts.* Columbia U. Press, New York, 1956.

Rasmussen, Steen Eiler. "Neighborhood Planning." *Town Planning Review,* January, 1957.

Ratcliff, Richard U. *Urban Land Economics.* McGraw-Hill, New York, 1949.

Renne, R. L. *Land Economics.* Rev. Ed., Harper and Row, New York, 1958.

Roterus, Victor. *The Economic Background for Local Planning.* Proceedings, Annual Meeting of American Society of Planning Officials, Chicago, 1946.

Saarinen, Eliel. *The City: Its Growth, Its Decay, Its Future.* Reinhold, New York, 1943.

Segoe, Ladislas. *Local Planning Administration.* 1st ed., International City Managers' Association, Chicago, 1941.

Sharp, Thomas. *The Anatomy of the Village.* Penguin Books, Harmondsworth, Middlesex, England, 1946.

Siegel, Shirley. *The Law of Open Space.* Regional Plan Association, New York, 1960.

Smith, Paul E. *Shopping Centers: Planning and Management.* National Retail Dry Goods Association, New York, 1956.

Smith, Larry. "Space for the CBD's Functions." *Journal of the American Institute of Planners, February, 1961.*

Smith, Wilbur S., and LeCraw, Charles S. *Parking.* Eno Foundation for Highway Traffic Control, December, 1946.

Smith, Wilbur, and Associates. *Future Highways and Urban Growth.* The Automobile Manufacturers Association, 1961.

Snow, William Brewster. *The Highway and the Landscape.* Rutgers U. Press, New Brunswick, N.J., 1959.

Spengler, Edwin H. *Land Values in New York in Relation to Transit Facilities.* Columbia U. Press, New York, 1930.

Springfield, Oregon. *Springfield: Shoppers' Paradise.* August, 1957.

Stein, Clarence, and Bauer, Catherine. "Store Buildings and Neighborhood Shopping Centers." *Architectural Record,* February, 1934.

Stonorov, Oscar, and Kahn, Louis I. *You and Your Neighborhood.* Revere Copper and Brass, Inc., New York, 1944.

Strayer, George D. *The School Building Program: an Important Part of the City Plan.* Proceedings, National Conference on City Planning, June 1922.

Sutherland, Robert L., and Woodward, Julian L. *Introductory Sociology.* J. B. Lippincott, New York, 1937.

Tax Institute, Inc. *Tax Policy: The Impact of Outlying Shopping Centers on Central Business Districts.* Vol. 24, No. 8, Princeton, N.J., August, 1957.

Technical Committee on Industrial Classification. *Standard Industrial Classification Manual.* Office of Statistical Standards, Superintendent of Documents, U.S. Government Printing Office, Washington, D.C., 1957.

Terre Haute Chamber of Commerce. *Terre Haute: C.B.D.* January, 1959.

Thompson, Richard Grant. *A Study of Shopping Centers.* Real Estate Research Program, Institute of Business and Economic Research, U. of California, 1961.

Transit Research Foundation of Los Angeles, Inc. *City and Suburban Travel.* Issue 2X, Los Angeles, 1960.

Tratman, E.E.R. "Unification of Railway Passenger Terminals." *Engineering News-Record,* February 24, 1927.

Tulsa, Oklahoma Department of Highways. *Metropolitan Area Traffic Survey, 1954-1955.*

Tuner, D. L. *The Fundamentals of Transit Planning for Cities.* Proceedings, 14th National Conference on City Planning, 1922.

United States Bureau of Public Roads. *Parking Guide for Cities.* Washington, D.C., 1956.

United States Chamber of Commerce. *The Community Industrial Development Survey.* Department of Manufacture, Washington, D.C.

————. *Organizing for Community Industrial Development.* Local Chamber of Commerce Service Department, Washington, D.C., 1959.

United States Congress. *Control of Advertising on Interstate Highways: Hearings, March 10, 1958.* Senate Committee on Public Works.

―――――. *The Impact of Suburban Shopping Centers on Independent Retailers: a report, January 5, 1960.* Senate Select Committee on Small Business, 86th Congress, Senate Report No. 1016.

United States Department of Commerce. *Data Sources for Plant Location Analysis.* Business and Defense Services Administration, Office of Area Development, Superintendent of Documents, U.S. Government Printing Office, Washington, D.C., 1959.

―――――. *Federal Laws, Regulations, and Other Material Relating to Highways.* Bureau of Public Roads, August, 1960.

―――――. *General Location of National System of Interstate Highways.* Superintendent of Documents, U.S. Government Printing Office, Washington, D.C., 1955.

―――――. *Highway Transportation Criteria in Zoning Law and Police Power and Planning for Arterial Streets.* Bureau of Public Roads, Washington, D.C., October, 1960.

―――――. *National Airport Plan for 1958.* Superintendent of Documents, U.S. Government Printing Office, Washinton, D.C., 1958.

―――――. *Parking Guides for Cities.* Bureau of Public Roads, Superintendent of Documents, U. S. Government Printing Office. Washington. D.C., 1956.

United States Department of Health, Education and Welfare. *Elementary School Administration and Organization Bulletin 1960, No. 11,* Superintendent of Documents, U.S. Government Printing Office, Washington, D.C., 1960.

United States Federal Aviation Agency. *Small Airports.* Washington, D.C., January, 1959.

United States Small Business Adminstration. *Basic Information Sources on Downtown Shopping Districts.* Washington, D.C., December, 1955.

University of California. *Business Decentralization.* Bureau of Governmental Research, Los Angeles, 1960.

University of North Carolina. *Guidelines for Business Leaders and City Officials to a New Central Business.* Institute of Government, ed. Ruth L. Mace, Chapel Hill, N.C., 1961.

Urban Land Institute, Washington, D.C. *Automobile Parking in Central Business Districts: Technical Bulletin No. 6,* 1946.

―――――. *Technical Bulletin No. 42,* July, 1961.

―――――. *Community Builders Handbook.* Executive Edition, 1960.

―――――. *Conservation and Rehabilitation of Major Shopping Districts: Technical Bulletin No. 22,* February, 1954.

―――――. *Industrial Districts Restudied: An Analysis of Characteristics. Technical Bulletin No. 41,* April, 1961.

―――――. *New Aproaches to Residential Land Development: Technical Bulletin No. 40,* January, 1961.

―――――. *A Re-Examination of the Shopping Center Market: Technical Bulletin No. 33,* September, 1958.

―――――. *Securing Open Space for Urban America: Technical Bulletin No. 36, 1959.*

―――――. *Shopping Centers Re-Studied, Part One: Emerging Patterns.* February 1957.

Vernon, R. *The Changing Economic Function of the Central City.* Committee on Economic Development, New York, 1959.

Villanueva, Marcel. *Planning Neighborhood Shoping Centers.* National Committee on Housing, Inc., New York, 1945.

Voorhees, A. M., ed. *Land Use and Traffic Models. Journal of The American Institute of Planners,* May, 1959.

Wagner, Hulse. *The Economic Effects of Bypass Highways on Selected Kansas Communities.* Center for Research in Business, U. of Kansas, Lawrence, Kansas, 1961.

Waverly: A Study in Neighborhood Conservaton. Federal Home Loan Bank Board, Washington, D.C., 1940.

Weir, L.H. *Parks: A Manual of Municipal and County Parks.* A. S. Barnes Co., New York, 1928.

Weiss, Shirley F. *The Central Business District in Transition.* City and Regional Planning Studies Research Paper No. 1, Department of City and Regional Planning, U. of North Carolina, Chapel Hill, N.C., 1957.

Welch, Kenneth C. *Regional Shopping Centers.* City Planning Commission, Grand Rapids, Mich., 1948.

Westchester County Park Commission, *Westchester County Parks.* Annual Reports, Bronxville, N. Y.

Whitten, Robert, and Adams, Thomas. *Neighborhoods of Small Homes: Economic Density of Low-Cost Housing in America and England.* Harvard U. Press, Cambridge, Mass., 1931.

Williams, Wayne R. *Recreation Places.* Reinhold Publishing, New York, 1958.

Wilson, Leonard U. "Precedent-Setting Swap in Vermont." *Journal of American Institute of Architects,* March, 1974.

Wingo, Lowdon, Jr. *Transportation and Urban Land,* Resources for the Future, Inc., Washington, D.C., 1961.

Wood, Elizabeth. *A New Look at the Balanced Neighborhood: A Study and Recomendations.* Citizens' Housing and Planning Council of New York City, 1961.

————. *The Balanced Neighborhood.* Citizens' Housing and Planning Council, New York, 1960.

————. *The Small Hard Core.* Citizens' Housing and Planning Council, New York, 1957.

————. *Housing Design.* Citizens' Housing and Planning Council, New York, 1961.

Yeomans, Alfred. *City Residential Land Development.* U. of Chicago Press, 1916.

Yokley, E. C. *Zoning Law and Practice, vols. 1 and 2.* The Michie Co., Charlottesville, Va. 1958.

PART 5

Abrams, Charles. *Revolution in Land.* Harper & Brothers, New York, 1939.

Academy of Political and Social Sciences. *Building the Future City.* The Annals, Philadelphia, November 1945.

Adams, Frederick J. *Density Standards for Multi-Family Residential Areas.* American Institite of Planners, Cambridge, Mass., 1943.

Alterman, Rachelle and Hill, Morris. "Implementation of Urban Land Use Plans." A.I.P. Journal, July, 1978.

American City Planning Institute. *Control of Land Subdivision and Building Development: City Planning.* July, 1928.

American Institute of Architects. "Urban Design," *AIA Journal,* March, 1961.

American Institute of Planners, California Chapter. *California Planning Commissioner Handbook.* January, 1954.

American Society of Planning Officals. *Exclusive Industrial and Commercial Zoning: Planning Advisory Service Information Report No. 91.* Chicago, October, 1956.

_____. *The Restoration of Nonconforming Uses: Planning Advisory Service Information Report No. 94.* Chicago, January 1957.

_____. *Newsletter.* Monthly publication, Chicago.

A Standard State Zoning Enabling Act. Government Printing Office, Washington, D.C., 1926.

Bassett, Edward M. Zoning. Russell Sage Foundation, 1940.

Carnegie Institute of Technology. *Planning and the Urban Community.* Ed. Harvey S. Perloff, U. of Pittsburgh Press, Pittsburgh, 1961.

Chase, Stuart. *Rich Land, Poor Land.* New York, 1936.

_____. "Zoning Comes to Town." *Readers Digest,* February 1957.

Churchill, Henry. *Densities in New York City.* Citizens' Housing Council of New York, 1944.

Colean, Miles L. *American Housing.* Twentieth Century Fund, New York, 1947.

_____. *Renewing Our Cities.* Twentieth Century Fund, New York 1953.

Comey, Arthur C. *Transition Zoning.* Harvard U. Press, Cambridge, Mass., 1933.

Cornick, Philip H. *Premature Subdivison of Urban Areas in Selected Metropolitan Districts.* Division of State Planning, Albany, N.Y., 1938.

_____. *Premature Subdivison and Its Consequences.* Institute of Public Administration, Columbia U. New York, 1938.

Cullen, Gordon. *Townscape.* Reinhold Publishing Corp., New York, 1961.

Eckbo, Garrett. "Landscape for Living." *Architectural Record,* 1950.

Fagin, H., and Weinberg, R. C. eds. *Planning and Community Appearance.* New York Regional Plan Association, 1958.

Ford, George B. *Building Height, Bulk, and Form.* Harvard U. Press, Cambridge, Mass., 1931.

Gibberd, Frederick. *Town Design.* 3rd ed., Reinhold Publishing Corp., New York, 1959.

Goldston, Eli, and Scheur, James H. "Zoning of Planned Residential Developments," *Harvard Law Review,* December, 1959.

Goodman, Percival and Paul. *Communitas.* U. of Chicago Press, Chicago, 1947.

Haar, Charles M. and Hering, Barbara. "The Lower Gwynedd Township Case: Too Flexible Zoning or an Inflexible Judiciary?" *Harvard Law Review,* June, 1961.

Herrey, Hermann. "Comprehensive Planning for the City: Market and Dwelling Place, Part 1, Traffic Design." *Pencil Points,* April, 1944.

Higbee, Edward. *The Squeeze: Cities Without Space.* William Morrow & Co., New York, 1960.

Highway Research Board. *Parking Requirements in Zoning Ordinances.* Bulletin 99, Publication 347, Washington, D.C., 1955.

_____. *Zoning for Truck-Loading Facilities.* Bulletin 59, Publication 243, Washington D.C., 1952.

Home Title Guaranty Co. *Pitfalls of Zoning: A Guide for Attorneys.* New York, 1959.

Housing and Home Finance Agency. *Suggested Land Subdivision Regulations.* Division of Housing Research, Washington, D.C., 1952.

Hoyt, Homer. *One Hundred Years of Land Values in Chicago.* U. of Chicago Press, Chicago, 1933.

_____. *Structure and Growth of Residential Neighborhoods in American Cities.* Federal Housing Administration, Washington, D.C., 1945.

Hurd, Richard M. *Principle of City Land Values.* New York, 1903.

Land Value Taxation Around the World. Robert Schalkenbach Foundation, New York, 1955.

Lautner, Harold W. *Subdivision Regulations: An Analysis of Land Subdivision.* Public Administration Service, Chicago, 1941.

Los Angeles County Regional Planning Commission. *Exclusive Agricultural Zoning.* Uniform Zoning Ordinance Study, 1958.

_____. *Landscaping of Industrial Areas.* Uniform Zoning Ordinance Study, 1958.

_____. *Nonconforming Uses.* Uniform Zoning Ordinance Study, 1959.

_____. *Performance Standards.* Uniform Zoning Ordinance Study, 1959.

_____. *Signs and Outdoor Advertising.* Uniforn Zoning Ordinance Study, 1959.

_____. *Variances and Permits (Special Use and Conditional).* Uniform Zoning Ordinance Study, 1959.

_____. *Yards.* Uniform Zoning Ordinance Study, 1959.

Lovelace, Eldridge, and Weismantel, William L. *Density Zoning: Organic Zoning for Planned Residential Developments.* Urban Land Institute, Technical Bulletin No. 42, July, 1961.

Lynch, Kevin. *The Image of the City.* Techology Press and Harvard U. Press (publication of the Joint Center for Urban Studies), Cambridge, Mass., 1960.

Markeluis, Sven *The Structure of the Town of Stockholm.* 1956.

McHarg, Ian. *Design With Nature.* Doubleday, New York, 1971.

McHugh, K. S., Commissioner. *Local Planning and Zoning.* State of New York, Department of Commerce, 1960.

Merriam, Robert E. *The Subdivision of Land: A Guide for Municipal Officials in the Regulation of Land Subdivision.* American Society of Planning Officials, Chicago, 1942.

Metzenbaum, James. *The Law of Zoning.* 3 vols. and supplement, Baker, Voorhis, New York, 1955, 1961.

National Housing Agency. *A Check List for the Review of Local Subdivison Controls.* Washington, D.C., 1947.

National Industrial Zoning Committee. *Performance Standards In Industrial Zoning.* Columbus, Ohio, 1958.

New York City Planning Commission. *Zoning Maps and Resolution,* 1961.

_____. *Zoning Handbook,* New York, 1961.

Osborn, F. J. *Nothing Gained by High Density.* Town and Country Planning Association, London, 1953.

Owings, Nathaniel. *The Spaces In Between: An Architect's Journey.* Houghton Miffllin Co., New York, 1973.

Pomeroy, Hugh R. *Modern Trends in Zoning.* Municipal Law Section, New York State Bar Association, New York, January, 1960.

Ranes, Herman. "The Impact of Political Decision Making on Planning." Master's Thesis, Division of the School of Architecture, Columbia U., New York, 1959.

Redman, Albert E., Secretary, National Industrial Zoning Committee. *Steps to Secure Sound Zoning.* Columbus, Ohio, 1958.

Sanders, S. E., and Rabuck, A. J. *New City Patterns.* Reinhold Publishing, New York, 1946.

Santa Clara County Planning Department. *Exclusive Agricultural Zoning.* 1958.

Schulze, E. E. *Performance Standards in Zoning Ordinances.* Pittsburgh, Pa. Air Pollution Control Association, 1959.

Siegel, Shirley Adelson. *The Law of Open Space.* Regional Planning Association, Inc., New York, 1960.

Southwestern Legal Foundation —Continuing Legal Education Center. *Institute on Planning and Zoning.* Dallas, November 1960.

Spangle, Wm. E., Jr. *Model Zoning Ordinance.* Menlo Park, Calif., 1960.

Stanford Research Institute. *An Analysis of Organized Industrial Districts.* 1958.

Stanislaus Cities-County Advance Planning Staff. *Standard Terminology for Planning and Zoning.* Modesto, Calif., 1959.

State Laws Related to "Freeways." Public Roads Administration, Federal Works Agency, Washington, D.C., 1940.

Superintendent of Documents. *Suggested Land Subdivision Regulations.* U.S. Government Printing Office, Washington, D.C., July, 1960.

The Preparation of Zoning Ordinances. Advisory Committee on City Planning and Zoning, U.S. Department of Commerce, Washington, D.C., 1931.

United States Chamber of Commerce. *Zoning and Civic Development.* Construction and Civic Development Department, Washington, D.C., 1950.

United States Department of Agriculture. *Talks on Rural Zoning.* Argricultural Research Service, Farm Economics Research Division, Washington, D.C., 1960.

————. *To Hold This Soil.* Washington, D.C., 1938.

————. *The Why and How of Rural Zoning.* Bulletin No. 196, Superintendent of Documents, U.S. Government Printing Office, Washington, D.C., 1958.

PART 6

Abercrombie, Patrick. *Greater London Plan 1944.* His Majesty's Stationery Office, London, 1945.

American Academy of Arts and Sciences. *The Future Metropolis,* Wesleyan U. Press, Middletown, Conn., 1960. *Daedalus, Journal of the American Academy of Arts and Sciences,* Winter, 1961, issued as Vol. 90, No. 1, of the Proceedings of the American Academy of Arts and Sciences.

American Institute of Architects, National Policy Task Force:
Strategy for Building a Better America. December, 1971.
A Plan for Urban Growth. January, 1972.
Report of Constraints Conference. May, 1972.
Structures for Urban Growth. October, 1973.

Aronovici, C. *Community Building: Science, Technique, Art.* Doubleday, Garden City, N.Y., 1956.

Bauer, Catherine. "Cities in Flux." *The American Scholar,* New York, Winter, 1943–44.

Bernarde, Melvin A. *Our Precarious Habitat.* W. W. Norton, New York, 1970.

Bronson, William. *How to Kill a Golden State.* Doubleday, Garden City, N.Y., 1968.

Cahn, Robert. *Where Do We Grow From Here?* Christian Science Publishing Society, Boston, 1973.

California Chapter of the American Institute of Planners. *The Nature and Control of Urban Dispersal.* Ed. Ernest A. Englebert, 1960.

California Roadside Council, Inc. *More Attractive Communities for California.* San Francisco, 1960.

Cobden-Shanderson, T. J. *Art and Life, and the Building and Decoration of Cities.* London, 1897.

Chamber of Commerce of the U.S. *Balanced Rebuilding of Cities.* Statement Issued by the Construction and Civic Development Department Committee, Washington, D. C., 1937.

Chase, Stuart *The Road We Are Travelling.* The Twentieth Century Fund, New York, 1942.

_____. *For This We Fought.* The Twentieth Century Fund, New York, 1946.

Cheney, Charles. *Architectural Control of Private Property.* Proceedings, National Conference on City Planning, 1927.

Chicago Plan Commission. *Building New Neighborhoods: Subdivision Design and Standards.* Chicago, 1943.

Collection ASCORAL. *Les Trois Etablissements Humains. Denoël,* 19 Rue Amélie, Paris, 1945.

Comarc Design Systems, Inc. *Computer Graphics Planning Information System.* San Francisco, Cal., 1978.

Copenhagen Regional Planning Office. *Preliminary Outline Plan for the Copenhagen Metroplitan Region.* August, 1961.

Crane, Jacob. *Urban Planning—Illusion and Reality: A New Philosophy for Planned City Building.* Vantage Press, New York, 1973.

Creighton, Thomas H., Ed. *Buildling for Modern Man.* Princeton U. Press, Princeton, N.J., 1949.

Committee for Economic Development. *Guiding Metropolitan Growth.* New York, 1960.

Dash, Jacob and Efart, Elisha. *The Israel Physical Master Plan.* Ministry of the Interior Planning Department, Jerusalem, 1964.

Dahinden, Justus. *Urban Structures for the Future,* Praegar, New York, 1972.

Dickinson, R. E. *City, Region and Regionalism.* Grove Press, New York, 1954.

Directive Committee on Regional Planning. *The Case for Regional Planning with Special Reference to New England.* Yale University, Yale U. Press, New Haven, 1947.

Downs, Roger M. and Stêa, David. *Image and the Environment.* Aldine Publishing, Chicago, 1973.

Duff, A. C. *Britain's New Towns.* Pall Mall Press, London, 1961.

Duncan, Scott, Lieberson, Duncan, Winsborough. *Metropolis and Region.* Resources for the Future, Inc., Johns Hopkins Press, Baltimore, 1960.

"Environmental Assessments for Project Level Action." HUD, Washington, D.C., 1974.

Fagin, H., and Weinberg, R. C., Ed. *Planning and Community Appearance.* New York Regional Plan Association, 1958.

Ferris, Hugh. *The Metropolis of Tomorrow.* New York, 1929.

Forshaw, J. H., and Abercrombie, Patrick. *County of London Plan.* London County Council, Macmillan & Co., Ltd., London, 1943.

Fortune: The Exploding Metropolis. Doubleday., New York, 1957.

Freilich, Robert H. and Ragsdale, John W. Jr. *A Legal Study of Control of Urban Sprawl in the Minneapolis-St. Paul Region.* Twin Cities Metropolitan Council, St. Paul, Minn., 1974.

Freilich, Robert H. and Greis, David T. "Timing and Sequence Development." Unpublished draft, 1974.

Friedmann, John and Alonso, William. *Regional Development and Planning.* M. I. T. Press, Cambridge, Mass., 1964.

Futterman, Robert A. *The Future of Our Cities.* Doubleday, New York, 1961.

Goodman, Robert. *After the Planners.* Simon and Schuster, New York, 1972.

Gottman, Jean. *Megalopolis,* The Twentieth Century Fund, New York, 1961.

Greer, Guy. *Your City Tomorrow.* Macmillan, New York, 1947.

Gropius, Walter. *Rebuilding Our Communities.* Paul Theobald, Chicago, 1945.

Gruen, Victor. "The Emerging Urban Pattern. *Progressive Architecture,* July, 1959.

Guttenberg, Albert Z. "City Encounter and Desert Encounter: Two Sources of Regional Planning Thought." AIP Journal, October, 1978.

Hawley, Amos H. *The Changing Shape of Metropolitan America: Deconcentration Since 1920.* Free Press, Glencoe, Ill., June 1956.

Hegemann, Werner, and Peets, Elbert. *Civic Art: The American Vitruvius.* Architectural Book Publishing Co., New York, 1922.

Heller, Alfred. *The California Tomorrow Plan.* William Kaufman, Los Altos, California, 1972.

Herrey, Hermann; Herrey, Erna; and Pertzoff, Constantine. "An Organic Theory of City Planning." *Architectural Forum,* April, 1944.

Hiberseimer, Ludwig. *The New City.* Paul Theobald, Chicago, 1944.

————. *The Nature of Cities: Origin, Growth, and Decline; Pattern and Form: Planning Problems.* Paul Theobald, Chicago, 1955.

Honikman, Basil, Ed. *Responding to Social Change.* Dowden, Hutchinson, and Ross, Inc., Stroudsberg, Pa., 1975.

Houstoun, Lawrence O., Jr. "Saving Urban Charm." *Planning, The ASPO Magazine,* December, 1974.

Hughes, Michael. *The Letters of Lewis Mumford and Frederic J. Osborn.* Praeger, New York, 1972.

Huxley, Aldous. *On Living in a Revolution.* Harper & Brothers, New York, 1944.

Inter-County Regional Planning Commission. *Metropolitan Growth Plan,* 1970–2000. Denver, 1959.

————. *Standards for New Urban Development.* Denver, 1960.

Isard, Walter. *Location and Space-Economy,* John Wiley & Sons, New York, 1956.

Isard, Walter, and Coughlin, Robert E. *Municipal Costs and Revenues Resulting from Community Growth.* Federal Reserve Bank of Boston and American Institute of Planners, Boston, 1957.

"Israel Builds." State of Israel Ministry of Housing, Jerusalem, 1973.

Isserman, Andrew M. "The Location-Quotient Approach to Estimating Regional Economic Impacts." AIP Journal, January, 1977.

Jacobs, Jane. *The Death and Life of Great American Cities.* Random House, New York, 1961.

Justement, Louis. *New Cities for Old.* McGraw-Hill, New York, 1946.

Knecht, Robert W. "Coastal Zone Management Comes of Age." *Practicing Planner,* AIP, December, 1978.

Kuenzlen, Martin. *Playing Urban Games.* Braziller, New York, 1972.

Lewis, Harold MacLean. *Planning the Modern City, Vols. 1 and 2.* John Wiley & Sons, New York, 1949.

Lilienthal, David. *TVA: Democracy on the March.* Harper & Brothers, 1944.

Los Angeles County Regional Planning Commission. *Landscaping of Industrial Areas.* Los Angeles, 1958.

Los Angeles Regional Planning Commission. *Freeways for the Region.* Los Angeles, 1943.

Lynch, Kevin. *The Image of the City.* Cambridge Technology Press and Harvard U. Press (Publications of the Joint Center for Urban Studies), 1960.

McKaye, Benton. *The New Exploration: A Philosophy of Regional Planning.* Harcourt, Brace, New York, 1928.

McKenzie, R. D. *The Metropolitan Community.* McGraw-Hill, New York, 1933.

Meyerson, M., and Terret, B. "Metropolis Lost, Metropolis Regained." *American Academy Political and Social Science Annual,* November, 1957.

Mitchell, Robert B. *Metropolitan Planning for Land Use and Transporation: A Study.* U. of Pennsylvania, Philadelphia, 1961.

Mumford. Lewis. *The Urban Prospect.* Harcourt, Brace & World, New York, 1968.

National Resources Committee:

    Regional Factors in National Planning. December, 1935.

    Regional Planning, Part 1: Pacific Northwest. May, 1936.

    Our Cities: Their Role in the National Economy. June, 1937.

    Technoligical Trends and National Policy. June, 1937.

    The Problems of a Changing Population. May, 1938.

    Consumer Incomes in the United States. 1938.

    Suggested Procedure for Population Studies by State Planning Boards. Washington, D.C., 1938.

    Residential Building, Housing Monograph, Series No. 1. Industrial Committee, 1939.

New Towns and Old. The Swedish Institute, Stockholm, 1975.

New York Metroplitan Region. Harvard University Press:

    Vernon, Raymond. *Metropolis 1985.* 1960.

    Lichtenberg, Robert M. *One-Tenth of a Nation.* 1960.

    Robbins, Sidney M. and Terleckyn, Nestor E. *Money Metropolis.* 1960.

    Hoover, Edgar M. and Vernon, Raymond. *Anatomy of a Metropolis.* 1959.

    Chinitz, Benjamin. *Freight and the Metropolis.* 1960.

Niering, William A. *Nature in the Metropolis.* Reginal Plan Association, New York 1960.

Northeastern Illinois Metropolitan Area Planning Commission. *Land Use Handbook: A Guide to Understanding Land Use Surveys.* Chicago, 1961.

Owen, W. *The Metropolitan Transportation Problem.* Brookings Institution, Washington, D.C., 1956.

Packard, Walter E. *The Economic Implications of the Central Valley Project.* Adcraft, Los Angeles, 1942.

Perloff, Harvey S., Dir. "The Arts in the Economic Life of the City." Unpub. paper, National Endowment for the Arts, 1979–80.

Pooley, Beverly J. *The Evolution of British Planning Legislation.* U. of Michigan Law School, Ann Arbor, Mich., 1960.

Progress in Regionalism. Arizona State Advisory Council on Intergovernmental Relations, Phoenix, 1972.

Regional Plan Association, Inc. *Planning and Community Appearance.* Henry Fagin and Robert S. Weinber, New York, 1958.

Regional Survey of New York and Its Environs. Russell Sage Foundation, New York, 1927–31

    Vol. I. Major Economic Factors in Metropolitan Growth and Arrangement.

    Vol. II. Population, Land Values and Government.

    Vol. III. Highway Traffic.

    Vol. IV. Transit and Transportation.

    Vol. V. Public Recreation.

    Vol.VI. Buildings: Their Uses and the Spaces About Them.

    Vol. VII. Neighborhood and Community Planning.

Vol. VIII. Physical Conditions and Public Services.

Regional Plan, Vol. I, The Graphic Plan.

Regional Plan, Vol. II, The Building of the City.

Rodwin, Lloyd. *The British New Towns: Policy, Problems, and Implications.* Harvard U. Press, Cambridge, Mass., 1956.

————. *The Future Metropolis.* George Braziller, Inc., New York 1961.

Saarinen, Eliel. *The City: Its Growth, Its Decay. Its Future.* Reinhold Publishing Corp., New York, 1943.

Sanders, S. E., and Rabuck, A. J. *New City Patterns: The Analysis and a Technique for Urban Reintegration.* Reinhold Publishing Corp., New York, 1946.

Sive, Mary Robinson, Ed. *Environmental Legislation.* Environmental Information Center, N. Y., 1976.

Soleri, Paolo. *Arcology: The City in the Image of Man.* M.I.T. Press, Cambridge, Mass., 1969.

Stephenson, Gordon. *New Town Policies in Great Britain: A Brief Description.* Department of Civic Planning, Liverpool U., Liverpool, 1948.

Stein, Clarence S. *Toward New Towns For America.* Reinhold Publishing Corp., New York, 1957.

Tulsa Metropolitan Area Planning Commission. *1975 Metropolitan Tulsa.* Tulsa, Okla., 1959.

Tunnard, C., and Reed, H. H. *American Skyline: The Growth and Form of Our Cities and Towns.* Houghton Mifflin, Boston, 1955.

United States Chamber of Commerce. *A Brighter Future for America's Cities.* Washington, D.C., 1954.

United States Housing Authority. *Planning the Site.* Department of the Interior, Washington, D.C., 1939.

University of California International Urban Research Institute of International Studies. *The World's Metropolitan Areas.* U. of California Press, Berkeley, 1960.

Uthwatt Report: Report of the Expert Committee on Compensation and Betterment. Minister of Works and Planning, London, September 1942.

"Urban Design," *AIA Journal*, March, 1961.

Wagner, Richard H. *Environment and Man.* W. W. Norton, New York, 1971.

Weiss, Shirley. *New Town Development in the United States.* New Towns Research Series, Center for Urban & Regional Studies, U. of North Carolina, Chapel Hill, 1973.

Wenkam, Robert. *Hawaii.* Rand McNally, Chicago, 1972.

Wood, Samuel E., and Heller, Alfred E. "California, Going, Going." *California Tomorrow,* Sacramento, 1962.

Wolf, Peter. *The Future of the City.* Watson-Guptill Publications, Cincinnati, 1973.

INDEX

WITHDRAWN

WITHDRAWN

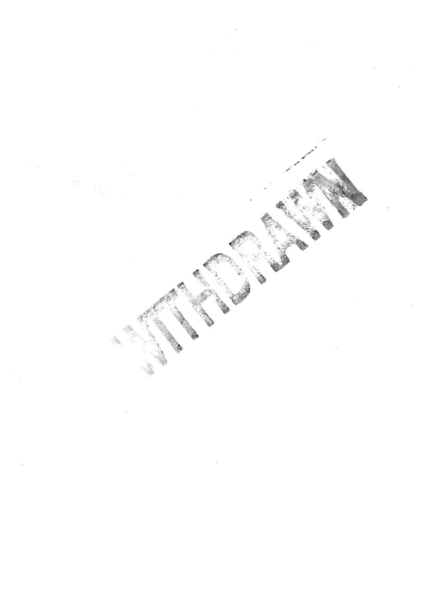